HUMAN RESOURCES MANAGEMENT

in the Corporate environment

Terry McIlwee & Ivor Roberts

ELM PUBLICATIONS

British Library Cataloguing in Publication data

A catalogue record for this book is available from the British Library.

CONTENTS

LIST OF FIGURES

LIST OF TABLES

Dedication

To our wives and families, who have listened patiently to so much
of this detail, and supported us throughout its production.

IVOR ROBERTS has spent most of his working life at Board level, in major commercial companies, initially as Personnel Director and then as a profit-responsible Operations Director.

He has had wide consultancy experience in both industry and commerce, and is also a Principal Lecturer in Applied Behavioural Science at the Polytechnic of West London where he is a member of the Programme Directorate team for Personnel Management programmes.

TERRY McILWEE is a professor and director of Personnel Management Programmes at the Polytechnic of West London. Before entering the education world he had personnel experience in engineering, tyre manufacture and the electronics industry. He is also Chief Examiner — Professional Competence for the Institute of Personnel Management.

INTRODUCTION

This book focuses on the organisational and environmental context of human resource management. This is done by examining the objectives and functions of business and public service organisations and the role of modern organisational management. The major functions of personnel maangement are discussed, together with the means for measuring its contribution and evaluating its success. The main features of the external environment are studied which influence the manner in which personnel specialists operate — especially political, social, governmental, labour market and legislative pressures.

Covering the Human Resources Management syllabus of the IPM Stage 1 examination, *Human Resources Management* will be useful to students on BTEC Business Studies courses and on other programmes which cover the management of people at work.

This third edition has incorporated material up to the end of August, 1991 and is the successor to two editions of *Personnel Management in Context.*

Alexander Pope: *Essay on Criticism*

'A little learning is a dangerous thing;
Drink deep, or taste not the Pierian spring;
There shallow draughts intoxicate the brain,
And drinking largely sobers us again.'

CHAPTER ONE

THE BUSINESS ENVIRONMENT

1. INTRODUCTION

The term "Business Environment" as applied to Organisations, is much broader than the physical and geographical location of the Business.

In managerial terms, the Organisation must, of course, consider the physical and geographical location, but, in addition, must also consider the economic, political, social, cultural, legal, technological and demographic factors which relate directly to the Business.

In this respect, those organisations which operate in overseas markets must apply these factors to each and every country they trade in, or export to, a task requiring both tact and detailed planning, plus constant evaluation, in order to monitor significant changes which could, ultimately, affect the overall business strategy.

To successfully formulate a viable business strategy, top management must allocate a considerable amount of time to the task of gathering information on each of the factors referred to above, but, in addition, must give careful thought to three other important business influences, namely, Customers, Competitors, and Suppliers.

The exhaustive evaluation of all the factors which can, and do, affect a business, leads, initially, to the formulation of the Strategic Business Plan, from which both the Corporate objectives and, ultimately, the Divisional or Departmental objectives can be agreed, monitored and, finally, achieved.

It follows, therefore, that this whole area is one which must be recognised, by all levels of employees, as being of primary importance to the future of the Business, and given sufficient time for in-depth investigation, throughout the Organisation, before any final plans are made and actioned.

Let us now study each of these factors in more detail.

2. THE ECONOMIC FACTORS

In recent years, we have seen the United Kingdom economy swing, dramatically, between recession and progression, and watched both interest rates and inflation being, first, brought under control then escalate to unacceptable levels, in a relatively short period.

These movements, together with a widening gap in the balance of payment deficit, have had direct, and for some small businesses, terminal repercussions, on trading conditions, and a great deal of management time has had to be devoted to the design, evaluation, and redesign of business strategies, in order to maintain a viable business base.

Growth in consumer demand for what have been called "Luxury Goods" and the comparatively easy access to credit facilities, for almost anyone who requests them, has further complicated the money markets, and has, almost inevitably, had a negative effect on interest rates, in an effort to curb individual expenditure. A situation of this type, if prolonged, has an serious impact on planning, in all businesses, as cash flow becomes tighter with the reduction in consumer spending power, and activities have to be curtailed, or forward expansion plans shelved.

A major area of economic concern in the United Kingdom, in recent years, has been the unacceptable level of unemployment and the lack of job opportunities in some parts of the Country, for those actively seeking work.

Government figures seem to indicate that the number of people unemployed is declining, month by month, and, in January 1989, the published figure fell below the two million mark for the first time in four years. 1991 has seen a progressive increase in the number of unemployed to just over 2.3m in August 1991.

The availability of manpower, particularly skilled manpower, has a direct impact on the economic performance of organisations as they strive for profitable results, and even apparently well structured and evaluated strategies can fail, when insufficient time has been given to a thorough investigation of the availability of human resources. Conversely, in times of poor National economic performance, with rising interest rates and inflation leading to tighter monetary supplies, businesses find themselves in the unhappy situation where job shredding must take place to reduce costs and retain competitive viability — creating further employment.

Although an organisation may be solely based in the United Kingdom, it is by no means immune to international economic pressures. Those who market their goods and services overseas must constantly monitor the changes in the economic status of the "Host" country, in order to evaluate positive/negative pressures on existing strategies, and be in a position to take whatever corrective action would be necessary to maintain strategic viability.

In most circumstances, that action may only be a revision of trading options, up or down, in terms of cash flow projections and resource requirements, but, in extreme cases, those options may mean immediate steps to withdraw from the location, in total, accepting the cash flow implications of such a decision.

Factors for consideration could include:

(a) inflation and escalating wage rates in a Host country which could impact on the supply of goods or services to the U.K. or any other trading location.

(b) inflation and escalating wage rates in a Host country which could affect the ultimate performance of a subsidiary company based there.

(c) exchange controls which may be applied by either the United Kingdom Government or the Government of the Host country, impacting directly on to the price of goods or services to be imported or exported.

(d) Corporate and personal rates of taxation which may be subject to adverse change in the Host country.

(e) the effect of international trade agreements, particularly within the EEC, which could have a negative effect on the Corporate objectives of the Organisation.

(f) trade barriers which the Host country may impose, in an attempt to protect indigenous industries from foreign competition.

(g) a major political power shift in the Host country.

One essential activity, for any business organisation, is in the complex area of *Environmental Forecasting* which is the process whereby key economic variables, which assist top management in making sensible assumptions about the future of the Business, are isolated and fully evaluated. The techniques to be used will depend, very much, on the size of the Organisation, and the nature of the markets it serves, and they will range from informal discussions with the "City" to detailed analysis of the entire economic spectrum, related to essential resources, by either in-Company experts or retained Consultants. The value of this is considered questionable by many small companies, but major organisations recognise the value of thorough research into National and International economic trends, whilst accepting that a "forecast" is really informed guesswork!

3. THE POLITICAL FACTORS

Government Policy impinges directly on to the Strategic Stance of all organisations, in both a positive and a negative way.

In a positive sense, legislative or political changes can create opportunities for those organisations which are flexible and reactive enough to grasp them, e.g. in terms of Regional Development programmes, Privatisation programmes, Defence Contracts and Educational programmes.

In a negative sense, Government Policy, at both National and Local level, can restrict or control company operations by legislative changes, particularly in relation to environmental matters, although it must be said that even these changes can create opportunities for business expansion.

In the last twenty years, we have seen the influence of political factors reflected in Government attitudes toward Trade Unions, with a perceived bias towards Trade Union power in the 1970s, and a continuing policy directed at restricting that power since the arrival in office of the Conservative Party in 1979.

Both these periods have presented Management with problem areas which needed to be taken into consideration, in planning Manpower Strategy and total Business Strategy.

We must accept that all organisations operate within a political environment on a day to day basis, but it is the factor of political change, which produces uncertainty in the activity of planning for future results.

Political change is not confined, solely, to legislation, and many companies trading in overseas markets have had to make major directional changes, in terms of operating strategy, in the aftermath of Military Coups, or Religious groups taking a direct role in the Government of the Host Country.

Political intervention in business policy formulation has also become a fact of life for participating countries since the inauguration of the European Economic Community, and input from Brussels, in respect of harmonisation programmes, has become an accepted part of policy planning.

The onset of 1992 will cause many organisations to totally review their business strategies, and the way in which their internal systems support the achievement of business objectives.

Many European countries have fully embraced the concept of *Total Quality Management,* an operational system long used by Japanese companies, which recognises that each part of an organisation is both a supplier and customer of internal services, related to the effective production of whatever good or service that the organisation provides.

This means that every part of the organisation, and every individual within those parts, must be fully aware of the total business objectives and, more importantly, be fully committed to their achievement, irrespective of departmental bias.

Long before 1992 arrives, U.K. based organisations must accept the principle of *Total Quality Management* (TQM) and ensure that their business plans are based on this method of operation, which requires continuous commitment, from top to bottom and an acceptance that this is the only way the organisation can ensure a viable future in World markets.

This system is no "flavour of the month" management fad, but rather a serious change in the way businesses go about their objective achievement in a fiercely competitive market, and it will be a very foolish and irresponsible Board of Directors which chooses to ignore this.

4.   SOCIAL AND CULTURAL FACTORS

Recent years have brought tremendous changes to the normal working practices of the United Kingdom.

THE BUSINESS ENVIRONMENT

We have seen a concerted movement towards a shorter working week, reduced daily working hours, increased holiday entitlements, and early retirement programmes.

Business organisations are, additionally, affected by the expectations and attitudes to work of all levels of employee, from Top Management to the latest joined junior, and those expectations have steadily increased as time has past.

On a broader basis, social change related to the influence of music and fashion, particularly, have created business opportunity for many organisations, and the changing shopping requirements of consumers in these major areas and other more basic areas, has brought about a rethink in the location and design of mid-town shopping centres and out of town complexes.

Leisure is an important growth area in the U.K., in terms of the need for sports facilities, clothing, equipment and holiday locations, both home and abroad, and with the changes in working patterns, referred to earlier, will remain an area of major business opportunity for the 1990s.

Many writers on business matters have commented on the changed attitude of todays worker, away from the "Protestant work ethic" where hard work and devotion to duty was considered a central fact of life, to one where pursuit of self interest and leisure is more prevalent — indeed it is sometimes referred to by the media as the "British disease".

In the U.K. there has also been a steady decline in Manufacturing employment, and an equally steady growth in Service industry employment, the "blue collar" element of the work force therefore becoming much less significant in both numerical and influence terms.

Cultural change has seen the growth of full time female employment, particularly in managerial occupations, and, as a direct result of redundancy in many geographic locations, we have seen an increase in "role reversal" situations where the husband remains at home and the wife pursues a full time career, as the only part of the family that can find employment.

There has been a concerted move, in the 1980s towards ensuring that businesses accept their social obligations, in relation to the way the daily life of the business is conducted.

In relation to this, consideration must be given by senior management to their policies on employment, particularly in the areas of Equal Opportunities and the eradication of all forms of Discrimination.

In addition, policies relating to company attitudes towards customers, suppliers, debtors and creditors, competitors, home based subsidiaries and overseas subsidiaries, and the impact of the business on local communities, must be given every consideration if the business wishes to retain a substantial image in the eyes of the business world and existing and potential shareholders.

In social responsibility terms, any business which ignores the growing influence of environmental pressures, now constantly in the public eye as the "green policies", is heading for an area of potential conflict, both with Government and with the community in general.

There are many well documented examples of this, river pollution by chemical factories, air pollution which impacts on the earth's atmosphere and damages the vital ozone layer which controls the climatic balance, off-shore oil pipelines which need to cross rural land and are now buried beneath green fields.

Social responsibility also extends to those who carry passengers whether on land, sea or by air, and there is a growing demand for much greater care by operators, in terms of comfort and, more importantly, safety.

Particularly sensitive attitudes, relating directly to social responsibility, are required where a large company dominates the economy of a community, by having a relatively high proportion of the available work force in its employ. The impact of any decision to either reduce the work force, or to relocate the total business, must be considered in relation to the potential effect on the local community in terms of individual spending power, and impact on small businesses in the area.

Companies operating in overseas markets must also accept their responsibility for working conditions and employment policies which relate to indigenous workers, many of whom have been subject to exploitation in past years from foreign operators.

Reputations are hard won, and easily lost, in this sensitive area, particularly in relation to the practices known as "smoothing the path" or "oiling the wheels", in plain language, bribery of local officials by either cash or other means. Of course, in many Countries, this aspect of business life is both encouraged and accepted, but it is important to have a clear Company policy on these matters if the core business is to maintain an effective ethical image, in the eyes of both the host Government and the wider Business community.

In business life we recognise that each Company has its own type of culture, that all embracing ethos which is sometimes described as "the way we do it here".

Cultures can be *power based,* i.e. a top-down managerial style which, sometimes, emanates from one individual, or, at the other extreme, *task based,* i.e. the recognition that the only thing that is important to the Organisation is the total involvement and commitment of all employees to the achievement of objectives, irrespective of hierarchical status.

This latter cultural style evolved from the Japanese practice known as *"Quality Circles"*, the application of all employees, related to a process, to the solution of problems which impact on the successful production of the product, by free discussion and the acceptance of joint responsibility for the result.

The nature of business means that things do not stand still, and Quality

Circles have, in turn, been superceded by the all-embracing system known as *"Total Quality Management"*, a process whereby an organisation critically examines every aspect of its departmental operations, recognising that each element of the organisation is both a giver and receiver of services, to and from other parts of the organisation, and that those services should be of top quality.

This status being achieved, it follows, therefore, that the service given to any customer must, because of the internal process, be beyond reproach, but with this comes a recognition that this ideal situation is totally dependent on the continuous review of all internal processes, and the acceptance of the need to maintain those standards by every employee, irrespective of job or rank.

To finally refine this process, each supplier to the organisation is also required to achieve the same high standards, a process which must improve business practice, as a whole.

5. THE LEGAL FACTORS

Business organisations, and the people who work within them, no matter what status they enjoy, are subject to a series of Legal constraints which apply to the total framework of the business.

These constraints emanate from Government decisions, and, in recent years, much emphasis has been placed on the creation of legal parameters which relate to both the treatment of employees and to the operations of Trade Unions.

Other legislation relates to the manner in which a business conducts its trading operations, i.e. laws on consumer protection, or to the description of the goods or services it purports to supply, the wording of Contracts, and the requirement to provide information on annual performance to both Shareholders and to the Registrar of Companies.

Businesses are, of course, subject to legislation concerned with Taxation, and equally importantly to legislation relating to the Health and Safety at work of those employed in the business, and of those who come in contact with the business, a process which was strengthened by the introduction, in 1989, of stringent requirements related to the control of substances which could be hazardous to health, in any way.

The growth of the "Green Movement" in the 1980s has had a great effect on those businesses who have waste products to dispose of, either into rivers or sea, into the air, or on to the land, and we can expect to see this form of pressure growing at a constant rate, through environmental groups and Government action.

6. TECHNOLOGICAL FACTORS

In order to maintain a competitive stance, an organisation must both understand and work within the pressures known as "Market Forces".

In essence, this means keeping pace with competitors, in every way, including, where necessary, the introduction and development of new technology, and the processes related to it.

The highly charged business environment of the later 1980s brought this need sharply into focus, and there can only be an escalation of this situation throughout the 1990s, as world competition grows.

In order to compete successfully in those world markets an organisation must accept that high technology is a necessity, in investment, manning and training terms, and also accept the fact that this investment can have a negative effect on their employees — high technology can reduce the need for people!

Where an organisation operates in a business environment where constant technological change is the norm, management must ensure that there is a high element of flexibility in their thinking, particularly in strategic terms, in order to react quickly to new demands of the market.

Organisations may introduce technical change for a number of reasons:

(a) to improve productivity and reduce costs;

(b) to improve product image, quality of service;

(c) to reduce the size and cost of the workforce;

(d) to improve the speed of product delivery;

(e) to offer new products and services;

(f) to gain competitive advantage;

Particular examples of this strategic activity are to be found in the Automobile industry, where robotics have had a significant effect on both the speed of production and the size of the workforce, and in areas of Office Administration, where the development of computers and word processors had reduced the need for large filing facilities and for clerical support, in both the general office practices and in the accounting area.

7. DEMOGRAPHIC FACTORS

In order to operate any kind of business, an element of human resource is required, and the study of human resource trends and availability, is related to demography – the study of population.

The changes in age distribution, within any country, are of prime importance to strategic business planners, in that they call for flexibility in strategy, structures, attitudes to recruitment, and for flexibility in product type and availability.

Currently, in the United Kingdom, we are faced with a downward trend in the availability of younger workers, and a growth in the number of older workers and the number of those who have reached retirement age, and these factors call for a great deal of flexible and innovative business thought.

There has been a direct impact on recruitment, in that older workers are now being seen as valuable, and offered both re-training and, where early retirement has occurred, re-employment by many organisations who are concerned at their inability to find staff of the right calibre.

We hear constant reference to the "North/South Divide" and the movement of skilled employees to the booming industries of the southern counties, from the unemployment blackspots of the North, although, in fairness, there is a steady growth in employment in that part of the Country.

This movement in population and the change in the overall age balance of the population has serious implications which the business planner would be ill advised to ignore, in that the demand for products and services has also changed. Older age groups are in the ascendancy and this brings a shift of product emphasis, in terms of health care, housing, household goods, leisure facilities and holidays, and clothing.

In pure marketing terms, the study of demographics is the key to product development, the creation of new services, the content and thrust of advertising campaigns, and, in Managerial terms, the clear need to remain alert and fully flexible to the changing needs of the market.

8. CUSTOMERS, SUPPLIERS AND COMPETITORS

The Customer is King, in terms of business success, and the days are long gone where, once a product or service has been paid for, there is no real redress for the purchaser.

Consumer protection is a major element of Government legislation through for example, the Sale of Goods Act, and the essential factors of good marketing practice demand that customer needs are taken seriously, mainly due to the basic fact that there is little business sense in producing a product or service which no-one wants, or one which is out of step with current pricing policies in the market place. The consumer, as the ultimate end user of the product or service, has the particularly powerful sanction of being able to transfer purchasing power to a competitor, if the original supplier fails to provide satisfaction, or changes marketing policy in such a way as to reduce the original attraction, in the eye of the consumer, and management would be well advised to remember this when they are formulating policy for future operations.

Suppliers, of materials or services to other businesses are, of course, subject to these factors, but, in addition, have the power to either support success or to withdraw support, in the case of business decline or failure.

Good relationships with suppliers pay dividends, in terms of service, whilst poor relationships mean shortages leading to missed delivery dates, end user dissatisfaction, loss of hard won reputation, and, ultimately, loss of customer! There are still a number of managers who firmly believe that accounts from suppliers should remain unpaid for as long as possible, going to great lengths to fend off all enquiries.

That practice is diminishing, as businesses come to realise that both consumer and supplier should form an effective team that can lead to success in the market place, followed by additional business for both companies.

Competitors are always ready to seize opportunities, developing from the weakness of another business, and any forward thinking company keeps itself fully briefed on the immediate competition. Those already in the market will be well known, and subject to constant evaluation, but the wise organisation remains aware of possible new entrants to the market, for new entrants mean extra products in circulation, aiming for a share of the existing market, and that share can only come from those already in the market.

The business environment of today requires a quality product or service at a competitive price, with good support, and this, in turn, means a thorough grasp of market forces, particularly where low margins prevail and the possibility of change of supplier exists, as the penalty for poor service.

The business environment is, therefore, a complex collection of factors, each of which can impact on the ultimate profitability of an organisation, and those who are to be successful in their endeavours must never lose sight of any of these factors. The key to business growth is flexibility, but the management of an organisation can only achieve this if they are aware of the interplay of all the facets of the market, and this is what this chapter has tried to illustrate.

9. BUSINESS AND THE GREEN ENVIRONMENT

In June 1990, Peat Marwick McLintock's consultancy arm conducted a survey amongst senior managers related to their knowledge of environmental issues, and the current government initiatives.

The results, not too surprisingly, indicated that of 63 chemical companies, 25% of senior managers had never heard of the new bill and a further 60%

said that they were 'not very familiar' with it!

In recognition that consumers will now buy 'green' commodities, many major companies have developed corporate strategies for environmental issues, and B.P. in particular has adopted a high-profile stance on the subject.

Tesco has sought to promote itself as a green retailer, and its competitors have rushed to follow suit, but environmentalists have recently pointed out a major inconsistency, in that Tesco's strategy is based on the development of large out-of-town stores, having plenty of parking space, thereby using up land resources and encouraging customers to use more petrol!

Hard line environmentalists believe that none of the major oil companies can be said to have concern for the environment, due to the nature of their core business. Shell faced a huge outcry after the Mersey oil disaster in 1989, resulting in a £1m fine, and the United States has now produced a code called the *'Valdez Principles'*, after the major pollution problem in Alaska.

This Valdez Principle asks firms, who wish to present an acceptable public image, to sign a commitment to the new environmental code, guaranteeing to disclose in full all accidents with environmental implications, and agreeing to rectify all damage, before being considered for ethical investment. There is growing pressure on institutional pension schemes to adopt this hard line in the U.K.

A major problem is that the U.K. is in grave danger of being left behind, in relation to environmental issues, mainly by virtue of regarding it as a threat, thus brushing the subject under the carpet, rather than developing effective policies, like other European companies, and there is therefore considerable danger, post 1992, to both import and export markets.

There is no doubt that industry *must* take these matters seriously, history holds many illustrations of the disastrous consequences of uncontrolled activity, on human beings – Chernobyl, Bhopal, to name but two.

Europe is by no means blameless, a 200 year old chemical company, in Marktredwitz – West Germany, was forced to close in 1985 after revelations of an appalling history of major environmental pollution, involving widespread mercury contamination. To date nearly 3000 tonnes of contaminated soil and other material, including arsenic, cadmium and cyanide, has been placed in underground storage, but the final total to be removed is estimated to be as much as 80,000 tonnes.

The German taxpayer will foot the clean-up bill, put at more than Dm 50m, for the collapse of the company means that liability of the originator does not apply, although two former managers were brought to trial and fined Dm 910,000 and Dm 80,000 respectively for having failed to respect environmental regulations.

The chemical industry is in the forefront of environmental surveillance, products from this area are an indispensable part of normal life, from clothing to plastics, and toiletries to medicines, but this places an enormous responsibility on to the industry, which on one hand is a valued provider, and on the other, a source for disaster.

These pressures call for deliberate changes in strategy, placing environmental matters high on the management agenda, and can produce economic advantages, after new anti-pollution systems reduce the need for disposal of waste products.

The electricity industry is also very concerned about its impact on the environment, particularly after the June 1990 agreement, by European ministers, to reduce sulphur dioxide emissions from power stations by 60% before the year 2003.

Britain has an 80% reliance on coal-fired electricity production, and faces a huge bill for bringing installations up to date, having already put aside £1 bn to bring the first 13% of its generating capacity in line. As an additional part of the anti-acid rain programme, the Central Electricity Generating Board is already involved in a £170 m programme to fit low nitrogen burners in all coal burning power stations.

The water industry faces a number if E.C. Directives, covering areas such as surface and underground water standards, and the protection of fish, but the two most pressing issues relate to drinking water and bathing water quality.

The drinking water Directive was agreed in 1980, with a five year delay factor on implementation, and fixes maximum advisable concentrations of more than 60 undesirable substances, in water for water consumption, and from 1985 the regulations became even tighter, in that every sample taken *has* to pass a series of tests, related to taste, smell and colour, in addition to permitted concentrations of undesirable elements.

The bathing water Directive was agreed in 1975, with a 10 year implementation period, and laid down minimum standards for designated bathing beaches, which many U.K. beaches fail to meet still.

There are not easy solutions to any of these environmental problems, but rather a need for initial assessment of the scope of the problem, in any given industry, followed by well structured plans for rectification, the establishment of effective controls, and a concerted effort in both management and employee awareness training.

The environment belongs to all of us and we must *all* accept our responsibility for it, both for ourselves and the future of mankind.

CHAPTER TWO

THE STRUCTURE OF CORPORATE OBJECTIVES

1. INTRODUCTION

There are a number of people in the business world who will tell you that there can only be one corporate objective for any type of business organisation — that of profit maximisation. Whilst accepting this as the ultimate goal, what that very condensed statement fails to illustrate is, that in order to achieve that desirable objective, a number of significant, and quantifiable, activities must take place throughout the organisation, i.e. the achievement of pre-determined objectives by all major functional areas of the organisation, based on a clearly defined strategic plan aimed at achieving total vertical and horizontal interlock of all activities within the Company.

The full process of corporate objective setting is a time consuming and complex issue, requiring a great deal of careful thought, clearheaded analysis of all the hard data available, in respect of past performance of all sections of the Organisation, and realistic projections of future intent, based on a detailed analysis of the business environment surrounding the Organisation.

In this Chapter, we shall examine the task of management, in establishing viable corporate objectives, and take note of the constraints which, if ignored, all too often prevent those objectives being achieved.

2. THE CORPORATE MISSION

The "Mission" of an organisation lies at the very core of its being, a clear identification of what it exists to do, the important reason towards which all resources are directed, and upon which all objectives are based. It would be reasonable to assume that the Mission was established when the organisation was originally formed, in that those initial objectives were the subject of detailed discussions, by the founding Directors, and this is certainly true, within the original time frame, but time and changing business pressures can, and do, cause the original Mission to assume different forms, as the organisation progresses.

The Mission of any organisation is subject to both internal pressures and external pressures, related to economics, technical innovation, legislation, market forces, and the impact of the human resource, within the organisation, on total performance and the agreed strategic objectives, and the combined influence of these can cause an organisation to move away from the original Mission.

By way of illustration, take the case of a major dairy group who, one might say, has the clear Mission of supplying milk to the customers doorstep, on a daily basis, and this was most certainly true some years ago, but consider what service the average milkman brings to the customer now, in relation to the supply of eggs, cheese, bread, chickens, potatoes, yoghurt etc, and accept that the original Mission of the organisation has broadened considerably, over time.

It is, therefore, essential to examine and clarify this important area, prior to any attempt to formulate strategy, set objectives, or determine resource requirements, and management must be prepared to allocate time, on a regular basis, to undertake a thorough examination of all the activities going on within the organisation, which, together, form the overall Mission of the business, prior to formulating any strategic plans.

3. OPERATIONAL ANALYSIS

Organisations stagnate, just as people stagnate, they become complacent and fail to recognise that circumstances surrounding them have changed and moved in different directions over time, a case of "let sleeping dogs lie" is all to often the prevailing ethos within organisations of all sizes in all sectors, in other words, a highly developed resistance to change exists. Those organisations which recognise this, and do regularly examine all sections of the company for efficiency of performance, are the ones who stand out in the business community, but regrettably, the majority of organisations still resist change.

A well validated system for business analysis is that which is known as "SWOT ANALYSIS" – the detailed analysis of four main areas which have a direct impact on the Organisation:

STRENGTHS.... WEAKNESSES.... OPPORTUNITIES.... THREATS (SWOT)

These four specific areas are usually plotted on a "Crucifix" chart (as Figure 1 below) and all activities of the organisation are evaluated separately, and placed under one of the four headings, on the chart.

Strengths	Weaknesses
Opportunities	Threats

Figure 1 : SWOT Analysis Chart

Essentially, this activity assists management in answering basic questions like:

(a) what are we good at? (Strengths)

(b) what are we not good at? (Weaknesses)

(c) how effective is our Senior Management? (Strengths/Weaknesses)

(d) how effective are the control systems of the organisation? (Strengths/Weaknesses)

(e) how do we compare with out competitors in the market? (Strengths/Weaknesses/Opportunities/Threats)

(f) what financial resources do we have available to us? (Strengths/Weaknesses/Opportunities/Threats)

(g) how effective is our human resource element, at every level? (Strengths/Weaknesses/Threats)

(h) can we compete effectively, with our present equipment? (Strengths/Weaknesses/Opportunities/Threat)

These, and many other questions need definitive answers, if the organisational analysis is to form a secure base for future planning, and it is here that many Managements fall short of achieving a reliable format, due to the entrance of emotion, entrenched or defensive positioning, and inability to face up to unpalatable answers, into the discussions. All, of course, will enter enthusiastically into a discussion of Strengths and Opportunities, and, perhaps, even try to isolate Threats, but the main stumbling block always seems to be the area of Weaknesses, because this means admitting failure!

The ground rules for successful completion of this form of business analysis are clear, i.e. build on and maximise Strengths, seize and exploit Opportunities, plan a defence against Threats, and, ERADICATE WEAKNESSES as soon as possible, and it is here that Managements often avoid the unpalatable — particularly if it involves major change or the removal of a senior executive, but it is a valuable asset to an imaginative and courageous management group, with determination to act in each area.

4. CORPORATE OBJECTIVES

To be fully effective, corporate objectives must reflect the controlled linkage of a series of clearly defined separate objectives, either Divisional or Departmental, which, together, form the total expectations of the organisation, as a whole.

There are a number ground rules for this process which cannot be ignored, and it is essential that those involved should be full aware of them, otherwise a less than successful conclusion will be achieved! All objectives must be QUANTIFIABLE, i.e. capable of being accurately measured, rather than subject to a form of measurement which is predominately QUALITATIVE, i.e. based on value judgements of individuals, no matter how experienced. The reasons for this are related to the very natural influences that all humans are subject to, their habit of liking, or disliking another human being, and, therefore consciously or unconsciously, allowing their judgement to be biased, one way or the other, in matters related to that individual.

Further emphasis must be placed on the need for any objectives to be ACHIEVABLE, by, first, the organisation as a whole, and, second, any department or individual within the organisation allocated a task. There have been a number of organisations who approach the process of objective setting by the simple method of either just allocating an arbitrary requirement, without consultation, or by changing any projection submitted, again usually without discussion, and both of these, of course, fail to gain any form of commitment from the people concerned. The overriding requirement, in setting corporate objectives, is the need to ensure that all objectives clearly relate to the Mission of the Organisation, for without this, all concerned are involved in a series of unrelated activities, which are of little benefit to the organisation, in the long term.

In terms of positive viability, therefore, the total agreed collection of both primary and secondary objectives, related to the strategic intent of the organisation, must firmly lock together both horizontally and vertically, in order to achieve corporate success (Figure 2). This, effectively, ensures that not only does the control of top management cascade down through the organisation, and return as an viable flow of information for further decision making but also that there is cross fertilisation between all divisions and departments of the organisation, to ensure cooperation and avoid duplication of effort, and the resulting financial losses which that would bring. The total effort of the organisation is therefore harnessed into an effective and efficient forward drive, from which positive results must surely flow.

Figure 2: Corporate Objectives Model

The value of fully communicating the benefits of this structure of organisational linkage, is related to the process of making each division or department fully aware of the aims and specific objectives of all other sections of the organisation, with the very clear intention of ensuring that no part of the organisation by virtue of decisions or actions it may take, during the course of normal activity, or, indeed, in times of pressure.

In terms of the determination of Corporate Objectives, a series of well validated parameters are necessary, and each must be given sufficient time to ensure that all possible factors have been fully considered, and that logical, and unemotional, conclusions have been reached, and the action plans are both realistic and capable of being achieved. The following factors need careful consideration:

(a) Clarity of definition

Many businesses fail to fully achieve their Corporate Objectives due solely to one primary error, i.e. failure to ensure that their future intentions have been clearly defined.

There are many business executives who will insist that there can only ever be one Corporate Objective for any organisation, and that is profit maximisation, and whilst that certainly will feature on any list of priorities, in itself, it is not sufficiently detailed, as a statement of intent, to be accepted as the sole organisational objective. All objectives are expressed as statements of intent, fully supported by necessary detail, related to the achievement of the Mission of the organisation, and should provide a set of performance parameters, against which informed judgements, and decisions, can be taken to ensure those objectives are achieved.

The Board of Directors must therefore give considerable time and thought to the process by which a limited number of primary objectives, related to the overall Mission of the organisation, can be agreed, an important proviso being that they should ensure that these main objectives are capable of being sub-divided into clear operational objectives for all major sections of the organisation.

Some typical areas for such consideration would be:

(a) a policy of business growth through acquisition;
(b) the development of overseas markets, using existing products;
(c) the development of overseas markets, using new products;
(d) an increase in market share by higher emphasis on the quality, value for money, and attractiveness of current products;
(e) the introduction of new technology within the business;
(f) the improvement of physical resources related to the business;
(g) the improvement of Managerial & Worker performance levels;
(h) the reduction of areas of the Organisation, in size and cost.

The areas listed are not exhaustive, but given as an illustration of the need for specific objectives to be arrived at, rather than a bland statement of intent expressed as "growth" or "improved profit", or "survival", regrettably all to often used in statements of top management strategy for the year to come, but almost incapable of being translated into viable action plans, by those who have to achieve those intended results.

(b) Measurement

A great deal of valuable time can be wasted, by arriving at objectives which are measurable only in qualitative terms, and therefore by subjective judgement only, a fallible situation! The golden rule, in terms of objective setting, is to arrive at a limited set of *Primary Objectives* which are "quantifiable", i.e. able to be measured with a high degree of accuracy, by both the management and those charged with achieving the tasks.

A group of three basic questions, which can be applied to all primary objectives, may prove to be the most practical approach to this problem:

(a) who will benefit, if we achieve this objective?

(b) what form will the benefit take?

(c) in quantifiable terms, how large, or small, will that benefit be?

These questions are devised to induce detailed thinking to the process of objective clarification, by adding a requirement for the evaluation of the actual expected return, in each case. Once this process has been completed, some serious effort must be made to establish completion time-scales for each objective, for failure to do this will allow the inevitable erosion of the activity patterns, due to their being overtaken by other "pressures" in the daily task of running a Department or Division.

(c) Capability

Earlier, we referred to the need for "unemotional" decisions, in relation to any aspect of organisational strategy, and this was for important reasons, related to the capability of the organisation to achieve the objectives it finally arrives at.

In the Boardroom, or indeed at any number of business meetings, when ideas flow freely, it is very human to be carried along with the tide of optimism and enthusiasm, relying on the informed judgement of a specialist manager, who, because, perhaps, the idea originated from his part of the organisation, and it will enhance his image, or profitability, will seek to gain the support of the others at the meeting for a series of activities to take place. It is, however, essential that any such action is subject to detailed discussion, and evaluation, prior to full approval being given. Some top managers, sadly, seriously overestimate the capability of their Organisations in such areas as Market Position, Production Ability, Manpower Skills, and Financial Flexibility, or their ability to absorb another Company, by acquisition, without stretching the resources of their own organisation, and this can be a recipe for Corporate disaster!

Within every organisation, there is a great deal of hard data available to assist the process of arriving at practical conclusions, related to the ability, and capability, of the organisation to achieve specific objectives. This hard data can consist of previous organisational performance, in the area under debate, or the performance of the relevant market, or of specific products in the market, plus the performance of individual managers and staff in similar tasks in recent months or years, plus the available data related to the National and International economic trends.

In the case of acquisitions, particularly where the projected target is in an unfamiliar Market, the capability of Top Management to, firstly, evaluate the prospective acquisition with any degree of certainty, and, secondly, to direct and control operations, post acquisition, is critical, and these two factors could decide the successful outcome of the activity. It therefore follows that both the "capability" and "ability" of top management needs critical evaluation, in a cold, unemotional, and logical way, prior to embarking on the acquisition trail-for there is no room for rose tinted spectacles, or inflated egos, when such an important activity is contemplated, and such realism must be present for all organisational objectives, the same parameters for success, or failure, apply.

(d) Flexibility

Many well intentioned organisations spend considerable time, and effort, in arriving at their Corporate Objectives, in discussing those objectives with relevant managers, and obtaining their agreement, in communicating with staff and ensuring full understanding by issuing comprehensive manuals to all sections concerned with the objectives, and establishing performance monitoring systems. Initially, progress appears to be satisfactory, and all systems seem to be working well, justifying the original time spent in the opening discussions, but, suddenly, things start to go wrong.

At first there is low key concern, coupled with an expectation that this is "only a temporary blip", but the system fails to react effectively and the problem grows, causing a rash of management meetings, to both isolate and deal with the crisis, in order to return to the previously defined path. An isolated incident may, indeed be effectively dealt with in this way, but, perhaps, the single incident is far more critical than it initially appears to be, and could, be the first indication that major changes will become necessary, and this is where the need for flexibility, in both managerial thinking and organisational ability to react, is of paramount importance.

THE PROCESS OF OBJECTIVE SETTING

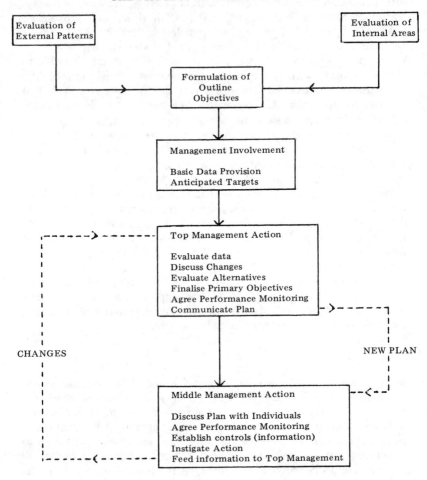

Figure 3

All organisations are subject to pressure, from two distinct sources, first, the external environment in which it operates, and, seconds, the internal environment, within the organisation, and both have equal ability to force change upon an organisation. Some examples are given, below:

THE STRUCTURE OF CORPORATE OBJECTIVES

1. The external environment:

> National and International economic change;
> All forms of Government action, at home and abroad;
> Market changes, due to competition activity;
> Changes in consumer buying habits, particularly in economic downturn
> periods when spending is restricted;
> Problems with suppliers (missed deliveries or material shortages);
> National or International transport problems;
> National or International industrial relations problems.

2. The internal environment:

> Loss of key Management;
> Shortage, or loss, of skilled workers;
> Internal industrial relations problems;
> Major machinery breakdown in a critical area;
> Quality control problems;
> Shortage of working capital;
> Poor stock control, leading to critical production shortages.

In each case, both internal and external problems need prompt and decisive management action, which may result in a total change of Corporate policy, which, in turn, will impact on the original objectives.

The wise organisation will have recognised that flexibility is the key to success in reaching objectives and an effective use of management time, spent in both arriving at the original group of objectives, and, in the same process, in evaluating a number of alternative strategies which may be needed in the future, should problems arise with the original objectives. The ability to move to "plan B" when any problems arise, is an essential requirement for top management strategic objective planning, and time spent training managers, in flexible thinking, can yield rewards, in times of organisational stress. It is a clear fact of life that in the fast moving business environment of the 1990s, the potentiality for change is always present, and managers who recognise that a "problem" today is tomorrow's "opportunity", and build flexibility into their organisational thinking, are the ones who, ultimately, will become the winners in the quest for increased performance and profit.

5.   THE HIERARCHY OF BUSINESS OBJECTIVES

We have established the need to create a limited number of Primary Objectives, statements of organisational intent for the immediate and medium term future, and discussed, briefly the division of these objectives into, first Departmental, and then, individual objectives with clear performance monitoring parameters. The total activity of Corporate Objective setting must, as we have said earlier, relate to the "Mission" of the organisation, and all discussions with middle managers (heads of Departments) must ensure that the sectional, or sub-objectives, as they are often called, are segments of the total intent contained within the Primary Objectives, and that they, in turn, bear this in mind when discussing individual tasks.

6.   THE FORMULATION OF OBJECTIVES

It is the function of senior Management to select the primary objectives of an organisation, but these, essentially, must be in broad outline, initially, until sufficient data is made available to enable a more detailed analysis and evaluation to take place, prior to final approval being given. This basic data must come from the Departmental Managers, those who will, ultimately, be charged with achieving the Objectives, and the early involvement of these managers is an important factor.

There are two ways to arrive at Primary Objectives, one being to impose the decisions from above, without consultation, and this is called "Top Down management", an approach which gains little or no commitment from middle management, because of lack of discussion, and sometimes causes top management to make elementary mistakes due to lack of specialist operational knowledge, a situation which very often produces a great deal of derisory comment from managers, and certainly does not enhance the image of the Board!

A much better approach is to circulate the broad outline intent, and request managers to examine the proposals and quantify their Departmental ability to meet those proposals, or suggest alternative courses of action. This process is called "Bottom Up Management", and is designed to gain both the benefit of specialist input, avoiding unworkable decisions, and to also gain full commitment from the individual managers, by involving them in the planning of organisational activity, and, in the majority of cases, fulfilling the objectives set by themselves.

No strategic policy should be decided in isolation therefore, and although it takes time to request this basic detail, and evaluate the Departmental proposals, prior to the selection of Primary and Secondary Objectives, and the publication of the Organisational Strategic Plan, the end product, in terms of committed effort, is well worth the delay. A further element to consider, is the inevitable fact that the initial plan will be subject to either internal or external pressure, at some stage of its life, and that pressure will call for a flexible reaction, from the Organisation. By involving sectional Heads, initially, the process of directional change can be achieved far quicker, when flexibility is necessary, due to their detailed knowledge of the overall intent of the organisation, brought about by being part of the total planning process, and their commitment to achieving those plans. To retain that commitment, however, any changes of direction that are necessary must follow the same process of involvement and discussion that was such an essential element of the original planning process, for this is no managerial technique, to be given lip service by autocratic senior managers, in an attempt to motivate lower levels of management, whilst the "real" decisions are made in the Boardroom!

In the arriving at the initial broad outline statements, Top Managers could suggest areas such as:

Financial:
Improve total profitability;
Improve financial controls;
Improve return on capital employed;
Improve return assets;
Improve return on Shareholders capital.

Marketing:
Gain a wider Market share;
Move into optional markets;
Improve segmental market share;
Improve overall Corporate image.

Products:
Extend the product range;
Reduce the product range;
Improve new product launches;
Increase research and development activity.

Technology:
Introduce new equipment;
Increase production output;
Reduce production costs;
Improve production quality.

Management:
Improve performance;
Review areas of responsibility;
Ensure full accountability for actions;
Improve flexibility (by training);
Review ability and capability;
Reduce the Management structure.

Employees:
Improve performance and motivation;
Increase participation in decisions;
Review the total reward structure;
Improve career planning and training;
Reduce total costs.

Organisation: Review the structure;
Seek growth by acquisition;
Reduce the size of the organisation;
Improve total flexibility;
Improve communication;
Improve and streamline information flow.

External: Improve relationships with others,
Shareholders;
Customers;
Suppliers;
Government Agencies;
The Community.

This is not an exhaustive list, but an indication of some areas which have been used by many organisations, in the past, and is an illustration of the detailed thinking required.

7. ORGANISATIONS AND WORK

Our main concern is with people at work and their relationships within an organisation. We establish organisations to provide a product or a service for which a need has been identified by society.

(1) PRIVATE SECTOR FORMS OF ORGANISATION IN THE UK

There are a number of different legal forms of organisation in the private sector of industry and commerce:-

(A) Non-commercial organisations

Individuals may join together into organisations which are of a sporting or social type with rules and regulations drawn up in the form of a constitution and self-imposed, e.g. an archery or tennis club. They will probably acquire land and property and employ labour. The members are likely to appoint officers of the club who will operate as trustees in that they have the authority to acquire and dispose of the club's property within the articles and rules laid down, for the benefit of the members, but are not allowed to make profits for themselves. They are designated in law as unincorporated associations. Trade unions are a further example of this form of organisation.

(B) Sole traders

The simplest form of business in the UK, a sole trader is the owner and only controller and in law is held entirely responsible for the success or otherwise of the activity. He is responsible personally for any debts which the business has and any property or assets he has may be used to pay off these debts. This tends to curtail the scope of the operation and the growth in size of the business. Examples of sole traders include newsagents, jobbing builders, small car hire firms, photographers, etc., where the amount of capital and the number of employees required is small.

(C) Private partnership

A partnership is merely a collection of people who wish to operate the business together and agree to share the profits and the losses. Partners in many senses are in the same position as sole traders. The advantage is that it can allow for a combination of skills and expertise and often a greater availability of capital — the fact that each partner assumes an unlimited liability for the debts of the whole undertaking is an advantage when borrowing capital. Partnerships exist longer than the sole trader type of enterprise because the firm is not dependent upon the life of anyone individual, although the death or retirement of a key partner is liable to bring the partnership to an end. Most solicitors, accountants, doctors and dentists operate this form of business relationship.

(D) Private limited company

The limited liability company was an extension of the partnership principle but was brought about largely because of the inability of most partnerships to obtain sufficient capital to expand. Such a company comes into existence when a number of people, who may even be unknown to each other, join together to invest their money in a common enterprise. The company is for legal purposes a separate entity, distinct from the individuals who set it up. In the event of the failure of the company, the liability of each investor for the debts of the company is limited to the amount of his original investment. Each shareholder in a limited liability company receives a share of the profits each year — a dividend — depending on the amount of money invested. Whereas the shareholders own the company, it is the company that carries on the business and the company alone that can enter into contracts and be asked to pay the business debts. The Companies Acts underpin the basic legal regulation of such enterprises. To form such a company certain documents have to be completed and lodged with the Companies Registration Office in Cardiff. These are:-

(a) The Memorandum of Association, which states the company's name, its objectives and details of how the shares are organised.

(b) The Articles of Association, setting out the internal rules of the company, as to the way it is to be run; it sets out the powers of directors.

(c) A declaration that the legal requirements of the Companies Acts concerning the formation of a registered company, have been complied with.

(d) A statement of the nominal share capital of the company and the way in which the shares are divided up.

Private limited liability companies are restricted in whom they may sell shares to; they must first offer them to one of the existing shareholders of whom there can be no more than fifty.

In 1988 there were some 921,000 private companies listed by the Registrar of Companies according to the Department of Trade and Industry.

(E) Public limited liability company (PLC)

There are several main differences between public and private limited liability companies:-

(a) the shares of a public company are quoted on the Stock Exchange and are available — normally via brokers — to the general public; whereas there are restrictions on transferring shares in a private company;

(b) the number of shareholders in a public company is unlimited, but there must be a minimum of seven shareholders.

(c) there must be more than one director in a public company;

(d) before public companies are formed they must issue a prospectus setting out details of their financial records and their directors;

(e) investors' capital is more liquid because shares are bought and sold easily on the Stock Exchange;

(f) it is especially suitable, where returns may take a long time to appear, e.g. developments in balloon transportation, where a number of people can be encouraged to invest small amounts with prospect of no immediate returns;

(g) they are able to use the services of experts with keen business ability, but no capital. Thus the functions of the capitalist and the entrepreneur can be separated.

There are some disadvantages to public limited liability companies. The only link between the undertaking and the worker is a cash one in that the worker gets a wage and has little contact with those who actually own the assets of the company. In addition shareholders are in practice able to exercise little control over the actual operation of the company and over many policy matters. A further problem tends to arise, especially in these days of institutional shareholding, for the ease with which shares are transferred makes the company liable to speculative dealings on the Stock Exchange which have little to do with actual investment in a specific product or organisation.

Table 1: Percentage distribution of shareholdings in PLCs 1963-1989

Source: Share Register Surveys: various

Shareholding	1963	1969	1975	1981	1989
Individuals	54.0	47.4	37.5	28.2	21.3
Charities	2.1	2.1	2.3	2.2	2.0
Banks	1.3	1.7	0.7	0.3	0.9
Insurance Companies	10.0	12.2	15.9	20.5	18.4
Pension Funds	6.4	9.0	16.8	26.7	30.4
Unit Trusts	1.3	2.9	4.1	3.6	5.9
Investment Trusts	11.3	10.5	10.5	6.8	3.2
Companies	5.1	5.4	3.0	5.1	3.6
Public Sectors	1.5	2.6	3.6	3.0	2.0
Overseas	7.0	6.6	5.6	3.6	12.4
	100.0	100.0	100.0	100.0	100.0

In 1988 there were some 6,600 PLCs registered in Britain.

Table 2: The 30 Largest Companies in Britain by Turnover

Source – The Times 1000 1988–1989

COMPANY	MAIN ACTIVITY	TURNOVER (£m)	employees
British Petroleum Co	Oil industry	34,932	126,400
Shell Transport & Trading	Oil industry	23,924	n/a
BAT Industries	Tobacco, retailing etc.	11,255	168,949
ICI	Petrochemicals, Pharmaceuticals, etc	11,123	127,800
Electricity Council	Electricity suppliers	11,118	131,891

British Telecomm	Telecommunications services	10,185	235,633
British Gas	Gas suppliers	7,610	88,469
Hanson	Consumer products	6,682	88,000
Shell UK	Oil industry	6,677	13,636
Grand Metropolitan	Hotels, brewers, milk products etc.	5,706	129,436
Unilever	Food products, detergents etc.	5,428	155,000
Esso UK	Oil industry	5,398	5,352
General Electric Co.	Electrical	5,247	159,579
Ford Motor Co.	Motor vehicle manufacturers	5,211	47,000
Dalgety	International merchants	5,003	23,966
Dee Corporation	Wholesale, retail, cash & carry	4,837	84,240
J. Sainsbury	Retail food distribution	4,792	82,601
Marks and Spencer	General store proprietors	4,578	68,450
British Coal	Coal mining	4,515	162,800
Allied Lyons	Brewers, vintners, hoteliers etc.	4,236	78,178
BTR	Construction, energy and electrical	4,149	81,800
Tesco	Multiple retailing	4,119	71,262
British Aerospace	Aircraft etc. manufacturing	4,075	86,800
Saachi & Saachi Co.	Advertising	3,954	15,630
Gallagher	Tobacco, optics, pumps & valves	3,887	32,540
British Airways	Transportation	3,756	43,969
Post Office	Mail and parcel services	3,473	188,732
British Steel Corporation	Iron and steel manufactures etc	3,461	54,650
RTZ Corporation	Mining, industrial, metals & fuel	3,397	78,705
Bass	Brewing, drinks & pub retailing	3,213	79,348

(F) Cooperatives

These may take three main forms in this country:-

(a) EMPLOYEES' COOPERATIVES: workmen own and manage an organisation to derive profits as well as wages. The worker is freed from the position of a hired employee who sells his labour.

(b) RETAIL OR DISTRIBUTIVE COOPERATIVES: this generally takes the form of cooperative stores in which a number of retail shops combine to buy foods collectively at wholesale prices, sell at retail prices and divide some of the surplus among the members in proportion to their purchases. The remainder of the surplus is often devoted to social and benevolent purposes.

(c) WHOLESALE COOPERATION is the formation of cooperative wholesale societies to provide retail stores with goods on the same principles as the stores provide goods for their members. The members' of the wholesale societies are the individual retail stores who share the surpluses in the same way as the stores' members share their profits.

(2) PUBLIC SECTOR FORMS OF ORGANISATION IN THE UK

Public Services are a significant part of the economy and perform a role in providing an infrastrucutre of the management of the country, provide essential services and various measures to provide support for members of the community. The conservative government in office from 1979 onwards was keen to reduce the scope of the public sectors and increase the involvement of the private sector in providing some of the services ostensibly to imporve competitiveness and performance. Some 5.5m people are employed in the public sector including the armed services and nationalised industries.

(A) Central Government

The Civil Service

Civil servants are employees of the Crown whose salaries are paid through monies voted from Parliament. They work for the Government departments, either centrally or in the regions. Or they may work in some other independent body set up by Government, e.g. ACAS, Certification Office, Equal Opportunities Commission, or the Commission for Racial Equality. The major departments in 1990 were:

Agriculture, Fisheries & Food	Lord Advocate's Department
Defence	Lord Chancellor's Department
Duchy of Lancaster	Northern Ireland Office
Education & Science	Paymaster-General's Office
Employment	Privy Council Office
Energy	Scottish Office
Environment	Trade & Industry
Foreign & Commonwealth Affairs	Transport
Health & Social Security	Treasury
Home Office	Welsh Office
Law Officers' Department	

Each Government department is headed by a Minister, some of whom are members of the Cabinet, e.g. Department of Employment, Education and Science, Home Office, etc. The departmental minister works closely with the most senior civil servant in his department, the permanent secretary (or permanent-under-secretary if the minister is a Cabinet minister) who is responsible to the minister for administrating and directing the work of the department and its finances. A civil servant, in carrying out his duties, must be politically neutral. Yet because they are permanent members of the administration, it is true to say that senior civil servants have an important role not only in implementing policy but also in formulating it.

(B) Local Government

Not all matters can be handled by Central Government because of the sheer weight of issues. In addition different parts of Britain have different needs: thus only by a form of Local Government is it possible for priorities to be established to reflect the needs of the local community. The structure of Local Government in England and Wales in 1990 was as follows:

Figure 4: Structure of Local Government in England and Wales

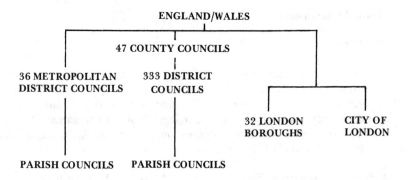

Local authorities have a wide range of services, some of which, e.g. education and the fire service, they are obliged by law to provide, whereas others, such as parks and recreational facilities, are at local discretion. We could split the services into three broad categories:

i)   those offering protection to the community, such as the fire service, police service, consumer protection, environmental health (including refuse collection and disposal and street cleaning); and

ii) those concerned with the welfare of the community, such as education, social services, housing, transport, roads and local planning; and

iii) those providing communal facilities, such as parks, recreational facilities, cemeteries, libraries and museums.

Each different tier in the Local Government system has responsibilities for services, some of which are common (e.g. some roads are the responsibility of the County Councils or Metropolitan Councils and other roads are the responsibility of the districts or boroughs), and some of them are specific to a tier (e.g. the police and the fire service are the responsibility of the County Councils or the Metropolitan Councils, whereas housing tends to be the main responsibility of the districts or boroughs). The distribution of functions between the various councils can vary based on local catchment and local need.

Local Government authorities have powers to raise funds through Community Charge and loans and are also allocated Central Government block grants, which enable them to finance their activities.

Generally the powers of Local Government are limited by Acts of Parliament and the Government can also influence their activities via the allocation of the block grant and by the granting or withholding of permission to borrow funds. Some Local Government services are also influenced by Central Government departments, e.g. education by the Department of Education & Science, and the fire services and police by the Home Office. One major trend in recent years has been the reduction of the role of the local authorities as direct providers of services. Thus the 1988 Local Government Act required local authorities to offer for competitive tendering many of the services previously provided by directly employed local authority labour e.g. maintenance of parks and borough properties, catering services, street cleaning, refuse collection etc.

(C) National Health Service

The National Health Service was established by the National Health Service Act of 1946. Until 1974 local authorities were responsible for provision of personal health services including ambulances, health care, some nursing and midwifery, family planning, vaccination and immunisation, and hospitals were administered through Regional Hospital Boards, with dental services and the family practitioner service being administered through local executive councils. From April 1974 these services were amalgamated in a major reorganisation of the Health Service when 14 Regional Health Authorities replaced the Regional Health Boards, and (due to a further reorganisation in 1982 cutting out a tier of Area Health Authorities) these are now supported by 201 District Health Authorities. The structure from 1985 therefore is shown on page 32 Figure 5. This structure derives from the Griffiths Report, published in 1983. The NHS Management Board, with members from business, the health service and the civil service, plans the implementation of policies approved by the NHS Supervisory Board and manages the health service within the budget agreed by the Supervisory Board and Parliament.

Figure 5: Structure of the National Health Service

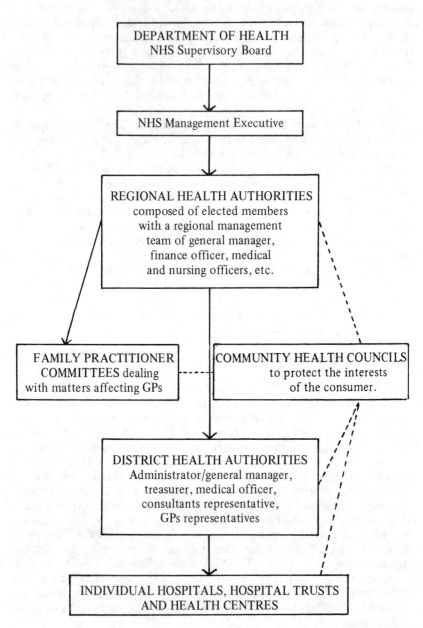

The functions of the Regional Health Authorities are to draw up plans for the allocation of resources amongst the District Health Authorities who are responsible for planning, organising and administering the district's needs. The Community Health Councils act as a channel of communication between the health authorities, the consumers and the public and are consulted by the District Health Authorities on their plans.

The latest initiatives in the NHS are to encourage decentralisation by allowing the creation of hospital trusts and by allowing general practices to become budget holders and to purchase hospital treatment for their patients from the most efficient and cost effective source.

(D) Police authorities

These are based on the county unit, although where counties are small or have a small population they may cover more than one county.

(E) Public corporations

In their early days companies engaged in supplying some form of public utility, e.g. gas and electricity, were encouraged by Government to compete with each other, for it was considered that such a policy would give the general public the best possible service at lowest cost. Gradually it was argued that duplication of activity was inefficient and it was decided for political, social and economic reasons that certain activities were best controlled by the State. Most of the previously nationalised industries were formed between the war and 1950. Acts of Parliament were passed to put such activities as coal mining, electricity generating and supply, gas supply, transportation and air travel into the hands of public corporations e.g. British Rail and British Coal.

Public corporations are not synonymous with the nationalised industries, few of which remain after the privatisation of the conservative government years in the 1980s. Those privatised included British Aerospace, 1981 (Rover Group joined in 1989), National Freight Corporation, 1982, Britoil, 1982, Associate British Ports, 1983, Enterprise Oil and British Telecomm in 1984, British Shipbuilders, 1984 and subsequent years, British Gas, 1986, British Airways, 1987, and Regional Water Authorities and Electricity 1990. The arguments used in favour of nationalisation include:

— reduction of the role of the State in the market and commensurate savings for public sector borrowing and the taxpayer;

— The democratisation of share ownership for members of the economy and employees of the company — but have shares been sold too cheaply?

— encourage efficiency and management responsibility for success;

Those who argue against the sale of these industries would argue that,

— the taxpayer has taken the losses over the years and should benefit from the success;

— they are powerful monopolies and should be controlled for the benefit of the community;

— they could be (and should be) more efficiently and effectively run for the benefit of the community as public organisations.

The legal status granted to public corporations was intended to give them a commercial freedom not traditionally granted to government departments. They were created either by statute or Royal Charter — were able to enter into contracts in their own right. They thus enjoy a degree of self control with targets established by the government and their responsibility is via a Minister to Parliament to the general public. Each Minister has considerable financial control over the corporation and can regulate their borrowing, reorganisation and development pricing and can demand levels of profitability in the public interest. Although the Minister lays down general policy, the day-to-day operation of the corporation is left to the Board of Management which is appointed by the Minister, selection for which is based on the individual's previous experience and ability. Each Board has to present, via the Minister, an annual report to Parliament to permitting day-to-day matters to be raised and discussed. This is especially necessary as most of the State corporations are monopolies and care has to be taken to protect the interest of the consumers from inefficiency and profligacy.

Table 3: Main public corportions — years of formation (excluding Nationalised Industries)

Source: *Various*

British Broadcasting Corporation (set up by Royal charter)	1927
Scottish Special Housing Association	1937
New Town Development Corporations	1946

Bank of England	1946
Commonwealth Development Corporation	1948
Covent Garden Market Authority	1961
Highlands and Islands Development Board	1965
Northern Ireland Transport Holding Company	1968
Passenger Transport Executive	1969
Northern Ireland Housing Executive	1971
Independent Broadcasting Authority	1972
Trust Ports (Northern Ireland)	1974
Royal Mint	1975
Scottish Development Agency	1975
Land Authority for Wales	1976
Northern Ireland Development Agency	1976
Crown Suppliers	1976
Welsh Development Agency	1976
Development Board for Rural Wales	1977
Pilotage Commission	1979
Her Majesty's Stationery Office	1980
British Technology Group	1981
Urban Development Corporations	1981
Water Authorities Association	1983
Audit Commission	1983
Oil and Pipeline Agency	1985
English Industrial Estates Corporation	1986
Local Authority Airport Companies	1986
Local Authority Bus Companies	1987

8.   DEVELOPMENT OF ORGANISATIONS

To operate organisations we need to employ people.   At first a small organisation may require little specialisation and the people concerned with it get on with whatever task is most urgent, but gradually organisations recognise a need to add other individuals with particular expertise to the labour force.

When an organisation starts it probably has an 'ideas' person who has identified the societal need. He rarely has cash to spare and usually finds someone who will finance him.   Dependent upon the 'product' of the organisation, whether it be to make motor cars, print cards, bake bread or sell holidays, some technology may be required and our ideas person may not have much in the way of technical knowledge, so he attempts to find someone who can provide that necessary skill.   To begin operating the organisation suitable premises must be found and then he may want some appropriately-trained workers.

Thus, as an organisation grows necessary expertise is acquired — marketing experts, salesmen, development engineers, social workers, nurses, doctors or whoever is required to fulfil objectives. We hire people for their strengths and we combine them with other people who individually have complementary strengths. We can view organisations as entities which attempt to maximise their use of each individual's strengths whilst, at the same time, minimising their weaknesses by employing others to cover these skill deficiencies. Gradually a hierarchy will develop as we establish control within the organisation by means of an authority network to coordinate the division of labour we are creating. As organisations grow, the complexity of control becomes greater and organisations differ from each other in their methods of coping with these complexities. It is possible to define the common elements of organisations and for this a good statement is given by Schien in *Organisational Psychology* 3rd edn Prentice Hall, 1980 who defined an organisation as:

'the planned coordination of the activities of a number of people for the achievement of some common explicit purpose or goal, through division of labour and function and through a hierarchy of authority and responsibility.'

This definition examines the essential elements of organisation:

1. Organisations have *purposes* and these purposes have to be made clear to all workers so that they can work collectively.

2. To carry out the purposes of the organisation *division of labour* is required to use the expertise of each individual to the full.

3. *Authority* is required to ensure that individuals work consistently towards the organisation's objectives.

4. Organisations employ those 'activities' of people which help in attaining objectives and, although individuals can belong to a number of different organisations, only some activities are relevant to each organisation.

Thus each organisation produces a different working environment. One of the essentials of human resource management is the recognition that this environment influences the behaviour of the individuals working in it. We have to understand the particular influences which exist in our own organisation and how they affect the behaviour of the individuals working there.

Organisations are composed of people with different sets of values, beliefs and skills; they have structures with different characteristics, depending upon the type of product produced, the technology used and the tasks performed. This creates different kinds of relationships between people and their work. The processes and structures are concerned with authority, communication, goal setting and the decision making necessary to fulfil the task of the organisation whilst, at the same time, considering the objectives of the human resources.

9. OBJECTIVES OF ORGANISATIONS

To define the objectives of an organisation at any one moment is not simple. Any organisation may have multiple goals, for the immediate priorities of organisations change due to pressure from the environment in which they operate. These goals may overlap in their effect. For example, if we examine a business organisation, at one time the priority may be an increase in profits. This could be achieved by an increase in price, but the organisational ability to benefit from such an increase will depend on the nature of competition in the market. A different strategy could be an increase in efficiency, which in turn will be influenced by the commitment of the employees or the ability to purchase or introduce technological change. A parallel emphasis, however, could be on gaining a larger share of a particular market. This may only be obtained by freezing and even lowering prices, which could actually reduce profitability in the short term. In a different period, the objective could be compliance with new health and safety legislation, again necessitating a reduction in profits as cash is used to fulfil this objective. Perhaps, at another time, the use of resources may be necessary to develop new products, as consumer research shows a fall in demand for the current range.

(a) Objectives of private sector organisations

A list of a business organisation's objectives could include the following:

— do research,
— make a profit,
— diversify,
— develop new products,
— control other organisations,
— maximise sales,
— provide an enhanced range of products,
— move into new national or regional markets,
— provide a healthy and safe working environment,
— offer education and training,
— minimise unnecessary expenditure,
— have the best terms and conditions of employment,
— promote the personal growth of individuals within the organisation,

— create jobs,
— serve the community,
— survive,
— grow,
— protect the environment etc.

all of which may operate together or individually from time to time.
The following examples illustrate stated company objectives:

The Unigate company objectives were stated as follows in their 1981 Company Report:-

'It is our intention to continue to upgrade our manufacturing and distributive facilities and services to customers, despite the temptation to delay vital investment until the economic climate appears more favourable ... We place the highest possible priority on the elimination of waste and of inefficiency in order to derive maximum benefit from our assets.'

Bass PLC. in their Annual Report for 1989 outline their company philosophy

'To provide a high standard of product and service to our customers at a fair price,
To provide our employees with the security of working for a successful company with job satisfaction, good remuneration, and good working conditions, acknowledging their right to be informed and consulted on all matters which affect their work.
To earn sufficient money after tax to provide an adequate return on the savings that our shareholders have entrusted to our care, after reinvesting enough capital in the business to maintain the value of their assets and to ensure the healthy long term growth of the company.
To conduct our business with due care for the environment and for the interests of the consumers and the general public."

The ICI Group purpose as outlined in the 1989 Annual Report states

'As The chemical industry is a major force for the improvement of quality of life across the world. ICI aims to be the world's leading chemical company, serving customers internationally through the innovative and responsible application of chemistry and related sciences.
Through achievement of our aim we will enhance the wealth and the well being of our shareholders, our employees, our customers and the communities we serve and in which we operate.
We will do this by;

- seeking consistent profitable growth;
- providing challenge and opportunity for our employees, releasing their skills and creativity;
- achieving a standard of quality and service internationally, which our customers recognise as being consistently better than any of our competitors;
- operating safely and in harmony with the global environment."

Nowadays, public sector organisation aims are reflecting those of the private sector, especially in the competitive industrial situation of the media. We can see this in the following statement.

Marmaduke Hussey, Chair of the BBC, said in the Annual Report and Accounts for 1990;

'The fundamental issue we face is to reconcile an adequate and competitive staff remuneration with the investment necessary to retain and continually improve the quality of our programmes.... . The guiding principle of the BBC must be what it always has been – to provide the widest range of quality programmes across the full range of licence payers' tastes, interests and enthusiasms, or as the Charter outlines, to inform, educate and entertain."

The complexity of objectives and the interdependency between them is illustrated in the following statement by Eliot Jaques on the objectives of the Glacier Metal Company, which was given in *The Changing Culture of a Factory* Tavistock, 1951:-

'The purpose of the Company and those working in it shall be the continuity and expansion of the working community the coordination of which will enable its members to serve society, to serve their dependents, to serve each other and to achieve a sense of creative satisfaction.

This purpose will best be accomplished by:

1) seeking the maximum technical ability;
2) seeking the utmost organisational efficiency;
3) seeking to establish an increasing democratic government of the company community, which will reward fair responsibilities, rights and opportunities for all its members, consumers and shareholders;
4) seeking at all times to earn such revenue that the company will be able:
   - to provide such reasonable dividends for its shareholders as to represent a fair return on their capital investment for the speculative risk incurred;

- to undertake research and development in order to enable the company to attain a high position in the competitive market;
- to provide those who work in the company with working conditions which will promote their physical and mental well being;
- to improve its equipment to enable those who work in the company to do so with the greatest possible effectiveness;
- to raise wages and salaries in order to enable those who work in the company to live full and happy lives;
- to improve the company's service to its customers by reducing the price or improving the quality of its products;
- to make reserves to safeguard the company and those who work in it.'

Objectives of public sector organisations

Organisations in the public sector have a variety of different objectives. We look to the State and the public bodies to:

- educate children, young people and adults,
- build and maintain roads and streets,
- dispose of refuse,
- provide cemeteries and crematoria,
- offer services for consumer protection,
- supply transportation including railways, bus services and an airline,
- establish a stable money supply and control the banking system,
- establish weights and measures,
- predict the weather,
- keep society safe by providing armed services, the police and a fire service,
- control traffic,
- reduce crime,
- operate postal services,
- inspect restaurants and licensed premises,
- represent our interests abroad,
- conserve the environment and reforest land,
- help to encourage research by the provision of funds,
- provide basic social services and prevent people starving,
- provide hospital and health care services,
- provide rehabilitation services for the handicapped and disabled,
- maintain parks and other recreation areas and amenities,
- create jobs or provide compensation for the unemployed,
- guarantee free speech,
- guarantee the individual's freedom to worship.

THE STRUCTURE OF CORPORATE OBJECTIVES

These are only a few of the aims of public sector bodies operated directly by the State, Local Government bodies, the Health Service and the public utilities and corporations. For example, the primary objective of the Health Service is defined in the National Health Service Act, 1946, Section 1(1) as:

'to secure improvement in the physical and mental health of the people ... and the prevention, diagnosis and treatment of illness.'

The specific objectives of the hospital services are stated in the Act, Section 3 (1):

'to provide... accommodation and services of the following description:-
(a) hospital accommodation;
(b) medical, nursing and other services required at or for the purpose of hospitals;
(c) the service of specialists...'

In addition the Act states the duty of teaching hospitals in Part II Section 12 (3)(a):

'to provide for the university with which the hospital is associated such facilities as appear to the Minister to be required for clinical teaching and research.'

However, it is left to the statutory hospital authorities to define specific objectives so that the hospital service remains effective. These tasks can include:

(a) the provision of beds, meals and other services for patients;
(b) the provision of general nursing services for patients;
(c) the provision of specific nursing facilities for patients, as prescribed by doctors;
(d) the provision of medical diagnosis, prescriptions and appropriate treatment by doctors;
(e) the provision of other services for patients, including medical social services, occupational therapy, chiropody and physiotherapy;
(f) in teaching hospitals, the provision of training facilities for medical students;
(g) in training hospitals, the provision of training facilities for nurses;
(h) the provision of research facilities for doctors and scientific and other technical staff;
(i) in psychiatric hospitals or psychiatric wings of general hospitals, the provision of facilities for detaining patients under compulsory orders of the Mental Health Act, 1959;

(j)   the provision of medical laboratory services to General Practitioners;

(k)   to continually assess and review the services offered by the hospital in response to the needs of the patients it is likely to serve and consequentially to provide the relevant building and technical facilities and the required medical, nursing and other services.

The Royal Commission on the National Health Service, reporting in 1979, argued that the National Health Service should have the following objectives:

— encourage and assist individuals to remain healthy;

— provide equality of entitlement to health services;

— provide a broad range of services to a high standard;

— provide equality of access to those services;

— provide a free service at the time of use;

— satisfy the reasonable expectations of its users;

— remain a national service, responsive to local needs.

The objectives of any organisation are a function of the environment in which it operates and are the result of a combination of internal and external factors. Organisations are essentially open systems which influence their environment and are influenced in turn by it; they exist in a highly interdependent relationship of exchange with their environment and other organisations. They utilise a wide variety of inputs of people, materials, machines and capital and their ability to operate depends on the availability of these inputs and their ability to adapt to the changing demands of their customers. Thus a tyre manufacturer will be affected by the customer's demand for a long-lasting tyre but also by the availability of the raw materials he uses and the efficiency with which he can manufacture the product.

The particular objectives at a given moment are a feature of the internal and external forces on the organisation at that point in time. This is illustrated in Figure 6 on page 43.

The State may itself provide products or services which it feels producers in the private sector might not. In the UK these products include transport facilities, postal services, education, health and defence.

THE STRUCTURE OF CORPORATE OBJECTIVES

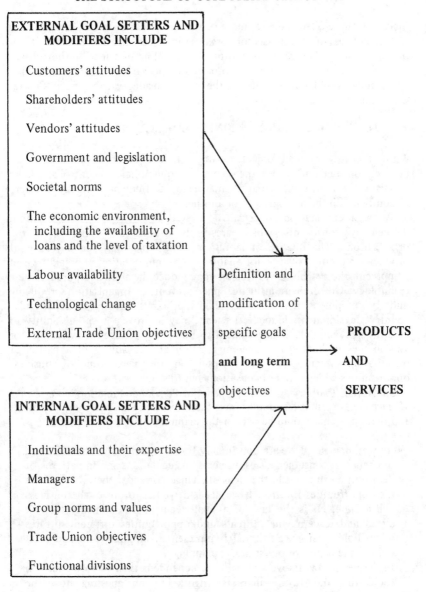

EXTERNAL GOAL SETTERS AND MODIFIERS INCLUDE

Customers' attitudes

Shareholders' attitudes

Vendors' attitudes

Government and legislation

Societal norms

The economic environment, including the availability of loans and the level of taxation

Labour availability

Technological change

External Trade Union objectives

Definition and modification of specific goals **and long term** objectives

PRODUCTS AND SERVICES

INTERNAL GOAL SETTERS AND MODIFIERS INCLUDE

Individuals and their expertise

Managers

Group norms and values

Trade Union objectives

Functional divisions

Figure 6: Internal & external forces on the organisation

As we can see, from the example of the public corporations, in all sectors the objectives of public sector organisations are heavily influenced by political policy. The actual operation and spending of a local authority will be influenced by the 'members' who sit on the various committees which agree budgets and policy, and by the money made available from Central Government.

10. NEED FOR CLEARLY DEFINED OBJECTIVES

Without clearly defined objectives the activities of an organisation may become confused and erratic, the resources required hard to control and keep in balance. It is also likely that the management of one process may interfere or conflict with the management of another.

An organisational objective can be viewed as a field of possible action, defined by constraints, which are both internal and external to the organisation. The quality of labour available constrains the objective of producing a product of superior quality, or the minimisation of breakdown in equipment; the availability of finance may reduce the ability to purchase new technology; Government influence may prevent an organisation producing military equipment being able to sell its products directly to a particular country; developments in medical science may improve a hospital's ability to cure the sick; and cuts in Government spending may reduce the availability of jobs in the public sector. The imagination and capability of a particular organisation's management may result in the perception of business opportunities which other organisations fail to see.

Sir Adrian Cadbury in "How I see the Personnel Function", *Personnel Management* April 1982, emphasised the importance of renewing objectives and that personnel should be part of the planning team:

'In planning ahead we are continually trying to determine the direction of change in consumer tastes, in costs, in regulations and in patterns of distribution. If we read the signs of change correctly, they will provide the opportunities for growth we need; if we fail to do so, the business will decline. It is the task of a small team in the company to look ahead and discern what threats and opportunities different futures might hold in store. Personnel is represented on that team and so is right in the centre of our strategic planning...

In the next 20 years we will be more dependent than ever, not just on forecasting our future markets aright, but on guessing how the behaviour of individuals as customers and as employees will change and what constraints on society and the pressure groups within it will exercise on our business. On these interpretations of the future we will build our plans and agree our aims. From there we have to develop patterns of organisation which will enable those aims to be carried out, this means devising structures which encourage change, allow for individuality, and operating autonomy and yet fit within a policy framework.'

Any individual working within an organisation is selecting courses of action within a set of constraints determined by the objectives which are set by the executives. Thus each department sets sub-goals for the members of that department, which reflect the higher overall goals of the organisation. There is thus a hierarchical structure of ends or goals, ranging from broad general ones at the top of the organisation to more specific ones at lower levels. We might represent these as follows:

Figure 7: Hierarchy of organisational objectives

Overall objectives

Divisional objectives

Departmental objectives

Sectional objectives

Individual objectives

Thus for example, we would probably find that the specific goal of profit is unlikely to be found among the goals of a foreman at Metal Box, British Airways or British Gas, but we do find foremen very interested in reducing costs, which for them is a logical objective within the constraints set by the overall objective of profit.

We can, therefore, argue that the objectives of the organisation are paramount in determining the nature of work within it. They will also determine the capital and monetary resources required. If we wished to establish an organisation with the aim of producing cheap family motorcars, the finances required would be much greater than if we wished to produce and sell bread in a small village. The objectives also influence the types of technological equipment we need. The technology required for the mass production car market is much more advanced than that required to produce custom-built cars from bought-in components. The type of equipment required will, in turn, influence the qualifications or skills of the people we require; the nature of the training we will need to give; the systems of reward; and the size of the labour force. Objectives will influence the channels of communication and the kinds of information we develop to control and monitor the success or otherwise of our activities. There is a direct relationship between objectives and the structure which is consequently adopted for the organisation. This in turn, influences its systems of control and the provision of information for management decision making. It is necessary, for the efficient operation of organisations in society, that the employees are made aware of the general objectives so they can relate their efforts to the resultant success.

There is no general magic blueprint, for each organisation has different needs and influences, although there are common elements like legislation and the economic and social environment. Each organisation comprises individuals whose skills and expertise differ. The strengths of each individual need to be considered when deciding how to spread responsibilities to ensure fulfilment of organisational objectives. For instance, the Chief Accountant may be a fine financial and budgetary administrator, but have no concept of the needs of marketing or production. It is important to develop a team of people who are sensibly organised and skilfully led so that together they will succeed in developing and managing a successful organisation.

The organisation structure may change, dependent upon the key objectives of the moment. For example, project teams may need to be created to cope with specific challenge but may be disbanded when that challenge has successfully been met. Individuals need to change as new roles and functions arise and as they themselves develop through training and maturation. Growth in size always demands organisational changes, both to be able to respond to outside factors and because growth requires that the structure and methods of management which people adopt must adapt to cope with the increasing volume of information and the greater complexity of business problems with objectivs of public and private sector organisations being affected by market place pressures, both sectors are having constantly to review their policies and objectives therefore human resources continue to make the difference between success or failure. Without clearly defined objectives, employee committment and cooperation will be difficult to encourage and develop.

11. AUTHORITY AND CONFORMITY

When tasks are delegated some responsibility is of necessity also delegated and the Manager recognises two important features:
- Firstly that the individual taking over part of the responsibility from another member of the organisation will not and cannot do the job in the same way as it was done in the past.
- Secondly that information will be required to enable the manager with overall responsibility to monitor the efficiency with which the delegated task is being accomplished and to ensure that the task holder is contributing efficiently towards the organisation's overall objectives.

These twin problems of how much and what authority and responsibility to delegate to whom, and of how to obtain sufficient information to control what is happening in delegated functions, are key issues, especially for large organisations.

The problem is compounded when we consider organisations which operate on more than one site. For example, control is more difficult for a large Building Society where autonomy may be given to each Branch Manager to make key decisions on loans and to decide who is hired and fired. How can we ensure fairness and equity in decision making, whilst at the same time allowing a large degree of local autonomy?

Any individual, when joining an organisation in a new role, needs to be made aware of certain facts about it. Some of these may be expressed in the job specification; some may be included in the terms of reference of budget responsibilities; some can only be communicated by word of mouth; and others will depend on the progress, expertise and derived experience of the individual postholder. We can all probably recognise elements in our own jobs which have developed because of our individual abilities and which are often not captured within any existing formal job specification.

Among the things an individual holding a particular job needs to know are:

(a) a knowledge of which people are directly responsible to him;
(b) knowledge of the tasks he is expected to perform and the responsibilities he has;
(c) what results he is expected to achieve and the time span within which they are to be achieved;
(d) what are the parameters of his authority on such matters as wages and salaries; prices; disciplinary action; responsibility for engaging staff; obtaining and purchasing supplies etc;
(e) what figures must be prepared on the performance of his function, in what form and how often should these figures be presented;
(f) what information he is entitled to from the activities of the other functions within the organisation; how often should he be furnished with it; and from whom does he obtain it.

The more precisely an individual can be told what job he has to do, the objectives he has to achieve and the constraints on his actions and methods of reaching those objectives, the more likely he is to be able to contribute effectively to the operation of the organisation and the attainment of its objectives. Therefore, the individual responsible for making decisions and performing his task, within the overall objectives of the organisation, should know what norms and values the organisation has and what specialist assistance he can obtain. This is important because the amount of specialist assistance varies, with greater specialisation tending to occur in large organisations.

Organisations use a number of methods to ensure that each individual uses his expertise to work towards the objectives. It has been argued by Schein (in *Organisational Psychology* 3rd edn Prentice Hall, 1980) that when an individual joins an organisation he enters into a *psychological contract*. Thus the organisation and the individual himself have expectations about the required behaviour of the other, not only on the amount of work which is wanted but also on the whole pattern of rights, privileges and obligations which are attached to employment within the specific organisation.

To ensure that individuals perform to the required standards, organisations develop a series of rules and regulations which control the behaviour of the individual while at work. The amount of discretion allowed to each individual often depends on the nature of the work which he is performing. For example, someone working on a continuous process assembly line is likely to find that their ability to determine when they go for a cup of tea or to fulfil natural bodily functions is dependent, either upon specific break times, or upon the ability of the supervisor to provide a substitute while they are absent from the line. They are also likely to find that if they do not arrive at work on time or if they are late back from a break they may be subject to a sanction of loss of wages or some other form of disciplinary action which is specified in some formal rule or procedure. The organisation thus imposes authority on the individual employee. Employees in turn, however, expect that the organisation will be reasonable in the exercise of that authority and, for example, not unnecessarily withhold permission for them to leave the production line.

Individuals accept, when they join, the authority relationship which is granted to their superiors and the rules and regulations on hours and the amount of work expected for payment. The psychological contract for individuals is implemented through an expectation that they can, either through individual or collective action, influence the organisation's treatment of them and be treated in an acceptable manner. What is considered acceptable treatment inevitably changes as the norms and values of society change. Nowadays, many of the minimum standards are laid down by statute law.

Individuals in joining a particular organisation thus accept a reduction of their freedom of action. As discussed earlier, the actual duties and responsibilities may be transmitted to the individual by means of job specifications, etc. which attempt to establish the expected roles, duties and behaviour expected. Organisations also use a number of other devices to ensure individual conformity, e.g. works rules, collective agreements etc.

12. SOCIALISATION OF INDIVIDUALS

Within the recruitment and selection process the organisation is attempting to select those with the required skills, knowledge, experience and attitudes to fit the need, and will reject those who are not considered suitable.

Organisations attempt to portray the desired traits and expected behaviour through the induction process, which is designed to explain the aims and objectives of the specific organisation, the rules and regulations which apply to the individual and the benefits which will accrue because of his employment. Superiors, subordinates and colleagues in the department in which the job is located further act as transmitters of group norms and values within the organisation. These norms will not only include formal standards expected by the organisation but also the informal ones to which the individual must conform to become accepted as a member of the work group or team.

Socialisation continues through initial skills training which establishes the patterns of acceptable output and the work methods which are to be adopted. With time, the individual's behaviour continues to be moulded by the workplace environment. He finds that his ability to obtain merit-related wages increases, to be granted his holidays when he wants them, to be considered for promotion, to be encouraged and developed for wider responsibilities or transfers, depends primarily on the acceptability to his superiors of his overall pattern of behaviour and his willingness to conform to the standards and rules.

The socialisation process attempts to ensure that the individual is clear about the objectives of his work and enters into what the organisation considers appropriate activities, minimising his attempt to attain inappropriate personal objectives which may perhaps interfere with those at work.

13. MEASUREMENT OF ORGANISATIONAL SUCCESS

Analysis of success in carrying out work or tasks will be inadequate if individuals have no idea of the objectives of the organisation or they do not know how successful or unsuccessful it is in reaching them. As we have implied, the basic reason for having an organisation in the first place is that there are objectives which cannot be attained by the efforts of individuals alone or resources are required beyond the skills, knowledge, experience and finance possessed by individuals or capable of being used by individuals in isolation.

To examine whether an organisation is moving in the right direction and fulfilling its objectives we must consider its performance in the light of the available resources and environmental constraints which influence it. We could for instance, measure the success of a hospital in terms of the number of patients who regain their health; yet this is not a suitable measure for those units or hospitals which care for the terminally ill or for the small cottage hospital which is faced with a 'flu' epidemic in an area where the general population are in the main elderly.

Consider also profitability of a business enterprise as a measure. We would inevitably expect a higher level of profits from a well-established organisation than perhaps from one which is only just entering into a particular market and is not yet known. Profitability is also something which is influenced both by internal efficiency and by the general economic environment which prevails. In a period of depressed economic activity we would expect profits to be lower than in a boom. The level of profits demanded can also vary from organisation to organisation. For instance, we may demand high profitability in the oil industry to be able to fund future investment, whereas we may only demand break-even profitability from British Rail.

Profits may also be easier in industries where demand for the product is little affected by increases in price, because the product concerned is essential to the consumer, e.g. water. Where the product is not essential, but a luxury item, e.g. video recorders, prices may have to be low because of other manufacturers' competition.

Our objective may be to increase our share of a particular market and we may need to undercut the prices of our competitors. Yet, if we consider this objective in isolation, without considering profitability, we may find that this leads to our firm going out of business. A well known example of this was the electronic calculator market.

A further objective which could be measured is that of level of sales; yet high sales are not merely a result of an organisation's efficiency and success. For example, high sales of umbrellas could result from unusually high rainfall. We may use the wrong measures to analyse success. For example, firms which use returns of discount vouchers on items bought in shops may find, when these vouchers are counted and measured against items actually supplied, that there is a discrepancy, because some stores are less honest than others in being strict about the named items for discount.

It may at times be difficult to measure success because of the interdependency of factors which impinge on ability to attain objectives; yet organisations will need to constantly monitor their progress to ensure that the structure, labour force, products manufactured, quality of those products etc. are adequate to cope with the opportunities in the market place. Certainly personnel departments are becoming increasingly involved in analysing the success of current organisational structures.

14. ORGANISATION STRUCTURES

An organisation differs from an uncoordinated interrelationship of people because it has a structure which is specifically derived for it to be able to reach its objectives. The prime concern of organisations is getting work done, but work is done by people. One of the major problems for an organisation is to create a structure which aids communication and the attainment of work objectives. Structure comprises a series of hierarchical relationships which establish the accountability and responsibility of individuals in the organisation and are designed for the organisation to achieve its objectives. It thus groups jobs in a particular pattern and the people filling those jobs are expected to carry out a collection of specific activities to cope with a variable workload. There is no best or 'right' structure in a particular situation, but there are certain arrangements of jobs which are likely to be more effective than others for organisational success whilst providing individuals with an acceptable degree of attainment of their own aims and aspirations. Structures also need to be flexible as organisations are continuously and inevitably changing in line with market or product conditions and the general attitudes of society on the morality or immorality of business operations.

Patently a business cannot remain static or it will not survive; it needs to adapt and respond to its opportunities and to minimise the effects of external threats. We cannot talk of organisation structure as if it is a static thing; it is dynamic. Organisation charts imply rigidity and this is enhanced when we consider that often job descriptions may be removed and dusted off from time-to-time and used when a vacancy occurs, without being examined to see if they are currently or futuristically viable. Such actions overlook the human influence. Inevitably jobs grow and shrink because of the nature of the person in post as well as due to reactive changes in the organisation.

Think of your own job and those around you and see if they have changed recently, either because you or others have matured or grown more experienced and examine these jobs against the current job descriptions.

Many books on organisation seem to start from the premise of freezing the organisation at a moment in time and dissecting it, rather like the examination of a cadaver on a mortician's slab, to see what has gone wrong and terminated its existence.

We cannot do this as easily with organisations, for the very investigation process itself often changes the nature of the organisation and because organisations are dynamic living entities which are always undergoing subtle changes over time. Certainly we may be able to see how well the organisation was coping or is coping today by examining particular incidents, but these occur in the context of slow, and in some cases, hardly-perceivable change.

J Child in *Organisation: a Guide to Problems and Practice,* Harper & Row 1984, argued that the following are essential elements for consideration in designing and reviewing organisation structure:

— to allocate jobs to individuals giving them some personal control over the methods of working and the utilisation of resources.

— to clearly formalise the hierarchies within the organisation and the breadth of spans of control.

— to unite individuals together into divisions which fit logically and contribute loyally to organisation objectives.

— to delegate authority where most appropriate and procedures developed so that the parameters of decision making could be monitored for success or failure.

— to design communication systems to be efficient and effective in coordinating effort and encouraging involvement in the decision making processes.

— to design systems which motivate individuals to give of their best and which rewards them appropriately for doing so, perhaps by linking where appropriate appraisal of performance with reward.

With these factors in mind let us examine some of the most common forms of organisation structure.

(A) Functional structures

The classical structure which is commonly used in organisations of all types is the one which is formed around the primary tasks which require to be done. An example could be given as in:

Figure 8: Classical form of organisation structure

In this structure work activities are organised into separate departments. Such a structure often tends to be centralised for the purposes of decision making. This structure is very common in small companies or in large companies with a small product range. It tends to be found in situations where the environment is changing slowly and there is little need for the organisation to react quickly to market opportunities.

This form of structure has lasted for a long time and has the advantage that the Managing Director is in close touch with all the operations and can thus coordinate the whole enterprise. Lines of command are relatively simple to understand and control and people are grouped together on the basis of their technical or specialist expertise, which provides clearer opportunities for promotion and career development. One of the strengths of this form of structure is that people with certain skills or disciplines tend to be managed by those with similar skills or disciplines; thus attention to specialist career planning and training tends to be good.

There are disadvantages with this type of structure:

(i)   Internal conflict and competition can occur as sectional interests develop, for example, over budgets or available resources; perceived departmental needs may conflict with the needs of the organisation as a whole and loyalty may be given to the departmental or specialist function.

(ii)   This structure is difficult to adapt in situations of growth and diversification, either of product of geographical location, as the total responsibility falls on the Chief Executive for ensuring overall profitability and it is difficult to split up this responsibility without creating greater potential internal conflict. Thus, for example, projects which require the involvement of all functions, like new product development, tend to provide stresses for the organisation as no one function has overall responsibility for the task.

(iii) Due to the inherent specialisation within this form of structure it is more difficult to develop successors for top management who have the necessary across-the-board organisational skills and expertise.

(B)   Division structures

As organisations develop and outgrow the functional type of structure or where that type of structure is not as apposite, as in, for example, local authorities or the Health Service, the trend is towards divisionalisation. This is a popular form in organisations with a wide range of products or services where fairly identifiable splits can be made between profit or cost centres. There are two main ways of creating divisions depending on the type, emphasis and size of the organisation concerned:

(i)   One frequent form is *divisionalisation by product or market* where fairly clear product or market differentiation is possible. For example, in local authorities, the Chief Executive has responsible to him Chief Officers who run the various services, within the budgets allocated centrally, e.g., as in Figure 9.
       In the National Health Service the key groups of employees − doctors, nurses, paramedical and ancillary staff − are organised around the service provided, e.g., prenatal and natal, psychiatric, dentistry, general surgical, orthopaedic and so on.
       This form of organisation is also found in many large private organisations, e.g. ICI has separate product divisions for Paints, Alkalis, Dyestuffs, Pharmaceuticals, etc.

(ii)   *Geographical divisions* may be formed where differentiation between types of customers is considered important or where distances or communications costs favour this type of structure. It is usually adopted where essential decision making is better handled locally. Examples of this form of organisation occur in the brewing industry and amongst pharmaceutical companies, e.g., as in Figure 10.
       Within such a structures it is usual to find a group of senior functional managers or directors located at headquarters to provide centralised

direction and guidance for regional managers in the performance of their line function and to provide help to functional managers in each region on aspects which need to be handled on a company-wide basis. Yet each region or product division acts in an autonomous way in producing and marketing the products developed, within the overall control of the head office functional specialists.

Divisionalisation is the most common form to be found in large organisations in both the public and the private sectors of industry. The advantages of a divisionalised structure can be listed as follows:

(i)   More products or services can be encompassed within the organisation by creating new divisions;

(ii) Where technological change is faster in one product sector of the market than another, differential adoption can take place, the appropriate expertise can be developed and specialised equipment purchased in each major unit without creating major problems for other units;

(iii) With both product and regional divisionalisation, profit responsibility can be delegated down the chain of command allowing the main activities of the organisation to be separately evaluated and major decisions can be taken nearer to the interface with the appropriate market;

(iv) It is easier to acquire and dispose of major activities within the organisation;

(v)   A team is developed with loyalties to product or knowledge of an area;

(vi) More scope is provided to develop divisional managers, who have overall control over sections of the organisation, for succession to top management posts.

Yet disadvantages also accrue to such structures:

(i)   Where product divisions are created, there is a danger that each General Manager could promote each product group in a way which creates problems for other product divisions or the organisation as a whole, e.g. retail — and wholesale — type sales departments at the fringe of the two markets could find themselves competing with each other on discount policy. Some form of centralised control may be necessary without reducing the motivation of such General Managers to produce satisfactory results themselves.

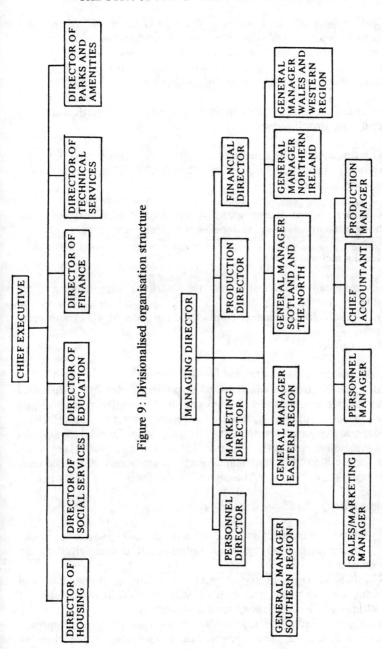

Figure 9: Divisionalised organisation structure

Figure 10: Geographicaly divisionlised organisation structure

(ii)   Conflict between divisions may occur, e.g. as above, where they compete against each other in the same markets, or where transfer prices have to be negotiated for internal trading between them, perhaps where the product of one division, whilst having a market of its own, is also an important bought-in-part of another division.

(iii)   There may be conflict between short term divisional objectives and long term company objectives.

(iv)   With divisional profit structures the effects of recession may hit some regional or product divisions harder than others and may lead to stress between divisions.

(v)   A further problem is that specialist functional experts may be spread through the organisations and feel isolated from each other.

(C)   Mixed structures

With increasing complexity and size of organisations, many companies are attempting to develop structures which incorporate elements of both the functional and divisional to reduce conflict and optimise the use of resources:

(i)   *Project structure*

A structure which may be found in the high technology industries, such as aeronautics and electronics, which are given powers to demand and control resources and are created and superimposed on the existing functional and divisional structure of the organisation. People with the relevant skills, knowledge and experience are brought together, perhaps for product development or some other multidivisional or multifunctional purpose. They work together for the life of the particular project and are usually disbanded once the team is no longer necessary, the extant structure reasserting its control.

The main advantages of such a structure are :

(a)   It utilises the mix of skills within the company and in so doing helps to develop management teams for the future benefit of themselves and the organisation;

(b)   By getting managers to work together on a common project it aids in helping them to understand more of each others' skills and reduces the mystique which can surround specialist functions;

(c)   If all groups within the organisation realise that a common approach has been developed, there is greater likelihood of cooperation when the outcome of the project has been determined.

There are also potential problems with such an approach:

(d)   There may be conflict between the line units which continue to operate during the life of the project and the project teams as to responsibilities and accountability, creating control problems. For example, those who are not members may resent the involvement of such a team in those areas which they perceive as their long-term responsibility.

(e)   There is also the danger that the best managers will become overloaded with work and will neglect either their permanent jobs or their projects as a result.

(ii) Matrix structures

A matrix structure usually combines a functional form with a project-based structure. It differs from a project structure in so far as project teams (as described previously) are disbanded at the end of the project, whereas a matrix structure tends to be operated on a permanent basis. A project manager will coordinate and be responsible for the work carried out by the project team and he will deal with the client. This, for instance, is often seen in civil engineering contracts. He is still responsible to his own departmental manager, but will be functionally involved with other departmental managers, depending upon the complexity of the specific project. These managers will provide his with specialists responsible to him for the specific project, but responsible for departmental matters to their own managers. Matrix structures combine vertical and horizontal lines of communication and authority. Thus, a division of an engineering organisation, which has four projects being undertaken simultaneously, may have a matrix organisation as in Figure 11.

Project managers, whilst having responsibility for funding and budgets, planning, scheduling and quality control of the project, usually have more responsibility than formal authority for the staff, hence they often get results by persuasion and informal appeals for cooperation.

Advantages claimed for the matrix structure include:

1.   It enables the organisation to improve the quality of decision making over particular projects because decisions are made by the project leader who is in direct contact with the client.

2.   It encourages functional managers to understand the contribution they are making directly to each project, because the focus of effort becomes the project, and not departmental functional needs.

3.   Interested departments are involved from the inception of the project and thus in the decision making process from the first phases.

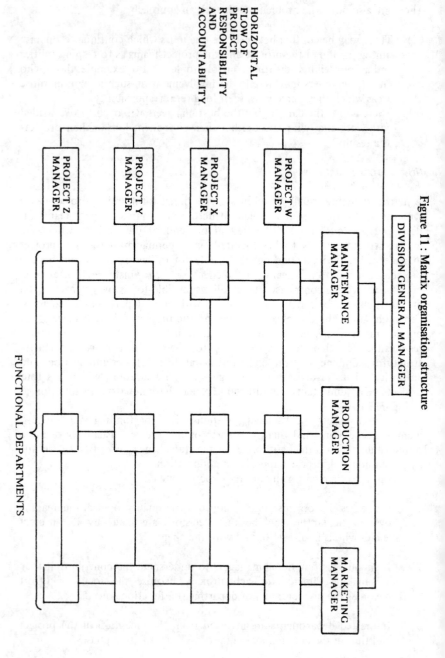

Figure 11 : Matrix organisation structure

As in the other types of organisation structure mentioned, disadvantages do accrue. These include:

1. Decision making may take longer as the consultation process often takes time.

2. It may be felt that there is a dilution of functional specialist responsibilities within the organisation and, consequently, managers of functional departments may feel their authority as 'experts' threatened.

3. Potential conflicts may arise over the allocation of resources and division of authority between functional groups and project groups.

4. There is also potential danger that individual members of project teams may feel their loyalties divided between their project manager and colleagues and their own functional manager and specialist colleagues.

15. CENTRALISATION AND DECENTRALISATION

The trend towards increased specialisation of function leads to a diffusion of accountability and authority to attain organisational objectives. An organisation's structure requires the allocation of authority to those responsible for undertaking specific activities; and consideration of how much power and authority should be allocated to the various activities and key roles. In every organisation which has multiple levels of management in the hierarchy and multiple specialism, there is delegation. The question is not whether it occurs, but how much it actually takes place. With centralised structure, the major decisions on all significant aspects of the organisation's work are made at the top. A decentralised structure, on the other hand, places the authority and decision making process as close as possible to the level at which the work is done. Only very small organisations can maintain a centralised structure where effective authority can be retained at the top by one individual or by a small group of senior executives.

Whether a particular organisation is managed on a centralised or decentralised basis depends on a number of factors:

(i) The absolute size of the firm or organisation is a key factor. It is very difficult to coordinate all day-to-day decision making in a large multi-product organisation, in a local authority or a large general hospital. The number of units or different specialisms and the total number of employees controlled are significant factors. Efficiency and the ability to respond quickly is improved by making subordinate units semi-autonomous with long term planning being coordinated from the top.

(ii) The nature and history of the organisation can also be a significant influence. If there is only one product and the organisation is located on only one site, then centralised control is likely. If, on the other hand, the organisation is a multiproduct conglomerate, operating on a number of different sites nationally or internationally and it has grown through mergers and takeovers, it is much more likely to have a decentralised structure. In such a diverse organisation, the speed and efficiency of decision making and the flexibility of the organisation in responding to customer requirements are enhanced through a decentralised authority network.

(iii) A further consideration is the philosophy and personality of top management. Thus, for example, Henry Ford used to make all the major decisions in the Ford Motor Company and this centralised control is also familiar in many other owner-managed organisations. If the Chief Executive is autocratic in his control and also owns a substantial proportion of the enterprise's assets, a centralised form of control will tend to prevail.

(iv) In practice some management functions are more easily decentralised than others. In large multiplant organisations such functions as financial planning, research and development and some aspects of personnel can be usefully centralised — albeit there are people who carry out some aspects of day-to-day control at each site — whereas cost accounting, purchasing, production, quality control and some marketing and sales functions are probably decentralised.

The main *advantages* of decentralisation can be listed as follows:

1. It permits speed in decision making by enabling line managers, who are closer to the work in hand, to take local decisions without waiting for decisions from the highest authority.

2. It enables local management to be flexible in their approach to decisions, in the light of local market opportunities or needs, and thus to be more adaptable in situations of change.

3. It prevents top management being overloaded with minutiae, by freeing them from operational matters, and enabling them to concentrate on the essential strategic decisions which are necessary for an organisation's long term survival and competitiveness.

4. It encourages subordinates at each level in the structure to exercise greater initiative and ingenuity and can contribute to staff motivation by enabling middle and junior managers to take and be responsible for local decisions. This ensures the development of capable managers groomed for more senior coordinating posts.

5. Problems of coordination, communication and bureaucracy are reduced, thus cutting down on local management frustration.

6. It focuses attention on cost control and profitability locally, which enhances management awareness of cost effectiveness and success in reaching revenue targets, thus minimising the ability to blame others where difficulties are encountered.

For all the advantages which decentralisation of decision making can bring, there are *disadvantages* which must be considered and the repercussions of which must be controlled if the organisation is to reach its long term objectives. These have been identified as:

1. It requires an appropriate and adequate control system if major errors of judgement are to be avoided by local management. Decentralisation can only succeed with competent, well-trained managers who are able to judge when centralised advice is required.

2. It requires coordination from senior management to ensure that individual parts are not working so that their objectives conflict with those of the organisation as a whole.

3. The decisions made by individual units may lead to inconsistency in the treatment of employees and of customers or clients.

4. There is a danger that loyalty may be encouraged to individual units and unit managers rather than to the enterprise.

5. Local units may fail to utilise the expert services which are available centrally: there is the danger of duplication of effort by local units who may try to solve problems from scratch, which have already been adequately solved in another unit.

To reduce some of these disadvantages it is essential that decentralisation should be adequately planned, and not happen by default. The managers who operate with local autonomy must be well trained and made aware of the overall aims and objectives of the total organisation on a regular basis. Logical decisions must be made on which types of decision will be decentralised and what the limits of discretion are. The more competent and effective the key employees are in their individual unit, the more likely it is that problems will occur with decentralisation and the more difficult it will be to control the organisation. The main difficulties likely to occur are influenced by the differing views of the extent of autonomy of each unit; the inter-actions between key central and key subsidiary staff; and the different styles of management and different cultures that may develop between the main organisation and the individual operational units, especially where there is geographical separation between the units and head office.

The degrees of autonomy allowed to specific units can vary from organi-sation to organisation, depending on the nature of the market served. This relationship can vary along a continuum from the individual unit having complete freedom of action, controlled only by levels of investment and a laid down profit objective, to that where the subsidiary unit is completely controlled by the parent organisation, having little freedom of action except over day-to-day operations. The most important element is not where the freedom of discretion lies along the continuum but that the parties mutually understand the amount of licence which is allowed.

16. LINE VS STAFF MANAGEMENT

In small organisations all employees tend to be line personnel, but as organisations grow it becomes necessary to employ specialists who give technical advice and provide support services for line personnel. The terms line and staff are usually explained in two senses: firstly in the sense of functions which contribute towards the organisation's overall objectives, and secondly as authority relationships.

Line positions and the individuals employed in them contribute directly to the provision of the goods and services which are demanded by the customer or client. Generally the organisation could not operate, even in the short term, without the functions which comprise the line. In a manufacturing organisation manufacturing and sales functions are line functions; in a department store both buying and selling are line functions; and in a hospital so are both nursing and medical. They are seen as primary functions and they act to ensure that objectives are met. Line authority is central to the chain of command and members of line functions have direct authority over others.

Staff functions can be split into two categories, specialised staff and service staff:

Specialised staff functions provide planning, advice and control: engineering, research and development, legal, finance, audit and personnel departments fall into this category. Such departments are usually composed of people with technical and professional expertise. In addition to providing advice and control functions for all line departments, they are also involved at senior levels in policy formulation. They have direct authority over others in respect of their specialist functions only. Thus there tends, for example, to be a hierarchy within the personnel department of superior-subordinate relations, and there are line responsibilities within specialised staff functions. Because line authority is not totally dependent on line functions, it can be better understood as a central feature of the total chain of command within the overall organisation structure.

Service functions aid the organisation in the predominantly physical sense and some give technical counsel and perform control functions. Examples of service staff are purchasing, maintenance, inspection, quality control and typing pools.

It is most sensible to consider the concepts of line and staff in terms of authority relationships rather than in terms of functions and their direct contribution to products or services. This is because most organisations have complex relationships between functions which are often dependent on each other to a greater extent than direct classification into traditional staff or line compartments would imply. Some areas of the staff function may merely provide services, e.g. recruitment, market research, legal advice and guidance, whereas others may establish key standards of performance for other sections of the organisation, e.g. setting and monitoring key quality standards for the customer or installing and controlling industrial relations procedures to maintain common standards of treatment of employees. It can be argued that staff managers have functional authority in relation to agreed aspects of their own particular expertise. Thus, the personnel manager of a company is not only responsible and accountable for the conduct of personnel matters, but may also have authority to ensure that line managers adhere to the organisation's procedures and policies in their treatment of staff individuals and groups within their departments. This overall authority for personnel matters inevitably reduces the power of line managers to exercise their own discretion but, given the external pressures of legislation and Codes of Practice in the 1980s, it is only by having expert advice that organisations can fulfil the responsibilities demanded of them by society.

The amount of actual power to enforce his authority which a functional staff manager has varies from organisation to organisation, dependent on the particular traditions which have evolved.

Certainly the relationship between line and staff personnel has the potential for disagreement and conflict:

1. A potential cause of such conflict is the dual authority that can exist when members of staff or advisory departments attempt to give instructions to line management. For example, a safety officer who is a member of a personnel department may order a foreman to shut down a defective piece of equipment because there is a potential danger for the operator. The foreman's line manager may have instructed the

foreman to keep the machine running because she/he considers the dangers minimal to the experienced operator in charge of the machine. Unless the safety officer has earned the respect of the foreman and line manager, conflict can result if higher levels of the executive hierarchy are asked to adjudicate.

2. The task of many staff units is to initiate improvements and change in an organisation's operation, policies and procedures. Line personnel often have a different orientation; their job is to produce a product or provide a service within an appropriate time-span and, to do this, they may prefer stability to changes for which they cannot immediately see a return.

3. A specialised staff function usually consists of staff who are expert in a limited field and who have often undergone professional or specific technical training. A line manager, on the other hand, tends to be a generalist who has obtained his position because of hard work within the organisation. There are likely to be conflicts because of different perceptions of the value of practical experience compared with further education and training.

4. Different staff specialists may be called upon to help solve the same problem in a line department and may offer different solutions. For example, if a specific department's accident record is poor, the plant engineer may advise improvements in the fencing and guarding of equipment, whereas the personnel and training officer may recommend improvements in, or intensification of, safety training for the operators and departmental supervisors. The line manager must then reconcile the differences and determine an appropriate solution.

5. Staff departments also serve as an instrument of top management to control the performance of operating managers and others. This monitoring of performance against objectives and standards, for example, — How are payroll costs rising? What levels of overtime are being worked? How high is labour turnover or absenteeism? — can cause problems between line and staff functions unless cooperation occurs and constructive diagnosis and recommendations are made jointly.

Line and staff managers should work together in solving problems and in attaining objectives; the degree of staff advice to line managers and the degree of functional authority within the structure varying from organisation to organisation.

17. THE MEASUREMENT OF ORGANISATIONAL PERFORMANCE

(A) INTRODUCTION

Earlier, we looked closely at the process of arriving at a series of agreed organisational objectives, and emphasising the importance, in terms of gaining commitment from those within the organisation who have to achieve them, of full discussion of the tasks and required results.

Whilst this process of analysis and planning is taking place, reviewing the impact of all major resource areas in the Organisational Strategic Plan, one further vital area must form part of the discussion – that of *Performance Monitoring*. Without making provision for such a system, with its clearly specified requirements, in terms of standards and timescales, no objective would be accepted as meaningful, and no sense of organisational urgency would exist, related to objective achievement, and, therefore, Corporate failure would be a real possibility. There are, of course, many organisations who look upon the annual budget, and four-weekly Management Accounts, as the most effective way of monitoring performance, and, in a very narrow sense, this may be true, but to accept that this is the only action necessary to monitor progress and performance is courting disaster. Before moving on, let us therefore examine Budgetary Control, as an organisational performance measure.

(B) BUDGETARY CONTROL

(a) The effectiveness of Budgetary Control

The formulation of the Annual Budget is a time consuming task, undertaken by most business organisations, but the most important factor, initially, is to consider how that Budget is to be created in the first place. We discussed the process of "Top Down" and "Bottom Up" decision making earlier, and the formulation of the Annual Budget is closely related to these systems, in that a wise management team will seek to pursue the latter course.

The fact that a Manager has not been consulted about potential results and costs of his area, can, and does, lead to loss of senior management credibility, in that the imposed financial parameters have been arrived at without detailed knowledge of the strengths and weaknesses of the area in question, in terms of market forces, production capabilities, people skills, and other directly related specific environmental factors which could have an impact on final performance. These situations become more important where the organisational area in question is a Division, geographically separate from the headquarters building, and market conditions very different.

The ideal system, therefore, is that no final decisions will be taken until each sectional Budget has been submitted, by the manager who must achieve the results, evaluated at Board level, and any changes agreed, prior to final acceptance. It follows, therefore, that any Budget, structured in this way, will be more related to reality, and, because of the joint discussion which has taken place, more likely to be achieved.

In many major organisations, whether in the public or private sector, there is a separate Planning Group, whose main responsibility is to both issue the guidelines, and to collect and discuss the initial draft submissions with managers, prior to final collation into a draft Corporate Budget, for evaluation by top management. The purpose of adopting this method of Budget creation, is to create a forum for analysis, between manager and planning group, seeking to identify potential areas of error, brought about by, perhaps, over-optimism, but it must be emphasised that the responsibility for data submission lies firmly in the hands of the individual manager, it is not the function of the planning group to devise Departmental Budgets, but to help and advise on any interpretation of the guidelines required.

The Planning Group is also involved with the communication of the final objective plan, together with ensuring that viable systems exist for performance monitoring, related to those standards, and timescales, which have been agreed with individual managers.

In summary, the benefits of a Budgetary Control System are:

1. Properly constructed, Budgetary Control should provide a one year financial plan for the Organisation, consistent with the Strategic Objectives.

2. By the process of involving Departmental Management in the formulation of their own projected results, it should assist in gaining commitment to the achievement of those results.

3. By being related directly to operational factors, it should also facilitate the establishment of realistic performance measurement, in each segment of the organisation.

4. The Corporate Strategic Plan should benefit, through the existence of what is now a factual programme for the full achievement of that plan.

5. Most importantly, a well structured Budget establishes the means for applying effective Corporate control systems.

6. Being operationally factual, the Budget should also assist inter-departmental co-ordination, where one part of the organisation either receives from, or supplies a service to another Division or Department.

(C) STANDARDS OF PERFORMANCE

Budgetary Control, as we have said, provides an effective means of measuring performance, throughout the organisation, against a factual plan. It is a recognised and widely accepted way of measuring the performance of managers, in all sectors of the economy, and, as long as it is based on input from those who, ultimately, will have to achieve the required results, it is also an effective means of both motivating, and gaining commitment from those same managers.

By the comparison of actual results achieved, to projected results, the Budget provides the organisation with a series of success/failure indicators, at the end of each four-weekly period of the accounting year, although one has also to recognise that this information is, essentially, historic, and reflects, perhaps that a problem arising in week one, or two, may well be four weeks old, in information terms, allowing for a time lapse at the end of the period for final accounting work.

There will, of course, be good operational reasons why some results may appear to fall short of requirement, in one particular period, but the fact that this variation has been highlighted will draw attention to the shortfall, and, perhaps, prompt some initial investigation into the causes of the problem, and form the basis of remedial action, if required, to bring results into line again.

The system of Budgetary Control can also be used, in every element of the organisation, to increase performance by the introduction of a competitive atmosphere, providing, as it does, a means of direct comparison, and therefore, a competitive edge between those Divisions or Departments engaged in similar activities. Whilst accepting this fact, it is also worthwhile noting that this comparison is solely in Financial terms, and that other factors of measurement must be taken into account, to produce a truly factual means of comparing one part of the organisation to another, using, perhaps, sales volume or units of production.

In establishing meaningful standards of performance, due allowance must be made for those factors which can have a direct impact upon the final result. Many businesses are subject to marked seasonal fluctuations in their patterns of trade, and this indicates that the Budget must be realistically structured, and that any performance standards set must take these patterns into consideration, and these, of course, will be indicated in any Budgetary projections drawn up by operational managers, and should be taken into consideration in structuring the final Budget requirements. Seasonality of trading patterns presents innovative management with opportunities for alternative products, rather than becoming an accepted downturn of income "because of the business we are in", and more organisations are recognising this.

There is a small school of thought, thankfully diminishing, which looks upon seasonality as having a minor impact on the total year, and supports the method of Budgetary Control which takes all costs and revenue items and divides them equally across the thirteen four-weekly accounting periods of the year. This certainly makes for neatness, but ignores the fact that real life does not always work that way, but those who favour this method argue that the end result is the only important factor, and what happens in between is only a numerical exercise, the reason for the diminution of these organisations probably being that they have gone out of business!

Standards of performance are effective only when the individual concerned accepts that the required target is achievable, perhaps with a great deal of effort, but certainly within their ability. Anything other than this negates the purpose of the system, as does the failure, on the part of management, to give clear responsibility for achieving the result the individual, plus the required level of authority and resources necessary to facilitate the successful outcome.

(D) THE MONETARY FACTOR

Budgetary Control expresses all results in financial terms, and it is useful to compare the advantages, and disadvantages, of working this way.

(a) Advantages

The majority of managers are familiar with the use of Budgetary Control as a measurement of performance, and the fact that their results are expressed in financial terms, for in-Company comparison of performance, of Divisions or Departments. There are well established links, between ultimate profit levels and control of cost factors, within all parts of an organisation, enabling a manager to isolate, and deal with, any apparent deviation from plan. These variations are clearly indicated as "savings", "overspends", shortfalls/increases (against target), and are therefore recognisable to both Accountants, and non-Accountants, as areas for concern and control, for savings can quickly disappear and costs escalate.

(b) Disadvantages

By reducing everything to a monetary base, the Budgetary Control system ignores all non-financial factors, which contribute to the final achievement of an objective. In particular, factors, used within Departments to measure success, can apparently have no similarity to other Departments, for they relate only to the operational tasks of that particular section of the organisation. Ultimately, the financial factors are, of course, perceived as most important, for they are the final comparator of organisational results.

It is essential to recognise some of these factors, as valuable inputs to the assessment of performance within organisations, from a total managerial control viewpoint. Transport sections may express efficiency in terms of route cost per mile, or cubic capacity carried, cost of spares, cost of driver hours, whilst the Production section may talk in terms of machine capacity available/used, machine "down-time", labour utilisation, total units produced, or material wastage. Sales sections will be vitally interested in sales per salesman, new business secured, sales per product line, cost of salesforce, whilst the Personnel Department will be interested in staff turnover factors, absenteeism cost of recruitment, skill shortages, and labour cost. The financial factors, expressed in the Budget, are the way the organisation compares results, but in setting standards of performance, individual managers will wish their objectives to be expressed in the terminology which relates closely to their own particular operational tasks, as factors for control within the Department, and these are much more meaningful to them than pure monetary factors.

We earlier referred to the rigidity of the four-weekly accounting patterns, and it is important to emphasise, again, the fact that all operational tasks will not conform, precisely, to these neatly packaged periods, but may have critical measurement points which fall before, or after, the period end. Recognising this, the experienced manager will set up control indictors which relate, solely, to the Department in question, expressed in terms which show where action is necessary, without having to be translated into monetary terms.

Budgetary Control is, therefore, a basic, and much used, way of initially measuring the performance of the managers of an organisation, and it is not our intention to be little the value of the system, but rather to show that it is the basis of a system of measurement that must be developed, in detail related to specific activities of all sections of the organisation, if it is to be accepted as a meaningful way of involving managers in the achievement of objectives.

(E)   ADDITIONAL MEASUREMENT FACTORS
We can clearly establish a basic principle, against which all performance measurement factors are reflected:

"PERFORMANCE MEASUREMENT LINKS THE PLANNING AND CONTROL ELEMENTS OF ALL ORGANISATIONAL ACTIVITY, AND IS THEREFORE VITAL TO THE ULTIMATE SUCCESS OF THE BUSINESS"

THE SYSTEM
1. Agreeing objectives and required standards   (Planning)
2. Measuring achieved results   (Control)
3. Isolating variances   (Control)
4. Agreeing action plans to correct variances   (Planning)
5. Re-setting performance standards   (Planning)
6. Monitoring performance to goal achievement   (Control)

THE STRUCTURE OF CORPORATE OBJECTIVES

ANALYSIS:

1. Agreeing objectives and required standards.

Standards are closely aligned with decisions, taken by the Board relating to organisational objectives, and indicate performance levels for every section of the organisation which must be achieved, if the total Plan is to be realised. Matters cannot, however, be allowed to remain on such a broad basis as that, as both objectives and their related performance standards must be stated as specific Departmental or Divisional objectives, in order to elicit a meaningful response from senior operational management.

Within each of these operational sections of the organisation, the objectives must again by sub-divided into sectional objectives which will be the responsibility of individual managers and/or supervisors, and it is here that performance standards are particularly relevant, for they form the solid base from which, ultimately, organisational objectives can be achieved.

Individual objectives and performance standards must be subject to discussion and agreement initially, but the process does not stop at that point. By agreeing a set of objectives and standards with an individual, the manager concerned must also recognise that there is a continuing requirement for input of relevant information, in order to enable the individual to maintain positive forward momentum. Equally importantly, such information allows for the isolation and actioning of variances, in order to achieve the required result, with the agreed timescales.

Senior Management must also distinguish between two other important factors, in the analysis of the actual performance of individuals:

(a) Manageable Variances
(b) Uncontrollable Variances

(a) Manageable Variances

Those factors relating to operational performance which fall directly within the control of the person concerned, and for which they must accept personal responsibility for success/failure. Examples of this could be:

Sales team performance,
Unit costs of production,
Transport utilisation costs,
Control of wage budgets,
Stock of wage budgets,
Stock loss levels.

(b)   Uncontrollable Variables

Those factors relating to operational performance which do not lie within the direct control of the individual, and therefore cannot be included in any performance measurement activity. Examples of this could be:

Total failure of material supply,
Industry-wide industrial relations conflict,
The effect of dramatic economic downturn.

Taking action to correct a variance is an additional expense, in terms of both time and money, and it is, therefore, sensible to investigate all the factors of the situation, prior to initiating a course of action to correct matters. Some of the real reasons for the apparent variance may be obscured by other, less important, factors which would lead only to dead ends and add to the timescale and cost, if followed.

(F)   SUCCESSFUL MEASUREMENT FACTORS

The most ineffective performance measurement practices are those which depend, largely, on the "informed judgement" of one person in respect to another individual, for all of us have the innate ability to either like, or dislike, another person quite deeply. This *like/dislike* effect, sometimes referred to as the *"Halo/Nimbus"* element in relationships, and can seriously colour our thoughts about another individual, and can therefore either enhance or reduce our view of their operational performance, if taken as the only measurement.

Organisational performance factors, at all levels, directly impact on the eventual success or failure of the total business, and must therefore be based on the most unbiased parameters available, ones which are founded in FACT rather than in "judgement".   The accepted terminology for this is QUANTITIVE MEASUREMENT, as opposed to QUALITATIVE MEASURE-MENT, which refers to the use of subjective judgement.

Performance measurement, related to organisational objectives, should therefore have target areas which can be formally measured, in Quantitative terms, confining the elements of judgement to areas of little or no impact. Examples of Quantifiable Targets would be:

Allowed cost factors (labour/Materials/Fuel);
Projected Sales Revenue:
Projected Material utilisation;
Timescales (Production and Delivery);
Labour utilisation (Man hours).

Examples of Qualitative Judgement would be:

> General attitude of an individual;
> Standards of personal appearance;
> Dedication and Morale/motivation.

In addition to these parameters of measurement, there are two further areas related to the subject of "performance" which are worthy of consideration, and these are the elements of EFFICIENCY and EFFECTIVENESS.

> Efficiency = Doing things right.
> Effectiveness = Doing the right things.

Efficiency can be summarised as "the ratio of output quantity as an element of input resources", in other words, what was produced, and at what cost!

Organisational effectiveness has two important areas for consideration:

(a)   Total actual combined performance against total targets
(b)   Achieved performance of individual managers against targets

In terms of subsidiary targets, every organisation should be aware of the possibility of some managers sacrificing long term success for short term gain, in order to enhance their own prestige. This, in effect, means that deliberate action is taken to exceed initial targets, by perhaps bringing essential resources forward, thereby reducing their availability for future operational needs, and causing problems later in the plan year, not only for themselves but for other managers also.

(G)   ORGANISATIONAL FACTORS

Each section of the organisation is required to make a positive contribution, in terms of measured performance against Quantifiable factors related specifically to its own areas of operational responsibility.

Financial Departments: Cash flow,
                            Debtor control,
                            Investment return.

Sales & Marketing: Volume sales in total,
                            Individual product performance,
                            Media cost/benefit analysis,
                            Market share percentage,
                            Cost of the sales team.

Production:	Labour costs and utilisation, Material cost and utilisation, Units produced against target, Delivery timescales achieved.
Personnel:	Recruitment costs/benefits, Reaction time in recruitment.
Purchasing:	Discounts achieved, Continuity of supply, Quality of materials supplied.
Distribution:	Transport operating costs, Load efficiency (cube capacity used), Control of driver hours/costs.

All sections of an organisation must, of course, control their departmental budget, in terms of allowed cost parameters and revenue requirements, but within those budgets there exist specific areas where effective, Quantifiable, performance can be measured, and this is the essential core of true organisational performance measurement.

18. CONTEMPORARY ORGANISATION STRUCTURES

The past 10-20 years have seen a remarkable degree of change within organisations. Apart from the influence of technological innovations, such factors as mergers and takeovers have led to new structures developing. Organisations have combined with others horizontally, vertically and laterally.

Horizontal combination or integration occurs when firms making the same kinds of products merge to become more competitive in the market-place. One example was the combination of the separate motorcar manufacturers to form British Leyland. The aims of such combinations are to reduce price cutting and competition; to encourage economies of scale by increasing efficiency; and to buy raw materials and sell a broader range of products.

Vertical combination or integration occurs when organisations acquire the different stages and processes of production perhaps back to raw materials or essential components or forward to the point of sale to the customer. The aims of this form of combination are to reduce costs, by cutting out the middleman or wholesaler; to obtain the sources of raw materials; to reduce the likelihood of failures in supply due to other purchasing competition; and to obtain the economies of linked processes and unified control.

Lateral combination or integration occurs when firms producing allied or complementary products, or products for different markets, join together.

The aims of this form of amalgamation are to be able to reduce the effects of loss of markets for one particular product and to increase profits.

Such combinations rarely take only one form and many large companies have practised all three. Such amalgamations can cross national boundaries and lead to the increased development of international multiproduct organisations, which practise division of operation across national boundaries to increase efficiency; to reduce their reliance on one individual economy; and to increase their penetration of difficult markets. Well documented examples are Ford, Alfa Laval, ICI and the major oil and chemical-producing companies.

These combinations have forced organisations to change their structures to take advantage of the benefits. Traditional centralised functional or divisional structures will not be effective in such organisations and a mixture of forms is often to be found. These past trends will still be discernible in the next decade as organisations attempt to maintain competitiveness, by shedding their unprofitable units and consolidating their operations.

This is likely to cause a trend towards intermediate matrix-type structures as groups or teams form or reform to do different tasks or work processes change with technological innovations. Organisations will face pressures to change and to be flexible; to adapt to such changes, on the one hand, whilst retaining stability and coherence of objectives on the other. The structures will have to be developed against the background of the human need for stability, career development and participation in organisational decision making. Adequate communication systems will need to be created so that people do not lose sight of the overall long term goals of the organisation and are able to operate in ways which can be seen to be contributing fully to those objectives.

Obviously not all organisations will have to develop new structures; the traditional functional or divisional systems are still suitable for many, especially those where market changes take place slowly.

The trend towards decentralisation of operations is likely to continue especially in the public sector to increase the consciousness and entrepreneurial ability of the decision makers in units which can respond to the needs of the client. This will increase the speed with which organisations can respond to technical innovation, which will occur at different rates from sector to sector and process to process.

At present it would appear that organisations will either have to grow or they are likely to stagnate in the competitive market of 1992 onwards. Growth, however, is unlikely to be in terms of expansion but rather in terms of increased efficiency; better use of resources; better quality of output; and greater awareness of client needs. This will require more effective management, both in terms of efficiency in decision making and awareness of human needs and fears. Information flow will increase with developments in computer technology — it is thus likely that organisations will have to become more participative and democratic in their decision making.

It must thus be recognised that if an organisation is to survive, its structures, policies, operations and style of management must be developed by deliberate design and must be reviewed continually, consciously and critically. Techniques of organisation development will, therefore, be required as part of the personnel management role, and organisational culture will have to be constantly monitored.

19. ORGANISATIONAL CULTURES

A great deal has been written about Corporate Culture, and the impact it can have on the effectiveness of the organisation, and its relevance to strategic issues, and it is therefore important for us to review the subject in detail.

"Culture", in organisational terms, refers to the collection of systems, practices, and values, which exist within the organisation, and which influence the daily working life of all levels of staff, in short, it can be best described as "the way we do it here". These cultural factors can influence the behaviour of those in management, in terms of decision making, planning, and the way in which employees are treated, and can also reflect the behaviour patterns of separate departments, in respect to specific tasks.

It could, therefore, be thought that culture is an unchanging pattern of influence within an organisation, evolving over a number of years from hard learned experience, but this is not altogether true, as significant changes at senior management levels bring new practices and values into play, leading, in some organisations which are subject to frequent change, to a state of confusion which exerts a negative influence on strategic plans.

In seeking to implement significant strategic change, within an organisation, sufficient time must be allocated to the study of existing norms of behaviour, and the identification of the actual dominant culture which exists, which, we have already established, is probably based on both historic events and the strongly held beliefs of those in senior management positions. The way individuals behave in organisations is directly related to the way systems and procedures have been operated, over a number of years, and the successful introduction of any change is, therefore, dependent on spending time in changing the beliefs and behavioural patterns of those involved – major cultural change is not achieved simply by top Management issuing instructions!

In addition to the historic evolution of systems and procedures, organisation culture is directly related to the developed values of the management, in terms of impact on strategic change. Those organisations which have forward thinking, progressive managers, will have an ethos which is flexible and accepting of change, whereas those which have managers who believe that change is disruptive and dangerous, unless subjected to the test of time, will be much more difficult to move, strategically. A further cause for consideration is that managers tend to build teams around them which reflect their own values and beliefs, and this, also, impacts on successful strategic change.

20.   THE FUNCTIONS OF ORGANISATION CULTURE

Apart from indicating to all employees the way in which systems are to be operated, within the organisation, Culture has some other, equally important areas of influence:

(a)   To provide a basis of stability;
(b)   To provide a guide to expected behaviour;
(c)   To provide a sense of Corporate identity for all levels of employee;
(d)   To indicate communication channels to be used;
(e)   To provide a basis for control of individuals;
(f)   To provide a structure for the integration of new employees;
(g)   To clearly indicate the decision making process for all those in a management function.

Each organisation has a set of cultural beliefs which are unique to itself, and whilst some basis exists for the belief that there are four generic types of culture, this does not detract from the ability of an organisation to develop its own version of one of these models. Each industry, also, has influences on the culture of organisations within it, in that it exerts external environmental pressure on each set of strategic plans, produced by each of them, and, to some extent develops a set of industry-wide behaviourial norms, in terms of systems and terminology, which have developed over time.

21.   TYPES OF ORGANISATIONAL CULTURE

Organisational Cultures have been described as a group of deep beliefs which are directly related to a number of specific areas of organisational operations:

(a)   The way in which work is structured;
(b)   The way in which authority is exercised;
(c)   The way reward and incentive systems work;
(d)   The way in which people are controlled;
(e)   The extent to which formality exists;
(f)   The way planning is done (if at all);
(g)   The extent to which individual initiative is allowed or encouraged;
(h)   The expected standards of dress and individual behaviour, at all levels;
(i)   The way in which working hours are operated;
(j)   The extent of formal rules and procedures;
(k)   The extent to which individual control is allowed, in relation to task;
(l)   The type of office building or workshop used, particularly related to layout and equipment;
(m)   The education and socio-economic status of those normally employed by the company.

Reviewing this list of cultural factors leads to the need for acceptance of three other important areas of understanding. We have already established that each Organisation develops its own specific culture, but it must also be accepted that, to be successful, each of those cultures requires clearly defined types of people within it, those who can work well inside the framework of values and systems which have developed over time. Finally, we must also accept that strong cultures evolve into easily identifiable "Tribes" which have their own traditions, jargon, rituals and what has been referred to as "clannishness", that element of exclusivity or superiority that some specialist organisations or sections of the business community use to set themselves apart form others, more often than not, deluding themselves, rather than those they seek to impress!

We earlier referred to the four generic types of culture which have become recognisable, over time, and these can be described as:

POWER CULTURES - ROLE CULTURES - TASK CULTURES - PERSON CULTURES

These four generic types of culture have specific factors which distinguish them form each other, and, as referred to above, each of them tends to attract those sorts of employees which feel comfortable within that culture, employees which they must have in order to achieve their organisational objectives.

Let us now go on to examine each of these cultures in detail.

(A)   THE POWER CULTURE – THE "WEB" STRUCTURE

The illustration indicates the familiar pattern of the spiders web, and this graphically describes the way this type of organisation is operated.

The most prominent factor is that there is only one source of Power, within the organisation, and that is one individual, placed at the centre of the web, from whom, and to whom, all decisions relate, and by whom all functions are controlled, usually via well regulated middle managers. The success of the organisation depends on the receipt of regular information, from the source, and a sense of trust in the decisions taken by that individual, together with an almost telepathic sense of the way the power source would expect an employee to behave, in any given situation - a case of understanding the boss!

To be really comfortable in this type of organisation, the employee concerned must "fit" with the boss, and failure to do so leads to a very rough ride, usually culminating in the departure of the individual, either voluntarily or with assistance. When one accepts that the management team will be selected in the same image as the power source, this type of organisation tends to both be, and to attract, abrasive individuals, and those not happy with this style of behaviour would not be encouraged to, or wish to join such an organisation.

There will be few rules and procedures, and minimal bureaucracy, in this type of operation, the central source reserving the right to make changes, at any time, to suit the prevailing needs of the business, the overriding factor being the need to conform. These tend to be highly "political" businesses, related directly to the ethos of one power source, and the need, therefore, to gain influence with that source, and in recognising this fact, the person at the central power point can influence all operations, and create a competitive atmosphere between executives, simply by manipulation of their need to gain influence.

In terms of reaction time, because of this central decision making ethos, the organisation can be effectively flexible if danger looks like impacting on plans, particularly as executives are used to frequent change and straight line control — they simply obey the orders given!

This is a tough, abrasive climate, and could lead to a situation of low morale, and high staff loss, at all levels, for the organisation will not encourage individualism, in any way. The ideal type of employee is either happy to take orders, or a risk taker who enjoys a rollercoaster ride, or one who enjoys a game of organisation politics (again a risk taker). Growth, however, brings a need for more formal structure and this can lead to organisation collapse, ultimately.

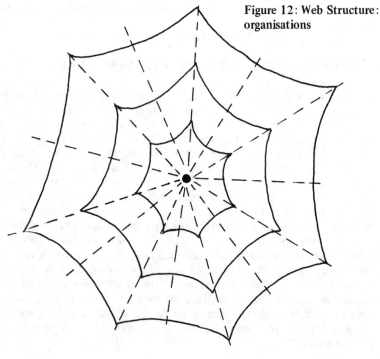

Figure 12: Web Structure: organisations

(B)   THE ROLE CULTURE – THE "GREEK TEMPLE" STRUCTURE

The usual comment that is made about this culture is that, more than any other, it works by an all pervading sense of logic and rationality. It is a culture that is to be found in many major organisations, particularly those which have been established for many years, basing their systems and operating procedures on practices which, in their view, have stood the test of time. This type of culture tends to regard the modern trend for speed of decision making and total flexibility with deep suspicion, preferring to evaluate all pertinent factors, over a period of time, before committing the organisation to action.

The structure of the organisation is a series of well defined hierarchic levels, through which the decision process must pass, and also through which aspiring executives must make their way, in terms of career progression. In this Culture, the job function is more important than the individual, and people are selected in relation to their ability to fulfil the job description, rather than on personality and future career potential. High performance, above the job requirement specified, is not a prime requirement, and those who aspire to personal power will be reminded that the only access to power comes from "position", that which has been achieved through satisfactory service over a period of some years – this is definitely not the organisation for the thrusting young go-getter!

The strength of the Culture comes from the effectiveness of the specialist functions, as indicated by the doric columns which support the roof structure of the Temple (illustrated), and these functions are clearly strong, as individual groups of key staff, in their own right. Co-ordination of these specialist functions is the sole province of the Senior Management Board, and interaction between them is controlled by:

(a)   Clearly defined role procedures (job descriptions)
(b)   Clearly defined communication channels and systems (many of which are clogged up with copy memos!)
(c)   Clearly defined disputes procedures, covering both staff and interdepartmental activities

In this Culture, "efficiency" is equated to the "rational allocation of work", a phrase which typifies the ethos of it.

From an employee point of view, working for an organisation which operates in a Role Culture mode, there is much benefit to be gained, in terms of job security, the predictability of the working patterns, the clearly defined reward systems and promotion paths, and, of prime importance to many people, and organisation which does not ever demand the sacrifice of private life for company business.

However, the impact of environmental changes, of any sort, which weakens one of the specialist functions, could have a major effect on the continued smooth running of the organisational systems, and ultimately cause the hierarchic foundations to shake, and, possibly partially collapse. The rather ponderous control mechanisms would be slow to respond and the situation could take the organisation into unfamiliar waters, leaving a long-term wound which would take time to cure.

Figure 13: Role culture structure: organisations

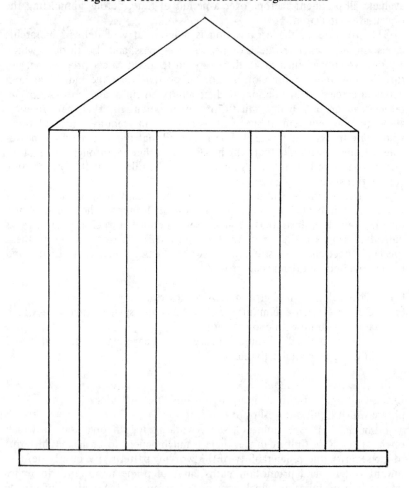

(C) THE TASK CULTURE – THE "NET" STRUCTURE

The Task Culture is the one which most modern managers prefer their organisations to adopt, in that the total emphasis is always on "getting the job done", rather than becoming hide bound by procedures. In strategic terms, this Culture lies at the heart of the ethos of relating all organisational activity to the achievement of those objectives, and it could, therefore, be quite rightly described as the Cultural style for the 1990s.

Because of the constant emphasis on objective achievement, the Culture links all available resources to the tasks, and the organisation can be seen to have dynamic forward drive, a positive atmosphere that can literally be sensed, as you enter the building.

You will find no rigid hierarchic structures in an organisation which is committed to Task Culture, rather, you will find that tasks are approached by the formation of project teams, made up of specialists from different sections of the organisation, the strength factor coming from the wide pool of expertise that therefore is made available to achieve the ultimate objective. In this respect, recognition, inside the Organisation, comes solely from being seen to be good at what you do, rather than the position you occupy, within the structure.

The Cultural activity relies heavily on the maintenance of Team Identity, with all individuals locked into corporate objectives, being supported by a free flowing communication system, and it follows, therefore, that there must be, and is, high individual task control, with few restrictions.

Senior management exercise control through the initial allocation of people, and other resources, to specific tasks, sure in the knowledge that those tasks will be carried out effectively, by staff who will know when to refer back for advice and assistance. Organisations engaged in highly competitive markets, or who have products with short life cycles, are particularly suited to the Task Culture, requiring, as they do, fast and flexible decision making, in a volatile market place, from executives with the expertise and responsibility to take the right decision, without reference back to committees!

The Task Culture is called the "Net" structure because the whole organisation is likened to a fishermans net, the total strength coming from the linking of all parts together, with particular strength at the points of the net, where lines cross each other, i.e. the Project teams from specialist sections of the organisation.

The dynamic forward drive, which exists throughout the organisation, can, however, lead to problems when resources are tight. With the emphasis being firmly on task achievement, and career success being also linked to those same tasks, there is a danger of inter-group conflict, and organisational politics, when resources are denied to any section of the organisation, the total drive for achievement tending to sometimes obscure a realistic appraisal of the true situation facing the organisation.

Apart from this, the Task Culture is one which all modern organisations see as the ultimate pinnacle to aim for, and a prime function of the strategic planners must be to foster a total conversion to this culture.

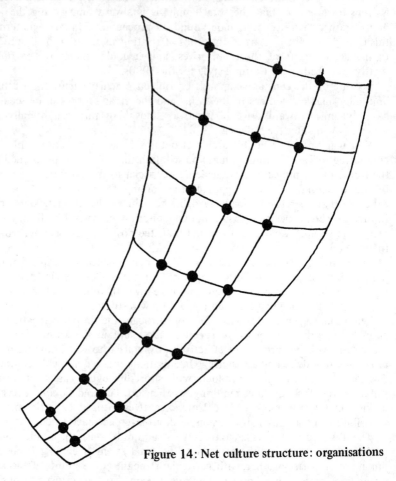

Figure 14: Net culture structure: organisations

(D)   PERSON CULTURES

The structure of an organisation involved in a "Person" Culture is unusual, in that the structure only exists to support the work of those individuals within it, for they are all equal. The Culture is formed by individuals who have similar aims, in terms of the career that they wish to follow, and the structure is controlled through a process of mutual consent.

Figure 15: Person culture structure: organisations

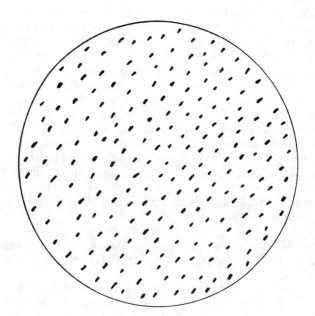

It is said that such a structure is subordinate to the people within it, and a "Psychological Contract" exists between them, in that they each work for the benefit of the others, without hierarchic control being necessary. An individual can leave the group, but the group has no power to dismiss, for all are equal, influence being shared, and any power base which exists is based on individual expertise and input potential.

Anyone joining such a group normally has no drive for personal power, and indeed, the group would not accept anyone with such aims. Success, in organisational terms, brings growth, and growth brings the need for more formal structures and procedures, and this, in turn, creates a need for seniority to be established, removing the original concept of all being equal. The original concept group, with success, could therefore have a short life cycle, but with careful handling, that original ethos can be preserved, within the systems and attitudes of a larger, but still select, group.

THE STRUCTURE OF CORPORATE OBJECTIVES

SUMMARY

Each of the Cultures outlined within this chapter, relate to specific types of organisations, which continue to exist in the 1990s. The Power Culture is found within those organisations where the founder still survives, and, having built the business, is still reluctant to delegate ultimate decision taking to others, failing to recognise that growth means that all the reins cannot continue to remain in the hands of one individual. By trying to maintain this situation, the person concerned is only contributing to the complexity and time span of decision making, slowing down potential future growth, but it is always hard to convince such a person that the Culture must change.

The Role Culture still exists in many organisations, particularly those with many different subsidiaries, and also in the way that the Civil Service, Education, Local Government, and the Church still operate today. Whilst accepting that some of those would find it difficult to adapt to commercial pressures, and, perhaps, find it unnecessary to do so, there is little excuse for true commercial organisations who still refuse to change slow and cumbersome structures, and decision making processes, in the fast moving business world of the 1990s.

The Task Culture, as referred to earlier, is the one most suited to today's business operations, and constantly moving markets, but it, too needs regular examination, to ensure that elements of either Power, or Role Cultures do not gain a foothold.

Finally, the Person Culture will always exist, in the form of GP Group Practices, Accountancy firms, Barristers Chambers, Architectural partnerships, and lastly Management Consultants, where a small number of qualified people decide to form themselves into a supportive partnership, with no hierarchic structure being needed.

Culture is important to any organisation and they all have them, the secret is to identify which form is being used!

Examine your own organisation against the background of this chapter. What objectives does it currently have in the short term and long term? How and why have these objectives changed? What structure does it operate? How centralised or decentralised is it? What degree of autonomy is allowed to each division or branch? What staff/line conflicts exist? What significant changes will it face in the future? What do you believe will be the resultant employment and employee relations issues? What culture is being operated? What is the organisation's mission?

CHAPTER THREE

THE MAJOR FUNCTIONS OF ENTERPRISE : MARKETING

Personnel management occurs within the context of organisation, alongside other functions and contributes with those other functions to the attainment of organisational objectives. Before we examine the nature of personnel management itself, it is worth examining two of the major functions of business — marketing and production. In this chapter we shall examine marketing and, in the next, production.

1.   WHAT IS MARKETING?

Marketing is a major function of the management of an enterprise which is more concerned with what is happening outside the particular organisation than inside. Marketing as an activity has been described in a number of different ways. Here are some examples:

1. The British Institute of Management (BIM) defines marketing as:

> 'The creative management function which promotes trade and employment by assessing consumer needs and initiating research and development to meet them. It coordinates the resources of production and distribution of goods and services, determines and directs the nature and scale of the total effort required to sell profitably the maximum production to the ultimate user.'

2. Peter Drucker in *The Practice of Management* (1954) has said:

> 'Marketing is...looking at the business through the customer's eyes.'

3. The Institute of Marketing, (1966) stated that marketing was:

> 'The management function which organises and directs all those business activities involved in assessing and converting customer purchasing power into effective demand for a specific product or service and moving the product or service to the final consumer so as to achieve the profit target or other objectives of the company.'

The origins of marketing can be traced back to the period following the Industrial Revolution when, for the first time, there were indications that the means of production were capable of meeting and even surpassing the actual stated demand for goods. Before techniques of mass production were developed, there was generally a shortage of manufactured goods and this demand and supply lag meant that most products and services were assured of an immediate sale. Productive processes were given a great stimulus by the two World Wars and, despite an increasing population (because of medical developments and enhanced survival prospects) by the early 1960s, in developed industrial countries, the supply of manufactured goods had outstripped demand. Companies found that competition had increased; they could no longer sell all that they made. The position had changed from one in which the manufacturers had to a great extent determined the quantity and the type of goods supplied, to one in which the consumer had a choice — especially affecting the consumer goods industry — the cash to be able to purchase goods and was able to discriminate in his purchases.

For businesses to sustain their share of the market and to grow it was necessary to conduct research into the needs of the consumer and to develop products of a price and a quality that was acceptable. This has been recognised for years. Adam Smith wrote in his *Wealth of Nations* 1755:

'Consumption is the sole end of production'.

In this lies what has been termed *the marketing concept*: the appreciation that far from being the last link in the business chain, it is the customer who initiates the whole business cycle. This does not mean that the customer is always right, but that customer need should be the starting point for the organisation's corporate strategy. Wealth is only created when goods are sold, not when they are made and goods are sold when there is an identifiable consumer need which can be satisfied by the organisation. It is the first concern of marketing to identify those needs and, having defined them, to devise methods of meeting them at a profit.

One important differentiation needs to be made. In marketing there is an identifiable difference between people's *needs,* which can be defined as the physical and psychological drives which stem from being human, e.g. the need for food, clothing, shelter, etc. and to differentiate these from people's *wants* which are the specific fancies which are directed towards satisfying those needs. Thus, the need for food can be directed by a confectionery firm into a specific fancy for jelly babies or liquorice allsorts rather than another organisation's food products. Marketing often concentrates on creating and changing people's wants to satisfy their human needs.

The specific elements in the marketing function can be represented as in Figure 16.

Figure 16: Elements in the marketing function

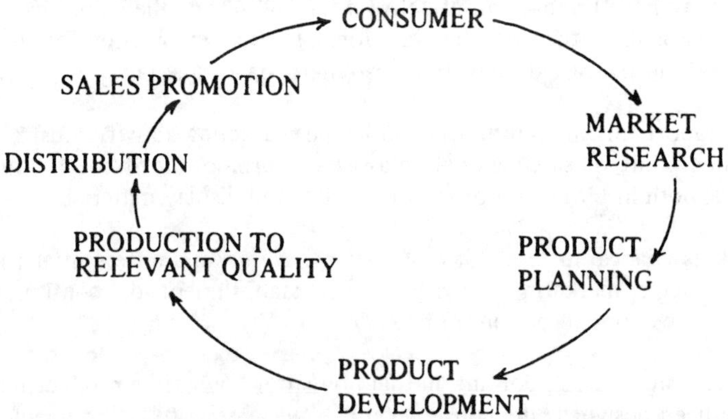

2. STRATEGIC MARKETING

The primary role of management, in relation to marketing activities, is to design a series of strategies which will enable the organisation to create, build and maintain specific target markets, directly related to the achievement of objectives.

In order to do this, management must complete a group of specific tasks:

a) Conduct a disciplined analysis of their own market area, in terms of customer requirements, competitor activity and dominance status, and the market share of each of their products, together with their relative positions in the product life cycle.

b) They should review the relevance of each product to the market requirements, designing specific products to either fill gaps in the range, replace products nearing decline stage, or break new ground.

Price structures should also be reviewed and changed, if necessary, to conform to, or take advantage of, conditions in the market place.

c) Marketing is directly related to the process of "persuading customers", and there is little point in developing an attractive product range, at an attractive price, if no-one has taken time to develop an effective customer communication strategy.

This can range through TV advertising, Sunday colour supplements, specialised journals, radio, local and national newspapers, down to leaflet campaigns, perhaps including a customer price incentive or discount.

d)   In line with the communication activity, management should ensure that they have arranged an effective means of getting their products to the customer, either via the traditional showroom or shop, by mail order or, in the case of industrial customers, via a trade fair.

To support this distribution network, the marketing activity must also include point of sale material to assist the promotion of the product range, both in terms of information leaflets and display material.

e)   Markets change, in terms of customer behaviour, and an essential part of strategic marketing activity is the establishment of continuous product performance monitoring systems.

These systems are important, in that no matter how well a product may have been designed, the consumer may find reasons to either reject it, initially, or lose interest in it, in preference to a competitor product, or due to a repetitive fault which develops.

Performance monitoring is an integral part of organisational strategy, and marketing activity forms a major part of this, for failure of a keynote product can cause the organisation to fall short of target, and management must be aware of this.

f)   Competitors exist, in every market, and they rarely allow another company to take their market share, for any length of time.

Continuous monitoring of the total market place is therefore vital, in terms of competitor reaction to new product launches, or their activity in bringing a new product of their own to the market, or taking action to seize advantage by price adjustment.

3.   THE STRATEGIC MARKETING PROCESS

The strategic marketing process can be compared to the normal structure of organisational strategic planning, indeed it is part of that mainstream activity. The impetus for any marketing action must stem from an awareness of opportunities which exist in the particular market, related to the organisation.

Before any action is taken, these potential opportunities must be matched against the established objectives of the organisation, for perfect fit, for there is little point in instigating action which will not combine well with mainstream objectives and, perhaps, detract from them.

Having established a 'fit' then the process of devising the strategic marketing plan can commence, in terms of designing the detail plan, which will achieve the strategic objectives and specify the action to be taken, and

Figure 17 : The strategic marketing process

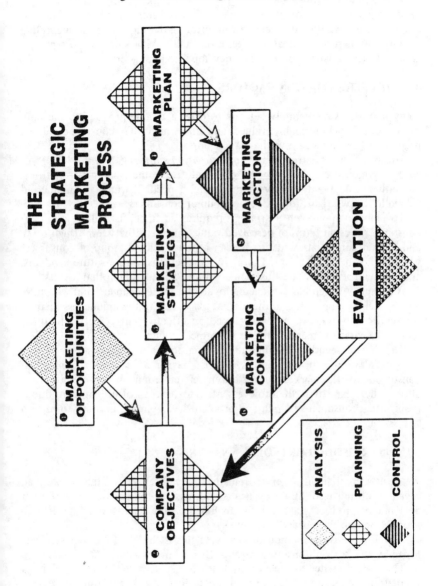

the marketing control systems to ensure that those objectives are achieved.

Throughout the timescale of the total strategic marketing plan, there must be an on-going evaluation process, not only of the actual marketing plan, but also of the organisational objectives, monitoring the impact of the marketing activity on these vital areas of operation, and taking steps to correct any apparent plan variances, before they develop into a long-term threat.

4.   DIFFERENTIATION FACTORS

Many companies deliberately set out to offer a unique product to the consumer, one which is highly valued and for which that consumer will be prepared to pay prices above the market norm.

This practice is referred to as *"differentiation strategy"*, and this is *not* yet another jargonistic term for being different from other, competitive, firms, but rather a deliberate policy of producing a product which is unique and valued in its own right, for a specific group of consumers.

To embark upon such a strategy requires an in-depth understanding of consumer needs, in terms of perceived value, price sensitivity level (high/low), and market conditions, and success can produce a loyal group of consumers who will not be easily tempted away by competitors, via substitute products, and who will accept price adjustments without a reduction in that loyalty.

A company which has attracted a loyal group of consumers, and who have a well established position in the market place, due to the uniqueness of their product, can be said to have developed an effective entry barrier to those seeking to enter the market, due to the projected high cost of entry.

The fact of securing this unique position does not, of course, mean that the organisation can rest on its laurels, having a 'captive audience' of consumers, for the market place is a dynamic environment and predators are always there, and it is therefore essential to have a pattern of continuous monitoring, consumer research and product development, in order to remain successful.

5.   MARKETING PORTFOLIO ANALYSIS

We have seen that, in order to remain at the forefront of the market, an organisation must continuously assess and reassess the performance of their portfolio of products, taking decisions based on the relative standing of each product, within their overall market share.

A well established method of achieving this is the portfolio matrix, developed by the Boston Consulting Group (BCG), known as the *"Boston Box"*.

The matrix invites the marketing team to classify their products under a set of four categories, which, in turn, relate to four other factors concerning the relative market share position and industrial growth rate. The four basic product categories are:-

a) 'STARS'   Those products which are producing rapidly increasing sales results and therefore have a high share of a growth market. These are products which command high organisational support, in terms of cash and effort.

b) 'QUESTION MARKS' Products which could pose potential problems, in that they have only attracted a low share of a high growth market. The remedy may well be a further cash injection, for increased sales promotion, or a price repositioning decision, or an element of repackaging or redesign — certainly an area for market research activity.

c) 'CASH COWS'   These products tend to be well established and in the maturity stage of the product life cycle. They have a high share of a low growth market, and can be relied upon to generate cash, with relatively low support. Their cast generation status ensures that funds are available to support the 'STARS' and take action on the 'QUESTION MARK' products. They are often referred to as good company servants.

d) 'DOGS'   These products have a low share of a low growth market and are therefore prime candidates for deletion from the range, once a replacement has been developed.

The Boston Box is a very useful marketing tool, in that it requires a series of clear decisions, taking a detailed review of the performance of every product, as a precursor to developing an action plan, and it therefore assists in the development of marketing strategy.

Figure 18: Market share: the Boston Box

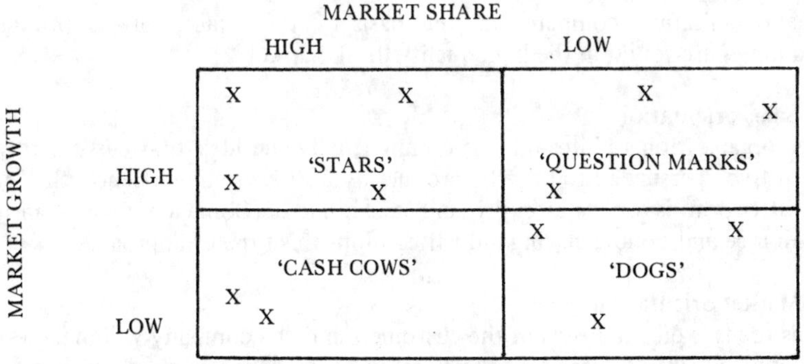

MARKET SHARE

	HIGH	LOW

HIGH (MARKET GROWTH)	X X
	
	X 'STARS'
	        X
		X
		                X
		'QUESTION MARKS'
		X

LOW	'CASH COWS'
	X
	  X
		X X
		'DOGS'
		        X

The BCG Growth/Share Portfolio Matrix (Boston Box)

6.   MARKET ENTRY STRATEGY

In certain situations, usually to maximise opportunities and achieve positive diversification, an organisation may decide to break into a new market.

There are potential problems to this, in that those already established in the market will not welcome a new entrant, due to the effect of entry on their market share, and will therefore, go to considerable lengths to devise entry barriers to ward off the predator, perhaps by adjusting prices, or by exerting influence on suppliers and distribution channels.

There is, therefore, a strong case for entry into a target market by the acquisition of a company already established in that market, preventing entry barriers being raised and allowing for rapid expansion, backed by in-depth knowledge of the market, in the form of in-house management.

Such an acquisition may also help to achieve economies of scale, in terms of production, purchasing, or distribution, and certainly reduces the risk of entry to a more acceptable level.

7.   COMPANY ORIENTATION

Organisations can take a variety of orientations towards their customers and potential customers in the consumer market. The four most commonly identified are:

1.Production orientation
The organisation concentrates its attention on efficiency of production and distribution and maintaining low costs to encourage customers to purchase their products.   Mass production car manufacturers tend to adopt this approach.

2. Product orientation
The organisation competes on the basis of the quality of its products. Examples are found in the high quality 'hi-fi' market.

3. Sales orientation
The organisation's philosophy is dominated by the idea that customers will need to be persuaded to buy the product by positive selling. Hence, the focus of attention is on sales skills and techniques.   Some companies in the insurance and double-glazing industries adopt this type of approach.

4. Market orientation
This focus is on the needs of the customers and the company will make every attempt possible to ascertain their real wants. It then responds to customer demand. This is quite common in the kitchen design industry.

8. IDENTIFICATION OF THE MARKET

The first task of marketing, however, is to identify what the market is. It is not just Shepherds Bush or the UK or the World; used in the context of modern marketing, the word 'market' is taken to mean people or groups of people having in common the need or desire for a particular commodity or service. Two broad categories of market can be identified:

1. *Industrial markets,* which may represent a relatively small number of customers who require technical advice and support after the sale has taken place and who may require products tailored to individual requirements. Some industrial and commercial markets do purchase large quantities of similar products.
2. *Consumer markets,* where lower costs of producing and selling may be influential in tempting people to buy.

Marketing managers have a special interest in classifying potential consumers, whether of the industrial or private kind, to discover differences in taste, spending habits and attitudes, which may be used as the basis for designing relevant marketing programmes.

The term *market segmentation* is based on the idea that most, if not all, markets are composed of different types of customers with distinct product preferences. Segmentation identifies that consumers are different in some way; they may buy the product at different times, or for different reasons, or perhaps the product can be put to a different use in a segment which is not general for the rest of the market. The most frequent methods of segmenting a market are based on demographic, geographical and buyer-behaviour variables, which may overlap. Figure 19 illustrates these variables.

Figure 19: Variables affecting market segmentation

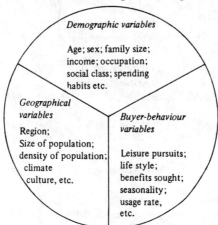

1. *Demographic variables.* A convenient way of classifying the population is according to social class on such characteristics as occupation, education and income. This has a correlation with spending habits and life style. The common classification of classes and approximate percentages of the population in such categories is given in Table 4. The categorisation has a weakness as it tends to be based on the occupation of the head of the family.

   Magazines, newspapers and journals are examples of products which can be directed towards carefully segmented markets and this is of interest to advertisers who will choose the medium which is orientated towards the consumer groups they are trying to reach. What characteristics do you think consumers have who read the following?

The Observer	The Independent	The Sun
Playboy	The Economist	Woman's Realm
The People	The Financial Times	Woman and Home
New Society	Daily Telegraph	Cosmopolitan

Table 4: Social Classes – Broad Classification

Code	Broad Category	Occupation of Head Household	Approx. Percentage of Population
A.	Upper middle class	Professional and senior managerial	16%
B.	Middle class	Intermediate managerial administrative or professional staff	
C.1	Lower middle class	Junior managerial, supervisory, senior clerical	22%
C.2	Skilled working class	Skilled manual	33%
D.	Working class	Semi-skilled and unskilled manual	29%
E.	Subsistence levels	Persons living on pensions and social security or in casual work	

2. *Age* is a further basis of segmentation because of the different attitudes and preferences between age groups and because of the different domestic circumstances which ageing brings, e.g. clothes can be aimed at different age groups.

3. *Geographical segmentation,* which covers aspects such as regions and their density of population, has significance for suppliers of such goods as pork pies, which are more popular in the Midlands and North, and clothes, which are required to deal with certain variations in climatic conditions. Attempts to maximise sales without segmenting the market would probably lead to wasted effort. Large retail stores are only likely to establish shops in areas with high population density, to gain maximum returns.

4. *Buyer-behaviour variables.* Such items as the frequency of use of particular products or seasonality may have major repercussions in some industries. For example, small off-licences are likely to keep a small stock of liqueurs throughout the year but are likely to increase their stocks around Christmas and Easter when families are more likely to indulge. Some industries may also be affected by weather patterns, e.g. certain brands of beer are more likely to be purchased in good weather or hotels may have to improve their attractions for year-round guests. Other examples of products with a seasonal demand include bedding plants and Christmas cards. Seasonality factors are of considerable importance in relation to production schedules, distribution and storage arrangements.

Thus the nature of a particular market is likely to have profound effects on the techniques employed in identifying the needs of each sector.

9. THE MARKETING MIX

An important element in every marketing strategy is (termed in the 1940s by Professor Neil Borden of Harvard University) the *Marketing Mix.* It identified twelve key influences on marketing programmes. Borden's model has since been refined and the variables have now been reduced to four, product, promotion, price and distribution. Once the decision has been made to penetrate a particular market, the influence of these variables operating together on success is crucial. The Marketing Mix can be represented in Figure 20. These various elements are outlined later in the chapter.

Figure 20: The Marketing Mix

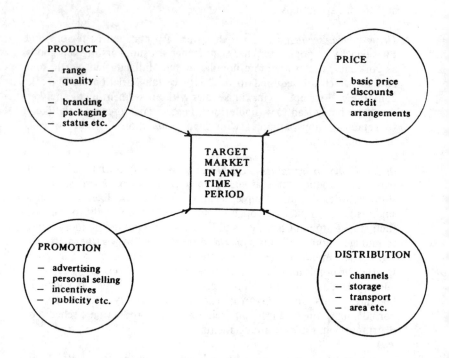

10.   MARKET RESEARCH

Market research attempts to acquire and analyse information to make marketing decisions.   Thus information is gathered which tries to answer the following questions:

1.   What products are being sold?
2.   In what quantities?
3.   Where?
4.   How?
5.   When?
6.   At what price?
7.   What is the total potential size of the market?
8.   Is it an industrial or consumer market or a mixture of both?
9.   Is the market growing, saturated or declining?

10. What are the characteristics of competitors' products?
11. How successful are advertising strategies?
12. Do customers require an after sales service?
    — and so on.

Thus it is concerned with assessing the demands for new products and the acceptability of existing products. In both instances, it will study the organisation's position and that of its competitors. The data which forms the raw material of market research falls into two broad categories, primary and secondary:

1. *Primary data* — is gathered directly from the customers and those handling the commodity, e.g. wholesalers and retailers. This data is most frequently collected by means of surveys, which may either be based on questionnaires or on interviews. Often surveys are undertaken by specialist research organisations who use trained interviewers asking structured questions to ensure comparability of data. Questionnaires have the advantage that they obtain wide coverage at a relatively low cost, but this is offset by the usually low rate of response. Interviews have the advantage that they are more flexible than questionnaires and the target population can be effectively controlled, but they have the main disadvantage that they are costly and time consuming.
2. *Secondary data.* There are two main sources of secondary data — firstly, external information from Government statistics, trade reports, and press and private marketing research agencies; secondly, internal data can be obtained from sales information including field sales reports and letters from consumers.

11. PRODUCT PLANNING AND PRODUCT DEVELOPMENT

This translates customer needs, as identified by market research, into acceptable products or services which can be sold to the consumer to meet that need. People, as we have already mentioned, do not necessarily purchase products for their intrinsic value, but because they believe their needs will be satisfied by the product. For example, people buy motorcars for what they provide in terms of convenience and comfort as a means of transport, but also possibly for psychological reasons of status or self-expression.
    Product planning is concerned with any or all of the following:

1. Completely new products
2. Changes in existing products
3. Extensions to an existing range of products
4. Introducing an established product from another market.

Market research will establish the nature and extent of the potential market and will also evaluate the extent and quality of competitive activity. If the findings are favourable for a new product, the preliminary product specification will be passed to the Research and Development department for production of a prototype for testing. At the same time, preliminary costings will be calculated so that estimates can be made of the profit margins. Tentative advertising and sales plans will be prepared and, depending upon the results of product testing (perhaps with potential consumers) and evaluation of the results, a decision will be taken as to whether to launch the product or not. Production capacity and equipment will be necessary for production of the appropriate quality and numbers.

Product quality may be designed into the item, so that benefits of reliability, long product life and value for money can be used in advertising and selling. In some products quality may not be important, e.g. certain types of disposable goods, like plastic spoons for picnics, do not need to be durable or aesthetically pleasing so long as they are hygienic and functional.

12. DISTRIBUTION

The objectives of distribution are to ensure that the right goods, in the right quantities, are in the right place. The producer must choose the most suitable *channel or channels of distribution* – a channel is a combination of organisation, transportation and storage. The most common channels can be depicted as in Figure 3:4.

The first channel is more often found in industrial than in consumer markets. Manufacturers of goods such as machine tools, turbines, computers and other large and expensive items tend to move them directly to the consumer without involving any middleman. Channel 2 is often found in mail-order business operations and large cash-and-carry warehouses which are increasingly developing their coverage. Channel 3 represents the situation where manufacturers sell direct to large national, retail chains who buy in bulk from manufacturers and distribute directly to their own retail outlets, e.g. Woolworth's, Marks & Spencer, British Home Stores and Sainsbury's. Channel 4 represents the typical chain for mass-marketed consumer goods where products are sold over a wide geographical area, perhaps both nationally and internationally, wholesalers buy in bulk from the manufacturers, store the goods and sell them in smaller quantities to individual retailers.

Three major influences affect the physical storage and distribution of goods from the manufacturer to the customer:

Channel

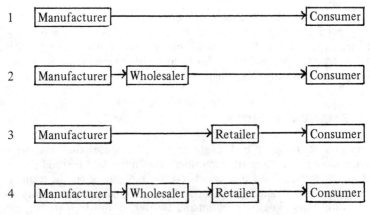

Figure 21: Common Distribution Channels

1.   Market considerations

Some examples are:

(a)   The channels of distribution chosen to satisfy the industrial sector of the market will usually differ from those chosen for the consumer sector.

(b)   Where seasonal demand cannot be met by seasonal production, storage facilities may be required for the goods which are accumulating as a result of continuous production — these stocks can be known as *buffer stocks.*

(c)   Variation in purchasing habits between different parts of the country will have an effect on distribution methods and costs.

2.   Product considerations

The composition, size, weight or technical complexity of the product can all affect distribution. For example:

(a)   Perishable products will require special transport and storage facilities.

(b)   The actual size and weight of the product can also impose limitations and some products may need to be shipped partially-assembled for final reassembly at the point of sale.

(c)   Complex products may require installation by qualified technicians and perhaps after-sales service, including the distribution of spare parts.

3. Economic considerations

In Europe, distribution accounts for between 35% and 50% of the retail price of the product. Capital is tied up in finished goods and so a manufacturer will tend to choose a channel of distribution which does not necessitate his holding an inventory and thus releases, and perhaps even reduces, the working capital he requires for his business.

13. SALES PROMOTION

Every product needs to be brought to the attention of the customer in the market-place and its benefits identified. One important method used to sell benefits is termed *branding,* which can be thought of as the naming of a product to give it appeal and recognition. Famous brand names include Coke, Biro, Mars, Wilkinson Sword and Hoover, all of which are synonymous with particular products. Thus, for instance, most domestic vacuum cleaners are referred to as Hoovers, whether they are made by Hoover or not. Branding is used a lot in selling beers, cigarettes, detergent, and perfumes. Some of the large retail stores successfully sell products manufactured by other well-known suppliers under their own brand name, e.g. Sainsbury's, Woolworth's, Marks & Spencer and Iceland.

Sales promotion is merchandising the product in such a manner that it attracts prospective customers and induces them to buy. This may take a variety of forms with different emphasis, according to whether they are used for consumer or industrial markets. The principal methods are:

1. Advertising
2. Personal selling
3. Incentives
4. Packaging
5. Sponsorship and publicity.

1. Advertising

This communicates information about the product or service by means of the written word, the spoken word and visual material. There are five principal media of advertising:

(a)   Newspapers, magazines, journals, trade publications, etc.
(b)   Television
(c)   Direct mailing
(d)   Commercial radio
(e)   Hoardings, transport advertisements, trade and country fairs etc.

In the UK something like 70% of advertising is via the press and about 30% on commercial television. There are various options open to an organisation in deciding how much to spend on advertising. It can be based on a relationship of advertising expenditure to sales expenditure, on what competitors are spending and on special budgets to increase awareness of particular products. Examine the impact of advertising by listing some products of which you are aware and try to analyse why the advertising is a success.

2. Personal selling

Personal selling is an important adjunct to advertising. Personal selling is especially important in the industrial market. The basic sales process contains five elements or stages:

(a) Arousing interest in the product;
(b) creating a preference for the organisation's product rather than that of another organisation;
(c) establishing contact with the customer;
(d) encouraging interest in a sale;
(e) completing the sale;
(f) keeping the business.

In consumer markets the first three stages are often handled by advertising, but in industrial markets it is more usual for representatives or salesmen to handle them. Companies allocate the following tasks to sales representatives:

(i) Communicating regular information to customers on the products and their uses and advantages;
(ii) obtaining new customers;
(iii) gathering information on customer satisfaction;
(iv) dealing with technical queries and ensuring delivery at the right time.

This requires knowledge of —
   — the range of products,
   — the customers and likely customers,
   — other organisations' products,
   — techniques of selling.

Sales forces may be organised on a number of different bases or combinations of different structures. These include organisation on:

— a geographical or territorial basis
— a product or range of product basis, where specialist knowledge is important

— a customer basis, e.g. consumer or industrial markets.

The success of a salesman or representative can be evaluated in a number of different ways. These include:

— net sales achieved for product or customer
— number of calls made in a given period and value of sales per call
— number of new customers
— costs of selling as a proportion of sales achieved.

3.   Incentives

The offering of incentives to promote the organisation's product or service and to encourage customers to buy, is most common for consumer products. The hope is that various incentives will draw attention to a new product or improved product; encourage sales of slow moving items; and stimulate higher customer usage of particular items, which perhaps they have not used before. Incentives are also offered to trade purchasers to develop goodwill and encourage wholesalers or retailers to push' various items and to increase the amount they buy.   Incentives may take a number of different forms and include:

— free samples
— bulk purchase bargains
— temporary price reductions
— special discounts for the trade
— provision of display material
— stamp trading and gift catalogues
— competitions
— free demonstrations
— reductions on holidays etc.

4.   Packaging

This has two functions; firstly, it provides protection for the product, and secondly, it creates a brand image. Certainly packaging becomes important at particular times of the year, for example, Christmas, when many cigarette companies produce more large 200 boxes with wrappers which reflect the season and Easter, when the confectionery firms produce Easter eggs. Odd shapes or large packets with small objects inside produce problems of storage and distribution and this needs to be considered at the design stage.

5. Sponsorships and publicity

Some publicity, in the form of press-releases on new products or articles in trade or specialist journals, has the advantage that it often costs nothing. Other, more expensive forms include sponsorships of football, cricket, tennis tournaments and other sporting events. Organisations who sell products which have medical lobbies attempting to reduce consumption by individuals, often enter into this form of publicity.

14. PRICING

Price is important because it produces the revenue which is required for the organisation to remain in business. The main objectives of pricing policy are twofold :

1. To achieve a target return on investment;
2. To maintain or improve a company's share of the market.

Pricing policy can be subject to short term or long term considerations and price is particularly important when introducing new products or breaking into new markets. When a new product is introduced which has substantial development costs, the price may tend to be rather high yet, as the product attracts buyers and these initial costs are covered, prices may be reduced. One danger is to ensure that initial prices are not too high to deter customers. An example of a product which had a high initial price, but which dropped very rapidly as customers saw its advantages, was the biro.

Some products need to be sold at a higher price to retain credibility on quality. An example was Babycham which, when introduced at a very low price, was not purchased but, when prices were increased , sold more.

It may be necessary to sell a product at a low price to ensure market penetration: a bargain price may attract considerable sales and, at the same time discourage further competitors from entering the market. The cheap-fares policy attempted by Laker Airways in the 1970s was an example. The price was so low, however, that it failed to generate sufficient revenue to cover investment costs on new capital equipment.

Certainly we cannot underestimate the effect that competitors can have on pricing policy. For example, in the sale of petrol, prices change as each company attempts to increase their share of the market by reducing prices. Some companies, like Conoco, even operate a policy which insists that they undercut their competitors. Much depends on the sensitivity of the market to such price changes.

Demand patterns in the market may be categorised along a continuum from elastic to inelastic. Demand can be said to be *elastic* when demand can be increased or decreased by levels of price which may be affected, not only by internal pricing policy but also by economic, political and social considerations. For example, the market for motor cars tends to be elastic because the demand can be affected by such factors as hire purchase restrictions or Value Added Tax. Demand, on the other hand, tends to be *inelastic* when it is not subject to variation, as with the market for bread or salt.

Pricing policies can be based on a number of different methods as the following examples illustrate:

1. *Cost plus pricing* : This is pricing which is based on covering total costs and adding a margin of profit for each item sold. This method requires a very accurate knowledge of the structure of costs and the ability to distinguish how various categories of costs are likely to behave at different levels of output and over different time-spans.

2. *Contribution pricing* : This attempts to balance market demand and costs of production by developing tables which reveal the level of sales required to enable a company to break-even. Sales above this level make a contribution to profit. It is an important method of pricing for large items with heavy development costs, for example, aeroplanes. A graph can be derived as in Figure 22 – Break-even pricing.

Figure 22: Break-even pricing

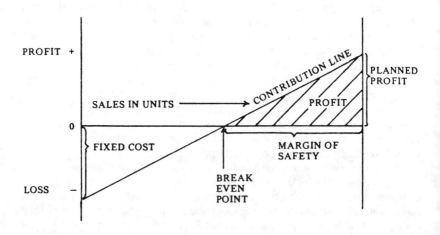

3. *Competitive pricing* : Prices are largely determined by competitors already established in the particular market. Newcomers have to judge their ability to penetrate the market by offering lower prices. Care

must be taken because they may find that customers have accepted a price structure which yields relatively high profits to existing organisations and to react to this by offering a new product at a substantially lower price may court disaster from two sources:

(a) the customers — who may not believe initially that it is as *good* as existing products, *or*

(b) the competitors — who may have the resources to undercut the organisation and force it out in a price war.

Where a range of products is offered, companies may use the 'loss-leader' concept, which means that one product in the range is reduced in price to below-cost levels with the objective of attracting attention to the range as a whole, and to establish the organisation's name in the market.

In pricing policies, companies need to keep a regular check on costs. Labour costs, for example, have changed from year to year in the post-war era; so have material costs for oil-based products, raw materials like copper and aluminium; and energy costs have increased substantially over relatively short periods during the 1970s and 1980s. Some cost increases may be offset by productivity changes, but the most crucial costs are those which can fluctuate upwards suddenly and which cannot easily be absorbed in the short term by productivity increases. Such changes pose problems for organisational marketing strategies.

15.   ORGANISATION OF THE MARKETING DEPARTMENT

The organisation of a marketing department depends on the way that the company views marketing and on its size. In small companies marketing may merely be seen as an extension of the selling function; in larger organisations marketing may be seen to have a much deeper and more general role and may give predominance to marketing executives over those in sales and separate out the functional specialisms within the marketing department. Figure 23 illustrates a possible structure.

In very large organisations where a divisionalised structure has developed because of geographical or product specialisms, the marketing function may be split into a headquarters function and regional or product functions with authority being delegated by top management, allowing a degree of autonomy to each subdivision. In organisations offering a range of products, a matrix type of structure may be developed with responsibility allocated to particular products or ranges of products, or even based on types of customer.

What sort of structure does your organisation have and what specialisms exist within the marketing function? How and where are the products marketed?

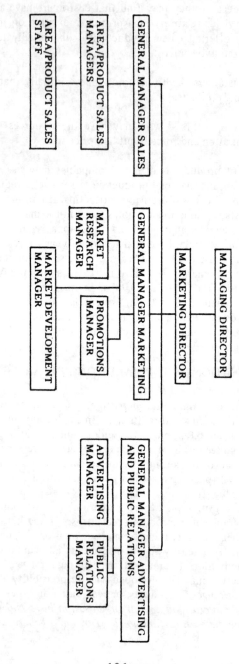

Figure 23 : Example of a specialised marketing department

CHAPTER FOUR

THE MAJOR FUNCTIONS OF ENTERPRISE : PRODUCTION

The production function has the objective of transforming the organisation's raw materials into finished products to make available the goods and services demanded by the customer. Modern production systems and processes are complex and can be costly to install and operate. People, materials and machines have to be integrated to develop a system which is efficient in both cost and human terms.

1. TYPES OF PRODUCTION SYSTEM

It is possible to distinguish four types of production system, normally determined by the scale of operations employed in the organisation. These are unit or job production, batch production, mass production and process production.

1. Unit or job production

A single product, often to customer's specific requirements, each product is a 'one-off job' which may never be repeated in that exact form, for example, the production of a turbine for a ship, a particular system of electrics, a particular market survey for an unusual product, or a civil engineering project. In job production in the first place the job is put out for tender and, in the case of specialised manufacture such as shipbuilding and some types of civil engineering work, only one or two specialist firms will be asked to submit proposals for the work. Thus, on large projects, it is always necessary for a great deal of designing and planning to be done in order for a tender to be submitted and one of the main problems is to decide how much time and money is to be spent in preparing the data for a contract which could be awarded to a competitor. The prime features of unit or job production are:

(a)   a relatively high-price product;
(b)   the use of highly-skilled labour;
(c)   relatively low capital costs of the production system — equipment often has more than one purpose;
(d)   the organisation requires a fairly high degree of flexibility of structure and amongst staff, as the sequencing of operations is not standardised;
(e)   centralisation of management, although employees are expected to show a high degree of discretion in their work;
(f)   unpredictability of demand for stores;
(g)   a comparatively large technical organisation

These conditions make production difficult to plan, control, sequence and accurately time. It is sometimes difficult to obtain manpower with the appropriate versatility of skills, as there is fluctuating demand for labour during the cycle of the work.

2.   Batch production

This type of production system is designed to produce a batch of standardised units, sometimes in small, sometimes in large, numbers, without continuous production. Unlike jobbing production, operations and sequences of work tend to be standardised. Examples of batch production items are aero-engines, components for the machine tool industry, and certain forms of electronic equipment.

Batch production is often used for goods for stock as well as to meet specific orders. One of the major problems is to ensure that too many units are not produced, especially where items are expensive and difficult to store, but that sufficient units are made to meet particular, urgent demand. The prime features of batch production are:

(a)   A relatively standardised set of operations, carried out intermittently, as production runs tend to be short, therefore there is a lack of balance in the workload of different departments;

(b)   equipment is generally grouped in batches of the same type;

(c)   although operatives tend to be less skilful than in job production, because there is less demand for adaptability, a relatively high degree of skill is still demanded;

(d)   emphasis is required on production planning and processing;

(e)   comparatively large product design department;

(f)   large production stores areas.

3.   Mass production

Production is continuous and all units of production are so highly specialised that each is employed continuously upon the same operation. The range of products made on each line of equipment is restricted and, consequently, output is very high. One operation follows on from another and leads to the next in a continuous flow. Mass production systems are heavily dependent on high market demand to maximise the utilisation of equipment and minimise costs. A highly developed marketing organisation is needed to make continuous production possible. Examples of mass production manufacture include the production of biscuits, soap powder, motor cars and washing machines.

Since mass production is production on a large scale, its prime features are in direct contrast to job production:

(a)   Production of a relatively low priced product;
(b)   product specifications are standardised;
(c)   high capital costs of production systems;
(d)   highly standardised methods, costs and materials, thus little flexibility of equipment;
(e)   long production runs for individual products;
(f)   a high proportion of semi-skilled and unskilled labour;
(g)   less centralisation of management and greater emphasis upon specialised services to management;
(h)   a tight system of production control;
(i)   strict control of flow of raw materials into the organisation.

Its greatest drawback, although it theoretically is an efficient way of producing large quantities of goods, is that it requires human beings to adapt themselves to the production process and this can bring reaction to the tedium and monotony of tasks.

4.   Process production

This is the continuous output of a product for weeks and months at a time. There tends to be a high degree of automation. Like mass production, process production requires an effective marketing organisation so that its expensive equipment can be employed without interruption. It also requires a steady supply of raw materials to avoid complete plant shutdown, owing to unforeseen shortages. Just as batch production can be seen as an extension of job production, so process production can be viewed as an extension of mass production, since the process production systems include oil refining, steel making, paper making, brewing and food manufactures.
   Its prime features are:

(a)   Production of a relatively low priced product;
(b)   high capital costs of production systems;
(c)   highly sophisticated mechanisms and procedures of control;
(d)   lower labour force than mass production, but a high level of technological skill as well as semi-skilled and unskilled employees;
(e)   little flexibility of equipment;
(f)   high levels of planning of essential raw materials.

2.   SCOPE OF THE PRODUCTION FUNCTION

The production function encompasses all activities directly concerned with the manufacture of goods and services. A typical production division within a company may be subdivided into Production Administration, Production Management, Production Design and Production Ancillaries. There is no ideal production structure and the organisation of any one will be largely a question of administrative convenience and company practice. The arrangements in any two organisations are unlikely to be identical and the titles of tasks in the function will probably vary from one organisation to another.

1. Production administration

Production administration is the process of planning and regulating the activities of that part of an enterprise which is responsible for the production of goods. It usually incorporates such activities as production engineering, production planning and production control.

(a) Production engineering

Production engineering determines and specifies work processes. The functions of a production engineer are:

— to investigate alternative methods of production and keep the organisation up to date on new methods;
— to design the processes of work including the layout of tools and equipment and the modification of tools and equipment, where necessary, within appropriate safety standards;
— to measure the rate of work flow by analysing the time span of each task, using work study and work measurement techniques.

Work study was developed in American industry during the 1920s by F W Taylor and others. It has been defined as:

'A generic term for those techniques, particularly method study and work measurement, which are used in the examination of human work in all its contexts, which lead systematically to the investigation of all the factors which affect the efficiency and economy of the situation being reviewed in order to effect improvement.' (British Standard BS 3138)

These techniques of work and method study are thus aimed at eliminating inefficient work methods and improving work methods to increase production, reduce costs, and increase the productivity of people and machines. They require the observation of working practices to ask — What is done? When is it done? How is it done? Who is doing it? Where is it done? and, How long does it take? Work study and method study are used to aid solutions to a variety of potential problems, including layout of work, handling of materials and efficiency of storage of materials, equipment design to increase efficiency and productivity.

Standard task times can be derived, which can be used as the basis of a wages system.

(b) Production planning

Production planning translates customer demand into short term and long term production schedules and programmes. This usually includes the maintenance of material and stock records, progress chasing and machine loading. Production schedules are usually detailed, specifying the timetable for precise operations and jobs and setting out the sequence of priorities. The major aim is to ensure that work is completed on time and within the laid-down cost budgets. Production planners have to work closely with marketing departments to ensure that customer needs are being met as to types of product, time of availability and quality, or where there are production difficulties, to keep the customer informed of progress. They will also have to work closely with purchasing departments to ensure raw materials are available on time.

To be successful production planning must be:

(i)   Geared to a suitable production policy; which is aimed at producing what is required, when it is required, at minimum cost.

(ii)   Realistic and based on facts; which requires that production schedules, machine loading schedules and labour schedules do not conflict with sales forecasts and are not based on sales delivery dates which are excessively optimistic.

(iii) Explained and a series of attainable targets set; so that the workforce have some idea of the objectives required.

(iv)   Flexible; so that inevitable delays can be offset.

(v)   Not merely for the short term; but based on medium and long term considerations to obtain a balance of work between departments.

(vi)   Subject to controls which enable adjustments to be made, when the plan runs into problems.

The order book shows the pattern of demand for the company's products in the coming months. Orders are often characterised by market (home or export), type of customer etc. as different standards may be incorporated into production plans.

If the order book shows a *decrease in demand,* production planners will have to make provision to compensate. Action taken could take several forms:

(i)   maintaining existing production schedules and letting stocks accumulate;

(ii)   discontinuing overtime;

(iii) introducing short time working;

(iv)   creating redundancy.

Where there is a sharp *increase in demand,* production planners will examine the following possibilities:

(i)   cutting stocks of finished products to a minimum;
(ii)   introducing rationing by permitting customers only a proportion of their orders;
(iii)   introducing overtime;
(iv)   sub-contracting work to other manufacturers;
(v)   looking at the need for long term expansion or re-equipment.

Production planners will need to liaise with the personnel function, as many of these strategies have manpower implications.

(c)   Production control

Production control ensures the progressing of orders through the production process and monitors results and efficiency. It is an inevitable consequence of the production planning activity. Any plan must incorporate controls to ensure that targets are achieved. In particular, there must be provision for managers to be informed of and to investigate, unexpected variances from the plan. In a large organisation a wide range of factors will be analysed and controls instigated:

(i)   Progress control – the control of production programmes and schedules to ensure that each department is maintaining its planned output at the right time;
(ii)   Cost control – control of budgets, including such aspects as material costs and labour costs and ensuring that significant variances do not arise;
(iii)   Machine utilisation control – ensures that planned maintenance takes place where appropriate;
(iv)   Stock control – the control of stocks of both raw materials and finished products to ensure that supplies are available as required and that raw materials are present in sufficient quantities.

2.   Production management

Production management ensures (in liaison with the personnel function) that the labour force involved in the actual production process is adequately trained, organised and supervised to achieve the required targets. These managers are responsible for the manufacturing and assembly processes and have to ensure that the work is carried out in accordance with the schedules prescribed and that employees are treated in a fair and equitable manner.

3. Production design

This area of production is concerned with the designing of products which consumers demand and which the organisation can produce. It will also be concerned, together with the production engineering function, with analysing equipment suitability for producing the new products developed. In those organisations operating with unit or batch production methods, the designer is likely to work closely with clients to meet their requirements. In some organisations the production design function is separated from the other production activities and given the umbrella title of *Research and Development* (R & D). This is likely to be a department in which expert scientific staff are organised to make the products of the future. One of the problems which R & D departments are likely to ignore is the production of an item at a reasonable cost. The production engineer may have to modify the prototype into a product which can be feasibly and cheaply made without major restructuring or reequipment of the organisation.

Two problems can occur with the use of a continuous research and development department:

(i) The results of research are not capable of accurate prediction. A firm might spend large sums on research, only to find no opportunity for its commercial application. For example, work on a new product may be negated and result in a financial loss because a rival firm reached the development stage first.

(ii) Costs may be considerable, not least in attracting suitably experienced and qualified staff.

4. Production ancillaries

A number of other departments may come under the production function. These may include purchasing departments, inspection and quality control and maintenance engineering.

(a) Purchasing

It is important that the necessary raw materials are available so that the production process is not impaired through shortages. The costs of bought-in materials and parts often represent a significant part of the total costs of production. The purchasing department has to liaise with the various sub-units of production and has to maintain links with avariety of external suppliers. A purchasing department can be said to have the following responsibilities:

(i) It should appraise the efficiency and reliability of suppliers and ensure that supplies obtained are of the appropriate standard and in appropriate quantities.

(ii) It will need to be aware of the current range of suppliers for each item and the reliability of their distribution methods.

(iii) It should purchase the relevant raw material and other inputs, representing the best value to the business in both the short and the longer term. For example, the cheapest supplier may not necessarily be able to provide appropriate quantities or be the most reliable in the long term.

(iv) It will have to ensure the maintenance of adequate stock levels, whilst, at the same time, being aware of the costs of storage and likely future trends in costs which might warrant larger purchases than normal.

(v) It will need to maintain good relations with all departments and with present and potential suppliers.

Depending upon the nature of the organisation's products, specialist purchasing officers may need to be employed who have technical knowledge of products and purchases.

(b) Quality control and inspection departments

The responsibility of checking the quality of the work on the shop floor is usually that of an inspection department whose staff ensure that standards are maintained. There are two main methods of doing this:

(i) All stages of the process can be inspected on a regular basis, against the appropriate laid down standards or

(ii) Inspection can be done by sampling batches of the product.

The standards of inspection required will depend on the degree of sophistication of the product.

Quality control tends to have a wider function. It involves itself with production engineering in building quality into the production system itself and in constantly reviewing the system to try to improve the process and work methods.

The aims of both activities are the same:

(i) To ensure that products are satisfactory to the customer in terms of quality and reliability and that the products are those which were actually demanded;

(ii) To ensure that the products are safe when sold;

(iii) To reduce the costs of wastage of raw materials and partially finished products and to ensure that the workforce are encouraged to take pride in the product.

(c)   Maintenance engineering

The prime responsibility of the maintenance engineering department is to ensure that production is not held up because of lack of serviceability of plant or equipment and that, if unexpected breakdowns occur, the equipment is repaired and returned to service as quickly as possible.

To achieve this the maintenance staff and production personnel must cooperate. Sometimes maintenance departments are organised so that each production area has a resident engineer, who is under the control of the relevant production manager, whereas, in other cases, the production manager has to call when appropriate for service from a separated department.

Maintenance can take a number of different forms, these can include:

(i)   Preventative maintenance, which regularly maintains equipment to prevent or reduce the likelihood of it failing. This can involve a planned programme of maintenance so that servicing and overhaul schedules are prepared and operated, with least disruption;

(ii)   Breakdown maintenance, which only deals with equipment when it physically fails. Such a policy can be very costly when compared with regular, planned maintenance.

One of the roles of the maintenance department will be to ensure that key spares are ordered and available so that delays can be reduced. This requires an analysis of machine failures so that common problems and problem parts can be identified.

The ability of a maintenance department to fulfil its role will depend on the nature of the productive process. Where process or mass production occurs, it will probably necessitate running maintenance being carried out while the plant continues in operation; shutdown of equipment, especially in a process organisation, may incur large losses.

Examine your own organisation if it is a manufacturing concern, and see which of these activities operate and how they are organised or structured and whether they are beginning to adopt Total Quality Management (TQM) principles and how successful they are.

CHAPTER FIVE

THE FUNCTION OF MANAGEMENT

The function of management has existed as long as organisations to accomplish work have existed; no one person alone can administer an organisation of any size. We read in the Book of Exodus, verses 13–26, the following:

'on the following day, Moses took his seat to administer justice for the people, and from morning till evening they stood around him. Observing what labours he took on himself for the peoples' sake, the father-in-law of Moses said to him, "Why do you take all this on yourself for the people? Why sit here alone with people standing around you from morning till evening?" Moses answered his father-in-law "Because the people come to me to bring their enquiries to God. When they have a dispute they come to me, and I settle the differences between the one and the other and instruct them in God's statutes and his decisions." "It is not right" the father-in-law of Moses said to him to take this on yourself. You will tire yourself out, you and the people with you. The work is too heavy for you. You cannot do it alone"... "choose from the people at large some capable and God-fearing men, trustworthy and incorruptible, and appoint them as leaders of the people: leaders of thousands, hundreds, fifties, tens. Let these be at the service of the people to administer justice at all times. They can refer all difficult questions to you, but the smaller questions they will decide for themselves, so making things easier for you and sharing the burden with you"... Moses took his father-in-law's advice and did as he said. Moses chose capable men from the ranks of the Israelites and set them over the people: leaders of thousands, hundreds, fifties, tens. They were at the service of the people to administer justice at all times. They referred hard questions to Moses, and decided smaller questions by themselves.'

There is no general definition of 'management', although the classic definition was given by Henri Fayol in 1916 when he said that:

'To manage is to forecast and plan, to organise, to command, to coordinate and to control.'
and these concepts have permeated all definitions of management since.

Peter Drucker has argued that management is:

'The organ of society specifically charged with making resources productive.'

THE FUNCTION OF MANAGEMENT

E F L Brech, in 1957, stated:

> 'management is a social process... the process consists of... planning, control, coordination and motivation.'

A manager is:

> 'Someone who directs the work of others and who does his work by getting other people to do theirs.' (Peter Drucker)

> 'Someone who decides what should be done and then gets other people to do it.' (Rosemary Stewart)

> 'A member who has subordinate to him authorised roles into which he can appoint members and determine their work; he is accountable for his subordinates' work in these roles.' (Wilfred Brown)

> 'Managers are those who use formal authority to organise, direct, or control responsible subordinates... in order that all service contributions be coordinated in the attainment of an enterprise purpose.' (Tannenbaum)

These statements are expanded in the Glacier Metal Co. Ltd's policy document which provides a specification of the work of a manager in controlling others, quoted by Wilfred Brown in *Exploration in Management* (1960).

> 'Assignment and Assessment of Work

> E.3. A manager shall be accountable for the work assigned to him including the work which he assigns to members under his command. In assigning work, a manager shall determine the extent to which he requires his subordinates to make reference to him before making their own decisions.

> E.4. A manager shall appoint, train and maintain at his immediate command a team of subordinates who are competent to carry out the work he requires of them and who conform to the generally acceptable standards of conduct. He shall assign and display an order of seniority among a sufficient number of his subordinates to ensure that his work is done in his absence.

>> E.4.1. He shall set standards of executive performance and attainment for his immediate subordinates and shall make these standards clear to them.

>> E.4.2. He shall assign work to his immediate subordinates consistent with the standards he has set.

E.4.3. He shall judge the executive performance of each of his subordinates in relation to the standards he has set, and their conduct in relation to the standards accepted by the company.

(a)   He shall ensure that each subordinate is rewarded at a level appropriate to the work of his executive role.

(b)   In the event of a subordinate performing below the standards he has set or contrary to the generally accepted standards of conduct he shall acquaint him of this fact and, in the event of continued inadequacy, he shall decide whether to retain him in his command

E.4.4. A manager shall limit his immediate command to a number of people he can effectively control, and amongst whom he can maintain cooperation...'

1. TRADITIONAL FUNCTIONS OF MANAGEMENT

There is apparently broad agreement amongst writers on management that the management function is comprised of the following activities: planning, organisation, control, coordination, motivation, communication and the development of the human resource within the organisation. Let us examine briefly each of these activities in turn.

(1)   PLANNING is that management activity which involves formulating the future strategy and policy of the organisation. Planning is concerned with the formulation and establishment of measurable objectives and is a decision making process. Once plans are implemented, results have to be monitored to provide feedback on performance.

(2)   ORGANISATION – Here the manager's task is to determine what activities are necessary to achieve objectives and to develop an appropriate organisational structure so the work is distributed logically and relevant responsibilities assigned.

(3)   CONTROL – Controlling activities are essentially concerned with measuring progress and correcting deviations from objectives. The basic functions within control are establishing standards of performance, measuring actual performance against standards and taking correcting actions, where appropriate.

(4)   COORDINATION – Coordination requires working with other groups and ensuring that subordinates work together in order to reach the desired results. The strengths of individual members of the department are exploited and weaknesses minimised.

(5)   MOTIVATION – In setting plans and in executing them managers have to gain the commitment of their subordinates. They must encourage staff to work towards objectives.

(6)   COMMUNICATION – Communication is vital to organisational success; managers must ensure that their subordinates are given sufficient data about the objectives of the organisation and the progress which is being made on each task to operate effectively. It is also important that they be made aware of their own strengths and weaknesses and how well they are performing.

(7)   DEVELOPMENT OF HUMAN RESOURCES – Peter Drucker and Wilfred Brown argue that training and developing his subordinates is one of the key elements of the manager's role. He is the one in the best position to develop strengths and help the individual to overcome problems and learn from experience.

Whilst it is easy to identify these traditional functions of management, it is very difficult in large scale modern organisations to classify easily the work done by managers as different responsibilities belong to different jobs, depending upon their position and level within the hierarchy. Some of the specific duties and responsibilities are stated in job descriptions. The only danger in using them to analyse managerial jobs however, is that job descriptions may be limited in that they often describe not what actually happens but what ought to happen or what people think is occurring.

2. FACTORS INFLUENCING MANAGERS

We can broadly identify the factors which are influencing the manager at any one moment as falling into three categories:

(a)   the *manager* himself, due to his experience, education, values and position in the hierarchy;

(b)   the *subordinates* who work for him, who are in turn influenced by the nature of their work, the skills they possess and the people with whom they work;

(c)   the *environment* of the organisation itself and the society in which it operates.

These features overlap with each other, varying over time, and can be pictured as in Figure 5:1 Factors influencing the manager.

Figure 24: Factors influencing the manager

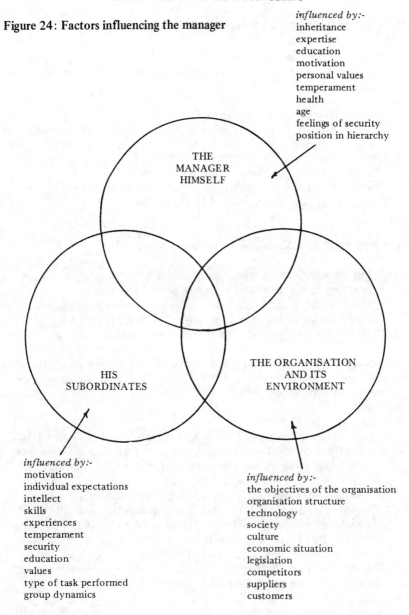

influenced by:-
inheritance
expertise
education
motivation
personal values
temperament
health
age
feelings of security
position in hierarchy

THE
MANAGER
HIMSELF

HIS
SUBORDINATES

THE ORGANISATION
AND ITS
ENVIRONMENT

influenced by:-
motivation
individual expectations
intellect
skills
experiences
temperament
security
education
values
type of task performed
group dynamics

influenced by:-
the objectives of the organisation
organisation structure
technology
society
culture
economic situation
legislation
competitors
suppliers
customers

The manager can be perceived as a PEST controller — that is he controls *people, economic factors of production, the structure of the organisation* and *technologies.*

3. WHAT MANAGERS ACTUALLY DO!

Attempts have been made to analyse the content of managerial jobs and how time is actually spent. Some of the questions which have been asked have included:

1. How specialised is the particular job?
2. To what extent does the job involve working with other people both inside and outside the organisation?
3. What work pattern does the task tend to impose?
4. What kinds of decisions does the job involve?
5. How much time is spent on different aspects of a manager's work?
6. What kinds of variety are provided by the job?

The three main approaches used by researchers have been:

(a) *Self reporting,* where manager are interviewed and estimate themselves how they spend their time between different activities.
(b) Managers are asked to keep *diaries* where they keep a record of what they actually do and record the data in specific time periods.
(c) *Observers* actually watch managers over an extended period of time.

One example of the problems which managers have in reporting what they actually do was quoted by Leonard Sayles in *Managerial Behaviour* (1964) where he gave the following account of a member of middle management who said:

'I have a terrible time trying to explain what I do at work when I get home. My wife thinks of a manager in terms of someone who has authority over those people who work for him and who in turn gets his job done for him. You know she thinks of those nice neat organisation charts... she also expects that when I get promoted I'll have more people working for me... Now all of this is unrealistic. Actually I have 18 people reporting directly to me. These are the only ones I can give orders to. But I have to rely directly on the services of 75-80 other people in this company, if my project is to get done. They in turn are affected by perhaps several hundred others and I must sometimes see some of them, too, when my work is being held up.

So I am always seeing these people, trying to get their cooperation, trying to deal with delays, work out compromises on specifications, etc. Again when I explain this to my wife, she thinks that all I do all day is argue and fight with people.'

This communication aspect of the manager's task has been further identified in the UK by Rosemary Stewart, in *Managers and their jobs* (1967), who supervised a major piece of research which included detailed studies from diaries kept by a sample of 160 managers employed by over100 companies. These were found to spend an average of 60% of their working time in conversation of one sort or another. The average timespent with their own subordinates was 26% of these contacts in their working week, (which averaged 42 hours) with 8% being spent with their own superior and 12% with fellow managers. In addition to communications activities, they spent on average 36% of their time on paperwork. Yet these averages do not represent all managers' tasks, for in the book Rosemary Stewart identified five different types of manager — the *emissaries,* the *discussers,* the *writers,* the *trouble-shooters* and the *committee men.*

(i)   The Emissaries — sales managers and general managers who spent a significant amount of time away from the company on visits to other companies, conferences and exhibitions, and hence spent a lot of time travelling and entertaining or being entertained.

(ii)   The Discussers — these managers spent most of their time with other people and colleagues solving the day-to-day problems of business.

(iii)   The Writers — who spent most of their time by themselves and who were less concerned with the day-to-day problems of business. Most of their contact was with only one other person, who tended to be a specialist adviser like themselves.   Often they were involvedin engineering or research and development activities.

(iv)   The Trouble-shooters — spent most of their time coping with crises concerned with industrial relations, man management, supplier shortfalls and work-in-progress. Most works and factory line managers fell into this category.

(v)   The Committee Men — spent most of their time in group discussions of both a formal and an informal type. Again many works and factory line managers fell into this category, as well as those in the designing and marketing function.

Many of the management jobs studied were shown to have a highly-fragmented work pattern with managers having to shift their attention every few minutes from one person to another. Very little of their working day was uninterrupted and there was little opportunity to give sustained attention to one problem or issue. This often meant that sustained attention was needed for problems away from the place of work.

Rosemary Stewart, in a later work *Contrasts in Management* (1976), suggested that managers' jobs differ in how far they demonstrate a recurrent work pattern, where the manager does work of a similar kind every day or every week, although in most there was a monthly or annual pattern imposed by reports and budgets which were required for company control purposes. This research studied 450 managerial jobs in industry and commerce, 16 of which were examined in depth. It identified the fact that jobs could be differentiated by the following characteristics:

— the duration of the activities undertaken;
— the time span of problems handled or decisions made regarding those problems;
— the periodicity and recurrence of work;
— the amount of expected, compared with unexpected, work;
— the incidence of urgent work and crises;
— the extent to which work had to be completed in a time period laid down by an external agency to the manager himself;
— the origin of work activities, whether these were determined by the need to respond to others whether they be employees, customers, superiors or other managers on the same level or whether work was self-generated.

In examining the jobs studied a matrix was derived as in Figure 25.

Figure 25: Type of work pattern: characteristics and sample membership
Source: Personnel Management, June 1976. Patterns of work and dictates of time, R. Stewart.

TYPE OF WORK PATTERN	1. Systems Maintenance	2. Systems Administration	3. Project	4. Mixed
Characteristics	Recurrent Fragmented Trouble-shooting	Recurrent Time-deadlines a. expected b. unexpected	Non-recurrent Sustained attention Self-generating Long-term	No dominant characteristics
Sample Membership	Works manager Production manager Production Supt.	a. Financial accountant b. Staff manager	Research manager Product sales manager Group product manager (some overlap with 1.)	General manager Area sales manager Head of admin. Production engineer
		2a/3 Management accountant Commercial manager		

THE FUNCTION OF MANAGEMENT

Definitions: The description of each type means that these characteristics are a marked feature of that type, not that they never occur in other types.

Recurrent: does work of a similar kind every day or every week;

Fragmented: switches attention from one person or problem everyfew minutes;

Trouble-shooting: has to cope with sudden problems;

Time deadlines: work to be done by a particular time which is not self-imposed;

Unexpected: the timing and precise nature of work which cannot be predicted;

Self-generating: work or systems originating with the individual, rather than in response to other people;

Long-term: One year plus.

1.   Systems Maintenance — a major task in some jobs is to handle exceptions, e.g. to keep operations within target completion times. Thus, the manager has to deal with problems that prevent completion on time. In addition, such managers need constantly tocheck that the system itself is retaining its efficiency. Most operational jobs fall into this type of work pattern.

2.   Systems Administration — is concerned primarily with the processing of information and the administration of the system. Such jobs are generally found in junior and middle management posts informally-structured organisations.

3.   Project work — is characterised by involvement in tasks very often of a unique type which have a long term time horizon. There is less imposition of structure from the organisation and there is a greater need for work to be self generated.

4.   Mixed work patterns — are less capable of rigid classification and include elements of the first three types. They are concerned with system design in reaction to environmental pressures rather than with operational problems.

THE FUNCTION OF MANAGEMENT

An alternative approach to studying managerial jobs, that of structured observation, was adopted by Mintzberg in *The Changing Nature of Managerial Work,* Harper & Row 1973. His studies emphasise interpersonal relations, the amount of time spent on obtaining or disseminating information, and the rather erratic nature of the managerial activity. Mintzberg showed through his studies of all levels of management, chief executives, administrative managers, sales managers, supervisors, etc. that major roles:

1. The interpersonal role — to ensure the task is accomplished:

   — the figurehead role — where the manager is the representative of the unit or specialism he manages, with people from both inside and outside the organisation;
   — the understanding role — where the manager interacts with his subordinates to motivate and encourage them to fulfil the task;
   — the liaison role — where the manager liaises with people inside and outside his specialism to obtain supplies, meet customer specifications, obtain data, etc.

2. The informational role of obtaining and giving information, which is probably the most important managerial function. This role sees the manager as:

   — a monitor, who gathers and stores information from all sources in the organisation;
   — a disseminator, who in his turn distributes information to others within his department which he has synthesised and which otherwise would probably not be available to them;
   — a spokesman, who fulfils the same role of disseminator to those outside his own area of control.

3. The decision making role — where the manager synthesises and translates the information he has obtained from all sources to make his decisions. Within this role he is:

   — an entrepreneur, who uses his expertise to make changes within his area of control, or within the organisation generally;
   — a disturbance handler, who is responsible for taking corrective action when the organisation faces unexpected situations which could not be planned for;
   — a resource allocator, who decides how to use any of the resources available to him at any moment;
   — a negotiator, who deals with those individuals and groups whose help, cooperation or consent is necessary for the oganisation to fulfil its goals.

These three major role groupings and ten major subsets encompass the managerial function, but the degree to which these are found in an individual manager's role will vary from task to task and from organisation to organisation. Mintzberg, however, concluded that there were eight major types of managerial jobs;

i) The contact man, who is a figurehead and liaises with outside organisations;

ii) The political manager, who spends much of his time external to the organisation trying to reconcile the conflicting forces that influence it;

iii) The entrepreneur, who seeks future opportunities and implements change within the organisation;

iv) The insider, who tries to build up and further internal activities by 'fire fighting';

v) The real time manager, who attempts to construct and maintain a stable system through time;

vi) The team manager, whose primary concern is to create a team which will work together effectively;

vii) The expert manager, who fulfils a specialist role advising other managers and who is consulted because of his expertise;

viii) The new manager, who has not found his feet yet and who lacks the interpersonal contacts and information channels of the other seven categories.

4. DIFFERENT LEVELS OF MANAGEMENT

From these studies we can see that it is difficult to talk generally about the manager's role, because management is not a unitary activity but is a feature of the organisation in which it takes place and changes according to the time and the environmental influences.

H I Ansoff in *Corporate Strategy* (1968) sees management as having three principal decision areas — strategic, operating and administrative. These can be differentiated as follows:

1. Strategic decisions: These are concerned with the examination of the external influences and opportunities which influence the organisation's objectives and the products and services it sells or provides. Such decisions set the principal goals and objectives of the organisation and determine the product mix and the markets in which it will operate. They will also tend to be non-routine and non-repetitive decisions which are frequently complex, especially in terms of the number of variables which have to be considered before final choices are made betweeen the alternatives available.

2. Administrative decisions: These are concerned with the structuring of the organisation's resources in such a way as to be able to reap the benefits of the opportunities available to it. Essentially they are concerned with structuring the authority and responsibility relationships; work flow; information needs and flow; location of the organisation; determining sources of raw materials and bought-in-parts; obtaining and developing the relevant labour force and the acquisition of the technology required to produce the goods and services. Such decisions arise from, and are subject to, the sometimes conflicting demands of strategic decisions and operational problems.

3. Operating decisions: These can be the short term decisions which attempt to maximise organisational efficiency on a day-to-day and a week-to-week basis. They settle issues, such as the scheduling of operations, manning levels of machines and departments, keeping a watch on performance and initiating appropriate action to enhance performance, by applying appropriate sanctions. They cover other key areas such as pricing, budgeting, stock inventory levels. Fewer variables are involved in the decision making process as they are reactive to situational pressures and the decisions themselves tend to be routine and repetitive. They generally aim to produce results in the short term.

The degree to which an individual manager becomes involved in these levels of decision making depends on his position in the hierarchy. Perhaps only managers at the highest level will have responsibility for deciding the future course of the organisation, but managers at all levels have the responsibility to ensure the success of the organisation in both the long term and the short term and to use resources effectively.

Dr John Adair has emphasised that there are three major areas of concern for managers at whatever level in an organisation; the task to be accomplished, the group who are performing the task and the individuals who comprise the group. Managers need to concern themselves with all three areas as neglect of any one area can result in adverse effects on the performance of work groups in achieving their objectives.

The key features of this *functional* model of leadership can be ilustrated as in Figure 26.

Figure 26: Functional model of leadership

THE FUNCTION OF MANAGEMENT

Achieving the task

Purpose	— am I clear what the task is?
Responsibilities	— am I clear about these?
Objectives	— have I agreed these with the group?
Programme	— have I worked out how to achieve the objectives efficiently?
Working conditions	— are these right for the job?
Resources	— are these adequate?
Targets	— has each member had these defined and agreed them?
Authority	— is the line of authority clear?
Training	— are there any gaps in the group's abilities?
Priorities	— have plans taken these into acount and the timing required?
Progress	— do I check regularly and evaluate?
Example	— do I set standards by my behaviour?

Developing the individual

Targets	— are these agreed and quantified, where possible?
Induction	— does the individual understand the organisation and his position in it?
Responsibilities	— is the individual aware of, and does he agree with, his job description?
Authority	— is this adequate for the task in hand?
Training	— has provision been made, where necessary?
Recognition	— do I emphasise success and give praise where earned?
Growth	— has the individual a chance to develop?
Performance	— do I perform regular reviews?
Grievances	— are these dealt with quickly?
Attention	— is enough given?

Maintaining the team

Objectives	— does the group understand them?
Standards	— does the group know what to expect?
Personality	— are the right people working together?
Team spirit	— is the job structured to encourage this?
Discipline	— is it reasonable? Is it impartial and consistent?
Grievances	— is the procedure sound? Are they dealt with quickly?
Consultation	— do I welcome and encourage ideas?
Briefing	— is this regular?
Support	— do I represent the feelings of the group?

Adair's concept is basically a contingency theory of leadership. It stresses that the manager's behaviour in relation to task, group and individual needs has to be related to the prevailing situation and task and, therefore, has to be adaptive. It recognises that management is a function of the situation. Management's task is to enable the organisation's purposes to be defined and fulfilled by adapting to change and by maintaining a balance between the various and frequently conflicting internal pressures.

This feature is summed up by Professor Handy in *Understanding organisations* (2nd edn 1981) where he suggests that the key variables a manager has to cope with are:

i)   People
ii) The nature of the work and organisation structures
iii) The prevailing systems and procedures which have been developed
iv) The organisation's specific goals
v)   The technology which is being used or is to be introduced
vi) The values and beliefs or the culture of the specific organisation.

In addition to the undoubted human relations skills which all managers need to possess, the knowledge and experience needed will vary dependent on the nature of the industry, the particular organisation in which they operate and the position which they hold within it. How much the knowledge and skills are organisationally biased and how much the environment needs to concern them depends on their job. Generally those managers making operational decisions are most concerned with the short term. Administrative decisions are concerned with three factors; the service which the organisation is receiving from its suppliers, the success it is having in meeting customer needs, and the changes which are being made in company strategy and their likelihood of affecting existing structures and procedures. Strategic decision making is far less concerned with the situation pertaining within the organisation, as that is the main responsibility of the other two levels of decision makers, but is extremely concerned with environmental pressures and their influence on the future. Some of these aspects can be illustrated as in Figure 27.

Each level has to be given the skills, knowledge and experience to cope with the predominant pressures. Thus the modern manager must be trained to cope with the technology of his particular industry and given administrative and personal communication skills. The higher up the organisation he progresses, the more knowledge he requires of the economic and social and political environment in which he operates.

As we have already inferred, when looking at the structure of organisations in Chapter 2, modern management now consists of a number of different functional specialisms. Each individual has defined for him the tasks and responsibilities that relate to his job and his position in the organisation.

Figure 27: Factors influencing strategic decision making

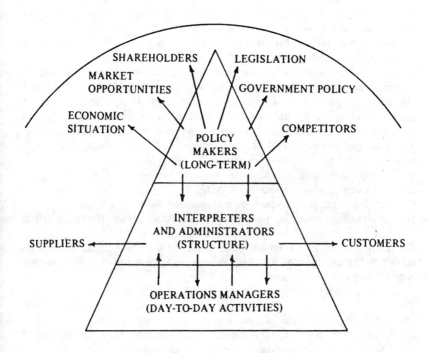

5. ORGANISATIONS OF MANAGERS

Most managers today are employees and there are few who own the organisation in which they work. Yet management has a different sort of task from other employees. Part of their job is to plan, coordinate and control the work of others and they have a responsibility to ensure that targets are met. They are granted authority and responsibility and use this for the benefit of the organisation. To their subordinates they are seen as the 'boss' and can be viewed as the employer — the hirer and firer. Within the structure of society, managers are given a status and class which significantly differentiates them from a shop floor worker or a clerk. Managers are also more likely to find their psychological needs are satisfied at work. Our society has seen a great proliferation of the task of management in large organisations. According to the 1981 census there were some 2.5 million managers in the UK — over 10% of the total labour force.

(A) MANAGERS AS PROFESSIONALS

This increase in management numbers, coupled with increasing specialisation, has brought into organisations people who have loyalties outside, especially to professional bodies, e.g. accountants, lawyers, engineers.

Alvin Gouldner in *Patterns of industrial bureaucracy* (1954), which studied an American factory, identified two types of company executive; the expert who had a wider loyalty than merely to the organisation and the company man who identified primarily with the organisation. According to Gouldner, 'experts' or cosmopolitans as he calls them, are less likely to identify themselves as company men because their previous formal training provides employment opportunities in a wide range of different organisations. The cosmopolitan often looks for recognition of his specialist abilities to the members of his profession. To summarise:

Cosmopolitans tend to have:
(a) a low degree of organisational loyalty;
(b) a high commitment to their own specialised skills;
(c) an identification with a peer group which exists outside the organisation.

Company men or 'locals' on the other hand are assessed on their loyalty and service to the organisation in which they work and are less mobile than those who are professionally trained.

Locals, therefore, tend to have:

(a) a high degree of organisational loyalty;
(b) low commitment to specialised skills, except those pertaining to knowledge of the organisation in which they work;
(c) an identification with a peer group situated inside the organisation.

Professions can be viewed as occupations in non-manual activity areas. The key to professionalism is competence. The professions each possess and foster a body of knowledge which enables them to establish high standards of practice to protect the client from incompetence. The important knowledge base is handed down via a rigorous training and education system and entry to the profession is regulated by the professional body by its membership policies. Explicit control of members is exercised over conduct and the profession itself recognises achievement by entry to higher grades of membership. It thus creates a power base which means that the professional organisation increasingly attempts to control rewards and expectations and constrains the performance and authority of the individual. Professional bodies thus seek to gain exclusive rights over particular areas of knowledge and socialise professionals in such a way as to diagnose problems in terms of the objectivity which education has sought to inculcate. We can summarise the characteristics of a profession as follows:

1. Professions are founded upon the existence of a systematic theory, i.e. a body of knowledge.

2. Professions establish a degree of professional authority based on the body of knowledge.

3. Professions have an established code of ethics or statements of appropriate behaviour by which the professional's behaviour and expertise is judged.

4. Professions often have a language of their own which is understandable to the professional and attain their professional knowledge in recognised, established training centres.

5. Professionals typically remain as members of the occupational group in which they have invested time and money and move from organisation to organisation as 'experts' in their particular field.

Carr-Saunders in an early work on *The Professions,* differentiated four major types of professions within society which are still valid today:

1. *The old-established professions* – founded upon the study of a particular area of learning which is used in the practice of the skills developed from that learning. Examples include religion, the law, medicine and education.

2. *New professions* – again founded on a body of knowledge which has developed, often because of new technologies and work environments. Examples include chemists, engineers and other natural scientists.

3. *Semi-professions* – which replace theoretical study of a field of learning by acquisition of a precise technical skill. Examples include nursing, pharmacy, social work and optometry.

4. *Would-be professions* – where members aspire to professional status. Examples include personnel, sales, business consultants, managers and estate agents.

We can also identify a fifth group which was not mentioned by him –

5. *Marginal professions* – which are comprised of those who perform technical assignments which are associated with professional roles. Examples are medical and laboratory technicians, draughtsmen.

THE FUNCTION OF MANAGEMENT

One of the most significant changes in our society has been the employment of professionals and semi-professionals in business, commerce, central and local Government. Most modern organisations tend to be based on what Weber has conceptualised as the idea of a bureaucracy, a system which is characterised by a rigid hierarchical structure where work activity becomes subject to rules which are laid down by the superiors within the hierarchy. This sort of structure can lead to conflict for the professional employed in a large organisation. Four areas of conflict can be identified:

   i)   the professional's resistance to bureaucratic rules;
   ii)   the professional's rejection of bureaucratic standards;
   iii) the professional's resistance to bureaucratic supervision;
   iv) the professional's conditional loyalty to the bureaucracy.

Professionals who participate in the two systems — the professional and the bureaucratic organisation — can find that their dual membership places important restrictions on attempts to deploy and control them in a rational manner with respect to the attainment of the organisational goals. Professions and bureaucracy are founded on fundamentally different principles of organisation; professions tend to be structured on a colleague basis with status being conceded to those with a greater knowledge of the particular specialisms. Thus, for example, the heart surgeon in a hospital will defer to the anaesthetist on matters of anaesthetics, whether he has higher bureaucratic status or not. Organisations, on the other hand, are controlled by rules and regulations and status is conferred by appointments to levels in the hierarchy.

If an organisation is to operate as a rational structure, it must to some extent be insulated from the surrounding environment, although we must remember that organisations can be classed as open-systems. Specifically the organisation will demand the power to select employees and promote them and control their contributions to implement and attain its goals. Yet organisations are often unable to fully control the criteria by which professional personnel are to be recruited; co-professionals are likely to demand some voice in the selection process, especially where the person to be recruited will work with existing professional staff who require complementary skills. Organisations may also have difficulty in controlling the efforts of professionals once recruited, in so far as they retain an identification with the profession and attempt to adhere to its norms and standards. In addition, the salaries which an organisation may have to pay to obtain people of the right calibre, may be influenced by the degree to which the profession limits entry.

A professional, therefore, comes with acquired skills which equip him to perform an entire task and he has internalised norms which control the application of those skills. He expects to direct those activities and be free from constraining regulations and interference. He demands autonomy and, at the same time, expects to assume responsibility for his decisions and actions. Bureaucrats, or 'locals' in Gouldner's terms, are less likely to come in contact with a set of standards other than those espoused by the organisation in which they are employed.

The following quotation, from *Fortune* magazine in 1965, serves to illustrate the problems which occur in integrating the professional manager into an organisational context. It was written by an industry-employed scientist:

'Research Directors sometimes fail to realise that the scientific standing of a scientist is determined primarily by the opinion of his colleagues in his speciality throughout the world. Actions that enhance his standing may bear little or no relation to actions that enhance his corporate standing. To achieve recognition from his professional colleagues he must communicate his research in the open literature, but publication in technical journals may be of little interest to the company or even damaging to it. To achieve company recognition, his research must lead to a marketable product or technique, but such research may not help his scientific reputation one whit. It is an error to think that all a creative scientist requires for happiness is to create. His creation exists scientifically if he can communicate it to his peers for evaluation. He not only needs to communicate his research, he wants it, and therefore wants himself to be thought of highly (by members of his profession)...'

Simon Coke in an article 'Putting Professionalism in It's Place', Personnel Management February 1983, also notes the emphasis of the professions on encouraging professional allegience and following professional methods:

'In the case of UK chartered accountants there is a long three to five year apprenticeship spent in auditing firms whose ethos and objectives are quite different from those of commerce and industry at large. A quick look through accounting examination papers suggests an emphasis on the highly technical and detailed aspects of the auditing function. No one can doubt the thoroughness of training given young accountants ... but these are formative years in their development. The particular emphasis paid on attention to detail, the need to check and check again, the cautious, considering approach are all ideal of course, for the business of auditing, but – I venture to suggest – not for the ideal company accountant. It militates against the creative instinct in top management decision making, kills any suggestion of justifiable risk taking, stifles the entrepreneurial spirit.'

A further problem for the professional is that organisations are demanding greater integration between specialist activities yet, as each profession widens its sphere of interest while at the same time trying to deepen and develop its specialism, this need is likely to lead to a higher degree of interprofessional conflict and hence problems in coping with interdisciplinary change.

(B) MANAGERIAL UNIONISM

An additional source of external influence on those in management positions is the increasing development of managerial trade unionism. We can identify four major determinants of managerial unionism:

1. There is little doubt that pay figures predominantly in managers' decisions to join trade unions. Particularly at junior and middle managerial levels, they are concerned to maintain or increase their standard of living and frequently to retain or restore their differentials over those that work for them.

2. Other managers are influenced by insecurity in job retention. The great expansion in managerial jobs has resulted in the paradox that, whilst there are more such jobs, the increasing consolidation of organisations when business is poor or depressed and the increasing numbers of mergers, takeovers and closures have led to organisations being increasingly prepared to make managerial jobs redundant. Often mergers take place to acquire productive capacity and managers are superfluous.

3. More management jobs also mean that the average manager is more likely to find himself stuck part-way down a bureaucratic pyramid with very little power to influence objectives and organisational behaviour.

4. Whilst promotion may be available in the early part of his career, the top posts in all types of organisations are limited and many a competent manager finds himself without promotion opportunities. His needs and problems can be easier resolved in a small organisation; in a large one he will tend to become entangled in bureaucratic procedures. Hence frustrations increase and managers become more willing to combine with others to represent their point of view.

These points were emphasised in the Commission of Industrial Relations Report on *White Collar Trade Unionism* (CIR study No.3) where it said:

> 'the need and wish for a collective voice can apply among managerial staff in particular when the organisation is large and where there are collective issues.. Increasing bureaucratisation and employment concentration are also affecting managers. The result is that in some circumstances quite senior managers are now finding it increasingly

difficult to air their grievances, especially where terms and conditions of employment, having become standardised, leave little room for individual negotiation. Moreover redundancies are no longer uncommon in managerial areas and many managers therefore see collective organisation primarily as an insurance policy in the event of redundancy or some other mishap outside their control.'

In examining the expansion of managerial unionism there is a distinction between general practice in the public and private sectors of the economy. In the public sector, since the Whitley Committee Report in 1918, trade unionism amongst staff at all levels has been accepted as a natural and normal development. This has been enhanced by the nature, size and structure of public service: in Central Government, Local Government, the health service and nationalised industries terms and conditions of employment have been developed in a rational way such that there is general uniformity of employment conditions, based on grade structures from the lowest to the highest levels. This has tended naturally to encourage collective representation. Unions like COHSE (The Confederation of Health Service Employees), NALGO (National & Local Government Officers' Association), NUPE (National Union of Public Employees), CPSA (Civil and Public Services Association), NUT (National Union of Teachers), RCN (Royal College of Nursing) and AUT (Association of University Teachers) have a long history of negotiation, and are now having to adapt to the rush towards decentralised bargaining.

In the private sector the norms and practices are generally different. Some employers still practice overt opposition to unionisation and many managers will not join a union against the known wishes of their superiors, either because they feel it is disloyal to do so, or from fear of the potential consequences to their career and their relationship with the organisation. Despite statutory protection against dismissal for union activity, the manager may feel it will affect his chances of promotion. Evidence suggests that supervisors and middle level managers are more likely to join trade unions than more senior levels of manager.

6. STRESS AND THE MANAGER

(A) INTRODUCTION

Human beings are both adaptable and deformable, and it is when they become "deformable" that we say that they are subject to stress. The reasons for the onset of stress are varied, but the most common accepted reasons are those related to tension, anxiety, depression. It is, however, widely accepted that most people work better with a minimal input of stress, a boost of adrenalin which enables them to rise to, and meet, a challenge, but it is when stress is a dominant factor that it becomes a source of concern, particularly in the work situation. Organisations have not taken stress seriously and been surprised at the disintegration of a member of staff, but by then the damage has been done and *two* problems have to be solved:

a)   the treatment of the individual

b)   ensuring that work continues in their absence

The task of management, therefore, is both to recognise and *manage* elements of stress within their organisations, and we shall investigate this in more detail in this chapter.

(B)   THE IMPACT OF STRESS

Excessive stress, in human beings, can be equated to stress in engineering terms and, in both cases, the impact is serious (Figure 28).

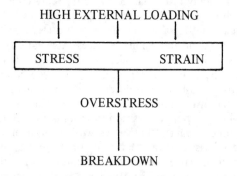

Figure 28: Impact of Stress

In humans the initial onset of overstress is typified by a general feeling of being tired and slightly unwell, resulting, probably, from broken sleep patterns, where the mind refuses to relax and continues to examine the problems of the day. This lack of wellbeing is brought into the work situation, and it is here that an alert manager can note the early symptoms of stress, now being expressed by loss of sharpness in problem solving, irritability and loss of sense of humour, coupled with physical signs of tiredness such as dark rings around the eyes or pale complexion.

Eating habits vary in those subject to stress and are therefore rather unreliable as indicators. One person will eat more than usual whilst another will eat virtually nothing, but an increase in alcohol intake, particularly in someone who rarely drank anything, is a more usual indicator. Management must be alert for these basic indicators which, if not checked, inevitable lead to more serious changes in behaviour patters related to interpersonal attitudes, both in the work situation and in social situations.

In work, normal behaviour may be disrupted by eruptions of almost uncontrollable rage, brought on by minor incidents, or withdrawal from group situations preferring their own company to that of others. This level of behaviour spills over into their social life where, again, isolationism is preferred to social interaction with friends or colleagues.

Prolonged stress can manifest itself physiologically in the form of stomach disorders, headaches, skin complaints or mental breakdown and these may take a great deal of time to resolve, and it follows, therefore, that prevention must be given top priority.

(C) CAUSES OF STRESS

Many incidents of stress have roots within organisations and these can be examined under a number of distinct headings, which relate to *ALL* workers, not only management.

a) Individual Causes

Some individuals bring stress upon themselves by virtue of their own personality and elements of this can be recognised within behaviour patterns. These may manifest themselves in terms of an unwillingness to recognise a gradual reduction in psychic energy brought about purely by advancing age, or a constant need to win or achieve outward success. Both of the latter could be said to have a dependence on adrenalin stimulation, a need to keep meeting and beating bigger and better challenges.

Lack of life-style balance is very often a pointer towards potential stress, in that all available energy is directed in one major direction, to the total exclusion of everything else, family or external interests, and those people often take great pride in being described as "workaholics", taking care to ensure that people they associate with are told about their long hours, refusal to take holidays and how much work they take home with them, most of it self-generated anyway!

A more serious situation, related to individual stress, is that brought about by being unable to accept that their career aspirations are over-optimistic and that they have reached *their* final organisation level, related to their experience and ability, and have to accept, perhaps, that younger people, or those with less service, are being promoted in preference to them.

Management needs to recognise and deal effectively with this problem if it is to both avoid creating stress in an individual, and still retain their contribution to the organisation, and it requires considerable human relations skill, and time, to effectively achieve a viable solution to the problem.

b) Causes Intrinsic to the Job

The most widely recognised cause of stress is that induced by overwork, bringing with it pressures related to deadlines, the need for decision taking on a wide variety of unrelated topics, and the need to cope with sheer volume of work in the course of a very extended working week.

To some managers, this may not seem an unusual set of circumstances, for most managers work under pressure for periods of their working week, but what we refer to as "overwork" is a set of circumstances over and above this situation, which form a continual and unrelenting source of pressure upon an individual, for a prolonged period of time. Less generally recognised as a stress-inducing problem is a situation of "underwork", i.e. reduced activity or involvement in decisions, allowing long periods of unpressured time when others, apparently, are more than fully occupied.

Situations of this nature sometimes arise when management feels that the individual can no longer contribute effectively unless their workload is reduced, possibly due to age, ill-health, or their inability to operate effectively in the broader sense. Stress-related problems often result because no-one has explained why those actions have been taken, leaving the individual to work it out for himself, usually coming to the wrong conclusion!!

There have, of course, been some situations when management have deliberately created this sort of situation in an attempt to induce the individual to resign, rather than having to go through a lengthy, and sometimes difficult, disciplinary process, but this is not related to the main substance of this chapter.

Stress can be induced, in any work situation, by adverse physical conditions, causing illness or mental pressure, brought about by the repetitive nature of the work being performed. In this context we must consider all the areas which could affect an individual's ability to work — heat, cold, ventilation problems, harsh or poor lighting, excessive noise or pressure generated by having to keep up with an unrelenting production line, as found in car production or electrical assembly.

c) Organisational Roles

Stress can often occur within organisations related to the level of authority or decision making involved in the role occupied by an individual.

In many cases, this is directly related to frustration in being unable to progress with an objective due to the inactivity or disinterest of someone senior to them who must be involved in the final decision. In other cases the blockage is caused by personality clashes with immediate colleagues leading to political manoeuvring between departments or divisions of the same company, creating pressures which, ultimately, can lead to the development of individual stress. In other situations, stress is induced by virtue of the non-inclusion of an individual in any process of decision making related directly to elements of their work or the people who work for them, this latter situation reflecting poorly on their perceived status in the eyes of subordinates. Cultural constraints concerned with the day to day work within an organisation are also causes of stress in that individual behaviour can be restricted by the overriding cultural beliefs, practices and behaviour patterns prevalent within the organisation, which can tend to mitigate against certain types of people in terms or organisational success.

d) Career Development

Organisational practices in relation to career development vary considerably within industry and commerce, from the highly organised development training and succession planning basis, to the, perhaps, more familiar factors of subjective judgement and 'face-fitting' appointments.

These latter systems are prone to areas of major error and, subsequently, the generation of elements of stress within individuals, from either over-promotion or under-promotion.

It is truly said that the responsibility for any failure, following a promotion, rests firmly with management, although it is more likely that the individual will receive most of the blame, mainly for not performing to expectation.

Little thought will be given to what could be the root cause of the problem, management's selection of an unsuitable candidate for promotion, perhaps due to inexperience or, more likely, there being no other candidate available at the time the appointment became available, due to lack of a formal system of succession planning. Over-promotion is, therefore, a very real source of stress, due to either a recognition by the individual that they simply cannot cope, or the result of a failure to recognise this, coupled with a desperate attempt to cope with a mounting tide of pressure, and loss of respect from subordinates.

At the opposite end of the scale is the equally serious source of individual stress brought about by under-promotion, that difficult situation whereby a very capable individual is restricted to an undemanding job, not being allowed to make full use of a broad range of talents and experiences, due to either the unavailability of a suitable appointment or the inability of the organisational human resource system to recognise and utilise capabilities in individual employees.

Unless this situation is resolved, it most certainly leads to lowered morale, loss of performance and, ultimately, could result in the individual leaving the organisation.

Both over-promotion and under-promotion engender a sense of lack of job security in the individual concerned and, particularly in an organisational climate of tight economic control and job shedding, can most certainly lead to the development of stress.

e) The Organisation and the Outside World

Many organisations lay heavy emphasis on company dedication and loyalty, usually related to a willingness to work long hours, particularly as an individual climbs the management ladder.

Whilst accepting the fact that management decisions do not usually fall neatly into a 9am–5pm time bracket, and that there must be demands on executive time outside these hours, a great deal of emphasis has, perhaps, been unrealistically given to the virtues of working long hours.

More enlightened organisations have recognised the fallacy of this thinking, preferring to measure their executives by performance rather than hours spent at work. However, where long hours have become part of company culture, there is the distinct possibility of an imbalance arising within the individual, either in relation to family commitments or to inability to pursue outside interests. Both situations contribute to stress, but the family situation is likely to have the more serious and wide ranging impact, both on the people concerned and on the organisation, in terms of performance, in that company versus family conflict does not contribute to executive effectiveness.

(D)   MANAGERS AND STRESS

Particular areas of managerial work are subject to stress-related problems and the diagram (Figure 29) illustrates these points, some of which have already been discussed.

Whilst some areas in Figure 29 have been covered earlier, four significant areas deserve further consideration:

a)   Lack of mobility

b)   Managerial obsolescence

c)   Subordinate job losses

d)   In-company politics

THE FUNCTION OF MANAGEMENT

SOURCES OF MANAGERIAL STRESS

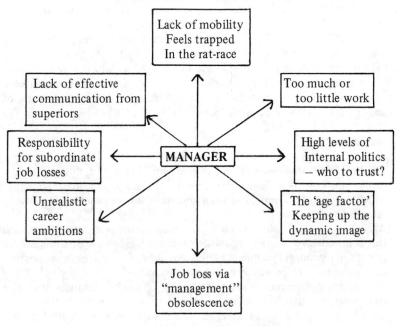

Figure 29: Sources of Managerial Stress

a) **Lack of Mobility**

This area of stress is often closely related to rising age levels, when the job opportunities become subject to that phrase "preferred age bracket is ..." and it has to be accepted that younger people are to be given preference. Many executives fail to accept this situation and become both bitter and highly critical of younger executives, forgetting, of course, that they also made mistakes as their career developed!

When mobility reduces, the manager has to accept, perhaps, that the current organisation will prove to be the basis of his future career, and the re-evaluation of personal aspirations is an essential factor in this process. Another problem arises when a manager has high level external financial commitments requiring a sustained level of income for the long term future, perhaps because of all the factors related to a growing family, house, clothing, schooling etc.

This situation produces pressure because of the need to retain the current earning pattern, inducing an underlying fear of job loss, which manifests itself in long hours, working at home, and achieving what is sometimes called "face validity", i.e. being *seen* to be involved.

This set of circumstances reduces mobility in that managers are reluctant to seek other, perhaps less pressurised employment unless it is both "safe" and has higher income levels, which, of course will require even more involvement — a Catch 22 situation therefore exists. When pressure mounts, it is very human to want to alleviate it by moving away from the situation, but this is not always possible, particularly in the circumstances which involve family well-being, and managers have often described this situation as being like a hamster on a wheel, the problem is continuous, with no obvious means of escape and this produces stress ultimately.

b) **Managerial Obsolescence**

The business world today is one of constant change and this produces a regular flow of new information, both nationally and internationally, which a manager is required to keep abreast of if he is to maintain a highly effective profile.

Again, as age advances, coupled with pressures of day to day operations, this is not always possible, and the manager may be in a situation where newer (and younger) members of the management team are in possession of areas of knowledge way in advance of his own.

Far too many managers concentrate on the job to the exclusion of all else and, perhaps, rather look down on those who possess more formal knowledge such as business graduates, but this is sometimes an excuse for their own lack of academic ability. The fact remains, however, that this need for flexibility and advanced knowledge of technical subjects, produces a stressful condition in many managers and must be taken seriously in that a feeling of obsolescence may arise.

c) **Subordinate Job Losses**

Acceptance of a managerial appointment brings with it not only increased authority and financial gain but a wide range of responsibilities, not least of which are those which relate to the staff of the division or department they control. This responsibility includes aspects of recruitment, development training and team building and these activities bring an in-depth knowledge of each individual in the team, and a close-knit relationship, dedicated to task achievement, usually engendering a high level of group loyalty.

Given this situation, when circumstances dictate a reduction in staff numbers, it is sometimes not an easy task to both select those who must go, to carry out the process and, importantly, reassure and motivate those who are to remain.

There are very few managers who can deal with the reduction of a departmental team dispassionately, and the activity, for most managers, is a particularly difficult one, particularly where long service exists, and the fact that many managers find such a process stress-producing, should not come as any surprise.

d) **In-Company Politics**

It is said that learning the in-company political game is part of normal management practice but, whilst a manager should be aware of such activity, particularly when it could have an impact on his own area of responsibility, there comes a point when awareness is overtaken by a series of events which indicate that they have become a target for political attention, and this is where stress can develop.

In the early stages, increased awareness and vigilance can restore the balance but in highly competitive organisations this does not alleviate the problem and the pressure builds in a number of subtle ways. These can range from "off the record" comments to senior management, relating to a particular aspect of a department, unexpected questions at formal management meetings, or critical memoranda, copied to senior management, all designed to draw attention to managerial shortcomings, and improve the visibility of the instigator.

Concerted pressure of this nature, and other well known practices, place a manager under two major pressures, first to maintain normal work practices and, second, to keep one step ahead of the predator, and this combination is that which, if continued for a lengthy period, produces high levels of stress.

(E) EXECUTIVE "BURN-OUT"

Much work has been done, particularly in the United States of America, on the stress impact known as "burn-out". This is produced by high level exposure to constant pressure, perhaps where technological demand exceeds human capacity. Age, in this instance is not a specific factor, rather, the pace of the work situation creates such pressure that any potential weaknesses are subject to greater emphasis, the end result being a total breakdown.

These stress symptoms appear gradually, increasing in impact with prolonged exposure to the situation, and tend to follow a defined pattern of:
    a)   constant tiredness and loss of concentration
    b)   a general feeling of physical discomfort
    c)   loss of enthusiasm for both work and leisure pursuits
    d)   a growth of anxiety/increased loss of sleep/dread or work
    e)   constant gastric reaction/headaches/irritability
    f)   a craving for isolation/unsocial behaviour
    g)   breakdown
    h)   death (in extreme cases)

Whilst no occupation is exempt from some of those factors, highly pressurised situations, like those experienced by relatively young people working in the dealing room of City institutions, are a recognised source of "burnout", usually at a very early age, early thirties in some cases.

(F) AVOIDING THE IMPACT OF STRESS

Management must accept responsibility for both recognising and dealing with stress at work by reviewing work practices, workloads or, increasingly, providing facilities for staff to consult a stress counsellor, unrelated to the company, to maintain confidentiality. It lies with the individual to recognise the onset of stress and take steps to deal with the situation if possible. Initially, an in-depth review of personal strengths/weaknesses and career potential may help (providing the individual is able to recognise that stress exists at all) and this review should take into consideration:-

> Personal abilities
> Personal needs
> Realistic career aspirations
> Current lifestyle
> Personal habits
> Rigidity of thought

Following this essentially unemotional review, a conscious effort must be made to rebalance life interests versus work pressures and to take up a more relaxed posture, both mentally and physically. Within this process, due consideration should be given to dietary needs, to the consumption of alcohol and to smoking habits, but the importance of discussing the situation with an unbiased and "secure" listener cannot be overestimated, and the earlier reference to the provision of stress counsellors highlights a very real need.

Business is a pressurised situation and the manager of today must therefore accept that fact and take steps to maintain a balance — there is no future in death!

7. MANAGERIAL ORGANISATIONS

i) The British Institute of Management (BIM)

The BIM was established in 1947, and is an independent and nonpolitical organisation which is concerned with the development of the principles, practices and techniques of management and the encouragement of management education, training and development. The central policy and decision making authority of the BIM is its Council, which is comprised of nationally elected members and representatives of its local branches. The Council establishes and keeps under review the Institute's policies and objectives.

The BIM represents the views of management to Government and non-Government organisations. Its other activities include the provision of conferences and seminars on matters of interest to managers; in-company training provision; and the provision of an advisory service to the individuals and organisations who are members. It also publishes a range of books, management check lists, information sheets, information summaries, information notes and occasional papers on matters of interest and surveys of practices amongst organisations. Topics included are labour turnover, performance appraisal, management development and training, and employee relations. It publishes the monthly magazine, *Management Today*.

ii) The Institute of Directors (IOD)

The IOD was founded in 1903 and was incorporated by Royal Charter in 1906. It is the representative body for a considerable number of business leaders in the UK and abroad. It represents directors on the boards of over 90% of the country's largest organisations, including the nationalised industries. Its members are all individuals, there is no corporate organisation membership. It is dedicated to preserving free enterprise, although it claims to be a nonpolitical organisation. It's stated primary objectives are:

i) providing an effective voice for members both inside and outside Parliament;
ii) providing the help and encouragement the members need to improve their own competence as business leaders.

The Institute's Industrial Relations Advisory Service can be used by small companies who do not have an industrial relations department and provides guidance on legislation and general employee relations questions.

The Institute also provides a business information service which covers such matters as salary surveys, industrial relations, company law, taxation, financial planning and exporting. It has a Council as its governing body which has elected members and representatives of its branches. It publishes a monthly magazine, *The Director*.

iii) The Institute of Personnel Management (IPM)

The IPM was founded in 1913 and is an independent nonpolitical organisation which aims to develop comprehensive professional knowledge and experience in the field of personnel management. In pursuit of this objective the Institute aims:

- to provide an association through which knowledge and experience can be exchanged;
- to develop a dynamic body of knowledge in response to changing conditions and demands;
- to develop and maintain professional standards of competence and to issue codes of practice to further this;
- to encourage research in subjects of interest to the profession;
- to present a national viewpoint on personnel management and develop links with other bodies, both at home and abroad, which are concerned with personnel matters;
- to represent the views of its members to Government departments, employers' associations, trade unions organisations, and any other national or international organisations which concern themselves with manpower matters.

The Institute is governed by an elected Council drawn from the membership and its members are individuals. It collaborates with education establishments for education and training for personnel management, as well as offering a range of relevant short courses for both members and non-members.

The Institute, through its seven national committees on Education, Employee Relations, International, Membership, Organisation and Manpower Planning, Pay and Employment Conditions, and Training and Development, and its two standing committees on Public Services, and Discrimination, prepares and distributes a variety of reports and surveys on matters concerned with personnel policy and practice. It also publishes a wide range of books on management and personnel management topics and two magazines monthly, *Personnel Management* and *Personnel Management Plus*.

8. MANAGEMENT EDUCATION AND TRAINING

It is probably true to say that there was little formal management education prior to the Second World War. By the 1960s, however, larger companies were encouraging management education and training and a further boost was given by the levy/grant schemes adopted by the Training Boards established after the passing of the 1964 Industrial Training Act.

In 1969 a report by Alistair Mant "The Experienced Manager — a major resource" published by the BIM suggested that only 7-8% of British managers attended courses lasting more than one week. An additional criticism of the Mant report was that in many cases there was little attention paid to transferring learning from the classroom back to the workplace. He went on to point out that the most effective management education occurred where studies were closely linked to the manager's job via project work and assignments focussing on real problems and issues at work.

Many found the report thought provoking and moves were made to link management development activity into the practical world by most of the Public Sector educational establishments and training consultancies. The recessions of the mid 1970s and early 1980s, however further highlighted the apparant inability of UK organisations to adapt to the changes required to remain competitive and the spotlight was again focussed on the weaknesses of British managers.

In 1984 the Institute of Manpower Studies, in a report for the NEDC and MSC called "Competence and Competition" investigated on a comparative basis management education and training, in the UK compared with Japan, the USA and West Germany and concluded that all three of the comparator countries had identified a clear relationship between investment in the education and training spheres and competitive success.

A further report was conducted for the NEDC and MSC by Veronika Watson and Quentin Thompson of Coopers and Lybrand in 1985 "A Challenge for Complacency" and this highlighted that there was widespread ignorance by senior managers in organisations as to the amount of resources being used on training in their organisation or on the contribution training and education can mean for competitiveness and profitability. Broadly training was perceived as an overhead which was cut when the organisation was not performing too profitably.

Further confirmation was made of the lack of committment to end short-comings in the education of managers was provided in the publication of two further reports. One by Charles Handy for the MSC and NEDC "The making of managers" which compared the approaches to the education, training and development of managers in the UK with that of France, the USA, Germany and Japan and concluded that Britain did not take the preparation and development of managers as seriously as the other countries. Handy recommended a ten point agenda for action;

(i)   to expand the base of our education by educating more people for longer and that the education should be broader, which was the case in the other four countries;

(ii) to encpurage work experience as part of education, perhaps while still at school or in the gap between school and College;

(iii) to establish a study linked 'apprenticeship' or 'articles of management' as the initial phase of management development as in some German and USA organisations;

(iv) to provide an early grounding in the core subjects of business for all those in education who are likely to eventually have business or management responsibilities;

(v)   to encourage companies to provide a set number of days (5) for off the job training, each year, as in some USA and German companies;

(vi)   to encourage the development of further good practice in the development of managers by promoting the activities of the larger organisations and encouraging them to act as suppliers and contractors to others with their trainig services — a common feature of the Zaibatsu's in Japan;

(vii)   to develop both mechanisms for cooperation between companies and the business and management education providers e.g. the sort of encouragement and linking provided by Chambers of Commerce in France and Germany;

(viii)   to establish an official statistical and informational base to monitor what is happening by government and to disseminate good practice between enterprises as in France;

(ix)   to try and make individual study, reading and learning a more respectable and rewarded activity within organisations, as in Japan and the USA where the emphasis is on education as an investment;

(x)   to encourage firms to be discerning in their recruitment policies and practices and to give new entrants early responsibility and relevant training to promote their developmant.

Handy further advocated that companies should be encouraged to endorse a 'development charter' setting out a code of good practice for management development. This charter might call for a corporate management development plan, off the job training and education rights for every manager, a personal development plan for each manager, some form of reimbursement of tuition fees for approved self chosen education programmes, and a formal attempt to link education with work activities.

The second major report was that produced by John Constable and Roger McCormick for the BIM and CBI, "The making of British Managers". This also emphasised the low level of provision of management education and argued for a major publicity drive to increase the numbers taking advantage of the available provision. They recommended a basic foundation level course covering such subjects as accountancy and finance, interpersonal skills, economics, IT, people management and industrial relations for all those taking on their first job after completing higher education. They also recommended a growth in post experience management training to provide on the one hand basic knowledge and skills updating for existing managers who have had little or no previous exposure to training and on the other hand advanced education for those who were likely to be promoted into senior executive positions.

A direct outcome from these latter reports was the formation by a number of large companies of the Management Charter Initiative or MCI which is attempting to promote standards and a framework for management education and the development of core management competences. This will form part of the framework of national vocational qualifications set up by the National Council for Vocational Qualifications (NCVQ).

NCVQ was established in 1987 to introduce a new system of vocational qualifications based on the identification of the skills need of employers within a single hierarchical structure – the NVQ framework. It aims to provide a progression of learning opportunities which build on the competences and attainments achieved at lower levels. A feature of the NCVQs approach is that there is an emphasis on linking training and education with the real activities the individual is undertaking in the workplace so that people can do more than demonstrate theoretical knowledge but rather put that knowledge into practice.

Examine the management structures, roles and responsibilities within your own organisation against the ideas represented in this chapter. To what degree does your own organisation believe that management training and education is a good long term investment, what policies apply in this area and what do they say?

CHAPTER SIX

TOTAL QUALITY MANAGEMENT

1. INTRODUCTION

Total Quality Management (TQM) does not solely relate to the improvement of product quality, in a manufacturing situation, or to the improvement of a particular service, offered by a business organisation.

First, it must be seen as an entire organisational concept, fully embracing all levels and sections of the company in an on-going process, aimed at meeting the requirements of the Customer.

Normal interpretation of this would indicate that the "Customer" was, of course, external to the Company, but the TQM process brings that relationship inside the Company also, in recognition that all Departments are both Customers of, and Suppliers to, other parts of the Company, in the context of the need to seek continuous improvement in every aspect of their operations.

The staff of the Company have to accept therefore, the concept that every individual, as well as every Department, can be classed as both a giver and receiver of a service, from others, and that if these two activities reach a 100% quality level, then the service given to the ultimate, external, Customer must also be 100% effective.

This is a simplistic view of a far reaching and important area of Organisational life, one which will require a constant effort and a high degree of both internal change and commitment, at every level, if that ultimate 100% goal is to be achieved.

Philip B. Crosby, a recognised authority on this concept, clearly states that, in order to fully link both management and employees within the TQM process, five absolutes of Quality must be set up:

1. Quality means Conformance, not pursuit of elegance.
2. There can be no such thing as a "Quality Problem".
3. Economics and Quality are an unreal match, because it is always cheaper to do it right — first time!
4. Performance measurement, therefore, is solely the cost of achieving Quality.
5. Performance standards = Zero Defects.

Most well established TQM programmes have the following elements:

a) A continuous problem solving team culture.
b) A Quality structure which embraces the entire Company.
c) Well evaluated, quantitative, Quality controls.
d) An acceptance that Customers are both internal/external.

e) An effective training system, which, first, introduces the TQM concept, then is fully integrated as a constant support to the process thereafter.

2. THE DEVELOPMENT OF TQM

It would be understandable to imagine that TQM originated from the Japanese style of management, and indeed, a great deal of the current thinking has been developed and tested in Japan.

The original concept was, however, created in America, during the second World War, when Dr W Edwards Deming and J M Juran, working in the armaments industry, are credited with recognising that, putting quality first can both reduce costs and improve productivity, and that over 85% of quality failures normally stem from systems under the direct control of Management.

Later, an American industrialist, Phillip B Crosby, highlighted the importance of the human resource, within a business organisation, as a prime contributor to final quality standards, by their active involvement in the process of continuous improvement.

In the late 1970's the influx of quality products, at competitive prices, from Japan, caused many Western Companies to recognise that, to combat this incursion, they must review both their attitudes to, and their methods of, production.

Initially, many grasped the concept of "Quality Circles", believing it to be the key to Japanese success, building workplace teams which examined Quality problems, seeking solutions, rather than establishing the root cause of the problem, but still accepting that problems were a normal part of operations.

The limited success of Quality Circles is due, not to any failure of the concept, which in itself, certainly forms valuable workplace links, but rather to the narrowness of the process, due to:

a) Lack of continuous strategic Management involvement.
b) Lack of inter-departmental linking as a basic policy.
c) Being based on the acceptance that problems do occur.
d) Being inward looking, rather than Customer based.

A growing awareness of these limitations lead organisations to search for a more viable solution, one which permeated throughout the total structure, and could become a way of life, or in-house culture, rather than a system of control, and therefore, the concept of Total Quality Management (TQM) was created.

Initially, many organisations concentrated on improving customer service, as the main platform of the process, but quickly came to realise that this element was only a part of a far greater problem, because to achieve 100% Customer satisfaction requires a major change in the way things are done, within the company, and, perhaps more importantly, a radical change of attitude, at all levels, in accepting that 100% fault-free status is the only way to operate.

Professor Ishikawa, of Japan, clearly recognised that training is the firm foundation on which the total cultural change, required by TQM, can be achieved, and, in accepting this as a central and essential philosophy, it must be made clear that any training done must be specifically related to identified training needs of individuals, after the introductory sessions have been completed.

These individual needs will become apparent, as the teams are formed and start to assess the areas for improvement, and the whole basis of training activity must therefore be seen as an essential, continuous support structure to TQM.

It is important that the company must recognise that the central focus for all TQM activity is a communication structure which extends from the Managing Director downwards, and involves every level of the company in a positive drive for fault-free action, not by constant criticism and policing, but by the deliberate development of a method of operating which encourages a process of "Empowerment", the allocation of individual responsibility for the quality of work produced, and for the continuous improvement of systems.

Teams working on projects do, of course, have a responsibility for keeping senior management informed of progress, and for presenting any proposals for change in a detailed format, and many companies have built in Audit sessions to facilitate this, but these are not to be viewed as old-style control mechanisms.

Above all, it must be recognised that a Total Quality Management programme is not achieved by a concentrated burst of training activity, lasting, say, six months, but rather, it is an evolutionary process which can take up to five years to reach full maturity.

The initial cascade of introductory training must start with the top management team, moving steadily down through the organisation until all have been included, and only in this way will the required level of understanding and commitment be established.

Finally, an additional central tenet of TQM is the need to foster teamwork, and the formation of project teams which will work, as multi-discipline groups, involved and responsible for the resolution of specific problem areas which impact, directly on the level and quality of Customer service.

3. THE CENTRAL FACTORS OF TQM

1. "Prevent — rather than seek to detect and rectify"

Preventing failure is cheaper than correcting faults, and is more positive and cost effective than accepting that faults are an inevitable, and normal part of daily operations.

2. "Managers — fully involved and leading from the front"

The ultimate success of TQM, as an in-Company way of life, will be judged by the extent to which employees see that top managers are both involved in, and committed to the TQM concept.

3. "Responsibility belongs to everyone"

There is no one Department which is held responsible for the level of Quality, within a company, rather everyone accepts that this responsibility is a shared part of daily life.

4. "Right first time" is the only way

Customer satisfaction is gained by having zero defects, and this is the cornerstone of strategic success.

5. "Quality can have a cost factor"

Full emphasis must be give to the three basic costs of Quality:

1. Achieving prevention to allow "right first time."
2. The Audit process to ensure it will be right.
3. Failure = the cost of allowing errors to occur.

Failure costs occur in every Business organisation and can become the "Acceptable Norm if the true cost factors are unrecognised. Consider some of these important areas of potential cost:

Customer complaints	Loss of future orders
Cancelled orders	Returned goods
Warranty claims	Re-working faults
Wastage of materials	Disruption to production

6. "Quality first in all Departments"

Quality is not only Production's responsibility, it must also involve Accounts, Marketing, Transport and Personnel, in relation to the service they give others.

7. Finally — "A continuous improvement drive"

All results achieved must be subject to a process of continuous improvement, this is the progressive effect of a true TQM system.

4. THE ROUTE TO QUALITY

We have become accustomed to regarding Quality as a series of systems and procedures which must be followed. There are manuals of Work Procedures and detailed reporting documentation, most of which are geared to recording faults and planning for rectification, but these are costly ways of achieving Quality, and can also prove unpopular because they impose a system on people.

Engineering has usually recognised the role of the Inspection Department as a necessary in-Company process of isolating faults, prior to despatch, and the key weakness of this system is the full acceptance that faults are bound to occur! TQM seeks to achieve quality through the involvement of people who are perceived as assets to be developed and encouraged, given responsibility for their actions, and recognised as having a key role to play in adopting an organisation-wide cultural change, which accepts total quality, as a normal way of life.

5. WHO IS THE CUSTOMER?

Customers have one basic requirement — total satisfaction, and that means meeting all requirements without the need for later modification, first, however, identify "The Customer".

All businesses refer to their "Customers", but this is normally recognised as an entity outside that Organisation, who undoubtedly has certain specific requirements, in terms of Quality, service and delivery patterns.

TQM brings a wider interpretation of this entity, making people initially aware that, externally, there are three potential Customers:

a)   Shareholders,
b)   Purchasers of the product/service,
c)   Users of the product/service.

In addition to this, there must be a clear recognition that another, equally important, set of Customers exists, in every organisation — internal Customers of their Department, in other words, those members of the organisation who work in the other Departments, and who depend on them for effective performance, in order to achieve their strategic objectives.

An example of this could be the Production Department, who depend on the Purchasing department to ensure that all parts and materials, required for production are available, on time, to ensure that they meet delivery dates, and on the Design Department for the provision of accurate drawings to enable the production staff to make a fault free product.

An important factor to emerge from this internal/external comparison, is that the quality of service given to external Customers, is **TOTALLY** dependent on the quality of service produced within the internal Customer/ Supplier linkage.

This vital element is generally referred to as:

THE QUALITY CHAIN

This therefore means that "Customer First" attitudes must be applied, and accepted, with equal vigour, both inside and outside the Organisation.

Two internal rules must, however, apply:

1. As an internal Supplier, you must agree and fully satisfy the needs of your Customer.

2. As an internal Customer, you must establish your requirements, unambiguously, with your Supplier.

There is no room for "grey areas" in this respect, these only lead to disputes and lost, costly, time, possibly adversely affecting the ultimate customer. Therefore, all individuals, within each section of an organisation, become both customers and suppliers, within the Quality Chain, and the strength of the links of that chain ensure that the external customer receives 100% satisfaction.

"The end-user of a product, or service is the final judge of Quality – NOT the Supplier!"

This simple statement lies at the heart of the Total Quality Management concept, and must be accepted as a constant call for continuous improvement, indeed, I believe that it should be displayed, boldly, in every Department, as the reason for its existence!

6.   THE TQM PROCESS

There is no shortcut to Total Quality solutions for any type of project, the underlying requirement is for thoroughness and discipline, plus a quest for continuous improvement, once the initial solution has been achieved.

A clearly defined path, in addressing the perceived problem, is the only acceptable approach:

*   Clearly isolate the problem and its component factors.
*   List all possible causes of the problem.

TOTAL QUALITY MANAGEMENT

* Refine these down to specific causes.
* Produce a wide range of possible solutions.
* Thoroughly evaluate these solutions and rank them.
* Apply the prime solution and evaluate the results.
* Revise where necessary and implement fully.

Maintain controls and seek continuous improvement is mandatory.

During this definitive process, it is also important to ensure that the particular group of people concerned are fully capable of resolving the problem, using the finally approved methods, and this is where a supportive training system is essential.

There are two well proven techniques available to the group, as a means of arriving at a list of possible causes of the problem, and these are:

a) Brainstorming
b) Cause and effect diagrams

a) Brainstorming:

Brainstorming involves the rapid collection of ideas, from a group of people, all concerned with the resolution of a problem.

These ideas are to be subject to further consideration, therefore, initially, every idea no matter how strange, is recorded, usually on a flip chart.

Groups of business people do not easily disregard the process of disciplined thinking, with full consideration of all points BEFORE making any suggestion — Brainstorming demands a "Free wheeling" mental technique where everything is considered possible.

A) Create a comfortable, relaxed atmosphere, with no possible interruptions or telephone calls.
B) Select a good Leader and a Recorder.
C) Keep the group to a manageable size (say 8 maximum).
D) Clearly define the problem, before starting.
E) Write down EVERY idea, with no discussions or dissention.
F) Strive for a large collection of ideas.
G) Ensure that everyone makes a contribution.
H) Walk away from all the ideas at the end of the session evaluate and discuss at the next one (or two) sessions.

An important element of Brainstorming is that no member of the group should be subjected to any form of ridicule, in relation to ideas offered — this will kill the flow of ideas from others.

b) Cause and Effect Diagrams (Fishbone Analysis)

Cause and effect diagrams, sometimes known as "Fishbone Analysis" from the form of the diagram produced, are a valuable way of illustrating the apparent relationships which could exist between the separate causes of a problem, and therefore they assist in isolating them for closer examination.

These diagrams are produced in four main stages, illustrated in figure 30.

* Establish what the problem is.

* Identify the apparent prime causes.

* Isolate salient sub-divisions of the prime causes.

* Identify possible linkage factors between them.

A frequent problem, in crating these diagrams, is that they are drawn to a small scale initially, the identification of contributory factors therefore becomes confused, and difficult to follow and interpret – DRAW IT LARGE!

The concept must be viewed as one of "diagnosis", and not a "blame attaching exercise" the main purpose being to isolate apparent problem areas for both further study and final resolution.

In terms of contributory factor identification, it is also important to isolate MAJOR areas of potential problem, rather than seek many alternatives, because this will, inevitable, cause confusion and delay the achievement of a final solution.

An additional area of concern surrounds the analysis of any figures, produced in the problem definition process, because figures are easily misinterpreted, particularly by non-financial managers, and some basic guidelines should apply:

* Keep all figurework as simple as possible.

* Check all data for initial accuracy.

* Thoroughly evaluate all conclusions drawn.

* Look for linkages between separate groups.

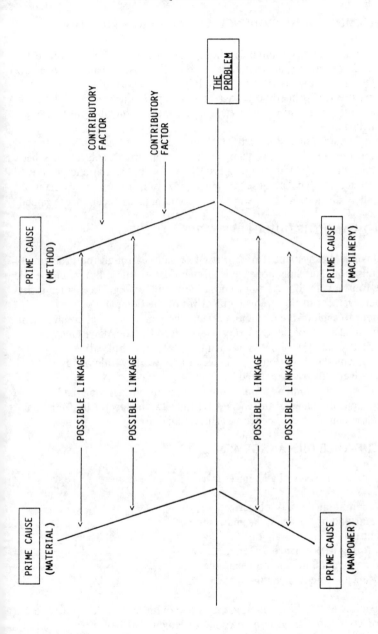

Figure 30: Fishbone analysis

7. EXAMINING THE EVIDENCE AND FINDING A SOLUTION:

Faced with a series of potential solutions to a problem, it is very easy to fall into the trap of settling for what appears to be the obvious solution, but care is needed, for the obvious solution is rarely the true answer!

The most effective method is to rank a group of alternative solutions, in initial priority order, and evaluate each of them separately, before reaching a final conclusion.

One final step remains, in that TQM emphasises the need to seek continuous improvement to any problem situation, even after a solution has been found, and this brings into the process a need for innovation and an unwillingness to accept that "because it now works well, there is no more to be done" - there are always better ways to do something, as experience is gained!

8. TQM AND THE HUMAN RESOURCE FACTOR:

Total Quality Management is not, in itself, a panacea for all the problems of an Organisation, standing alone, it is an inanimate system, but when people become fully involved in it, it becomes a powerful driving force which assists in the achievement of the strategic objectives of the Company.

In order to achieve the maximum effect, there must be total commitment, throughout all levels of the Company, clearly lead by Top Management.

It is rightly said that TQM is not really a "system", but rather a new way of life for any Organisation which decides to work within it, in short, a definite culture change is required.

There is early emphasis on teamwork, both in defining and solving problems, and in changing entrenched attitudes, a vital factor in gaining, and building the commitment needed to achieve objectives.

9. THE ROLE OF MANAGEMENT:

The accepted functions of a Manager involve:

* Clear communication of objectives.
* Planning and organising tasks and resources.
* Organising necessary training.
* Monitoring performance/actioning variances.
* Leading by commitment and example.
* Advising and encouraging the team.

TQM requires all of these functions, together with an innovative attitude, a drive for continuous improvement, and a recognition that the needs of the Organisation must come first, requiring, therefore, a willingness to work with other Departments in a positive way.

TOTAL QUALITY MANAGEMENT

The Manager should carry out an on-going review of all quality related activities under his/her control, giving assistance and advice where necessary, and giving time to each team, in order to support their progress towards positive results.

Some of the areas which could require analysis could include:

* The level of Customer complaints.
* Product failures during production.
* The failure of support services (internal/external)
* Areas of Inter-departmental conflict.
* Isolating time consuming errors/tasks.

Within TQM, a Manager has to accept that the old values, epitomised by the system of "Management by control", have to change, there is no room for:

Product orientation only.   Quality by inspection.
Inflexibility of attitude.   "People are expendable."
              Role and power hierarchies.

An important element of TQM is the process now being called "Empowerment", i.e. the deliberate encouragement of employees to accept full responsibility for both the quality of their work, and for seeking, always to improve not only their own task area, but also those which directly relate to it.

Empowerment has a direct, and beneficial, effect on employee attitudes, motivation, commitment, and the development of effective teamwork.

By creating a policy of publicising successful projects, Management will not only add to team motivation, but also encourage others, perhaps initially less committed, to join the drive for total Quality improvement.

A major factor in the achievement of attitude change, is the process where managers progressively reduce the level of checking on progress, emphasising the fact that people are HELD RESPONSIBLE for the Quality of their work, in a TQM Organisation.

The people of any work group all have different skills, abilities and knowledge and an important managerial role, within TQM, is the analysis of individual training needs and the organisation of training, to meet those needs.

True, the process of Empowerment requires employees to accept responsibility for the Quality of their work, but this also requires Management to prepare them to accept this wider responsibility, by providing training, and this will always be a factor, as new tasks and procedures are created by teams.

TQM has, at its core, the requirement for fault-free work, and training plays a vital role in this, in developing skills and finally, a positive attitude change.

10. THE TEAMWORK CONCEPT:

An effective team has balanced abilities, a willingness to work as a cohesive group, no personal barriers (personality clashes) and good leadership.

To ensure this group of people are fully effective, the Organisation has an important role to play in:

* Isolating projects for study and resolution.
* Communicating objectives for those projects.
* Providing full resources and training.
* Clearly "Empowering" the team to control projects.
* Agreeing report-back times/final completion dates.
* Clearing indicating the relevance of the project ot the total objectives of the organisation.
* Maintaining an effective communication channel, in relation to the activities of other project teams, particularly where their results impact on the team.

Contrary to popular opinion teamwork does not involve endless meetings and "talk shops", in fact, the total team does not always need to attend a meeting, the system encouraging individual and small group work, within overall plan.

Full team meetings are for the initial briefing and task allocation, within the group, for reviewing the progress of sub groups, planning new work areas, as the project develops, and applying the combined talents of the team to the resolution of major obstacles to success.

A great deal of frustration is often caused by badly planned and handled meetings, usually due to lack of any formal agenda, or poor pre-preparation, on the part of the person calling the meeting.

A good meeting agenda is issued well in advance, clearly states the subjects to be covered, is supported by any necessary documentation, lists the names of those attending, the time, date, and location of the meeting, and most importantly, indicates the probable length of time required for the meeting, time costs money!

Full contributions should be encouraged, from all participants, and firm control exercised to ensure that new, or irrelevant, issues are not introduced, regrettably, there are those who like to prolong meetings in order to impress others with their own opinions, which, often are of little value!

11. TQM... AN ON–GOING CULTURE

Total Quality Management is not designed as a quick-result technique, but rather as a central and permanent part of future organisational culture.

It will require patience, total commitment and a positive will to change attitudes at every level of the organisation, and equally importantly, to maintain those new attitudes as part of normal practice.

Once the decision to encourage Empowerment has been taken, and put into practice, the continuous support of management must be clearly seen to happen, and all improvements accepted as permanent steps to more effective working practices.

New systems are initially uncomfortable to live with, as old habits and methods must be cast aside, and the new ones accepted in full, and there must therefore be a system of follow up, until the philosophy of Empowerment becomes an integral part of the normal behaviour of the organisation.

Remember — to assist the process of change, all necessary communication and training support must be made available, plus any other required resources to achieve the objective.

Initially, TQM will be regarded as "just another Management system" and the cynics, which exist in every Organisation, will stand on the sidelines, waiting for it to be replaced by something else, as normal, in many Companies.

A fully effective TQM system may take up to five years to become integrated and accepted as a part of daily operating practice, and much hard work and patience is needed to reach that stage.

TQM must be seen as a way of life, not just a management inspired and controlled system, related to Quality and as resistance to change is an ever present factor in all walks of life, time must be given to achieving that change, ensuring that employees know:

*   Why is it necessary.

*   How will they be involved.

*   That full training will be available.

*   How they may benefit from the result.

*   That Top Management are fully committed and involved in achieving change.

These factors are important requirements of an effective Total Quality Management system, and they are vital to the eventual success of the concept, within an Organisation.

They cannot be rushed, there is no way to short circuit the development process, and management must be prepared for set-backs, in the early stages, when some resistance to change still exists, and results seem a long time in coming, but tenacity pays off, and success breeds success — the long term results are very much worth the effort!

TOTAL QUALITY MANAGEMENT

12. TQM PAYS OFF

British Airways Engineering Division:

Engineers at the base at Nantgarw, working as a dedicated TQM team, decided to seek improvements in the process of crack detection in engine parts, a major bottleneck.

They separated the process into three distinct parts:

a) The lifting facilities.
b) The work flow.
c) Improving the use of electrostatic booths.

By accepting individual responsibility for parts of the study, and working as a team on the collection and evaluation of results, they devised new systems, equipment, and working practices which have achieved savings in the region of £48,000 per annum.

National Westminster Bank Plc:

A study in the early 1980s helped Nat West to recognise that, in order to remain competitive, they had to achieve much higher levels of Customer service.

A campaign was designed, based on TQM, with four distinct elements, the first two focusing on how staff dealt with various Customer situations, the third on identification and elimination of complaints, whilst the fourth element invited the Customers to give their views on the service they now received.

Nat West regards what they now call their "Quality Service Programme" as a never ending drive towards improving service Quality, weaving Quality into the framework of the Company through detailed planning, training, standards, and constant market research.

Quality service action teams, of 6-10 staff, are voluntary groups, charged with the task of continually analysing Quality issues at their location, and devising effective solutions for implementation, whilst steering groups, at regional level, ensure full support and strategic direction is maintained.

The TQM system has been welcomed as an integral part of the organisation, and over 58,000 staff have attended special workshops on the subject, devising/implementing 7,500 solutions.

CHAPTER SEVEN

MAJOR FUNCTIONS OF PERSONNEL MANAGEMENT

1. INTRODUCTION

The personnel function operates in different organisational contexts and its current activities are influenced by the history, the organisation culture, the ideology of senior management, the size, the geographical spread and the technology of the organisation concerned. All of these create expectations about the personnel department's role in decision making and the actual nature of its activities and major responsibilities. Thus the type of function which the organisation demands will influence what is done from day to day. Before we examine the major functions which can be identified in organisations, with varying degrees of importance and time spent on each, let us briefly examine some features of the history of the function.

2. HISTORICAL DEVELOPMENT AND GROWTH

The personnel function can be said to have begun life as a largely welfare-oriented activity. It emerged first in firms which operated a primarily paternalistic philosophy. Examples included Quaker firms like Clark's, Rowntree's and Cadbury's.

Three factors can be identified in the development of personnel management:

(a) First the need for a human concern or welfare function developed with the Industrial Revolution and the rapid extension in the use of machine power, which resulted in work being transferred from agriculture, small factory workshops and cottage industry to the creation of large factory units reliant on large numbers of unskilled employees. Although the overall prosperity of the nation developed, it was mainly the engineers and the new middle-class entrepreneurs who benefited, whereas the working classes lost their traditional agricultural skills and became appendages to machines, prone to the diseases which developed with the overcrowding and slums of the new urban industrial areas.

In the latter part of the 19th Century family firms were being replaced by limited liability companies where ownership and management became divorced from each other. The owners and shareholders had little knowledge of the lives, thoughts and needs of the workpeople employed by their companies. Paid managers acting as the agents of ownership were in more contact with the employees, but they seldom had the familiar personal knowledge of the individual workmen which the employer had under the old family-run system and were generally more concerned with efficiency of technological processes and work output than with the people who operated the processes. The increased size of firms, the size of operations and the numbers of workmen thus made personal relations difficult.

(b) In addition, the welfare and well-being of workpeople became a public issue when the debate occurred over Lord Althorpe's Factory Act of 1833, which set legal limits on the working hours of children and young people. Its provisions were enforced by the appointment of Factory Inspectors, who had powers of entry into the factories and textile mills.

The British Factories Regulation Act, Circa 1835

The new Factories Regulation Act applies to all cotton, wool, flax, tow, hemp or silk-mills, of which the machinery is driven by steam-engines or water-wheels. Where the machinery is moved by animal power, the act does not apply, not to bobbin-net lace factories.

No child can be employed at all before it is nine years old.

No child younger than eleven must work more than forty-eight hours in any one week, or more than nine hours in any one day.

After the 1st March, 1835, this restriction extends to children under twelve; and after the 1st March, 1836, to children under thirteen.

To render these restrictions effective, no child must remain on any pretence more than nine hours a day in any working apartment of the factory.

Persons under eighteen years of age must not work more than sixty-nine hours in a week, or twelve in a day; nor at all between half-past eight o'clock at night and half-past five o'clock in the morning.

Children under nine may be employed in silk-mills.

One hour and half must be allowed for meals to all young persons, but that time is exclusive of the nine or twelve hours' work.

Two entire holidays and eight half-holidays are to be allowed to all young persons who are under the restrictions.

Every child restricted to forty-eight hours' labour in the week must attend a school for at least two hours a day, for six days out of the seven. The mill-owner is not allowed to continue in his employment any child who does not regularly attend school as above stated; for which purpose he must be certified every week of the child's attendance by the teacher.

Source: Andrew Ure, *The Philolsophy of Manufacturers*, 2nd ed.
(London: Charles Knight, 1835), pp.358-359.

Out of this Act grew the Ten Hour' Bill of 1847 which limited the daily working hours of women and children in textile factories to 10 hours. This principle of regulation was extended by a series of Acts to other areas of work, e.g. Lord Shaftesbury's Mines Act of 1842 by which the underground employment of women and children was forbidden.

(c) A third influence was the development of trade unions which were concerned with the improvement of working conditions and themselves were struggling for life.

Early welfare workers were mainly women because it was the plight of women and young people which had caused most societal concern. They were primarily of the upper middle-classes and were the output of university social work courses which focused on overall social, and not industrial, issues. No-one was very clear what they should be doing to raise standards of welfare at work, apart from trying to see that legislation was implemented, providing personal counselling when it was requested and looking after amenities such as canteens, recreation facilities, restrooms and administering benevolent funds as they developed. Some managers and owners, however, found that their welfare workers, far from being innocuous easers of conscience, actually wished to contribute reforms to the employment conditions in factories. Ann Crichton in *Personnel Management in Context* (1969) said on this point:

'One cannot blame the paternal employers for their vagueness. The welfare workers were not helped to see what to do any more clearly in their courses of preparation at their universities. These courses were really intended for social workers and their theoretical studies were about social philosophy and social economics which encouraged them to be concerned about social justice and reform, hence very often they had considerable difficulty in realigning their objectives with those of the rest of management. They saw the need for an active management role in order to achieve changes and tried to press for major amendments in terms and conditions of employment, changes which were often unacceptable to management because they seemed unrealistic and visionary rather than practical and of immediate consequence.'

One of the early pioneers in the field of welfare work was Miss Eleanor Kelly who was successful in a firm of metal box manufacturers in Carlisle at the turn of the century. She persuaded management to install six wash-basins in the factory for the use of 1500 men and women employees. She went on in 1913 to found the Welfare Workers Association, the embryonic professional body, now the Institute of Personnel Management (IPM). Alongside the welfare-oriented function other areas of personnel work were also developing. The sheer number of employees in the growing firm led to the control needs of owners and management being met by the appointment of people to look after wages, addresses, other personal records and initial screening for employment. So men, either appointed from the shop floor or junior clerical positions, were employed as labour officers or employment officers (the title varied from one organisation to another) and were involved in recruitment and selection. Records were also maintained of discussions and agreements with trade unions so that matters in dispute could be compared with previous agreements. In some companies, therefore, these employment officers were also used within the collective bargaining function.

A major impetus to the welfare role was given during the First World War by various Government reports, in particular the Health of Munition's Workers' Committee which urged the appointment of Welfare Supervisors in all factories where women were employed. It was actually made compulsory to have welfare workers in all factories where explosives were used.

The main emphasis was still on work carried out by female workers, hence the proliferation of the welfare function, as more and more women were employed to replace the men who were away in the armed services. Occupational psychology also developed to meet the recruitment and selection needs of employers in allocating personnel to suitable occupations. Due partly to the work of the Industrial Fatigue Board, which investigated the effects of variations in hours of work, breaks and other working conditions, more serious concern developed for the working environment. At the same time, more formal apprenticeship schemes were developed so that they became not just a matter of serving time but also an educational experience. In fact the interest which was taken in those young people was to help the personnel function retain its credibility during the difficult years of the 1930s. Apprentices became supervisors and managers themselves and retained a close relationship with the employment and welfare officers over many employee matters.

The economic depression which followed the First World War led to the closing down of many welfare departments. As a result, especially in the older industries of mining, shipbuilding and textiles, the function of personnel lost ground as only the minimum standards of working conditions laid down by legislation were retained. It was not until the end of the 1930s and the beginnings of labour shortage, exacerbated by the Second World War, that there was sufficient concern for an improved evaluation of the personnel management function. Yet even during the 1930s the function was give credibility, especially in the new industries which supplied consumer goods like cars and electrical appliances.

In 1939 the Institute of Labour Management (as the IPM was known until 1946) defined the nature of personnel management as:

'that part of the management function which is primarily concerned with the human relationships within the organisation. Its objective is the maintenance of those relationships on a basis which, by consideration of the well-being of the individual enables all those engaged in the undertaking to make their maximum personal contribution to the effective working of that undertaking.'

and went on to list the activities of personnel specialists as:

'In particular personnel management is concerned with methods of recruitment, selection, training and education and with the proper employment of personnel; terms and conditions of employment; methods and standards of remuneration, working conditions, amenities and employee services, the maintenance and effective use of facilities for joint consultation between employers and employees and between their representatives and of recognised procedures for the settlement of disputes.'

The Second World War established the personnel function as an important specialism within management, recognised as such by Government, employers, employees and ther representative bodies, trade unions. Industry had a need to maximise production and so selection for appropriate jobs, and especially the training of staff, were recognised as essential features of the war effort.

The Engagement and National Arbitration Order ensured that work people in controlled occupations should have fair wages and reasonable terms and conditions of employment. The Schedule of Reserved Occupations specified essential jobs and labour officers were reserved, not having to join the forces, from the age of 25 (industrial welfare officers from the age of 35). Essential Work Orders prevented unnecessary labour turnover and people could only be sacked or move with the permission of the National Service officer. This led to the development of formal disciplinary procedures in many firms.

By the end of the Second World War, personnel management had been assured an essential place in industry and commerce and the state of full employment which prevailed for the next 30 years or so helped to maintain this importance. Organisations found themselves with a perpetual shortage of key skills and it became necessary to attract people to a firm, instead of picking and choosing from those who were looking for work. In many organisations wages were increased on an annual basis, from the early 1950s, and arbitrary dismissal was no longer a threat to the individual as there was inevitably a vacancy in another organisation desperate for the individual's skills.

As time went on the impact of full employment encouraged competition between employers for the scarce labour resources. Despite the warnings that were given by employers' organisations of the dangers of wage competition, firms and industries offered wage increases to gain and keep employees. Sir Ernest Field, Director of the Scottish Engineering Employers' Association, issued a circular in February 1952 which reflected the concern:

'All members are earnestly reminded that, in the interest of Federated firms in general and in their own ultimate interest, they should never offer inducements of any kind which may reasonably be expected to entice people away from a Federated employer ...

...Inducements take many forms –

Time rates higher than is normal for the job;

Overtime, which is not really necessary in the interests of production at the time;

Systems of alleged payment by results which bear little or no relation to effort and are in effect what are commonly referred to as 'gift schemes';

'Merit', 'Experience' or 'Ability' increments paid without any real regard to the possession of these qualities, or before there has been sufficient time properly to assess them ...

...I must also stress the proved fact that the results of enticement are of only transitory advantage to the firm and of boomerang effect: sooner or later, the labour position being what it is, th e losing firms are forced into the position of having to adopt the same methods to fill their vacancies, with obvious effect on the wage structure and costs ...'

Such problems made firms realise the need for sound and logical wages, salaries and fringe benefits packages and personnel officers became increasingly responsible for the monitoring of local rates and for advising on policy.

Partly because of the labour shortage, and partly because of the increasing complexity of technology and the need to have people who were unlikely to cause damage, through inexperience, to valuable equipment, training became more systematic and assumed greater importance during the 1950s. It was given a further boost by the Industrial Training Act of 1964.

The general pattern of industrial relations activity also changed in the post-war era. Trade union influence, credibility and bargaining power had increased during the Second World War and this continued during the next thirty years. From the 1950s, as we mentioned earlier, wages were negotiated annually and were under constant review. Whereas, before the war, much negotiation had been handled centrally by employers' associations and trade unions nationally, in the post-war era, the trend has been towards plant and company level bargaining with local lay workplace representatives or shop-stewards. Such local negotiation gradually tended to involve the personnel officer maintaining the industrial relations control function. This involvement was increased due to the criticisms of the Royal Commission on Trade Unions and Employers' Associations under Lord Donovan (1968) which urged a tightening up of local industrial relations practices and procedures. Paragraphs 94 and 95 of the Donovan Report emphasised the key role of personnel policies in improving industrial relations:

'(94)... If companies have their own personnel specialists, why have they not introduced effective personnel policies to control methods of negotiation and pay structures within their firms?

(95) Many firms have no such policy, and perhaps no conception of it. They employ a personnel officer to be responsible for certain tasks: staff records, selection, training, welfare negotiation and consultation. Many of the older generation of personnel managers see themselves simply as professional negotiators. Even if a personnel manager has the ability to devise an effective personnel policy, the director responsible for personnel (if there is one), or the board as a whole, may not want to listen to him. Many firms had acquired disorderly pay structures and uncoordinated personnel practices before they appointed a personnel manager, and the burden of dealing with disputes and problems as they arise has absorbed his whole time and energy.'

In Paragraph 179, Donovan argued for a more professional approach by specialists in industrial relations:

'(179) Over recent years growth in the size of companies has emphasised the unsuitability of the existing institutions of industrial relations to large companies. Most of them have factories in various parts of the country which do not fit into the regional or district structure of many employers' associations and collective bargaining procedures. This structure therefore fails to recognise the prime responsibility of boards of directors for industrial relations throughout their companies and it thwarts attempts to design company personnel policies. Even greater obstacles are placed in the way of the growing number of companies which operate in more than one industry. Large companies maintain, or should maintain, competently staffed and adequately equipped personnel departments. Many large companies are innovators and therefore in special need of negotiating arrangements linking improvements in pay with improvements in methods of operation. Many of them are pace-makers in pay and the problems which arise from the gap between industry-wide rates and actual earnings are therefore especially acute for them. Moreover competition for higher earnings between different factories within the company can be effectively controlled only by negotiating pay structures on a company basis, making agreed allowances for any appropriate regional differences.'

The recruitment and selection process also became more important, partly because the size of organisations was such that vacancies usually needed to be filled but also because of the increasing importance of new specialisms, particularly the increase in the numbers of administrative, technical and clerical staff.

During the 1960s it became clear that there was a trend towards the employment of specialist staff within the personnel function; recruitment and selection, training and development, industrial relations, wages administration, welfare etc. Personnel management also began to spread into Central & Local Government, health, education, nationalised industry and other service sectors of society. Even relatively small concerns employed personnel specialists. Reorganisations especially influenced the development of these departments, for example, in Central Government after the Fulton Committee Report in 1968, and with the reorganisations of both Local Government and the health service in the early 1970s. Influence can also be seen in these last two sectors due to the increasing activity of trade unions like COHSE, NUPE and NALGO and the recognition of the shop-steward role.

Finally, a further major influence on the development of the personnel management function over the last 20 years has been the need for organisations to conform to the increased amount of legislation in the employment field and the concomitant need for specialist advisers. From small beginnings there are now over 30,000 members of the Institute of Personnel Management alone.

3.   WHAT IS PERSONNEL MANAGEMENT?

Personnel management can be seen as that part of the management task which is concerned with the human resources of the organisation and their contribution to its effectiveness. It exists wherever one person employs another and can be said to be part of the role of everybody who is responsible for the work of others. The personnel management tasks which a supervisor performs in any factory or office throughout the economy are likely to be as follows:

— he participates in the selection of new employees;
— he very often inducts' the new employee into the organisational environment, explains what his duties and responsibilities will be and explains his rights and privileges;
— he outlines departmental objectives;
— he appraises performance and motivates employees;
— he counsels and helps employees with their personal problems;
— he recommends wages and salary increases, promotion and transfers;
— he enforces the rules and maintains departmental discipline, warning employees of unacceptable behaviour;
— he ensures safety standards are adhered to;
— he negotiates with shop-stewards representing work groups.

We can see that all managers have a responsibility of communicating with, and directing the activities of, individuals in the workplace. Thus, to emphasise a special function of personnel management runs the risk of undermining the personnel responsibilities of the managers. This makes personnel different from all other staff or advisory functions, whether in the public or private sectors, because the concerns of personnel specialists pervade the whole organisation: regardless of level, every manager who directs staff is in some sense a personnel manager.

Rules and problems in employing people are now so complex that many organisations feel that they need guidance in their interpretation and in designing adequate policies and procedures. They employ personnel specialists who provide an independent comprehensive expertise. In 1963 the IPM clearly stated that they did not see a conflict arising between the personnel professional's role and that of the direct management of human resources carried out by line managers:

> 'It is not the personnel manager's job to manage people but to provide the specialist knowledge or services that can assist the management team to make effective use of the human resources of the organisation' (IPM 1963).

Thus personnel specialists exist to help line or operating departments do their work more effectively.

In most organisations the personnel department has usually been established as an advisory or staff function, although there may be executive or line function over certain matters, for example, the final say in disciplinary or dismissal issues or the development of appropriate training programmes. The key role will be in establishing conformity of employment conditions and ensuring that all employees are treated in a fair and equitable manner.

Because there is an overlapping of responsibility in manpower matters, most personnel specialists experience some degree of suspicion, antagonism and resentment from the line managers that they service. This occurs for a variety of reasons. Line managers may feel personnel specialists are interfering and making their jobs more difficult by, for example, refusing to permit the sacking of an employee in a way that may be against company procedures. They may feel personnel are acting in a spying' role, looking for weaknesses on the part of individual managers in relation to their human relations skills. They may feel that personnel specialists are taking over duties which, historically, were those of line managers and so on. The extent to which personnel professionals gain acceptance from other managers depends very much on the quality of service which is given. As Tom Lupton said in *Industrial Behaviour and Personnel Management* (1964):

> 'The recognition of the policy making role of the personnel manager depends upon the extent to which he can demonstrate that he possesses a degree of expertise in the systematic analysis of the social consequences of economic and technological decisions which other members of top management do not possess. When his colleagues turn to him for professional advice in the same way as they would turn to an

accountant, an engineer, a market research man or an expert in operational research, and he is able to give such advice, he has become the new style personnel man to whom I have been referring. I am arguing that only if he has a good working knowledge of the theories of behavioural science and an ability to apply this knowledge to the analysis of the problems of organisation, he will generate confidence in his ability as a professional.'

In order for the organisation's objectives to be reached, however, both line and staff managers must work *together*. This was described realistically by Sir Alex Jarrett, Chairman of Reed International in *Personnel Management*, June 1982:

'It is my abiding conviction that individual managers in their own departments must carry the prime responsibility for industrial relations and the outcome of pay bargaining. No one else can carry that responsibility, though they can look to personnel for expert assistance and they may, in some cases, delegate the negotiating role itself. Further, it is no good having as I do, highly professional personnel staff, if I and my board and our senior line managers are not committed to the objectives and strategies they are pursuing.'

Personnel managers sometimes have difficulties in their relationships with trade union officials andd lay officers. This difficulty often concerns perceptions of the power of the individual personnel specialist to concede in collective bargaining. Personnel specialists should be given enough authority when they fulfil a negotiating role.

The success of the personnel function can probably best be evaluated by examining the use line managers make of the specialist services available and whether employees recognise its significance as part of management.

Three main principles tend to underpin the activities of personnel professionals in organisations:

1. That all employees should be treated with justice, i.e. that no favouritism or antagonism should be shown towards individuals and that there should be consistency of treatment of all employees, at whatever level or performing whatever function.

2. That the needs of the individual member of the organisation should be recognised, particularly in relation to personal development and job satisfaction.

3. That employees should be given knowledge of what is happening within the organisation and should be consulted when changes are taking place.

4. ACTIVITIES

The essential nature of a personnel department's functions can be summarised as:

1. Constructing and formulating a company's manpower policies in line with specific corporate objectives and ensuring that the policies and practices conform with the relevant statutory provisions and the collective agreements previously entered into with any representatives of the workforce.

2. Ensuring that the policies, where appropriate, are applied throughout all sectors of the organisation in a fair and equitable manner.

3. Assisting and guiding line management in the application of policy by providing advice and specialist services on manpower matters.

4. Constantly monitoring and evaluating the manpower policies of the organisation to ensure that they relate to the prevailing values of society and practices in other organisations.

Within these overall functions the general activities which may be encompassed by personnel specialists, depending on the size of the organisation, have been identified by the IPM as:

1. *Corporate planning:* This activity aims, by integrating with other functions in the organisation, to review the company's forward objectives and plans. It is concerned with specifying objectives, considering needs which arise from those objectives and planning methods of satisfying those needs.

2. *Organisation:* Examines the efficiency of the management structure and arrangements for authority and responsibility. It is concerned with job analysis; structuring of individual and groups of jobs; defining the roles within a job; and the allocation of intermittent tasks outside the normal job structure.

3. Manpower planning: This activity can be divided into four subsections:
   (a) Forecasting manpower requirements and manpower supply at all levels in the organisation, especially in relation to the number of people and the knowledge and skills required.
   (b) The recruitment and selection of employees, advertising, selection interviewing and testing.
   (c) Dealing with the transfer, promotion and termination of existing employees.

(d) Maintaining an administrative system to provide relevant information to monitor performance, e.g. labour turnover and absenteeism analysis.

4. *Manpower training and development:* Analyses and determines organisational training needs and individual development programmes; integrates training with other functional specialisms; and conducts performance appraisals.

5. *Remuneration:* Considers the total remuneration structures of the organisation, based on external relativities. This could encompass the monitoring of job evaluation, merit rating, pensions, and sickness pay schemes by local and national surveys.

6. *Employee relations:* Concerned with the relationships between employers and employees and their representatives and with overall productivity. Mainly concerned with trade union recognition and relationships, consultative machinery, and disputes procedures.

7. *Employee services:* The range of services relating to the health, safety and welfare of employees, including the prevention of accidents, the provision of medical and nursing facilities, canteens and employee counselling.

Shaun Tyson's article in *Personnel Management* in May 1985, 'Is This The Very Model of a Modern Personnel Manager?', suggests that there are currently three common models of personnel management activity in the UK.

(i) *The administrative support model:* personnel management is a routine activity which acts in support of line management and there is no real expectation that the function will contribute to major decision making in the businesss itself. It concentrates on the administration of recruitment and selection, wages administration, and health and safety. Probably the most typical of personnel roles and found in most small organisations, hotels and retail outlets, factories, and the subsidiary decentralised units of large conglomerates.

(ii) *The systems/reactive model:* a model which exists in more sophisticated environments and has a strong industrial relations bias. The personnel department's main activity and influence lies in the creation, and maintenance, of policies and procedures to control the work activity and the interface between the employee and the organsation. The function in such organisations thus, not only administers personnel systems and provides guidance on them to line managers, but also instigates and develops them.

(iii) *The business manager model:* here the personnel management function is integrated into business decision making, people are to be motivated to achieve the organisation's objectives and personnel policy objectives are perceived in the language of business ratios — value of sales per employee, value added per employee, employment costs as a percentage of profit, etc. Personnel policies are considered automatically in the achievement of the wider business organisation objectives and labour is manipulated to achieve these organisation ends.

5. STRUCTURE OF PERSONNEL DEPARTMENTS

The extent to which consideration of the above activities leads to subdivision in the personnel department structure varies considerably and is influenced by the size, the structure and the type of organisation which hosts the specialism. There are four main ways in which the department can be structured:

1. A central personnel office which provides a total personnel service for the whole enterprise. This is typical of the small firm and also in the retail trade where a company may have many branches but with none big enough to develop their own specialism. A personnel officer in this latter type of structure may find himself in a peripatetic role.

2. Central and branch personnel offices: In this structure a central personnel office, which establishes overall policies and procedures, is supported by branch personnel officers with executive responsibilities for routine staff acquisition and administration and who are responsible on a day-to-day basis to the senior line manager at the branch, but refer to the central functional organisation over matters which have broader ramifications.

3. Central and divisional personnel offices: Here one or a number of central personnel offices are supported at divisional, but not at branch, level with divisional personnel offices reporting executively to divisional senior managers. They have a functional responsibility to a central personnel officer or offices for overall policy. There can be many variations of this depending on the overall organisational form and structure. In some cases, divisional personnel offices may tackle local divisional policy as well as routine staff administration. This structure is seen in large organisations in both the public and private sectors.

4. Central, divisional and branch personnel offices: In this structure the personnel function is represented at all major organisational levels with, in each case, a specialist relationship to the central personnel office and executive responsibility to local management.

These four main ways of organising the personnel function represent increasing functional decentralisation and are largely a result of organisational size. Organisations usually develop a structure over time which is most appropriate for them.

Within these overall structures three common personnel department functional structures may exist. In some structures the personnel staff may be expected to fulfil a *generalist* role where they provide a total range of personnel skills in each division or plant, perhaps with the ability to turn for advice to personnel advisors or specialists in a central or headquarters function. These central specialists have the task of defining policy, but within this policy overall responsibility for all matters at branch or local level is left with the local generalist.

Some organisations prefer to organise the function at all levels into *specialist* units, for example, training, manpower planning, recruitment and selection, welfare, industrial relations. The few generalists are either in small units or in the top-line posts of the personnel function.

Finally, other organisations find it more logical to mix the two functional structures and have generalists and specialists represented at all levels.

The current trend is for a growing number of personnel departments to be organised on specialist functional lines, especially over such matters as training and development, manpower planning and wage and salary administration. Other tasks including, for example, recruitment and selection, industrial relations and health and safety at work which require continuous consideration, discussion and negotiation, may at local level be handled by generalist personnel managers with help from specialist personnel officers at local level and centralised advice from head office specialists.

6. LEVELS OF PERSONNEL MANAGEMENT RESPONSIBILITY

The number of levels of responsibility within the personnel function inevitably varies from organisation to organisation, depending on its size and the number of locations:

1. Clerical level: Responsibility at this level is for the maintenance of personnel records, for example, individual personal files; employee statistics by skill, location, job title salary level etc; absence figures; lateness figures; labour turnover statistics; and other control and 'organisational health' data. The task may also include other clerical, and perhaps also secretarial duties under the guidance of a senior personnel officer or manager.

2. Junior operational: This may include a title such as 'Personnel Assistant'. The job may include routine interviewing and routine training, perhaps emphasising induction training. A personnel officer, who carries overall responsibility, may delegate tasks.

3. Operational personnel officer: This may be a specialist or generalist post and will carry responsibility for the day-to-day personnel function. Policies and procedures determined by more senior levels will establish the boundaries.

4. Senior operational: This may be a senior specialist post, i.e. training manager, wages administration manager, or it may carry the title of 'Personnel/Human Resources Manager'. It may thus include those who carry responsibility for operational functions and also advise members of line management on the implementation of broad policy guidelines, but it may include those who are responsible for the derivation of policy, especially in specialist areas. It will also include responsibility of a line nature, in directing the work of subordinate personnel officers.

5. Policy maker: If the company has a personnel general manager or a personnel director he will direct and control the activities of the personnel department. He will also be involved in the creation and evolution of policy, especially personnel policy.

It is very difficult to differentiate these operational levels from job titles as job titles are often unique to the organisation. For example, a senior personnel officer within, say, British Gas will probably fulfil the same role as someone who is given the title personnel manager within a private sector organisation.

It will aid your understanding if you examine your own organisation against the structures outlined and the operational levels described.

7. PERSONNEL OBJECTIVES AND THEIR RELATION TO ORGANISATIONAL OBJECTIVES

Strategic and operational advice on personnel matters is directed towards the attainment of the organisation's overall objectives. As we have already outlined (and will expand in the next section) it covers issues such as manpower planning, the development of harmonious employee relations and the maintenance of individual and group motivation. It does so by developing appropriate and adequate personal and career development opportunities; maintaining and deriving equitable and fair remuneration packages and policies; and providing appropriate responsibilities within tasks required to perform the organisation's function in society. In addition, it requires the development of appropriate procedures for the control of employee behaviour, taking into account the structure of tasks in the organisational hierarchy, the relevant external values of society and legislation developed to protect the individual at work.

Finally, the personnel department will be required to contribute appropriately to the development of organisation structures to ensure that the implications of changed technologies and objectives are related to the needs of individual employees.

Ultimately the actual roles carried out by personnel specialists will be determined by the attitudes of senior management to the value of the personnel activity in helping to attain overall objectives. Where personnel is recognised as having something of value to contribute, then personnel specialists will be given a key role in operational and strategic planning. Where, however, personnel is seen primarily as a service function, providing advice and guidance, on demand, from senior managers, it will be given a routine administrative role and will only be called upon to demonstrate its expertise in crisis situations. Whichever role is given depends on the knowledge and credibility of the particular personnel professionals.

This has been emphasised by Karen Legge in *Power Innovation and Problem Solving in Personnel Management,* McGraw Hill 1978, where she looks at the personnel specialists power to implement policies and operate successfully, and lists the following factors which influence that power:

'1) The organisation's dominant ideology.
2) The areas of contextual uncertainty which are defined as being of crucial importance to resolve.
3) How (the organisation) defines measures and evaluates success.'
(1–3 being organisational factors)
4) The manager's own level of expertise in the areas of activity he undertakes, whether specifically personnel management or not.'

(N.B. If personnel managers are only prepared to develop expertise in their own functional specialism and not in a general business sense, they will lose credibility anyway.)

5) His right of access to those he needs to influence and from whom he requires information in order to design and implement policy.
6) His ability to establish credibility with those individuals he seeks to influence and from whom he seeks support.
7) The resource power his position commands.'
(4–7 being individual factors)

8.   OBJECTIVES OF THE COMMON PERSONNEL MANAGEMENT ACTIVITIES AND THE DIFFICULTY OF MEASUREMENT

The factors which have contributed to the growth of personnel management jobs and the enhancement of the status of the specialism are diffuse. We can identify two major contributors to this growth in the post-war era.

A primary influence until the mid 1970s was the simple fact that labour was a scarce resource. We had full employment and too few people chasing too many jobs. In that condition, the productivity of labour and the organisation's effectiveness in utilising its available labour force was of paramount importance. To this end it was hardly surprising that managements in both the public and private sectors of the economy paid enormous attention to any ideas and stratagems which could improve labour productivity. Thus, for example, training and development was seen as necessary; recruitment and selection skills were necessary and, as frequently turnover was relatively high and growth was occurring, there was a constant need for specialists; trade unions were powerful and hence specialists could relieve line management of many of the day-to-day pressures.

The second important feature was Government involvement in the social and economic protection of the individual employee. A succession of legislative measures were passed to increase this protection and personnel specialists were seen to be necessary as they were more able than line management to concentrate on these labour laws and ensure that appropriate policies and procedures were incorporated, leaving line management to manage the level of production or the effectiveness of the service provided.

As pressures on employment have been relieved over the last 7 years or so and legislation has become incorporated in most organisational procedures, the benefits of personnel management as a growing activity have increasingly come under scrutiny. Companies find it difficult to incorporate these benefits on a balance sheet and, unless personnel can demonstrate that it does contribute to profitability and efficiency over the next decade, there is a danger that its growth will slow down and its status may once again be questioned in the same way that Peter Drucker questioned it in *The Practice of Management* in 1961:

"Personnel administration... is largely a collection of incidental techniques without much internal cohesion'. Some wit once said maliciously that it puts together... 'all those things that do not deal with the work of people and that are not management...' As personnel administration conceives the job of managing worker and work, it is partly a file clerk's job, partly a social worker's job, partly fire-fighting to head off union trouble and settle it... the things the personnel administrator is typically responsible for — safety and pension plans, the suggestion system, the employment office, and union's grievances are necessary chores... I doubt though that they should be put together in one department for they are a hodgepodge... They are neither one function by kinship of skills required to carry out the activities nor are they one function by being united together in the work process..."

We should question our primary concern with what Herzberg has called the maintenance of hygiene needs of employees and ensure that we can demonstrate our ability to contribute towards motivation needs by involving ourselves more in job redesign, reviewing existing policies and procedures; and developing new ones to cope with the inevitable changes taking place in many UK organisations.

Let us examine each of the functions of personnel and consider the difficulties of measuring our effectiveness in real terms. At the same time we will consider the skills that personnel specialists need to develop to ensure their ability to cope with each objective. The objectives suggested are only examples and you should see if you can derive more adequate ones within the practices of your own organisation.

(a)   Organisation structure

This is developed as a direct result of objectives and future policy. Organisations have to constantly monitor existing structures to ensure that they are still viable when considering future plans and the needs of the individual members. It thus requires an examination of the levels of authority, the amount of delegation and the responsibilities given to each member of the organisation.

OBJECTIVE: The objective of the personnel department is to give advice on the adequacies and inadequacies of both the formal and the informal organisation of employees into working groups and how changes should be made to cope with future needs.

REQUIREMENTS: The personnel specialist will require knowledge of social psychology in industry and commerce and knowledge of the influence of technology and other job factors and organisation structure on individual motivation. He will require knowledge of the organisation's short term and long term objectives, considerable experience of the existing formal and informal relationships, job descriptions and their relevance, and work practices.

MEASUREMENT OF SUCCESS: Success can only be measured over time and will relate to other objectives which are determined by, for example, industrial relations, training and recruitment activities. Constant monitoring is needed to ensure that the appropriate jobs are handled at the appropriate times. Success will depend on the time-span of change and on the integration of all aspects of organisational decision making and success or failure will probably be dependent on a variety of internal or external pressures which may not be easily controllable. These pressures can be illustrated as in Figure 31 on page 185.

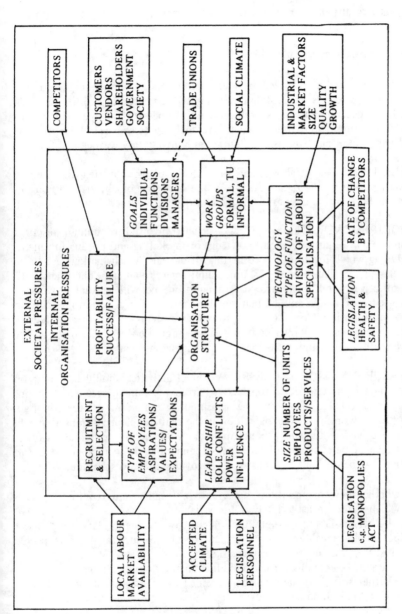

Figure 31 : Internal & external pressures on the personnel function

It is very difficult for the personnel department to justify and evaluate the success of its contribution in the short and medium term.

(b)   Human Resource planning

Manpower needs are derived from the determination of the organisation's long term objectives. This should result in the reduction of short term, crisis personnel decision making as strategems are planned with an eye to long term goals. Existing labour force numbers are analysed as well as an inventory of skills and potential patterns of voluntary and involuntary wastage.

OBJECTIVE: The establishment of realistic plans, covering the human resource needs of the organisation over the time-span of objectives to ensure that the human resources available match organisational requirements.

REQUIREMENTS: The personnel specialist involved in human resource planning will require detailed knowledge of marketing and production plans, including which products are to be phased out and which markets are to be developed, so that human resource requirements can be established both quantitatively and qualitatively. In addition, he will require a working knowledge of simple applied mathematical and statistical techniques and, in large organisations, knowledge of computer systems. He will also require reliable information about the future labour supply position, both within the organisation itself, and in the local or national labour market.

MEASUREMENT OF SUCCESS: Personnel activities should be based on short and long term objectives derived from the human resource planning process. Ideally success would be measured by examining whether the right people are working in the right jobs at the right time, performing the right functions efficiently and productively. Yet, our ability to be successful in this area of personnel work is again dependent upon a number of factors which may be difficult to forecast. Some of the influences include:

— whether new organisations move into a locality and require the skills which were forecast as likely to be available;
— whether the labour market situation changes. Suddenly, large numbers of potentially ideal employees become available due to the unexpected closure of a competitor for those skills;
— whether the economic situation reduces market opportunities;
— whether sufficient data can be obtained as to local authority plans for housebuilding and new roads;

and   so on. *Examine the factors which could influence your own organisation's ability to meet its future labour needs.*

(c)   Recruitment and selection

It is worth differentiating between these two functions. Recruitment is the process of attracting appropriately qualified candidates to the organisation in a cost-effective manner. Selection is the process of obtaining the right person from amongst the candidates, i.e. those who are most likely to fulfil the job requirements.

OBJECTIVE: This could be determined as the successful search for relevantly qualified and experienced personnel, the selection of the right individuals and the induction of the new employees to meet organisational needs.

REQUIREMENTS: The personnel professional will require knowledge of the most appropriate sources of potential employees and of the prevailing rates of pay for this category of job. He will want a knowledge of the future manpower needs of the organisation to ensure that he obtains employees who are going to be as necessary in the future as in the present. To select the appropriate candidate he will require a knowledge of interview techniques and appropriate selection tests. In addition, he will require a comprehensive working knowledge of the relevant statutory legislative requirements and of the organisation's own norms, standards and expectations regarding new employees.

MEASUREMENT OF SUCCESS: In the recruitment process the ultimate measure will be the presentation of appropriate and acceptable candidates. Care must be taken to ensure that, with the rising costs of advertising and the reduction of many advertising budgets, data is obtained and used in planning media coverage of the cost/benefit of relevant sources of candidates. Obviously the ability to attract applications is influenced by the availability of appropriate skills and experience in the labour market and the existing wages, salaries and fringe benefits package which the organisation is offering. Generally, in times of full employment, recruitment is likely to be more expensive for all levels of jobs whereas, with high levels of unemployment, costs for many jobs can be minimised.

Success in selection may be measured by examining the future performance of employees and the rate of labour turnover generally within the organisation. Yet turnover may be influenced by the state of the labour market and by prevailing competitors' wage rates. Future job performance may be influenced by the level of economic activity within the organisation concerned: an employee, for example, may be ideal when the organisation is not working at full stretch, but may be far less suitable if he is expected to work 'flat out'. Performance can also be affected by the adequacy of training activities and the speed of maturation.

These are only a few measures; *look at the advantages and disadvantages of other possible measures with specific reference to your own organisation.*

(d)   Training and development

The level of training and development activity since the early 1960s has been affected by legislative interference which has aimed to ensure an adequate supply of properly trained men and women at all levels in industry. In those areas affected by Industrial Training Boards, this area of personnel activity was one of the few in which some measure of success could be related to the amount of levy returned in the form of grant. With the reduction in the number of Training Boards, such measures will be less important, except in a few areas of the economy.

It is worth differentiating between three terms which are often applied in this area of personnel work; education, training and development.

(i)   *Education:* This usually refers to the basic acquisition of knowledge and skills to enable people to make the best of life in general and it tends to be broadly based rather than specific in its coverage (in occupational terms).

(ii)   *Training:* This term usually refers to the provision of specific skills, knowledge and attitudes which are related either to the current job of the person being trained or to the expected next job. It tends to be specific in its application.

(iii)   *Development:* This usually suggests a much broader view of knowledge, skills and attitude acquisition than training. It is less specifically job centred and more concerned with employee potential and career orientation. It thus develops employees for future roles.

OBJECTIVE: The efficient and effective training and development of all levels of staff so that they can contribute at optimum level to fulfilling the objectives of the organisation, and adequately developing their own skills to the mutual benefit of themselves and the organisation.

REQUIREMENTS: Specialists involved in the training and development function will require a knowledge of the future manpower needs and progression plans of the organisation. They will need an understanding of the relevant behavioural scientific research applied to training, and the skills necessary to undertake training needs analysis so that training meets the priority needs of the organisation itself. Where Industrial Training Boards remain they will require knowledge of the relevant Training Board requirements. They may also have to develop the relevant instructional and teaching skills for conducting training programmes, administrative skills for the training system and the ability to relate performance appraisal to the development of suitable training programmes.

MEASUREMENT OF SUCCESS: Evaluation of training is required as part of the control process to ensure that the relevant skills are being developed to meet the shortcomings discovered by training needs analysis. To establish the value of training, measurable objectives are needed. This is relatively easy when examining training which has the objective of improving, for example, the level of output of a particular individual machine operator or training a person in a skill in which he is not currently competent. It is more difficult to evaluate where development, as defined above, is being undertaken because it is hard to separate the effects of training from the effects of maturation or increased experience.

With the reduction in the statutory involvement of ITBs the value of training can no longer be judged on the level of grant return or on the retention of exemption from levy. It means that organisations will have to use other measures of value to ensure that sufficient funds are allocated to training and development and that adequate training will occur to fulfil objectives.

(e) Employee relations

This term is used to describe the regulation of the employment relationship between employer and employee. It is concerned with the whole complex of market and institutional processes which an organisation encourages or establishes to handle both formal and informal employment relationships. It is concerned with dynamic interactive relationships which, by their nature, change over time. It includes both individual contracts and collective agreements. In general terms the key issues encompassed are those of conflict, cooperation, rule making, authority and power, information disclosure, communication, motivation and control.

OBJECTIVE: The development and maintenance, in cooperation with line management, trade unions (or staff associations), and individual employees of a fair and equitable climate of employer/employee relationships to ensure the attainment of organisational objectives.

REQUIREMENTS: To further this objective, a personnel specialist must have a sound knowledge of the policies, procedures and objectives of the organisation and an understanding of the local trade union (or other) structures, objectives and agreements. He must be competent at interpersonal skills so that a relationship of mutual trust and confidence can be established with employee representatives. He may also need to be aware of the policies of employer organisations and trade unions locally and nationally.

MEASUREMENT OF SUCCESS: Traditional measures include the number of strikes or other forms of industrial relations breakdown which the organisation suffers, and the number of grievances and the speed at which they are processed. There are problems in using such measures; strikes may occur which have nothing to do with internal breakdown in procedures or internal relationships, but which are the result of Government, employer association, or trade union pressure from outside, or they may not occur not because of good internal industrial relations, but because of the prevailing weakness of trade unions generally. The number of grievances expressed may be a result of the general economic climate and the availability of alternative work in other organisations.

What other measures could be used and what are the problems with using them?

(f)   Remuneration administration

The personnel function has an important role in the designing and implementation of an appropriate rewards or remuneration package. In some industries, e.g. electrical contracting, Local Government, the Health Service and National Government, the basic structure may be determined by national agreements made outside the organisation, but in the manufacturing sector, e.g. engineering, chemicals, rubber manufacture, organisations often need to derive a structure which is appropriate to local circumstances and the perceived value to the organisation of specific jobs. Wages can provide a source of motivation for employees to perform effectively and wage and salary rates are certainly important to people considering whether to join an organisation or not. Key influences on remuneration structures are differentials and relativities. *Differentials* can be defined as the differences in reward patterns between one job and another within an organisation. *Internal Relativities* can be seen as the differences in wages and salaries between one bargaining group and another bargaining group within the same organisation. *External Relativities* can be viewed as the differences in reward patterns comparing jobs in one organisation with another.

OBJECTIVE: To give expert advice on wage and salary policies, including fringe benefits such as pensions and sick pay schemes, to ensure that differentials are logically derived and that the organisation is paying the market rate for skills to ensure its ability to obtain labour. To ensure that the schemes are administered effectively and to reduce the potentiality of creating anomalies.

REQUIREMENTS: The specialist will require detailed knowledge of local labour market and industry rates and of the relevant local and national wage agreements. He will need to be aware of the advantages and disadvantages of the various systems of remuneration, e.g. time rates, piece rates and bonus schemes and, in larger organisations, a knowledge of job evaluation techniques. He will require the skills necessary to conduct money and fringe benefit surveys and the ability to analyse and interpret the results. He must be able to settle the problems and queries which arise from specific systems of payment. At times, he will require knowledge of any applicable incomes policies and their effects.

MEASUREMENT OF SUCCESS: One of the main problems with evaluating the success of remuneration administration is that wage and salary negotiations are a dynamic process, hence at times relativities may be maintained, whereas at other times the organisation may find itself in advance of or behind its competitors. The ability of an organisation to reward its staff adequately can also be affected by the prevailing economic situation and the existence or non-existence of a Governmental incomes policy of a statutory kind. Measures which can be used, bearing these problems in mind, are:

— the ability of the organisation to obtain labour of the appropriate calibre;
— the number of anomalies that arise;
— reductions in the number of pay queries;
— the amount of concern expressed on differentials and relativities;
— the degree to which work effort is maintained;
and so on.

Whatever measures are used, it is important to administer a remuneration package which rewards all employees in an adequate and consistent manner and which appropriately reflects market forces.

(g) Employee services

These incorporate the 'welfare' aspect of the personnel function and include responsibility for canteen or restaurant facilities, medical and other personal services, e.g. dentistry and hairdressing, recreational facilities and helping with individual personal problems. It also includes the evaluation and monitoring of the organisation's compliance with relevant health and safety legislation and the design and administration of internal company safety and work practice policies.

OBJECTIVE: To ensure that the organisation complies with prevailing health and safety legislation and develops appropriate health, safety and welfare policies to promote the general well-being of its employees and that there is adequate liaison with safety representatives and safety committees (where they exist).

REQUIREMENTS: The personnel professional will require a current knowledge of the statute laws on health and safety and the Codes of Practice and regulations which apply in the industry. He will also need a detailed knowledge of the system of statutory sick pay and of the specific organisation's sickness provisions, medical facilities and welfare services. He will also need an up-to-date knowledge of the available Governmental, local authority and private welfare facilities. He will have to develop an aptitude for committee work and knowledge of the consultative machinery, policies and procedures in his organisation.

The extent of welfare facilities varies considerably. These can include subsidised canteens and restaurants; luncheon vouchers; protective or other clothing; a laundry service; medical services; convalescent homes; special transport facilities; company houses; loans, and counselling services. There may be creches, facilities for shopping, hairdressing facilities and leave of absence during school holidays.

MEASUREMENT OF SUCCESS: The success of personal welfare facilities to the organisation is difficult to measure, although labour turnover and general satisfaction may reflect some of their value. In terms of health and safety, measures include numbers of:

— accidents (perhaps differentiated between minor and lost time accidents);
— cases of industrial disease;
— cases of discipline over safety matters;
— improvement or prohibition notices issued by the inspectorate;
— days lost through illness;
and so on.

These measures can also be subject to criticism, for example, the numbers of days lost through illness are going to be affected by influenza epidemics. Lost time accidents may not adequately reflect the safety standards of the organisation, more relevant data may include the number of 'near misses'.

What measures are used in your own organisation? How useful are they?

(h) Ensuring the organisation complies with employment legislation

As previously stated, there is now a wealth of legislation in the employment field and the personnel function is often seen as the 'guardian angel' of the organisation in ensuring that legislation is implemented via rules and procedures and that line management is kept aware of the relevant provisions.

OBJECTIVE: To ensure that organisation policies are in conformance with current Government legislation and that the likely implications of proposed changes in legislation are considered.

REQUIREMENTS: The specialist requires detailed knowledge of the relevant Acts of Parliament and Codes of Practice and the effects they have on conditions of work, policies and procedures within the organisation. Where organisations do transgress rules, he should be able to write critical incident reports and possibly represent the organisation in Courts or Tribunals. He should also be able to communicate with other managers on the implications of legislation and be able to word collective and individual procedures to take legislative ramifications into account.

MEASUREMENT OF SUCCESS: Measures will include the ability to respond quickly to questions on legislation; lack of industrial tribunal or other court cases; and acceptable, easy to operate company procedures.

(i) Maintenance of personnel control and planning records and statistics

The production of meaningful manpower forecasts and planning depends largely on the availability of reliable and objective information about employees and their work records. The degree of sophistication and coverage of data will vary according to the size of the organisation. The method of collection and analysis will vary from manual systems to complicated computerised packages.

OBJECTIVE: The compilation and analysis of manpower records as a base for the optimum deployment of the organisation's human resources so that information can be retrieved efficiently and speedily to satisfy the requirements of internal decision making and external requests for information from Government departments, Government agencies, training boards, and other employers.

MEASUREMENT OF SUCCESS: the kind of analyses required to aid decision making will include employees' departmental distribution, occupational skills, age distribution, length of service, names and addresses and contact phone numbers; a register of accidents (both for statutory and control purposes); a register of disabled employees; assessment and performance appraisal reports; records of transfers and promotions; overtime levels, and labour turnover and absentee records; and sick pay records. Success can be ascertained by the availability of such data and the ease of obtaining it for the decision making process.

The list of roles, objectives, requirements and measurement of success is by no means comprehensive nor the only possible list, but it does highlight the problems of evaluating objectively the contribution which the personnel function is making to the success of organisations in the attainment of their objectives. The list also highlights the variety of roles and the skills and knowledge required to operate them. Theoretical knowledge of industrial sociology and psychology must be supported by practical skills, which can only be obtained through experience in the specialism. But what is equally important is an understanding of the environmental issues and pressures which affect organisation in the 1980s. (Some insight into these is attempted in the remainder of this book).

The current situation, which reflects the position summarised is illustrated in the written evidence of the Ministry of Labour in the Royal Commission on Trade Unions and Employers' Association which, although published in 1968, is still relevant:

'Personnel management in this country has succeeded in avoiding the criticism that it is an anti-union tool of management concerned with the manipulation of workers, which has been levelled at the profession in the United States and some European countries. However, the contribution which personnel management could have made and could make would be much greater if large sections of industry did not still regard it as something apart from the main stream of management and if the horizons of many personnel officers were not limited to the provision of limited common services or to dealing with day-to-day industrial relations questions...

...There are signs that this situation is changing. More personnel officers are assuming responsibilities in regard to clerical and administrative staff and management development, instead of confining their activities to the problems of manual workers. There is a trend towards the allocation of responsibility for personnel management to a member of the Board. Furthermore in an increasing number of cases the specialist personnel officer has been appointed to the Board.'

The status of personnel management has improved over the last ten to twelve years; the increasing professionalism of personnel staff has enabled them to demonstrate their contribution to overall organisational efficiency and profitability. Personnel management has expanded and is still expanding in Local Government, Central Government and the Health Service but, if the function expects to continue its importance and credibility, it must be seen to be a necessary part of all organisations. This will require the increasing adoption of a proactive role initiating change rather than a reactive role responding to problems and crises.

Those who wish to reach the top of the profession must obtain experience across the total spectrum of personnel work and cannot afford to become too narrow or specialist in outlook. Current personnel decision making requires an integration of knowledge and functional expertise across the spectrum of activities.

MAJOR FUNCTIONS OF PERSONNEL MANAGEMENT

Amongst the issues which personnel professionals need to address to ensure their continual relevance and effectiveness are the following:

i)   with trade unions being increasingly encouraged by legislation to be accountable for their actions, are existing bargaining structures and procedures relevant? Thus for example are we able to cope with moves towards decentralised bargaining expecially in the public sector?

ii)   with more demand for equal treatment in services and conditions between blue collar and white collar staff, are existing remuneration systems able to cope and do they still motivate people to perform well?

iii) do current practices and procedures enable us to cope successfully with the introduction of information technology?

iv)   do we still offer an appropriate and efficient recruitment and selection service?

v)   are we offering proactive advice on the range of employee relations issues?

vi)   do we have adequate communication structures which encourage involvement of staff and provide them with information so that they can identify with the values of the organisation and its objectives?

vii) are our training systems adequate and related to specific identified current and future needs, or do we merely jump on the latest bandwagon?

viii) have we adequate employee records and administrative systems in order to help us plan and control our manpower efficiently?

ix)   are we involved in identifying and analysing the motivational needs of employees and the design of appropriate methods of work and flexible work organisation?

x)   are we developing our own skills and expertise in our chosen profession, whilst at the same time developing general management skills and knowledge so that we can communicate effectively?

CHAPTER EIGHT

PERSONNEL MANAGEMENT AND THE LAW
OF EMPLOYMENT RELATIONSHIPS

INTRODUCTION

Until the last thirty years or so one of the distinctive features of the United Kingdom's employment system was the remarkable lack of legislation influencing the individual employment contract and the collective bargaining relationship. Yet there now exists a considerable amount of Statute law which influences the whole of the employment relationship and, in some cases, even the pre-employment situation e.g. the Race Relations Act 1976 and the Sex Discrimination Acts of 1975 and 1976 and the Employment Act of 1990.

Kahn Freund in his writings on labour and the legal relationship has usefully differentiated between *auxiliary* law, *regulative* law and *restrictive* law. *Auxiliary* law he saw as the legislation which provides support for the industrial relations system and which is primarily concerned with the institutions and procedures of collective bargaining e.g. the Trade Union and Labour Relations Act 1974 defines the term trade union and lays down their permitted activities and the Employment Protection Act 1975 creates some of the statutory institutions which 'help' in the process of collective bargaining, like ACAS. *Regulative* law gives rights to individual workers in the contractual relationship e.g. the Employment Protection (Consolidation) Act individual rights to redundancy pay and notice periods. *Restrictive* law lays down what is or is not allowed within either collective bargaining or the individual contract e.g. the ballot requirements in the Trade Union Act 1984 before industrial action, or the equal treatment rights in the Equal Pay Act 1970.

1. SOURCES OF INFLUENCES

The employment contract is influenced by a number of sources, these include;

(i) Common law rights and obligations both of employer and employee.

(ii) UK Statute law, which has gradually built what Lord Wedderburn has termed a 'floor of rights' into the individual employment relationship.

(iii) UK Statute law, referring to collective relationships, i.e. the relationship between trade unions and employers.

(iv) Collective bargaining and custom and practice arrangements.

(v) The Treaty of Rome, which we signed when we entered the EEC in 1973, and other laws and Directives which have derived from this.

(vi) Indirect influence from the European Convention on Human Rights and Fundamental Freedoms and the European Social Charter.

(vii)   The Conventions and Recommendations of the International Labour Organisation (ILO) .

(viii)   Codes of Practice, issued by ACAS, the Department of Employment, the Commission for Racial Equality, the Equal Opportunities Commission and the MSC.

(a)   Common Law

Before 1066 and the Norman Conquest, England was split up into several kingdoms and laws were generally local in application. The Normans however developed rules of law which could be common across the country, − hence the title *'common law'*. This has evolved since and Common Law now, to a limited extent, regulates the duties and responsibilities of both employers and employees under the employment contract. The relationship between the parties is tested in the civil courts against the background of 'precedent' in determining relationships which were established in previous cases. This ensures conformity in decision making. Nowadays, however, with the establishment of statute law and it's influence on the contract of employment, the common law aspects have begun to take a back seat in determining the rights and obligations. Thus, where statute law and common law appear to conflict, the duties and stipulations laid down by statute law prevails. Where, however, contractual relationships are not clear or where there is no statutory intervention, then the common law will be applied.

   Historically it can be argued that relative economic and social power in the master/servant relationship was in favour of the masters or employers. Hence the duties on the employee, as determined in precedents established under the common law, are more comprehensive than those duties of the employer. The rights and duties can be summarised as follows;

(a) Duties of the employer
 (i)   To provide work − but only where the employee earns his wages under a payment by results scheme or obtains recognition by the publicity he receives from a particular job.
(ii)   To pay agreed wages in return for the employee's willingness to work, and to pay wages in a manner which is not unlawful.
(iii)   To take reasonable care of an employee's safety.
(iv)   To treat the employee with proper courtesy.
(v)   To indemnify the employee for injury sustained while in employment.
(vi)   To be reasonable in maintaining the employment relationship.

(b) Duties of the employee
 (i)   To be ready and willing (sickness or other incapacity apart) to work.
(ii)   To offer personal service.

(iii)   To take reasonable care in the exercise of that service, including the duty to be competent at work and to take care of the employer's property.

(iv)   To not wilfully disrupt the employer's business.

(v)   To obey reasonable orders as to the time, place, nature and method of service.

(vi)   To work only for the employer in the employer's time.

(vii)   To disclose information to the employer relevant to the business.

(viii)   To hold for the employer the benefits of any invention etc. relevant to the business on which the employee is engaged.

(ix)   To respect the employer's trade secrets.

(x)   Generally to be of good faith and do nothing to destroy the trust and confidence necessary for employment.

(xi)   To account for all profits received in the course of employment.

(xii)   To indemnify the employer for loss caused by the employee.

(b)   UK Statute law on the individual relationship

Parliament is the supreme law making body in the UK and the Statutes it passes are interpreted by the courts. The statutes must be interpreted literally, except where to do so would be offensive to reason. Thus in some cases, individual interpretation may be used to modify the legislative impact. A large number of Acts of Parliament now influence the employer in his relationship with the employee. Examples of these include the, Race Relations Act, Equal Pay Act, Sex Discrimination Act, Wages Act, Employment Protection (Consolidation) Act, Rehabilitation of Offenders Act etc. We shall return to some of these and their main features in the next chapter.

The function of most of these statutes is broadly to prevent those who feel that they have been mistreated or feel that they are unsure of their duties and obligations from having to resort to the courts in order to obtain redress or settle a disagreement. The statutes, therefore, lay down legal duties across the whole spectrum of employment and provide remedies where transgressions arise. In most areas of individual grievance redress is normally available via the Industrial Tribunal system.

(c)   UK Statute law and the collective relationship

Statute laws concerning the rights of trade unions to operate in our society and the degree of freedom which they possess have been around in this country for 120 years. In their early years, trade union behaviour was severely constrained by a combination of criminal and civil laws. The situation began to change with the passing of the Trade Union Act of 1871 and the Criminal Law Amendment Act in the same year and the Conspiracy and Protection of Property Act 1875.

Since these Acts a series of legislative changes have been made which in some cases expanded trade union freedom and in others reduced it. Currently the key laws in this area are the, Trade Union and Labour Relations Acts of 1974 and 1976, the Employment Acts of 1980, 1982 and 1988, the Trade Union Act of 1984 and the Employment Protection Act of 1975.

These define what trade unions are; what protection they have from the civil liabilities of the economic torts when industrial action is contemplated or takes place; what rights officials of trade unions have to time off for trade union duties and activities; the requirements of consultation in situations of the transfer of the undertaking or collective redundancy; the provisions regarding disclosure of information to trade unions, and the ballot requirements in situations of potential strike action, election of officials and the operation of Political Funds.

(d)   Collective bargaining and custom and practice arrangements

These are the rules, both formally agreed and informally derived, which influence the parties in the employment relationship. They include national, local and workshop domestic arrangements made by trade unions and their representatives and by employers and their representatives through the collective bargaining process.

They also will include the specific work rules and regulations and joint unwritten understandings between workers and various levels of management, e.g. on decisions regarding the rota for overtime; which jobs an employee will be asked to perform; the employee who delivers the pay packets of those that are away sick and is paid overtime; informal job and finish arrangements; and the early finish before Christmas.

Custom and practice can be used in the courts to provide the substance of implied terms in the contract of employment; it may provide the basis on which collective agreements are incorporated into an individual's contract and the contractual status of certain works rules.

(e)   The Treaty of Rome and other EC legislation

The Directives of the EEC have had an influence on the development of UK law since 1973, especially in the fields of equal pay, sex discrimination, redundancy consultation and mergers or takeovers. Governments are obliged to implement the Directives although they can choose the relevant form and method of implementation. Examples include,

(i) The collective redundancy provisions of the Employment Protection Act 1975 were designed to implement in the UK EEC Directive No. 75/129 on "Approximation of the Laws of Member States Relating to Collective Redundancies".

(ii) The Transfer of Undertakings (Protection of Employment) Regulations, (Statutory Instrument No.1794) 1981 is the UK's response to the EEC Council Directive No.77/187 on "Acquired Rights of Workers on Transfer of Undertakings".

(iii) Article 119 of the Treaty of Rome provides for equal pay for equal work and this led to Directive No.73/117 on the "Approximation of the Laws of Member States Relating to the Principle of Equal Pay for Men and Women" which the Equal Pay Act 1970 covers.

(iv) Article 235 of the Treaty of Rome led to the development of Directive 76/207 on "the Implementation of the Principle of Equal Treatment for Men and Women as regards Access to Employment, Vocational Training and Promotion, and Working Conditions". The Sex Discrimination Act 1975 as amended in 1986, goes far in bringing the UK into line.

(v) Sections within the Employment Protection (Consolidation) Act 1978 on the employees' rights on the insolvency of their employer meant we had nothing to do to bring the UK into line when EEC Directive 80/987 was passed on "the Approximation of the Laws of Member States Relating to the Protection of Employees in the event of the Insolvency of their Employer".

(vi) The scope of EEC law does not extend to the issue of racial discrimination. However, the principle of the freedom of nationals to work anywhere within the Community was extended by Community Regulation 1612/68 on "Freedom of Movement for Workers Within the Community" and requires equality of access to all jobs for nationals of all member states. Certainly the Race Relations Act of 1976 embodies and fulfils the objects of the Regulation.

Parliament enacted that we should abide by the principles laid down by the European Court. Section 3(1) of the European Communities Act states;

"For the purposes of all legal proceedings any question as to the meaning and effect of any of the Treaties, or as to the validity, meaning or effect of any Community instrument, shall be treated as a question of law (and if not referred to the European Court) be for determination as such in accordance with the principles laid down by and any relevant decision of the European Court."

Wherever there is a conflict between the law contained in an article of the Treaty of Rome and an article or section of any law within a member State, the law of the Community will take precedence. Courts in the UK must therefore take note of any relevant European Court judgements.

(f)   European Convention on Human Rights and Fundamental Freedoms.

The European Convention on Human Rights of the Council of Europe provides for the protection of a whole range of freedoms for individuals and for groups. Thus, for example, it protects freedom of association and freedom of assembly in Article 11, which reads;

> "1. Everyone has the right to freedom of peaceful assembly and to freedom of association with others, including the right to form and join trade unions for the protection of their interests.
> 2. No restrictions shall be placed on the exercise of these rights other than such as are prescribed by law and are necessary in a democratic society in the interests of national security or public safety, for the prevention of disorder of crime, for the protection of the health or morals or for the protection of the rights and freedoms of others. This Article shall not prevent the lawful restrictions on the exercise of these rights by members of the armed forces, or of the police or the administration of the State."

The principle of equal opportunity is outlined in Article 14;

> "The enjoyment of the rights and freedoms set forth in this Convention shall be secured without discrimination on any ground such as sex, race, colour, language, religion, political or other opinion, national or social origin, association with a national minority, property, birth or other status."

The rights are not enforceable in courts in the UK but can be the subject of complaints to the European Commission on Human Rights in Strasbourg. If this body finds there is a case to answer it submits a report stating whether there is a breach of the Convention and if no voluntary settlement can be achieved, the matter may be referred to the European Court of Human Rights, either by the State concerned or by the Commission.

During the Court hearing, the Commission assists the Court by presenting and developing the arguments put forward in the report. The Court can make a majority decision on whether there has been a breach of the European Convention and can award compensation and costs to the winner of the case; States are bound by the judgements of the Court.

(g)   The Council of Europe's Social Charter

The European Social Charter seeks to secure protection for social and economic rights, e.g. time off and pay in relation to maternity; all workers should have two weeks annual leave; all workers should have rights to vocational training. States do not have to agree to be bound by every article in the Charter, they must however agree to at least 10 articles or 45 numbered paragraphs. The influence of the Charter could be said to be less potent than the Convention since there is no central European body to whom an individual may make a complaint. Compliance is monitored every two years when each signatory State has to submit a report on it's behaviour as regards the Charter to a Committee of Independent Experts. The Committee's conclusions based on the report are then passed to a Governmental Committee which has observers present from members of the European Federations of employers and trade unions who will soon contradict any elements where evidence has been reported by their affiliate members to the contrary. Those transgressing the Charter will then find themselves on the end of bad publicity.

(h)   Conventions and recommendations of the ILO

The International Labour Organisation (ILO) was initially created by the Treaty of Versailles in 1919. It was established as a tripartite body to bring together governments, employers, and trade unions to take united action to improve the social and economic well being of people throughout the world. It aims to encourage decent living standards, satisfactory conditions of work and pay and adequate employment opportunities through its conferences and other activities. It is financed by contributions from its member states.

The following principles underpin the work of the ILO and were adopted in 1944 and became known as the *Declaration of Philadelphia:*-

— labour is not a commodity,
— freedom of expression and association are essential to sustained progress,
— poverty anywhere constitutes a danger to prosperity everywhere,
— all human beings, irrespective of race, creed, or sex, have the right to pursue both their material well-being and their spiritual development in conditions of freedom and dignity, of economic security and of equal, opportunity.

In order to further these principles, the ILO has the following activities;

(i)   The formulation of international policies and programmes to help improve working and living conditions, enhance employment prospects, and promote basic human rights.

(ii)   The creation of international labour standards to serve as guidelines for national authorities in putting these policies into action.

(iii) An extensive programme of international technical cooperation to help governments in making these policies effective in practice.

(iv)   Training, education, research, and publishing activities to help advance all these efforts.

150 nations are members of the ILO. The annual (June) International Labour Conference is the supreme policy making body and provides an international forum for discussion of world labour and social problems, and sets minimum international standards. Each member country sends a four member delegation, two representatives from government, one representative of the trade union movement (nominated in this country by the TUC), and one representative from the employers (nominated by the CBI in the UK), each of whom may speak and, more importantly, vote independently.

Between these annual conferences the work of the ILO is carried out by it's governing body elected every three years at the Conference. It meets in February, June and November and comprises 28 government representatives and 14 representatives each of employers and trade unions. 10 of the government seats are held by the following countries, considered to be of chief industrial importance:-

Russia, USA, UK, India, Japan, West Germany, France, Italy, China & Brazil.

The International Labour Office in Geneva provides the operational headquarters, the secretariat, acts as the research centre and is the publishing house. Operations are also decentralised in regional, area and branch offices in over 40 member countries.The work of the Governing Body and of the Office in Geneva is helped by a number of tripartite committees which cover major industries and by a committee of experts on such matters as vocational training, management development, health and safety, worker's education, women and young workers.

One of the ILO's most important functions is the adoption by the International Labour Conference of *Conventions* and *Recommendations* which taken together are often termed the 'International Labour Code'.

Through Ratifications which are voluntary by individual member states, *Conventions* are intended to create binding obligations to put their decisions into effect. They become an international commitment by the country concerned to abide by the provisions of the Convention. Of the 160 Conventions in 1989 Britain currently ratifies 71 of them. Convention No.87 on Freedom of Association and Protection of the Right to Organise is the one Convention which it is expected that all member nations of the ILO adhere to without having to actually sign it.

A *Recommendation,* on the other hand, does not create any international committments but is designed to provide guidance to Governments on policy, legislation and practice.

A Convention comes into existence via the following stages;

(i) An issue is identified which requires action. It may be brought to the attention of the ILO by a government, a trade union, or an employer representative or even the ILO Office.

(ii) The Office raises the issue with the Governing Body at one of it's meetings.

(iii) The Governing Body having discussed it may decide to put the issue onto the Conference Agenda for discussion.

(iv) Concurrently, the Office consults with the member nations on their current practice and laws and uses this data to draw up a report indicating standards for the Conference debate.

(v) The report is discussed at conference and a decision made to draw up a Convention.

(vi) The Office draws up a draft Convention and Consults with member countries.

(vii) The draft then goes to the following conference to be discussed amended and agreed.

Thus it takes at least four years for an issue to be raised, pass through the various stages of consultation, discussion and refinement before a Convention is produced, and it is at that point when a member state decides to ratify the Convention or not.

In the UK, before deciding to ratify, the Government would produce a White Paper which sets out the Convention and discusses its status compared with existing UK law and the Government's policy. When this has been discussed in Parliament and a decision has been agreed, the Convention would be ratified. The fact that the UK Government has not ratified every Convention of the ILO does not mean that our standards are therefore lower than the Convention requires. In most cases it has been felt that either the Convention is no longer relevant in a UK context or we already have standards well in advance of the Convention concerned.

Once ratified and in force, a Convention can be denounced every 10th year if the Government so wishes. For example in 1982 the UK Government denounced Convention No.94, "Labour Clauses (Public Contracts)" so that it could remove the "Fair Wages Resolution".

In reality the ability to enforce compliance with Conventions is through publicity. Governments are required to communicate detailed reports to the ILO on a regular basis and copies of these are sent to the employers and trade unions in the country concerned for comment. It is likely then that any violations would be reported by the trade unions to the Office. These reports are examined by a Committee of Experts who could, if they feel there was a breach of a Convention, follow the report up by asking for clarification from the Government concerned or by conducting a formal investigatory visit, e.g. as it did in Poland when *Solidarity* was initially banned as a union.

The report of the Committee of Experts is then published and could be discussed at the Annual Conference and the country concerned censored. There is, however, no ability of the ILO to expel a member nation, they can only use adverse publicity and castigation as a weapon.

GCHQ Case

The relative weakness of the international provisions are illustrated by the GCHQ case. This concerned the international freedom of association provisions. The UK government withdrew union membership rights at the security establishment GCHQ in 1984 in order to avoid future potentially disruptive industrial action. This decision was challenged internationally both through the ILO and before the European Commission of Human Rights at Strasbourg. The Strasbourg Commission accepted that the UK's actions were justifiable and did not refer the issue to the European court of Human Rights.

At the ILO the relevant Conventions were 87,98 and 151, Article 2 of Convention 87 states

"workers.. without distinction whatsoever, shall have the right.. to join organisations of their own choosing without previous authorisation."

Article 1 of Convention 98 reads
"workers shall enjoy adequate protection against acts of anti-union discrimination... such protection shall apply more particularly in respect of acts calculated to
(a) make the employee subject to the condition that he shall not join a union or shall relinquish union membership;
(b) cause the dismissal of or otherwise prejudice a worker by reason of union membership."

Whilst Convention 87 applies to public sector employees, Article 6 of convention 98 expressly excludes public servants but it does say that this should not be seen as "prejudicing their rights... in any way".

Convention 151
"applies to all persons employed by public authorities, to the extent that more favourable provisions in other... Conventions are not applicable to them. The extent to which the guarantees... in this Convention shall apply... to employees (whose work is) of a highly confidential nature, shall be determined by national laws.."

Article 4 of the Convention provides for the same rights of protection from anti union discrimination as provided in Convention 98. The ILO's Committee on Freedom of Association (case no.1261 in 1984) judged that Convention 151 had been intended to complement and not to contradict or undermine the guarantees for workers in Convention 87 and therefore found that the British Government was in breach of the fundamental rights given by their ratification of Convention 87. The Government refused to take any notice of the judgement and the favourable result for the unions cannot be enforced.

The Conventions ratified by the UK

The current Conventions ratified by the UK are as follows:

Convention no.	Title of Convention
2	Unemployment 1919
5	Minimum age (industry) 1919
7	Minimum age (sea) 1920
8	Unemployment indemnity (shipwreck) 1920
10	Minimum age (agriculture) 1921
11	Right of association (agriculture) 1921
12	Workmen's compensation (agriculture) 1921
15	Minimum age (trimmers and stokers) 1921
16	Medical examination of young persons (sea) 1921
17	Workmen's compensation (accidents) 1925
19	Equality of treatment (accident compensation) 1925
21	Inspection of emigrants 1926
22	Seamen's articles of agreement 1926
23	Repatriation of seamen 1926
24	Sickness insurance (industry) 1927
25	Sickness insurance (agriculture) 1927
29	Forced labour 1930
32	Protection against accidents (dockers) 1932
35	Old age insurance (industry etc) 1933
36	Old age insurance (agriculture) 1933
37	Invalidity insurance (industry etc) 1933
38	Invalidity insurance (agriculture) 1933
39	Survivors' insurance (industry etc) 1933
40	Survivors'insurance (agriculture) 1933
42	Workmens' compensation (occupational diseases) 1934
44	Unemployment provision 1934
45	Underground work (women) 1935
50	Recruiting of indigenous workers 1936
56	Sickness insurance (sea) 1936
63	Convention concerning statistics of wages and hours of work 1938

64	Contracts of employment (indigenous workers) 1939
65	Penal sanctions (indigenous workers) 1939
68	Food and catering (ships' crews) 1946
69	Certification of ships' cooks 1946
70	Social security (seafarers) 1946
74	Certification of able seamen 1946
80	Final articles revision 1946
81	Labour inspection 1947
82	Social policy (non-metropolitan territories) 1947
83	Labour standards (non-metropolitan territories) 1947
84	Right of association (non-metropolitan territories) 1947
85	Labour inspectorates (non-metropolitan territories) 1947
86	Contracts of employment (indigenous workers) 1947
87	Freedom of association and protection of the right to organise 1948
92	Accommodation of crews (revised) 1949
97	Migration for employment (revised) 1949
98	Right to organise and collective bargaining 1949
99	Minimum wage fixing machinery (agriculture) 1951
100	Equal remuneration 1951
101	Holidays with pay (agriculture) 1952
102	Social security (minimum standards) 1952
105	Abolition of forced labour 1957
108	Seafarers' identity documents 1958
114	Fishermen's articles of agreement 1959
116	Radiation protection 1960
120	Hygiene (commerce and offices) 1964
122	Employment policy 1964
124	Medical examination of young persons (underground work) 1965
126	Accommodation of crews (fishermen) 1966
133	Accommodation of crews (supplementary provisions) 1970
135	Workers' representatives 1971
140	Paid educational leave 1974
141	Rural workers' organisations 1975
142	Human resources development 1975
144	Tripartite consultation (international labour standards) 1976
147	Merchant shipping (minimum standards) 1976
148	Working environment (air pollution, noise, and vibration) 1977
150	Labour administration 1978
151	Labour relations (public service) 1978
160	Labour statistics 1985

(i)   Codes of Practice

The use of Codes of Practice have developed since the publication of the, now removed, Industrial Relations Code of Practice in 1972. The purpose of a Code is to provide guidelines for the development of good practices in the employment relationship. Their introduction recognised that legislation could not hope to be totally comprehensive and that there was and is a requirement to voluntarily design procedures which, at the same time as being relevant for the particular work situation, incorporate the desirable qualities embodied in the Statute.

The general procedure adopted in producing a Code of Practice is that a draft is provided and circulated amongst interested parties. After these parties have given their advice and made representation, the final draft is given to the Secretary of State for approval of Parliament, before it becomes effective.

The status in law of such Codes is that, although failure to observe the provisions of the Code is not of itself likely to lead to legal proceedings before Industrial Tribunals or the Courts, they do have a legal significance in considering the case. The relevant judicial bodies are obliged to consider in their deliberations the relevant standards required by the Code or Codes in determining the rights or wrongs of the question at issue.

ACAS, in the past the MSC, the Health and Safety Commission, The Equal Opportunities Commission, the Commission for Racial Equality and the Department of Employment, under the direction of the Secretary of State, are authorised to produce Codes on a variety of matters;

(i)   The three Codes issued by ACAS are,

(a) Disciplinary Practice and Procedures, 1977.

(b) Disclosure of Information to Trade Unions for Collective Bargaining Purposes, 1977.

(c) Time off for Trade Union Duties and Activities, 1977

(ii)   The Health and Safety Commission has issued two particular Codes on,

(a) Safety Representatives and Safety Committees, 1978.

(b) Time Off for Training of Safety Representatives, 1978.

(iii)   The Codes of the Department of Employment are

(a) Industrial Relations Code of Practice 1972.

(b) Closed Shop Agreements and Arrangements, 1983.

(c) Picketing, 1980.

(iv)   The Equal Opportunities Commission Code is

— For the elimination of discrimination on the grounds of sex and marriage and for the promotion of equality of opportunity in employment, 1985.

(v) The Commission for Racial Equality Code is
- For the elimination of racial discrimination and the promotion of equality of opportunity in employment, 1983.

(vi) Before it was superceded, the Manpower Services Commission (MSC) issued a Code of Good Practice in the Employment of Disabled People.

2. INSTITUTIONS OF REGULATION

A variety of institutions have been established to administer the collective and individual employment legislation enacted in recent years. Some of these bodies administer judgements themselves, whereas others attempt to encourage the parties to resolve matters for themselves. These institutions have not totally replaced the trole of the civil courts, but they do have a significant role to play in judgements concerning statutory rights, leaving the Courts to deal with common law issues and matters which are referred to them by the statutory bodies.

(a) Industrial Tribunals

Industrial Tribunals (IT) were first established by the Industrial Training Act of 1964 to hear appeals by employers against the levies imposed on them by the Industrial Training Boards. Since that time their jurisdiction has been considerably extended to cover almost every other individual right which has been given by statute, although most cases are concerned with dismissal from the workplace. They can be regarded as, and have been referred to by the Court of Appeal as a 'type of industrial jury'.

Tribunals are organised on a regional basis and there are some 80 centres in Britain. They are used to provide a cheaper and less complex approach to statutory issues than the courts and their procedures are considerably less formal. Thus, in theory, neither side needs to be represented by a lawyer so that the costs of bringing a case is minimal and the costs of defending it are low. However, evidence suggests that more and more employers, especially, are utilising the services of a lawyer, hence costs are rising and greater legalism is creeping into the process. Unlike the courts, hearsay evidence can be accepted, leading questions can be addressed and they operate in a much less formal way throughout the proceedings.

The Industrial Tribunal panel consists of a legally qualified chair, who must have been a solicitor or barrister for at least seven years and can be full time or part time; and two lay members drawn from two panels appointed by the Secretary of State for Employment. These two lay panels are derived after consultation with organisations representing employers e.g. the CBI and organisations representing employees e.g. the TUC. Thus one panel consists of those with managerial experience and one panel consists of those with experience as employees or their representatives. Both panels are selected to ensure a spread of experience of industrial issues across the spectrum of industry, commerce and the public sector. There must normally be a representative of each side of industry sitting on a panel but the chair can sit with only one 'wing' present if both parties in the case agree.

Proof does not need to be absolute when an IT is considering a case. Tribunals are required to reach their decisions

"having regard to the equity and substantial merits of the case"

and taking into account the

"size and administration resources of the undertaking"

as the unfair dismissal clauses of the Employment Protection (Consolidation) Act 1978 states. Their main power, when finding in favour of an individual complainant, was expected to be the ability to recommend reinstatement or re-engagement but, similarly to other courts, they cannot force an employer to employ someone who the employer does not want, thus, they primarily award compensation for the individual's losses.

Procedure in Industrial Tribunals is regulated by the Industrial Tribunals (Rules of Procedure) Regulations 1985 (S.I.1985 No.16) (and in Scotland the Industrial Tribunals (Rules of Procedure) (Scotland) Regulations 1985 S.I. 1985 No.17). Witnesses are normally sworn in and the chair keeps a detailed rough-hand note of the evidence produced. The proceedings are relatively informal and an applicant may represent himself, or have a trade union official speak on his behalf or engage the services of a specialist lawyer. An employer can represent himself, call on an Employers Association official or lawyer, or engage a lawyer for himself. Legal aid is not available and costs as such are not generally awarded to the 'winner' but the Tribunal does have the power to award costs if one party is believed to have acted "frivolously or vexatiously". Tribunal hearings are generally held in public and the press may attend.

Tribunals are under no obligation to adhere to the decisions of other Tribunals faced apparently with similar evidence as each case must be considered on its individual merits. They must however follow the interpretations of the meaning of the Statutes as laid down by the superior courts.

Appeals against IT decisions are made to the Employment Appeal Tribunal (EAT) in the first instance and beyond the EAT to the Court of Appeal, and eventually, where appropriate, to the House of Lords. Some cases may even be referred to the European Court. Appeals to the EAT, in the majority of cases can only be made on a point of law, not fact. The only cases where appeals can be made on fact are against the decision of an IT to give, or refuse, a declaration in a case of unreasonable exclusion or expulsion from a trade union. Even in such cases appeals beyond EAT level can only be made on points of law. The EAT will only overturn Tribunal decisions if their conclusions were perverse; if the IT misdirected itself in law or misunderstood or misapplied the law; or where the IT exercised its discretionary powers, e.g. in assessment of compensation, based on the wrong principles.

An important feature relating to many of the individual claims to a Tribunal is that there are attempts at pre-hearing conciliation, which is carried out by conciliation officers of ACAS, who will approach both parties to try and encourage them to reach a voluntary settlement. Copies of all relevant documents including the tribunal application form (IT1) which states the reason for bringing the claim, and the employer's Notice of Appearance, which states the grounds on which the employer is contesting the claim, are sent to the ACAS Conciliation Officer. Any information given as part of this process of discussion with the help of the conciliation officer is confidential and cannot be disclosed at a later IT unless the party disclosing the information agrees. Thus, the conciliation and judgement stages are kept firmly separate.

The Conciliation Officer also possesses one very important power. Cases which have been initiated cannot be withdrawn, unless the applicant withdraws it or agrees to a settlement at the conciliation stage. No agreement which precludes a person from pursuing his claim at an Industrial Tribunal can be made by statute, except where a conciliation officer formally records an agreement made by the parties. The court of Appeal has held that where a conciliation officer has recorded the terms of an agreement by the parties on an ACAS form (COT3) and the parties have signed it, the employee is prevented from making a further complaint.

It is important that both parties should take any documents to the Tribunal hearings which might assist the decision making process. These documents will vary according to the nature of the case being considered, but are likely to include;

- the contract of employment or other documents which relate to the terms of employment.
- details of pay, e.g. pay statements or wages records, in both former and present employment, where relevant.
- documents relating to other benefits, including pensions, sick pay, travelling expenses, subsidised accommodation etc.
- documents relating to statements made by either party e.g. written warnings, relevant letters etc.

Industrial Tribunals will, in the main, announce its decision and the rationale behind the decision at the close of the hearing, but in complicated cases the decision may be deferred and given later. In every case both parties will be sent a document giving the judgement and the reason for it. Payment of any compensation or award will be made directly by the employer or trade union to the individual who is the recipient of it.

The time limit for complaints to the IT is generally 3 months, but is six months in claims of unfair exclusion or expulsion from a trade union or in cases of dismissal in connection with cases of a strike or other form of industrial action.

The Jurisdiction of Industrial Tribunals include;

(i)	Complaints of unfair dismissal.
(ii)	Applications for redundancy payments.
(iii)	References regarding written terms and conditions of employment.
(iv)	References regarding time off with pay for Safety Representatives.
(v)	References regarding time off with pay for officials on trade union duties.
(vi)	References for time off for trade union activities.
(vii)	Complaints regarding itemised pay statements.
(viii)	Complaints regarding guarantee payments.
(ix)	Complaints regarding suspension from work on medical grounds.
(x)	Complaints regarding trade union membership or non-membership.
(xi)	Complaints regarding maternity pay and maternity leave.
(xii)	Complaints under the Race Relations Act 1976.
(xiii)	Complaints under the Equal Pay Act 1970.
(xiv)	Complaints under the revised Sex Discrimination Act 1975.
(xv)	References regarding the right to be paid by the Secretary of State, debts owed by an insolvent employer.
(xvi)	Complaints by an recognised independent trade union that it was not consulted by an employer about proposed collective redundancies or a Transfer of Undertaking.
(xvii)	Complaints that a protective award ordered by a tribunal has not been paid.
(xviii)	Complaints that reasonable time off to look for work was not given in a redundancy situation.
(xix)	Complaints regarding action short of dismissal being taken by an employer.
(xx)	Complaints regarding the lack of a written statement being given where requested after dismissal.
(xxi)	References regarding time off for public duties.
(xxii)	Complaints of unreasonable exclusion or expulsion from a trade union.
(xxiii)	Appeals against 'improvement' or 'prohibition' notices issued under the Health and Safety at Work Act 1974.
(xxiv)	Complaints against non-discrimination notices issued under the Race Relations Act or Sex Discrimination Act.
(xxv)	References regarding secret ballots on employer's premises.

(b)   Employment Appeal Tribunal

The Employment Appeal Tribunal (EAT) was established by the Employment Protection Act 1975. Its function is to hear appeals from the Industrial Tribunals and some appeals from the decisions on trade union independence made by the Certification Office. Appeals are made to the EAT on points of law only, except in those cases where appeals are made against the findings of the Certification Officer and disputes over exclusions and expulsions from trade unions where consideration can also be given to factual issues. It can hold its proceedings anywhere in the country but generally sits in London or Glasgow.

The EAT consists of seven judges drawn from the High Court and the Court of Appeal, one of whom is appointed President. It also has lay members representing both sides of industry. In practice, these lay members are drawn from lists submitted to the Lord Chancellor and Secretary of State for Employment by the TUC or CBI. At each case heard there will be a judge and between two and four lay members sitting. It is thus paradoxical that a court which hears appeals generally only on points of law should contain lay members who theoretically are in a position to outvote the chair. Yet, it is argued, that their role is crucial because of their first hand knowledge of workplace relationships. Most decisions are unanimous.

At its hearings the EAT allows lay representation of the parties in making their case although in the majority of cases presentations are made by lawyers. Its deliberations are less formal than those of the higher courts. The legal aid system extends to the EAT and it has all the usual courtlike powers in requiring the attendance of witnesses, discovery of documents and punishing people for contempt of court. An appeal from the EAT goes to the Court of Appeal and from there to the House of Lords and the European Court, the EAT is, thus, bound by the decisions of these higher judicial bodies.

The majority of appeals dealt with at the EAT from 1976-1990 have been concerned with matters of unfair dismissal. The EAT laid down the guidelines of good industrial relations practice in the consideration of whether or not to dismiss an employee in *British Home Stores v Burchell* in 1980, these were:

- the employer must have genuine belief in the guilt of the employee;
- he must have reasonable grounds for the belief;
- before making a decision, he should have fully investigated the incident.

(c)   Court of Appeal

The Court of Appeal is split into two divisions
   (i)   the Civil Division,
   (ii) the Criminal Division.

The civil Division which concerns us, consists of the Master of the Rolls, who is President, and the Lord Justices of Appeal. It handles appeals on questions of legal interpretation of statutes from the judgements of the EAT in cases of employment legislation and common law. It can also hear appeals on judgements made by the Certification Officer.

(d) House of Lords

The House of Lords is the highest court of appeal in the land and produces the final definative interpretation of legislation and common law duties and obligations, although since we joined the Common Market appeals can now be made on some issues to the European Court.

(e) Advisory Conciliation and Arbitration Service (ACAS)

This organisation was initially established in 1974 as the Conciliation and Arbitration Service but was given a statutory identity and its current name of Advisory Conciliation and Arbitration Service (ACAS) in the Employment Protection Act of 1975. It is currently run by a tripartite Council composed of three nominees from the TUC; three nominees from the CBI; three independent persons; and a full time chair.

ACAS employs staff who are trained and have experience in employee relations matters generally. It is independent of government but has to produce an annual report on its activities and expenditure to the Secretary of State for Employment.

Schedule 1 Part 1 of the Employment Protection Act states;

"11.–(1) The functions of the Service and of its officers and servants shall be performed on behalf of the Crown, ... , the Service shall not be subject to directions of any kind from any Minister of the Crown as to the manner in which it is to exercise any of its functions under any enactment."

The Service exercises a comprehensive range of functions in relation to both individual and collective workplace matters. It provides the service of conciliation in claims brought by individuals to Industrial Tribunals. It also provides a variety of facilities in collective relationships in performing its general duty of

"promoting the improvement of Industrial Relations and in particular of encouraging the extension of collective bargaining and the development and, where necessary, reform of collective bargaining machinery." (Section 1 Employment Protection Act 1975.)

It tries to encourage the voluntary settlement of disputes through;

(i) *Conciliation:* this is the process whereby a third party tries to help the parties in dispute reach agreement. The conciliator attempts to help the parties discover points of agreement and the points of disagreement. By bringing a fresh mind to the dispute he attempts to get the parties to see 'the wood for the trees' and to keep them negotiating, to encourage them to reach their own mutually acceptable agreement. He works with them sometimes separately and sometimes together and attempts to merely help them clarify matters and work towards their solution, not to be too proactive in that solution.

(ii) *Arbitration:* this occurs when the parties to a dispute, having used all other available procedures open to them, including conciliation, recognise that their differences are so great that they need a third party to examine the evidence and provide them with a solution which they will normally agree to accept. There are two forms of arbitration in use;

(a) what could be termed 'split the difference' arbitration where the arbitrator suggests a solution which is somewhere in between the union's last demand and the management's last offer.

(b) what can be termed 'pendulum arbitration' (or flip-flop or last offer arbitration) where the arbitrator, with the pre-agreement of the parties, makes his judgement based either on the last offer or last demand position. In other words, one side wins and the other side looses.

(iii) *Mediation:* this process is somewhere between conciliation and arbitration. In mediation the third party tends to be more prescriptive than in conciliation but, although he provides a settlement formula, the parties themselves have to devise the fine detail of the agreement. This device is seldom used in the UK.

(iv) *Inquiry:* this is an attempt by third parties to establish the facts about a dispute which has occurred; to analyse the circumstances that have led to it; and to make a report that will lead to a settlement if one has not been found or, at least, to provide sufficient data and insight to prevent a dispute recurring.

In addition to the above services ACAS also offers an Advisory service to employers, employees and their representatives on any employment contract matter. It issues a range of advisory booklets on particular topics e.g. labour turnover, payment systems, communications etc. It also issues Codes of Practice, where requested to do so.

(f) Central Arbitration Committee (CAC)

The Central Arbitration Committee was established by the Employment Protection Act of 1975 and is a permanent body of arbitration, which, although financed by the Government is wholly independent of government influence. The CAC, although independent of ACAS, is served by ACAS staff. The Committee consists of a chair and members appointed by the Secretary of State for Employment after consultation with ACAS. The chair is a lawyer and the members, who are listed in two panels have academic or practical experience of industrial relations. The Committee can have a voluntary jurisdiction to arbitrate in cases referred to it by ACAS, with the agreement of the parties concerned, but it also has special jurisdictions under Statute and in these instances, its services can be invoked unilaterally by one party in a dispute.

These jurisdictions generally concern collective disputes and include;

— disputes relating to disclosure of information for collective bargaining purposes;
— sex discrimination in collective agreements and pay structures;
— and references under the Equal Pay Act 1970.

The Committee is empowered to regulate its own procedures, but it has no power to compel the attendance of witnesses, to take evidence under oath or to order the discovery of documents. The general practice is that the parties present written evidence to the Committee in advance of hearings and this data is clarified at the hearings themselves. The decisions on statutory matters made by the CAC are statutorily binding on the parties. Decisions are published, except where the Committee is handling a case of voluntary arbitration.

(g) The Certification Officer (CO)

The Certification officer is an independent statutory officer appointed in 1975 by the Employment Protection Act. A number of the functions now carried out by the CO were previously exercised by the Registrar of Friendly Societies. His main functions relate to the internal affairs of trade unions and employers' associations.

His is the sole jurisdiction in determining whether a trade union should be granted a Certificate of Independence, although a trade union has the right of appeal to the EAT. The criteria which the CO uses to determine independence include; history, membership base, organisation and structure, finance, employer provided facilities, and collective bargaining record. Only an independent trade union, as defined in the Employment Protection Act 1975, can avail itself of many of the statutory benefits, e.g. to demand information prior to redundancies and transfers of undertakings, and information for collective bargaining purposes.

The CO, in addition,

— maintains the lists of trade unions and employer's associations;
— receives financial returns from trade unions and employer's associations;
— hears complaints about the setting up, continuance and operation of trade union political funds;
— hears complaints about trade union mergers under the Trade Unions (Amalgamations) etc. Act 1964;
— hears complaints about ballots for the union's principal executive committee;
— and maintains the funds for reimbursing certain costs of trade unions in conducting ballots.

(h) The Equal Opportunities Commission (EOC)

The Equal Opportunities Commission was established by the Sex Discrimination Act 1975. It is independent of government but is funded by it. It consists of a number of Commissioners appointed by the Home Secretary. The Act makes discrimination against men or women, or discrimination on the grounds of marital status, unlawful in the employment situation.

The general duties of the EOC are;

— to work towards the elimination of discrimination;
— to promote equality of opportunity between women and men;
— to monitor and keep under review the operation of the Sex Discrimination Act;
— and to monitor and keep under review the Equal Pay Act.

In relation to these duties, its powers are to promote research and general awareness of the social and economic advantages of equal opportunity and to improve the societal climate to reduce the remaining barriers to foster and enhance opportunities for all.

The main powers of the EOC in enforcing the anti-discrimination laws include the right to carry out investigations and in so doing to require the production of documents and the giving of evidence. If, as a result of that investigation, the Commission is satisfied that there has been a breach of the law then it may issue a 'non discrimination notice' ordering the party to desist from the practice of direct or indirect discrimination. Employers have the right of appeal against such notices to an Industrial Tribunal.

This notice is retained on a register so that, if the employer continues to discriminate, the EOC may apply for an injunction against the offender in a County Court, providing that an Industrial Tribunal is satisfied that the act is unlawful.

The Commission is also empowered to give advice on individual problems and legal assistance in presenting cases to an IT or in Court proceedings. In most cases the EOC succeeds with informal discussions and threats that it will use its statutory powers. In 1985 it issued a Code of Practice on equality of Treatment.

(i) Commission for Racial Equality (CRE)

The CRE was established by the Race Relations Act of 1976 and replaced the former Race Relations Board and Community Relations Commission. The statutory duties and powers of the CRE are identical to those of the EOC. Over its life span it has tended to have initiated more formal investigations than the EOC. However, like the EOC it prefers to work through a process of persuasion and informal discussion to try and stamp out discrimination in the workplace. In 1985 it too issued a Code of Practice on Equality of Treatment.

(j) Health and Safety Commission

This Commission was established by the Health and Safety at Work etc. Act 1974. It consists of a full-time independent chair and nine part time commissioners, three nominated by the TUC, three by the CBI, two from the local authorities and an independent member. It is responsible to the Secretary of State for Employment and must follow directions from him.

The Commission has taken over responsibility for most occupational health and safety matters. It has a number of duties which include the following;
- To assist and encourage people to further the general purposes of the HASAWA;
- to make arrangements for, and encourage research into occupational health and safety;
- to promote training and the sharing of information relevant to health and safety matters;
- to itself act as an information and advisory service;
- to investigate the need for specific regulations under the Act and make recommendations as to their content and form;
- to draft and issue Codes of Practice with the approval of the Secretary of State.

In carrying out these duties the Commission has considerable powers to direct enquiries and investigations, to appoint staff and to publish information. Whilst control of broad national policy is the function of the Commission, the enforcement of the Acts and the administration of safety standards is the task of the Health and Safety Executive.

In its initiating role the Commission has outlined a number of recommendations which it advises organisations to follow in satisfying all parties that they are doing everything possible to control risks in the working environment. These include;

(a) The employer has drafted and published a comprehensive policy on health and safety;
(b) the appropriate resources are available for monitoring health and safety;
(c) management is trained and is competent in handling health and safety issues;
(d) specialist advice is available in house on health and safety;
(e) there is active involvement of any recognised trade unions in the health and safety system;
(f) employees, in general, have been trained and have a positive committment to their own and their colleagues health and safety;
(g) the organisation can demonstrate a satisfactory recent record on safety and ill health.

If this committment is evident in organisations the Commission believes that risks would inevitably be reduced and therefore the Health and Safety Executive could reduce its monitoring role and inspectors could be better utilised in providing advice and guidance.

(k) Health and Safety Executive

This organisation, answerable to the Health and Safety Commission, was created by the Health and Safety at Work etc. Act 1974, and consists of a director and two deputies, in addition to the staff it controls. It is an amalgam of the independent inspectorates which existed under previous legislation e.g. the Factories Inspectorate and the Mines and Quarries Inspectorate. The health and safety inspectors it appoints have powers to enforce the safety and health legislation and the required standards laid down. Inspectors are entitled to enter any premises at any time of the day or night to ensure that all regulations are being adhered to, they are also able to take samples of any substance for investigation. The main elements of enforcement open to the inspectorate, beyond exhortation, are 'improvement' or 'prohibition' notices which can be served when inspectors consider the law has been broken or there is danger to health or safety. Employers may appeal against these notices to an Industrial Tribunal. Non compliance with the notices can lead to prosecution in the civil courts and the imposition of fines or more severe sentences including imprisonment. The Executive is also responsible for issuing Codes of Practice under the HASAWA e.g. on Safety Representatives and Safety Committees and Time Off for the Training of Safety Representatives.

3. FUNDAMENTAL LEGAL CONCEPTS

(a) Contract

The Contract of Employment is of fundamental importance in the employer/employee relationship. Contracts are agreements with legal consequences and are in essence voluntary transactions which happen because the parties choose to enter into them.

Contracts can be made informally and are as valid when entered into verbally as when they are formally written down. It is presumed that contracts are made by parties with equal bargaining power, free to decide on the terms of agreement — although this may not be the case with employment contracts. For the formation of a valid contract the following elements must be present:

1. *Agreement;* this is demonstrated by offer and acceptance. The agreement must be free from any stipulations which render it conditional e.g. if an employee accepts a job offer but makes it conditional on th ability to find suitable accommodation, or an employer offers a job conditionally on obtaining suitable references.

2. *Consideration;* this can be perceived as the economic value of the relationship for example the promise of a certain level of remuneration in return for a particular level of work.

3. *Intention* to create legal relations; the parties to the contract must have expressly or implicitly intended that the contract should be legally binding. This is usually presumed when a contract of employment is concluded, but is statutorily not the case when a collective bargaining contract is made unless we expressly make it legally binding.

4. *Contractual capacity* in each of the parties; an individual generally has the capacity to enter into any contract he wants. He loses this capacity only if he is under the influence of drink or drugs or if he suffers from certain types of mental illness. Capacity will exist in the employment contract as long as the party agreeing to the contract on behalf of the employer is authorised to make that contract.

5. No mitigating factors such as, duress, undue influence, misrepresentation, mistake or illegality; both parties to the agreement must *freely consent* to the terms of the contract and the proposed contract must be legal in its object and the manner in which it is performed, e.g. a contract will be automatically invalid if the method of payment is chosen to deliberately defraud the tax authorities.

(b) Contract of service or contract for services?

A person employed by an organisation can either be employed by a contract of services i.e. as an employee as defined in Section 30 of TULRA 1974, or a contract for services i.e. as an independent contractor or a labour only sub contractor. It is an important distinction to make, because only those employed under a contract of service are granted the statutory legal right to,

— protection against unfair dismissal
— statutory redundancy pay
— minimum periods of notice
— a written statement of main terms and conditions of employment etc.

It is also important in considering entitlement to various state benefits, thus, for example, only employees are entitled to claim sickness and unemployment benefit.

A number of cases have considered the relationship between the two contractual devices, because of the importance of the designation of employee in obtaining statutory rights. Three main tests have been used by the courts in examining the relationship:

(i) The Control Test;

The initial test derived by the courts was called the 'control' test. This asks whether the person alleged to be the employer, both in respect to the work done, i.e. what to do, how to do it, and also in determining the required standard of performance. If the employer controls these things then the contract was determined as a contract of service, if not then the individual was an independent contractor. The difficulty was that the test was not completely satisfactory in the modern employment relationship in large scale organisations. People like doctors, nurses and lawyers are now employed in both public and private sector enterprises and their work, because of its specialism is not as subject to control as less specialised tasks. In order to cope with this problem the courts developed the second test.

(ii) The Organisation or Integration Test;

This test was used to explain the professional's employment within organisations and is decided on whether the individual is integrated within the organisation. Consequently, if a person is employed as part of the business and the work is an integral and essential part of the business in that the business would not exist without it, the court may then judge the person as an employee. This test did not cover all eventualities, therefore a third test was developed.

(iii) The Multiple or Economic Reality Test;

This is the most comprehensive test to date and takes into account both the previous tests and considers also the other circumstances of the relationship between the parties. It thus includes factors of control and the right to command; the right of selection and dismissal; whether the work is done as an integral part of the business; whether the worker is economically independent; and whether the other terms and conditions of employment are consistent with the contract of employment relationship. If the group of factors indicate that the relationship is on of a contract of service then the individual will be considered to be an employee and entitled to all the benefits that statute gives for this relationship.

(c) Dismissal

This means that the employee has had his contract of employment terminated by the employer with or without notice. It can also refer to the non renewal of a fixed term contract and also applies to the situation where, because of the employer's conduct the individual himself terminates the contract because mutual trust has broken down, with or without notice i.e. constructive dismissal.

(d) Unfair Dismissal

This was first introduced as a concept in the 1971 Industrial Relations Act and was retained in subsequent legislation. Its true meaning was best described by Justice Phillips in *W. Devis and Sons Ltd. v Atkins* in 1986 (ICR,196), when he stated,

> "It is important to note... that the expression 'unfair dismissal' is in no sense a commonsense expression capable of being understood by the man in the street, which at first sight one may think it is. In fact, under the Act, it is narrowly and, to some extent, arbitrarily defined. ... it is a form of words which could be translated as being equivalent to dismissal 'contrary to Statute' and to which the label 'unfair dismissal' has been given."

(e) Torts

The law of economic torts is concerned with 'wrongs'. They are deeds which result in civil actions being brought by the person or organisation harmed. The most common torts in industrial relations are the torts of inducing breach of contract, intimidation, conspiracy and interference, tresspass and public and private nuisance.

(f) Express Terms

These are where the worker and the employer have openly stated, in either written or oral form, the terms which comprise the contract of employment e.g. relating to pay, hours of work, pensions, sick pay, holidays etc.

(g) Implied Terms.

Where the parties do not refer to a particular contingency, trade usage and custom and practice may give rise to the implication of terms. Judges may imply terms which are necessary to give 'business efficacy' to the contract or where the term is one which would have automatically have been accepted by both parties if their attention had been drawn to it or other terms which the judges think is reasonable under the particular circumstances of the contract.

(h) Trade Unions

The definition of trade unions is laid down in the Trade Union and Labour Relations Act 1974 Section 28 as follows;

> "...'trade union' means an organisation... which either
> (a) consists wholly or mainly of workers of one or more descriptions and is an organisation whose principal purposes include the regulation of relationships between workers... and employers or employers' organisations, or
> (b) consists wholly or mainly of
> (1) constituent or affiliated organisations which fulfil the conditions specified above.... or
> (2) representatives of such... organisations."

(i) Independent Trade Union;

This is defined in the Trade Union and Labour Relations Act 1974 in section 30 as,

> "a trade union which
> (a) is not under the domination or control of any employer... and
> (b) is not liable to any interference by an employer..."

(j) Recognition;

This concept is defined in the Employment Protection Act 1975 in Section 126 as follows;

"recognition in relation to a trade union, means the recognition of the union by the employer, or two or more associated employers, to any extent, for the purpose of collective bargaining ..."

(k) Definition of a Trade Dispute

The basic definition is laid down in the Trade Union and Labour Relations Act 1974 Section 29, as amended by the Employment Act 1982 as;

"a dispute between workers and their employer which is concerned wholly or mainly with one or more of the following...
(a) issues and conditions of employment, or the physical conditions in which any workers are required to work;
(b) engagement or non engagement or termination, or suspension of employment or the duties of employment, of one or more workers;
(c) allocation of work......;
(d) matters of discipline;
(e) the membership and non membership of a trade union...;
(f) facilities for the officials of trade unions; and
(g) machinery for negotiation or consultation and other procedures, ...
including the recognition by employers or employers' associations of the right of a trade union to represent workers in any such negotiation or consultation or in the carrying out of any such procedures..."

(l) Secondary Action

This is defined in the Employment Act 1980 Section 17, as a situation where a person;

"(a) induces another to break a contract of employment or induces another to interfere with its performance, or
(b) threatens that a contract of employment under which he or another is employed will be broken or its performance interfered with, or that he will induce another to break a contract of employment or to interfere with its performance if the employer under the contract of employment is not a party to the trade dispute."

CHAPTER NINE

KEY ASPECTS OF CURRENT LEGISLATION

Statutory framework within which management operates:

The management of the human resource is an increasingly specialised activity. Over the last thirty years successive Governments have passed Statutes which influence the relationship between employers and employees. Whilst some would argue that this legislation has made the business of hiring, controlling and firing employees increasingly difficult, it would be more realistic to consider that the legislation, rather than being a hindrance, does no more than provide a framework for employment that emphasises the fairness and equity of treatment which all good managers should adopt in their dealings with employees. If you operate on the principle:

"do not treat your subordinates any differently than you yourself would expect to be treated by your superiors"

then 99% of the time you will not be breaching any Statutes.

The extent of the legal framework which relates to employment is a specialised study in itself. In this chapter we will only give a broad overview and describe the main points of each Act. For a more detailed examination of the intricacies of the law you will need to consult a more specialist text.

The major statutes

The primary legislation of which you will need a working knowledge can be listed in approximate date order as follows;

1. Disabled Persons (Employment) Acts 1944-1958
2. Factories Act 1961
3. Offices Shops and Railway Premises Act 1963
4. Employer's Liability (Compulsory Insurance) Act 1969
5. Equal Pay Act 1970
6. Fire Precautions Act 1971
7. Rehabilitation of Offenders Act 1974
8. Health and Safety at Work etc. Act 1974
9. Trade Union and Labour Relations Acts 1974 and 1976
10. Employment Protection Act 1975
11. Sex Discrimination Act 1975
12. Race Relations Act 1976
13. Employment Protection (Consolidation) Act 1978
14. Employment Act 1980
15. Transfer of Undertakings (Protection of Employment) Regulations 1981

16. Employment Act 1982
17. Trade Union Act 1984
18. Data Protection Act 1984
19. Wages Act 1986
20. Employment Act 1988
21. Access to Medical Reports Act 1988
22. Employment Act 1989
23. Employment Act 1990

1. DISABLED PERSONS (EMPLOYMENT) ACTS 1944/1958

This is one of the oldest pieces of anti-discrimination legislation. The objective of the Act was to help disabled employees to find work and to secure better employment. The Act stipulates that an employer with more than 20 employees must allot at least 3% of posts to registered disabled workers. It also specifies that some jobs,such as lift and car park attendants, should be reserved for the disabled. Records must be maintained of the numbers employed, their names, and their disablement number.

The definition of a disabled person given in the Act is;

> "a person who on account of disease, injury or congenital deformity is substantially handicapped in obtaining or keeping employment or in undertaking work on his own account, of a kind, which apart from that disease, injury or deformity, should be suited to his experience, age or qualifications."

The legislation confers no rights on the individuals themselves, it is only the disabled as a group, who are given some protection. The sanction for failing to fulfil the quota, where an exemption certificate does not lift the obligation, is prosecution, however such cases are very rare and the Act is recognised to be difficult to enforce. If an employer is not up to quota, he does not have to discharge 'fit' people but, when a vacancy does occur, he should engage a disabled person. Records must be kept of people employed under permits issued to enable employers to fill current vacancies if there are no suitably qualified disabled people available.

In November 1974 the Manpower Services Commission published a "Code of Good Practice on the Employment of Disabled People" which makes suggestions to ensure that all those who are disabled receive their share of the available employment opportunities. The code is purely a guidance document and the disabled have no redress to an Industrial Tribunal or other judicial body as individual appellents. The Code's approach is therefore encouragement and it provides employers with:

"a readily available means of determining how best to put their intentions into practice".

It attempts to provide encouragement for all disabled people, not just the registered.

The Code is laid out in two parts. The first part is aimed at those managers responsible for policy decisions and recommends specific policy objectives for the employment of the disabled. Regulations in the form of 'The Companies Directors' Report (Employment of Disabled Persons) Regulations' 1980 has placed a duty on all companies employing more than 250 people, to state in their Directors' Report company policy on the employment of the disabled.

The statement should include policy on;

— how to give full and fair consideration to the disabled who apply for jobs, taking into account their individual aptitudes and abilities;
— how to continue the employment of employees who become disabled while working for the company, and what training arrangements could be made for them;
— generally, how to develop the training, career, development and promotion possibilities of the disabled.

The second part of the Code is aimed at those responsible for putting the organisations policy into practice and covers the following areas;

— the legal requirements regarding the employment of the disabled;
— what the different characteristics of disabled people mean to employers;
— an examination of some employer concerns in recruiting the disabled;
— good practice in relation to training and promotion treatment;
— options for employees who become disabled;
— the role of employer and employee representatives on practices and procedures regarding the disabled;
— how to coordinate policy;
— sources of financial and other help, information and advice on the employment of disabled people.

2.   FACTORIES ACT 1961.

The Factories Act 1961 covers health, safety and welfare; the hours of work of young persons; and other miscellaneous provisions.

KEY ASPECTS OF CURRENT LEGISLATION

(a)   Health

(i)   Temperature — at least 16 degrees Centigrade after one hour; a thermometer must be provided and maintained in a workroom where work is done sitting and does not involve any serious physical effort. The Act does not specify any maximum temperature.

(ii)   Cleanliness — dirt and refuse must be removed daily; floors must be cleaned weekly; walls must be washed and whitewashed at least every 14 months; painting must take place every 7 years.

(iii) Ventilation — fresh air must circulate and workers must be protected from dirt and fumes.

(iv)   Overcrowding — each person must have 400 cubic feet of space and there must be a notice in each workroom specifying the maximum numbers who can be employed there unless the Inspectorate specify otherwise.

(b)   Safety

(i)   Accidents — the   Reporting of Injuries, Diseases and Dangerous Occurances Regulations (RIDDOR) unify all reporting arrangements for injuries causing more than three days absence and the immediate notification of all fatalities.

(ii)   Industrial Disease — also covered by the RIDDO Regulations.

(iii) Fencing — (or guards) to protect against moving machinery, pits or vessels containing dangerous liquids. How safe is safe? The duty to fence is absolute. One cannot use the words, as well as possible, conducive with use; if guarding moving machines means the machine cannot be used commercially, that is unfortunate.

(iv)   Drainage — all floors which are liable to be wet must be efficiently drained.

(v)   Inspection — of joists, lifts, chains, ropes or lifting tackle — every six months.
        — of cranes, every 14 months
        — of fire alarms, every 3 months.

(c)   Welfare

Employers must provide;
— drinking water
— washing facilities, including soap and towels;
— accommodation for outside clothes;
— a first aid box and one further box for every 150 employees. Where there are more than 50 employees, the box must be in charge of someone experienced in first aid;

— seating must also be provided, where necessary and practicable.

(d)   Employment of Women and Young Persons

(i)   **No woman or young person, under the age of 18, may clean any part of a moving machine;**

(ii)   A young person must be instructed in the dangers of a machine before that person is allowed to use it;

(iii)   Hours of work;
- Young persons can only work a maximum of 48 hours per week,
- No young person may work more than 9 hours per day,
- Young persons of 16-18 years of age must not work overtime of more than 100 hours per year or work overtime in more than 25 weeks per annum,
- Young persons (16-18) must not work nightshift without permission.

(iv)   Female young persons may not be employed in those parts of a factory in which the following processes are carried out:
- in certain processes involving the use of lead or zinc,
- in mixing or pasting in connection with the manufacture or repair of electric accumulators,
- in the cleaning of workrooms in which the above processes are being carried out.

(e)   General

(i)   The Inspectorate have the power to inspect any part of the factory by day and by night. They may ask for registers, may question any member of staff and may take samples for analysis.

(ii)   Notices to be posted:
(a) Abstract of the Factories Act;
(b) Abstract of any statutory Regulations;
(c) Notice in each workroom showing the maximum number of employees permitted to work there;
(d) Notice of the name of the person in charge of the First aid box;
(e) Notice of the addresses of the local Inspectorate and company doctor;
(f) Notice showing the hours of work and prescribed meal times of women and young persons;
(g) Notice, where relevant, specifying the clock by which the hours of work of (f) are to be prescribed;
(h) Cautionary placards under the regulations of certain processes;
(i) Placards as to the recommended treatment of electric shock, if voltage is above 125 AC or 250 DC;
(j) Notice in sanitary conveniences used by persons handling food, requesting them to wash their hands (Food Hygiene Regulations 1960);

(iii)   A General Register must also be kept with particulars of:
    (a) Young persons employed;
    (b) Washing, whitewashing and painting;
    (c) Every accident and industrial disease reported under RIDDOR;
    (d) Any exemption from the clauses of the Act allowed;
    (e) Inspection of hoists, lifts etc.

3.   OFFICES, SHOPS AND RAILWAY PREMISES ACT 1963

This Act broadly mirrors the provisions of the Factories Act —

- all furniture, furnishings and fittings shall be kept in a clean state;
- there must be no overcrowding — each person in a room shall have at least 40 square ft of floor space. (This does not apply in rooms to which the public have access).
- the temperature must be at least 16 degrees Celcius (after 1 hour) and a thermometer must be conspicuously displayed;
- sufficient ventilation for every room;
- adequate lighting;
- washing facilities including hot and cold running water and soap and towels;
- toilet facilities for each sex;
- accommodation for outside clothes;
- if employees in shops eat their meals on the premises, suitable facilities must be provided;
- fire alarm and means of escape;
- floors, passages and stairs must be properly maintained;
- first aid box must be provided and where there are more than 150 employees at one time, there must be more than one box;
- seating facilities must be provided.

4.   EMPLOYERS LIABILITY (COMPULSORY INSURANCE) ACT 1969

This Act aims to prevent an employee, who is owed compensation for injuries he has suffered while at work, from being unable to claim compensation due to the insolvency of the employer. Every employer must insure against liability for bodily injury or disease sustained by an employee in the course of his employment — failure to do so could lead to a £500 fine. Copies of the insurance contract must be displayed — failure to do so can lead to a fine of up to £200. Copies must also be sent to the Health and Safety Executive who enforce the Act. An offence is committed by any responsible person in the organisation who consents to, or connives at, violating the Act's provisions.

5. EQUAL PAY ACT 1970 – as amended by the Equal Pay (Amendment) Regulations 1983 (SI 1983 No.1794).

This Act aims to eliminate discrimination on the grounds of sex (for both men and women) in regard to pay and terms and conditions of employment. The Act came into effect on 31st December 1975 and was amended by the Regulations due to a judgement against the UK in the European Court of Justice in 1982 under the EEC 1975 Equal Pay Directive.

(a) Section 1 provides for the equal treatment of men and women when they are engaged in the same or broadly similar work, or where a woman's job has been rated as equivalent to a man's job through job evaluation, although the nature of the job is different; or where the work is considered to be of equal value to that of a man or woman although the work may be completely different. The comparisons used can be, for example, effort, skill, and decision making. Industrial Tribunals in considering cases may call a 'independent expert' appointed by ACAS to determine the equality of value of the work.

(b) Section 2 places the onus of proof on the employer to show, in cases of dispute, that the differences in terms and conditions of employment between a man and a woman claiming equal treatment are due to material differences between her case and his.

(c) Section 3 refers to collective agreements; if these contain discriminatory clauses they may be referred to ACAS.

(d) The woman may draw comparisons with men or with men's jobs only where the men in question are employed by her employer or by an associate employer. However, comparisons may be drawn with men in another establishment, if the terms and conditions of employment are common to the two establishments.

(e) Exceptions
– no equal treatment is required to the extent that women may enjoy special terms and conditions of employment when it comes to the birth or expected birth of a child.

Where an individual feels that the Act is not being complied with, *he or she* can complain to an Industrial Tribunal.

6. FIRE PRECAUTIONS ACT 1971

The Act governs fire safety in all places of work. Fire safety is now supervised by the fire authorities who control the issue of fire certificates. It is an offence to use premises as a place of work without a fire certificate, if Regulations have been passed bringing these premises into coverage of the Act. Fines can be up to £400 and up to two years imprisonment.

KEY ASPECTS OF CURRENT LEGISLATION

(a)Premises affected

The following premises are covered by the Act;
- factories, offices and shops;
- railway premises.

(b)Exemptions

For small factories, offices, shops etc. where;
- less than 20 people are employed (unless they are part of a large complex which overall employs more than 20.
- less than 10 people work above ground floor level (unless it is part of a larger complex).

If premises are outside of the Act's coverage, they will still have to comply with other regulations laying down minimum fire precautions, even though no fire certificate is required (under the Fire Precautions Non-certified Factory, Office, etc. Regulations 1976 SI No.2010).
These are:

(a)Doors from the building, or from any room where more than 10 people are employed must open outwards.
(b)Fire escape doors and windows must be clearly marked and must be easily opened, and passageways must be kept clear.
(c)Fire fighting equipment must be readily available for use.

(c) Certificates

Applications for new fire certificates are made to the fire authority. This will involve giving details of the use of premises, together with a plan, following which the fire authority will inspect to see if the fire precautions are as good as circumstances reasonably require.

The certificate will specify:

- the use of the premises which it covers;
- means of escape;
- ways by which the means of escape should be kept available;
- fire fighting equipment;
- fire alarm systems;
- other requirements deemed necessary.

Penalties, for not having an appropriate certificate or contravening fire certificates, are up to £400 fine and/or two years' imprisonment. Any company director, manager or secretary will also face these penalties, if the offence is done with their consent or connivance.

(d)   Enforcement

Fire authorities appoint inspectors who, in enforcing the Act, have the power to:

— enter and inspect premises;
— make necessary enquiries;
— require production of a fire certificate.

(e)   Special Premises

Special premises, where processes and the use of certain chemical compounds have a particularly high level of fire risk, are looked after by the Health and Safety Executive, who supervise them and issue fire certificates under the Fire Certificate (Special Premises) Regulations 1976 (SI 1976 No.2003).

7.   REHABILITATION OF OFFENDERS ACT 1974

The purpose of this act is to allow offenders, who have not been reconvicted of any offence for a period of time, to apply for jobs and take up job offers without the embarrassment of having to admit to past convictions. Thus, after a period of time from the date of conviction, providing another serious offence is not committed, the conviction can be counted as "spent" and, except in certain, specified cases, the individual cannot be forced to disclose that conviction, nor can it be used to dismiss the employee. Some sentences never become spent — life sentences of imprisonment, sentences of preventative detention and prison sentences of more than 30 months.

Exempted occupations and professions

Persons employed or seeking employment in any of the following categories are not at liberty to conceal details of spent convictions under Statutory Instrument 1975 No.1023, the Rehabilitation of Offenders Act 1974 (Exceptions) Order:

— registered teacher (in Scotland)
— medical practitioner
— barrister, advocate, solicitor
— chartered accountant
— certified accountant
— dentist, dental hygienist, dental auxiliary

— veterinary surgeon
— pharmaceutical chemist
— any profession to which the Professions Supplementary to Medicine Act 1960 applies
— certain judicial, local authority and education posts.

8.   HEALTH AND SAFETY AT WORK, etc. ACT 1974

Introduction

Employers' duties under the previous legislation, e.g. Factories Act 1961, Offices, Shops and Railway premises Act 1963 etc. continue. The aim of the 1974 legislation was to rationalise the situation pertaining to health and safety in the workplace.

The most important elements occur in the first 26 sections and the prevailing message in the Act is total involvement of all within the work situation. The intention was to alter the emphasis of the law from compensation after injury to one of agreeing and enforcing standards relevant to the particular workplace.

Prior to the Act, legislation was piecemeal. Enforcement machinery differed and also the defences which were available against an ultimate criminal sanction. One of the reasons for the generality of the legislation in 1974 was the fact that the more narrowly defined a legal duty, the more narrowly that duty will operate, and the more opportunity there will be for legal loopholes. Excessive reliance on legal technicalities was believed to be antithesis of true true safety.

(a)   Purposes of 1974 Act

1. Covers the whole working environment, without the need to differentiate between different premises.

2. Produce generalised definitions of those duties of the widest possible scope; details will be filled in by regulations issued under the Act.

3. The Act seeks to involve everyone — the employer and the employee who has to take the reasonable care for his own safety and also that of his colleagues and other persons.

4. Seeks to improve enforcement machinery, e.g. Improvement and Prohibition notices.

(b)   General Duties

It is simply provided in the Act;

> "it shall be the duty of every employer to ensure as far as is reasonably practicable the Health, Safety and Welfare of his employees".

Without prejudice to this general duty, the section then goes on to apply it to more specific functions, but again in a generalised form. Duty extends to;

> "provision and maintenance of plant and systems of work and to arrangements ensuring safety and absence of risks to health in connection with use, storage, handling and transport of articles and substances".

and

> "taking steps for the provision of such information, instruction, training and supervision which is necessary to ensure the safety and health at work of his employees".

He must

> "maintain any place of work... in such condition that it is safe and without risks to health and provide means of access to and exit from it that are safe and without such risks".

Finally, he must provide a working environment that is safe and adequate as regards facilities.

Systems of work are well defined in Common Law. It means the whole organisation of the job, management and layout.

Courts will always prefer to see action rather than excuses. Lack of money in the majority of cases, for example, will not be considered an acceptable justification for any legislative breaches. Also, the duty is there to require the employer to take reasonable steps to train the employees. The employer cannot blame the employees or their union if he has failed to take these steps. The Act requires the employee to cooperate with the employer.

(c)   Manufacturers and Suppliers

The Act establishes a duty on all those who manufacture, supply or import equipment and substances to ensure that safety and health standards are not breached and information on operation or use is supplied. This does not mean that the employer can rely on this; he is required to check himself.

However, in some cases the manufacturer can be prosecuted, not the employer, providing the employer has used the equipment or product in the way that the original manufacturer intended.

(d)   Self Employed

There are obligations on the self employed

"It shall be the duty of every self employed person as of every employer to conduct his undertaking in such a way as to ensure that it is, ..., free from risks to the health and safety both of himself and other persons who may be affected by it".

(e)   Controllers of Premises

Under the Act the controllers of premises must take reasonably practicable steps to protect the health and safety of people who are employed on or attend those premises.

(f)   Enforcement

The Act provided new, more direct, enforcement powers for the Inspectorate.

(i)   Improvement Notices; Section 21 provides for the use of Improvement Notices where the inspector feels that there is a contravention of a statutory provision, or a safety practice which could lead to a hazard. The notice will require the employer to remedy the contravention within a specified period — not less than 21 days. The machine concerned can be used during this period.
(ii)   Prohibition Notices; Where an inspector is of the opinion that there could be serious injury he may issue a Prohibition Notice whereby the activity must cease until the matter has been remedied.

Appeals against these notices can be made to an Industrial Tribunal within 21 days of the issue of the notice. The industrial Tribunal (Improvement and Prohibition Notices Appeals) Regulations of 1974 lay down the procedure to be followed.

Fines for failure to comply with Prohibition and Improvement Notices accrue on a daily basis.

(g)   Information

An employer is required to publicise certain information;

— a written statement of his general policy and attitudes to safety and health to each employee;
— information to persons who are not his employees but are liable to be affected;
— relevant warning notices
— information regarding training required and available.

(h)   Safety Representatives and Safety Committees

The Secretary of State has through Regulations provided for the appointment of safety representatives from amongst the employees. (Safety Representatives and Safety Committee Regulations 1977.) These safety representatives have a number of functions which they are entitled to perform and they are entitled to be paid while performing them;

— to investigate potential hazards and dangerous occurrences at the workplace;
— to examine the causes of accidents in the workplace;
— to investigate complaints by an employee he represents relating to safety, health and welfare at work;
— to make representation to the employer on such matters;
— to carry out inspections at least once every 3 months;
— to represent the employees in consultations at the workplace with the Inspectorate;
— to receive information from the Inspectorate;
— to attend meetings of the Safety Committee.

The Regulations also allow for the establishment of a Safety Committee if two safety representatives request one in writing. The Health and Safety Executive have issued a Code of Practice on Safety Representatives and Safety Committees.

(i)   Regulations

The general duties of the Act are supplemented by Regulations which modify and extend the scope of the legislation. The regulations issued include

— the Health and Safety (First Aid) Regulations 1981
— the Reporting of Injuries, Diseases and Dangerous Occurrences Regulations 1985

(j)   Codes of Practice

Regulations will only be made where Codes of Practice are felt to be inadequate or inappropriate. Consultation with those industries to be influenced will take place before codes are finally issued.

9. TRADE UNION AND LABOUR RELATIONS ACTS 1974/76

The Act was passed in 1974 and amended in 1976 but it has subsequently had its provisions modified by the Employment Acts of the 1980s.

(a) Its main purposes were to repeal the Industrial Relations Act of 1971 and to restore the status of trade unions and employers' associations to the pre 1971 position. The Act defines a trade union as follows (s 28(1));

"an organisation (whether permanent or temporary) which either
(a) consists wholly or mainly of workers of one or more descriptions and is an organisation whose principal purposes include the regulation of relations between workers of that description or those descriptions and employers or employers' associations; or..."

The Act defines an Employers' Association as (s 28(2));

"an organisation (whether permanent or temporary) which either
(a) consists wholly or mainly of employers or individual proprietors of one or more descriptions and is an organisation whose principal purposes include the regulation of relations between employers of that description or those descriptions and workers or trade unions; or..."

(b) Trade unions are imbued with certain corporate features in Section 2, thus;

— they are capable of entering into contracts;
— they are capable of suing or being sued in their own name;
— criminal proceedings can be brought against them;
— all trade union property must be vested in trustees who hold the property in trust for the union;
— court judgements, orders or awards are enforceable against the trust property.

(c) The Act defines an Independent Trade Union as one which is not under the domination or influence of an employer or a group of employers. Once a trade union has been certified as independent by the Certification Officer and it has been recognised, directly or indirectly, by the employer, it has the following rights;
— the power to request that an employer disclose information for collective bargaining purposes;

- the right to be consulted on proposals for collective redundancies;
- the employee has the right to join it and take part in it's activities;
- the right to time off for trade union duties and activities for it's officials and members
- the ability to appoint safety representatives.

(d) The Act states in Section 13 that any person "acting in contemplation or furtherance of a trade dispute" who induces a breach of any contract or interferes with the performance of any contract cannot be sued for damages or torts, provided that
- the actions are reasonably capable of furthering that dispute, or
- are taken predominantly in pursuit of the dispute and not for reasons unconnected with it.

(e) The Act contains the definition of what a trade dispute is in Section 29 which was amended by the Employment Act 1982. This reads as follows;
> (1) In this Act trade dispute means a dispute between workers and their employer, which relates wholly or mainly to one or more of the following, that is to say —......'

and then lists the following permitted activities;
(a) terms and conditions of employment, including the physical conditions of work;
(b) engagement or non engagement or termination or suspension of employment or the duties of employment of one or more workers;
(c) allocation of work between workers or groups of workers;
(d) matters of discipline;
(e) the membership or non membership of a trade union of a worker;
(f) facilities for trade union officials;
(g) machinery for negotiation or consultation or other procedures.

(f) Under Section 16 it is made clear that employees cannot be ordered to work or attend at their place of work by any court.

10. THE EMPLOYMENT PROTECTION ACT 1975

The Act had two major objectives — to introduce machinery to promote the improvement of industrial relations; and to introduce a new series of rights for employees and provide greater job security.

Most of this Act has either been repealed or its provisions transferred to the 'Consolidation' Act of 1978. However, some significant elements remain, as follows:

KEY ASPECTS OF CURRENT LEGISLATION

(a)   Statutory bodies

This Act created and lays down the general duties of the Advisory Conciliation and Arbitration Service (ACAS), the Central Arbitration Committee (CAC), the Certification Officer (CO) and the Employment Appeal Tribunal (EAT).

(b)   This Act imposes a general duty on employers to disclose to independent trade unions, on request, information which would lubricate the process of collective bargaining. This should be 'information which it would be in accordance with good industrial relations to provide' and which is in the employer's possession. An ACAS Code, issued in August 1977, suggests the sort of information which should be provided. If an employer fails to disclose information, the union can appeal to the CAC who would ask ACAS to conciliate. If the CAC upholds a complaint from a union, it has the power to require that employer to release that information.

There are limits set on the information which must be disclosed; the employer cannot be forced to disclose information which;

— would be against the interests of National Security;
— would cause substantial injury to the undertaking;
— has been communicated in confidence;
— was about an individual, unless the individual gives consent;
— was relevant to legal proceedings, or which it would be illegal to disclose;
— would involve a cost or an amount of work out of proportion to it's bargaining value.

(c)   Consultation regarding proposed redundancies

An employer planning redundancies is required to consult the appropriate recognised independent trade union about their implementation at the earliest possible moment. The employer shall disclose the information in writing and this information should include;

— the reasons for the redundancies;
— the numbers and description of the employees whom it is intended to dismiss as redundant;
— the total number of employees of any such description who are employed at present in the establishment in question;
— the proposed method of selection;
— the proposed procedure for carrying out the redundancy dismissals.

Where 10-99 employees are to be dismissed as redundant, the consultation period is a minimum of 30 days prior to the first of the terminations; for

100+ employees, the period is at least 90 days. Employers must also notify the Department of Employment within the same period.

Where an employer fails to notify the relevant trade union, the union or unions may apply to an Industrial Tribunal for a 'protective award' which will require the employer to pay normal wages to the employees covered by the award for the specified period.

(d)   Statutory Joint Industrial Councils

The Act also established the possibility of creating Statutory Joint Industrial Councils as a 'halfway house' between Wages Councils and free collective bargaining.

11.   SEX DISCRIMINATION ACTS 1975/1986

These Acts made discrimination unlawful in employment, training and related matters; in education; in the provision of foods, facilities and services and the disposal and management of premises. The Acts also;

— established the Equal Opportunities Commission (EOC);
— apply to discrimination against both men and women;
— apply to discrimination against married persons.

(a)   Exemptions

Excluded from the Acts are;

— employment which is wholly or mainly outside GB;
— provisions made in respect to pregnancy;
— religious orders;
— mineworkers who are employed mainly underground;
— situations where a person's sex or marital status are a Genuine Occupational Qualification (GOQ).

(b)   Definitions of discrimination

There are two types of action which are discriminatory;

(i)   Direct discrimination occurs if on grounds of sex or marital status a woman is treated less favourably than a man or vice versa;

(ii)   Indirect discrimination occurs if an action is discriminatory in effect, as opposed to deliberate intention, so that even if the same treatment is applied equally to members of either sex, the proportion of one sex who can comply is smaller than that of the other, unless the requirements are justifiable irrespective of the sex of the person to whom it is applied.

(c)   Discrimination in recruitment

The ways in which this can occur are;
— in the way decisions are made on who should be offered a job. A person who feels discrimination has taken place in an organisation does not need to have applied for the job in order to make a complaint;
— in relation to the terms and conditions offered;
— by refusing to offer a person employment;
— by omitting to shortlist someone for an interview;
— in the recruitment method and advertising literature and job descriptions.

(d)   Discrimination in treatment of present employees

(i)   It is unlawful to discriminate by not allowing access to or refusing to;
— promote, transfer or train employees.
However it is permissible to treat one sex less favourably than another in areas where it is necessary to overcome the effects of past discrimination against a particular sex.

(ii)   It is also unlawful to discriminate in dismissal, redundancy or layoffs, directly or indirectly, because of density of male or female employment.

(e)   Genuine Occupational Qualifications

A person's sex may be a GOQ for a job where;
(i)   the essential nature of a job calls for a man or woman for reasons of physiology (excluding physical strength and stamina), modelling clothes, or dramatic performances (for reasons of authenticity).

(ii)   considerations of decency or privacy require the job to be held by a man or woman, perhaps because of the likelihood of physical contact between the job holder and colleagues, or where the job holder is likely to work in the presence of people who are in a state of undress.

(iii)   the nature or location of the establishment makes it impracticable for the job holder to live in premises other than those provided by the employer and the only available premises do not provide separate sleeping and sanitary accommodation — unless it would be reasonable to require the employer to suitably equip or provide other premises.

(iv)   the job is in a single sex establishment or in a single sex part of an establishment, it will need to be shown, in relation to any particular job, that the character of the establishment requires that job to be held by a member of the particular sex.

(v)   the holder of the job provides individuals with personal services providing their welfare or education, e.g. some women might respond best to help offered by a female welfare officer.

(vi)   the job involves work outside the UK in a country whose laws or customs are such that a job can only be done, or done effectively, by a person of a particular sex.

(vii)   the job is one of two held by a married couple.

(viii)   the job is one covered by some legal restriction on one or other sex.

(f)   Enforcement

In the employment field an individual may make a complaint of unlawful discrimination to an Industrial Tribunal within 3 months of the alleged discrimination. Where an Industrial Tribunal has decided in favour of an employee it can issue an order;

(i)   declaring the rights of the parties;
(ii)   requiring the employer to pay the claimant damages;
(iii)   make a recommendation that the employer follows a particular course of action, e.g. promote the applicant, desist from using a particular test etc.

Where an issue is too complex for a complainant to deal with the issue alone or an issue is raised which has a wider public interest, the EOC could;

(i)   conduct formal investigations into the matter and, if it does discover behaviour which contravenes the SDA, it is empowered to issue a 'non discrimination' notice, and/or

(ii)   institute legal proceedings if the organisation persists with it's discrimination.

(g)   Code of Practice

'The Code of practice for the elimination of discrimination on the ground of sex and marriage and the promotion of equal opportunity in employment' of

April 1985, whilst it does not have the force of law, will be taken into account by Industrial Tribunals and has three main purposes;

(i)   to eliminate discrimination in employment
(ii)   to provide guidance on the steps an employer might reasonably take to ensure that their employees do not, in the course of their employment, act unlawfully contrary to the SDA;
(iii) to promote equality between men and women in the workplace.

The Code is divided into two parts; the first part is concerned with the role of good employment practices in eliminating sex and marriage discrimination and second the role of good employment practices in promoting equality of opportunity.

The Code sees as the key feature in promoting equality the establishment of a sound and realistic policy which

> "should be clearly stated and where appropriate, be included in a collective agreement; overall responsibility for implementing the policy should rest with senior management; and the policy should be made known to all employees....".

This policy and its implementation should be continuously monitored so that the organisation can at any moment justify that the policy is operating effectively and imbues every employment related decision at all levels within the organisation.   The Code also recommends positive action programmes through education and training to prepare people for promotion.

12.   RACE RELATIONS ACT 1976

The 1976 Act strengthened the law against racial discrimination in;

— employment;
— housing;
— education;
— the provision of goods, facilities and services;
— and extended the law to include discrimination by private clubs.

The Act closely follows the Sex Discrimination Acts.

(a)   General intention

(i)   To replace the Acts of 1965 and 1968;
(ii)   to harmonise the powers and procedures for dealing with sex and race discrimination to ensure genuine equality of opportunity in both fields;

(iii)   to provide for individual victims of discrimination fuller redress through both the Civil Courts and the Industrial Tribunal system;

(iv)   to establish a Commission for Racial Equality (CRE), which would fill a strategic role in tackling discrimination, promoting equality of opportunity, help individual victims of discrimination and to support and coordinate the work of local Community Relations Councils.

(b)   Definitions of discrimination

Part 1 of the Act defines two forms of conduct which may constitute racial discrimination;

(i)   Direct discrimination − This arises when one person treats another person less favourably on racial grounds than he treats or would treat someone else. 'Racial grounds'includes colour, race nationality (including citizenship) or ethnic or national origins. Such discrimination may be done not only openly but also by inference.

(ii)   Indirect discrimination − This involves practices which whether or not intentionally are discriminatory in their effect on a particular racial group and are not justifiable. Thus anyone is prohibited from applying a condition or requirement which, although also applied to those not in that racial group, meets all the following conditions;

− it is such that the proportion of that racial group who can comply is considerably smaller than the proportion of other people who can comply,

− the discriminator cannot show the condition to be justifiable, irrespective of the origins of the person to whom it is applied,

− it is to the detriment of that person because he cannot comply with it.

(c)   Victimisation

The definition of discrimination was also broadened to include victimisation of a person because that individual has asserted his rights under the legislation. However victimisation does not apply if people are badly treated when they have made allegations which are false or in bad faith.

Any employee who gives evidence in a Court or in a Tribunal on behalf of another who is alleging racial discrimination, is also protected against any consequential unfair treatment.

(c)   Employment

Part 2 of the Act applies to employment and related workplace matters thus;

(i)   it is unlawful to discriminate on grounds of race between job applicants or employees. For example, in selection procedures, employment terms, job offers, access to promotion and training, dismissal, earnings and redundancy;

(ii)   the employer is liable for any act done, with or without her/his approval, by any of her/his employees. Thus, the employer and the employee can both be held accountable for an unlawful act.

(e)   Exemptions

There are some exemptions;

(i)   where racial identity is a Genuine Occupational Qualification (GOQ);

(ii)   private households;

(iii)   small partnerships with less than 6 partners;

(iv)   seamen recruited abroad;

(v)   for employment training in skills for people not ordinarily resident in GB, where the employer intends those skills to be used outside GB.

(f)   Positive discrimination

The government was also concerned that the principle of non discrimination should not be applied inflexibly, so that the disadvantage experienced by some members of racial minority groups in employment and related matters was ignored. The Act, therefore, allows action to be taken to meet the special educational, training and welfare needs of members of particular groups. Employers and other training bodies are allowed to provide training for and encouragement to, members of particular racial groups to take advantage of opportunities for doing jobs in which they have previously been under-represented. There are similar provisions for positive action by trade unions, employers' associations and professional bodies.

(g)   Advertisements

Discriminatory practices (even where there is no actual victim), discriminatory advertisements, instructions and pressure to discriminate are all unlawful and a person who discovers such incidents, even if not personally affected, can make a complaint. The only exceptions are for Genuine Occupational Qualifications.

(h   Genuine Occupational Qualifications

These are not an automatic exception for general categories of jobs; in every case it will be necessary for the employer to show that, for the exception to be claimed, that the criteria set out apply to the particular task concerned. The GOQ's exist where;

(i)   the job involves participation in a dramatic performance or other entertainment in a capacity for which a person of the racial group in question is required for reasons of authenticity;

(ii)   the job involves participation as an artist's or photographic model in the production of a work of art, picture or film, for which a person of the racial group in question is required for reasons of authenticity;

(iii) the job involves working in a place where food or drink is provided to, and consumed by, members of the public or sections of members of the public, in a particular setting, for which, for reasons of authenticity a member of a particular racial group needs to be employed;

(iv)   the job holder provides persons of a particular racial group with a personal service promoting their welfare and those services can most effectively be provided by a person of the same racial group.

(i)   Other organisations

Other organisations which were specifically brought within the scope of the Act are:

— trade unions,
— the police,
— professional bodies,
— vocational training bodies,
— employment agencies,
— the careers service,
— the Training Agency.

(j)   Enforcement

Individuals have direct access to the Courts or to Industrial Tribunals. The remedies available from the courts are damages (including damages for injured feelings), a declaration of rights or an injunction. Complaints in the employment field will be referred by Industrial Tribunals initially to ACAS conciliation officers, who will try and promote a voluntary settlement before the case proceeds to the hearing. Where a complaint reaches an IT arrangements are normally made to specifically include a lay member with particular knowledge of race relations in employment.

(k)   Code of Practice

In April 1984 the Commission for Racial Equality issued a Code of practice for 'the elimination of racial discrimination and the promotion of equal opportunity in employment'.
The Code does not impose any legal obligations itself but, like all other Codes, its provisions will be considered in hearing cases in Courts or Tribunals. Like the EOC Code the most important feature highlighted to promote equality of treatment is policy established and enforced by senior management. The Code recommends that employers should,

> "make an ... analysis of the workforce and regularly monitor the application of the policy with the aid of analyses of the ethnic origins of the workforce and of job applicants."

Thus what has been termed 'ethnic monitoring' is felt to be the key to actively demonstrating the commitment to and successful integration of equal opportunity into the organisation.

13.   EMPLOYMENT PROTECTION (CONSOLIDATION) ACT 1978

This Act brought together into one piece of legislation all the individual rights of employees previously contained in separate Acts. The Act did not alter or amend the previous statutes but merely incorporated all the provisions in one document. Subsequently amendments were made by the Employment Acts of 1980, 1982 and 1988.

(a)   Written particulars of employment

The opening sections of the Act deal with the issuing of the particulars of the terms and conditions of employment, within 13 weeks of commencing work. The particulars should include the following;

— employer's name, employees name, date of contract, and job title
— scale or rate of remuneration and intervals at which payment will take place;
— terms and conditions relating to holiday pay and holidays, sickness and accident arrangements and payment for these, pension arrangements (and whether a contracting out scheme is in force);
— the length of notice to be given on either side, i.e. the employer must give, under the Act, one week after four weeks continuous service, two weeks after two years, three weeks after three years, and so on up to a maximum of twelve weeks after twelve years or more service; the employee only need give one week's notice.

- steps to be followed in any grievance which the employee might have;
- details of the disciplinary procedure and rules which apply to the employee;
- where relevant, the date on which a fixed term contract is due to end.

(b) Trade union membership and activities

An employee has the right not to be dismissed or have action short of dismissal taken against him to prevent him being or seeking to be a member of a trade union; preventing him taking part in the activities of an independent trade union at an appropriate time; or forcing him to become a member of a trade union. Dismissal in all these cases is automatically unfair and he can make a claim at an Industrial Tribunal within three months of the action.

(c) Time off for trade union activities

Employees who are members of recognised independent trade unions have the right to take time off without pay to take part in the activities of their trade union.

(d) Time off for trade union duties

The employees who are the officials of a recognised independent trade union have the right to take reasonable time off with pay, to pursue trade union duties relevant to the collective bargaining arrangements within the organisation or for relevant industrial relations training. The arrangements agreed between the parties should take into account the ACAS Code of Practice "Time off for trade union duties and activities" which came into effect in April 1978.

(e) Time off for public duties and to look for work

Employers are required to allow employees time off without pay to carry out public duties;

- as a Justice of the Peace;
- a member of a local authority;
- a member of a statutory tribunal;
- a member of a Health Authority;
- a member of a governing or managing body of an educational establishment;
- a member of a water authority;
- and to attend meetings or work on sub-committees of such bodies.

An individual is also entitled to reasonable time off with pay once he has been continuously employed for 2 years, or without pay if employed for less than 2 years, to look for work or to seek training on being declared redundant, before the expiry of his notice.

(f)   Maternity provisions

The basic rights are as follows;

(i)   Unless the woman is physically unable to perform her work or is working in a job where there is a statutory restriction on a pregnant woman performing that job, she must not be dismissed because of pregnancy. (N.B. in both the cases mentioned above the employer should always try and provide other work before considering dismissal).

(ii)   A woman who stops work because of pregnancy, who has worked continuously for the employer for two years and remains with the organisation until the 11th week before the expected date of confinement, is entitled to be paid maternity pay for the first six weeks of her absence, at 90% of her normal pay less State flat rate maternity benefit.

(iii) Employees are entitled to paid time off for ante-natal care;

(iv)   An employee who has worked continuously for two years, has asked in writing 11 weeks before she goes off for confinement, who works for an organisation employing 6 or more people, is entitled to return at any time up to 29 weeks after the baby has been born. This return can be delayed for up to 4 weeks by either party. The employer now has the right to request written confirmation of the continued intention to return to work 49 days after the expected date of confinement. The woman must reply in writing within 14 days in order to retain the right to return. The employee must also give 21 days notice of her intended date of return.

(g) Unfair dismissal

The employees right not to be unfairly dismissed was initially introduced in the Industrial Relations Act 1971 and is now consolidated into this Act. Some groups of employees are not protected from unfair dismissal, except where they are dismissed for an inadmissable reason, e.g. in connection with equal opportunities or trade union membership or non membership. Those excluded from the general provisions are;

— part time employees who work less than 16 hours per week unless they work 8 or more hours per week and have been continuously employed for 5 years or more,
— persons working under a contract for services,
— the husband or wife of the employer,
— those who are over the normal age of retirement,
— those who work outside of Great Britain and their work is administered overseas,
— members of the armed forces, police, share fishermen, merchant seamen.

A dismissal may be justified on the following statutory grounds;

— for reasons of capability or qualifications of the employee;
— for reasons relating to the employees conduct;
— for reasons of redundancy;
— where to retain the employee would contravene a statutory enactment or criminal law;
— some other substantial reason.

The reasonableness of an employer's behaviour will be judged taking into account the size and administrative resources of the undertaking. It will also be examined in the context of the ACAS Code of Practice "Disciplinary practice and procedures in employment" which came into effect in 1977. Where an individual feels that he has been unfairly dismissed or he suffers action short of dismissal, he may bring a complaint to an Industrial Tribunal within 3 months. The Tribunal has the power to make an award of compensation as a last resort. However the main thrust of the law was supposedly to ensure that the organisation which has treated the employee unfairly either re-instates (i.e. returns the individual to his old job with no loss of benefits) or re-engages (i.e. in some other post similar to the original one with no loss of benefits) the individual. Unreasonable failure to comply with an order for re-instatement or re-engagement will lead to additional compensation being awarded by the Tribunal.

(h) Redundancy

The objectives of the redundancy provisions are to reduce the impact of loss of job property rights and unemployment by compensating workers who have over 2 years service for thier job loss; to reduce hardship that may result from unemployment; and to encourage job mobility.An employee is dismissed for redundancy if;

"the dismissal is attributable wholly or mainly to —
(a)   the fact that an employer has ceased, or intends to cease, to carry

on the business for the purpose for which the employee was employed by him, or has ceased, or intends to cease, to carry on the business in the place where the employee was so employed; or

(b)   the fact that the requirements of the business for an employee to carry out work of a particular kind, or for the employee to carry out work of a particular kind in the place where he was so employed, have ceased or diminished or are expected to cease or diminish....."

The rights do not apply to those who are over the normal retirement age at the time of the redundancy or employees who work less than 16 hours per week, unless employed for 5 years or more and work 8 or more hours per week. In addition, share fishermen, crown servants and husbands or wives of the employer are not entitled to statutory compensation. The provisions for redundancy pay represent a statutory minimum standard. The legal minima are—

Age	Pay per year of service
18-21	1/2 a week

(NB. Service up to the age of 18 does not count, therefore an individual has to be 20 before he can benefit.)

Age	Pay per year of service
22-40	1 week
41-60(women) 65(men)	1 1/2 weeks

The maximum reckonable service for statutory redundancy pay purposes is 20 years, and there is a statutory maximum in terms of a week's pay. Between 59 and 60 for women and between 64 and 65 for men the total redundancy pay is reduced by 1/12th for each month over the age of 59 or 64. Employees do not have to pay tax on statutory redundancy pay.

(i) Employees' rights on the insolvency of their employer

Under the provisions of the Act, if and when an employer becomes insolvent, any payments owed to employees are to be given priority over all other debts that the organisation has. Application for sums owed should be made to the Receiver or the Liquidator and authorised by the Secretary of State for Employment, who may arrange for them to be paid out of State funds. The debts affected include;

— guarantee payments;
— payments for suspension on medical grounds;
— maternity pay;
— payment for agreed time off;

— arrears in pay for up to 12 weeks;
— statutory notice pay;
— holiday pay arrears up to 6 weeks;
— compensation under an Industrial Tribunal award;
— reimbursement of apprenticeship or articled clerk fees;
— the employer's payments into an occupational pension scheme.

(j) Guarantee payments

An employer is required to guarantee a payment to his employees should they be laid off or on short time working, providing the employee is willing and able to work and has been employed for 4 continuous weeks. A guarantee payment will however not have to be paid if the shortage of work is due to a trade dispute involving other employees of the employer or an associated employer, or if suitable alternative work is refused. The maximum amount of guarantee pay is limited by statute to only 5 days in any rollong three month period and the employer is only required to make the payment if a whole day's work is lost.

(k) Medical suspension

An employee who has been suspended from work under statutory regulations concerned with jobs exposed involving exposure to ionising radiation, lead and certain other chemicals, by an Employment Medical Advisor or an appointed doctor, will be entitled to be paid normal wages for up to 26 weeks. He is not entitled to this pay if, he has been offered suitable alternative work; he fails to fulfil reasonable conditions set by his employer regarding availability; he has not been employed continuously for 4 weeks or he is otherwise unable to work because of sickness or injury.

(l) Itemised pay statement

Every employee has the right to an itemised pay statement which should contain the following particulars;

— the gross amount of his wages or salary;
— the amounts of any variable or fixed deeuctions;
— the net amount of his pay.

14. EMPLOYMENT ACT 1980

The purpose of the Act was to redress the balance between management, trade unions and individual employees. It therefore, attempted to regulate the activities of trade unions and to relieve small businesses of some of the provisions of employment protection legislation.

(a) Secret ballots

The Act permits public funds to be made available through the Certification Officer to encourage and enable independent trade unions to conduct secret postal ballots of their members. The purposes include;

— obtaining a decision on calling or ending a strike, or other form of industrial action;
— carrying out elections allowed for in the union's rules;
— the election of trade union officials;
— amending trade union rules;
— making decisions on trade union amalgamations or transfers of engagements
— reviewing Political Funds;
— other purposes which the Secretary of State for Employment specifies.

Where more than 20 workers are employed, the employer is obliged, if requested to do so by the union or unions, to provide a place where the ballot can take place on the premises.

(b) Picketing

Picketing usually involves attempting to persuade employees to break their contracts of employment by not going to work and, because it disrupts the business of a picketed employer, the breaking of commercial contracts. Lawful picketing may occur, providing the following conditions are met;

— it must be in contemplation or furtherance of a trade dispute;
— it's purpose must be to peacefully obtain or communicate information;
— the person doing it must picket at or near his place of work.

Therefore what was termed secondary picketing anf flying pickets became illegal.

Under the Act there are three exceptions to the requirement that the person doing so could only picket at their own place of work, these are;

— a trade union official may accompany a member of the union whom he represents, and who is picketing at his own place of work or at another acceptable place;
— persons who do not normally work at one particular place, or for whom it

is impracticable to picket their own place of work, may picket the place from which their work is administered;
— unemployed people can picket their former place of work.

Even with these protections picketing remains subject to a wide array of other restrictions, obstruction, nuisance, trespass, conspiracy, assault and the pickets may face action for 'obstruction of the highway' or possibly 'obstruction of a police officer in the lawful execution of his duty'. Further guidance on picketing and the responsibility of pickets and picket organisers can be found in the Department of Employment Code of Practice on picketing.

(c) Secondary action

The Act further limits the immunities from actions in tort provided by the TULRA incases of secondary action, eg. sympathy strikes or blacking of goods or servives. If a person persuades employees of an employer who is not party to the trade dispute, to break their contracts of employment, therefore interfering with commercial contracts, this is secondary action. The organiser of such action has no immunity and can be sued or have an injunction taken out against him to cease the action forthwith.

To retain the immunity, the principal purpose of the dispute must be to put pressure on the employer by targetting either the first customer or first supplier of the firm in dispute or an associated employer of the one in dispute. In doing so the action must be targetted at a current contract between the employers concerned; it must also not affect others; and it must be capable of objectively influencing the outcome of the primary dispute.

(d) Acts to compel trade union membership

The Act removes immunity from prosecution for the employees of one employer who black' the work of employees of another employer, where the purpose of the action is to put pressure on the second group of employees to join a particular trade union. This does not apply where both groups of employees work for the same employer at the same premises.

(e) The closed shop

The provisions regarding the closed shop originally outlined in the Act have been made redundant by the Employment Acts 1988 and 1990 which make closed shop agreements impossible to enforce.

(f) Exclusion or explusion from a trade union

The Act also provides that, where a closed shop exists, individuals have a statutory right not to be unreasonably excluded or expelled from membership of a relevant trade union.

On admission policy the Closed Shop Code of Practice requires unions to have clear and fair rules on membership qualification which should include data on who has power to make decisions regarding membership; on what grounds can membership be refused; what appeals procedure is available to an individual seeking a redress from a decision; and the power to admit applicants when an appeal is upheld. Union rules on expulsions are expected to conform to the rules of natural justice, i.e. an individual must be informed of the charge against him in reasonable time; he must have the opportunity of being heard before an impartial Tribunal; and he must have a right of appeal to a higher authority in the union or the TUC.

Individuals, where they feel their rights have been abused, can appeal to an Industrial Tribunal within 6 months of the exclusion or expulsion.

15. TRANSFER OF UNDERTAKINGS (PROTECTION OF EMPLOYMENT REGULATIONS) 1981

The basis of these Regulations is to protect the employees' rights if the business for which they work is transferred from one owner to another as a going concern. The Regulations impose a duty on the employer to inform and consult with recognised independent trade unions prior to the transfer. The representatives shall be informed as soon as possible of;

(i) The fact that the transfer willtake place, the transfer date and the reasons for it.
(ii) The legal, economic and social implications of the transfer for the affected employees.
(iii) The measures (if any) the employer envisages he will take in relation to the affected employees.
(iv) The measures which the transferor envisages the transferee will take (if any) in relation to the affected employees.

The Regulations introduce the principle of automatic transfer of;

— contracts of employment;
— collective agreements and trade union recognition.

They also render automatically unfair, dismissal for any reason other than an economic, financial or organisational one connected with the transfer.

16. EMPLOYMENT ACT 1982

The Act includes the following provisions;

(i) It makes unions liable to be sued if they have organised unlawful industrial action. Thus the union will be held responsible for any unlawful act, such as industrial action ouside the s 29 TULRA definition, or secondary action, which is authorised or endorsed by a responsible official of the union, who may be one of the following;
   — the National Executive Committee;
   — the General Secretary or President;
   — any other person given power by the union's rules to call industrial action;
   — any official employed by the union;
   — any official of the union to whom an employed official regularly reports.

Unless the relevant official acted against the union's rules or the authorisation or endorsement is disowned in writing as speedily as possible.
Where an employer considers the union is taking unlawful industrial action, he can seek an injunction to prevent the action taking place or have it stopped and can claim damages from the union. There are, however, limits to the amounts which can be awarded as damages.
These are linked with the size of union, thus —

up to 4,999 members	£10,000 maximum
5,000–24,999 members	£50,000 maximum
25,000–99,999 members	£100,000 maximum
100,000+ members	£250,000 maximum

(ii) It made amendments to the definition of trade dispute. (see under TULRA 1974/6).

(iii) Amendments were made to the rules on dismissal in connection with industrial action. An employee who is dismissed while participating in a strike or any other form of industrial action cannot claim unfair dismissal if the following conditions prevail;
   (a) his employer has dismissed all those who were taking part in the action at the date of dismissal,
   (b) his employer has not offered re-employment to any of those dismissed within three months of the dismissal date without making him a similar offer.
The individual has six months to claim at an Industrial Tribunal.

(iv)   Union membership or recognition requirements as part of contractor's obligations in fulfilling a contract were declared illegal. The Act also declared illegal industrial action intended to put pressure on emloyers to maintain such contracts.

(v)   The Act introduced new rules for compensation for dismissal for union membership and non union membership. It specifies a minimum basic award for such cases; clarifies the circumstances when an employee's basic award can be reduced -
       — where the employee's conduct prior to dismissal merited a reduction;
       — where the employee has unreasonably prevented a reinstatement or reengagement order being complied with or refused such an offer, and further establishes a high special award where reinstatement or reengagement is requested by the individual or ordered by the Industrial Tribunal and compliance is unreasonably refused by the employer concerned.

(vi)   The Act requires that companies employing, on average, more than 250 employees in a financial year must include a statement on employee involvement in their annual report. This statement must describe the action which has been taken during the financial year to;
       — systematically provide employees with information of concern to them
       — consult employees or their representatives on a regular basis so that the employees' views can be considered where relevant in decision making
       — encourage the involvement of the employees in the company's performance through an employees' share scheme or by some other means
       — achieve a common awareness on the part of all employees of the financial and other economic factors influencing the performance of the organisation.
       If no action has been taken in any of these areas the annual report merely has to state this!

17.   TRADE UNION ACT 1974

The purpose of this piece of legislation was to 'return the unions to their members'.

(i)   Election of voting members of union Executive Committees

Part one, as amended, of the TUA imposes on unions the requirement that all members of a union's Principal Executive Committee should be elected by the membership and specifies how the election should be carried out.

These requirements, if not voluntarily adhered to, can be activated if an individual member brings an action. The members of the executive should be elected at least once every 5 years'

— in a secret ballot,
— by marking a voting paper without interference or constraint.

(b) Ballots before industrial action

The Act removes the TULRA immunities from both individuals and unions where a strike or any other form of industrial action has been initiated or endorsed without receiving majority support of those voting in a ballot. The ballot must be;

— of all those likely to be affected,
— held in secret,
— by the marking of a voting paper,
— held no more than 4 weeks from the commencement of the industrial action.

(c) Revisions to the Trade Union Act 1913 on Political Funds

Trade unions are now required to review the operation of their political funds at least once every 10 years and, if the ballot does not reestablish the political fund resolution, trade unions can no longer spend money on political objects. The Act also brought up to date the definition of political objects.

18. DATA PROTECTION ACT 1984

The purpose of the Act is,

"To regulate the use of automatically processed information relating to individuals and the provision of services in respect to such information".

The Act does not cover data which is processed by manual methods but it regulates the use of automatically processed data by a system of registration with the Data Protection Registrar. Registration lasts for 3 years and needs to contain the following information:-

(i)   The name and address of the data user;

(ii)   a description of the personal data held by the data user and of the purpose or puposes for which the data is held or used;

(iii)   a description of the sources of the data;

(iv)   a description of the person or persons to whom the data user intends or may wish to disclose the data;

(v)   the names of ant counties outside the UK to which data is to be directly or indirectly transferred;

(vi)   the provision of one or more addresses for data subjects who may wish to access the data.

It is a criminal offence to hold personal data without being registered or to knowingly use, obtain, disclose or transfer personal data in a manner inconsistent with the descriptions in the register entry.

The DPA lays down 8 Data Protection Principles which must be complied with. These are;

(i)   the information to be contained in personal data shall be obtained, and personal data shall be processed, fairly and lawfully;

(ii)   personal data shall be held only for one or more registered specified and lawful purposes;

(iii)   personal data held for any purpose or purposes shall not be used or disclosed in any manner inconpatible with the purpose or purposes registered;

(iv)   personal data held for any purpose or purposes shall be adequate, relevant and not excessive in relation to that purpose or purposes;

(v)   personal data shall be accurate and, where necessary, kept up to date;

(vi)   personal data held for any purpose or purposes shall not be kept longer than is necessary for that purpose or purposes;

(vii)   an individual shall be entitled;
- at reasonable intervals and without due delay or expense,
- to be informed by any data user whether he holds personal data of which the individual is a subject and
- to be supplied with any such data held by the data user.

— where appropriate, to have the data corrected or erased.

(viii) appropriate security measures shall be taken against unauthorised access to/or alterations, disclosure or destruction of personal data and against loss or destruction of the personal data.

19. WAGES ACT 1986

The expressed aims of the Wages Act are;
(i)   to facilitate the introduction of cashless pay;
(ii)   to repeal the Truck Acts;
(iii)   to modify and curtail the scope of Wages Councils;
(iv)   to remove the rebates to employers who make statutory redundancy payments except where they employ less than 10 workers.

(a)   Payment of Wages

(i)   From January 1st 1987 employers were free to introduce cashless pay systems for all new employees. However employees employed before that date are entitled to retain payment in cash if they so wish.

(ii)   Deductions from wages may only be made if the deduction is either by virtue of a statutory provision (e.g. income tax or national insurance) or by a provision in an employee's contract. Any deductions from wages on account of cash shortages or stock deficiencies payable by a retail worker cannot exceed one tenth of the gross amount payable to that worker for the day worked.

(b)   Wages Councils

The Act replaced the Wages Council Act 1979 and removed young people under the age of 21 from the scope of Wages Council regulation. In addition Wages Councils were limited to fixing a basic hourly rate, overtime pay, and a limit on deductions from pay that an employer can make for living accommodation.

(c)   Redundancy rebates

These were removed for employers who employ more than 10 people.

20. EMPLOYMENT ACT 1988

The 1988 Act was aimed at continuing the reform of industrial relations and established new arrangements for employment and training.

KEY ASPECTS OF CURRENT LEGISLATION

(a)   The rights of trade union members

The Act created a series of new rights for trade union members;

(i)   the right to restrain a union from organising any form of industrial action which is likely to involve them personally without there having been support from a properly coducted secret ballot;

(ii)   the right not to be 'unjustifiably' disciplined by a union, if they choose not to take part in or support a strike or other form of industrial action;

(iii)   the right to inspect their union's accounting records within 28 days of making a request to do so and to be accompanied by an accountant when doing so. This includes the right to take or be supplied with such copies or extracts of the accounting records as the members may require;

(iv)   the right of individual union members to take Court action to prevent the use of union funds for indemnifying unlawful conduct and to prevent unlawful use of the union's property by it's trustees e.g. for paying fines arising from criminal offences or contempt of court;

(v)   the right to require an employer to stop deducting union suscriptions from an employee's pay if that employee has resigned from the union.

These rights are legally enforceable either through an Industrial Tribunal or through the Courts. The Act also established a Commissioner for the Rights of Trade union Members to help members take action against their union in a court or tribunal.

(b)   The closed shop

The Act does not make the closed shop as an institution unlawful but it removes statutory protection from actions to enforce it.

(i)   The organisation or threat of organising industrial action to enforce union membership is made unlawful by removing the immunity from actions in tort previously given by Section 13 of the TULRA 1974. Thus employers and others e.g. the customers and suppliers of the employer affected, who might be damaged by such action are able to restrain the action or obtain compensation.

(ii)   Any dismissal of employees, or action short of dimissal for not being members of a trade union is automatically unfair.   Individuals are entitled to seek reinstatement or compensation.

(c)   Elections

The Act extended to the General Secretary and President of a union and to other non voting members of a unions's Principal Executive Committee the requirement to subject themselves to regular elections.

A non voting member is defined as one who may attend and speak at the executive committee meetings other than in a purely informatory or advisory capacity.

Candidates in elections are given the right to prepare an election address of 100 words or more and have it distributed with the ballot papers.

In addition the Act requires unions to subject union elections to independent scrutiny. The scrutineer is required to supervise the pro-duction and distribution of the ballot papers and must act as the returning officer. A written report is required on the conduct and result of the ballot.

(d)   Ballots

The Act made various changes to the requirements applying to a ballot for industrial action in order to preserve the immunity for organising industrial action.

(i)   Ballot papers must now contain the following words,

"if you take part in a strike or other industrial action you may be in breach of your contract of employment".

(ii)   Entitlement to vote must be given to all those who the union believes will be called upon to take part in the action and certain conditions are required if member's votes are to be aggregated across different places of work—
   — a separate ballot is required for each place of work and it became unlawful to organise industrial action at a specific workplace unless a majority are in favour at that workplace. Unless either
   — the union believes at the time of the ballot that the members work at the same workplace;
   or
   the union reasonably believes at the time of the ballot that the members have some factor in common which entitles the union to ballot the members and aggregate the votes across the different workplace e.g. similar terms and conditions negotiated in the same bargaining group.

(f)   Commissioner for the Rights of Trade Union Members

The Act provided for this appointment to be made, which is an independent post. The function of this role is to provide help to union members who are taking or who wist to take legal action against their union over the following:-

(i)   Failure to hold a ballot before industrial action;
(ii)   unlawful use of union property by trustees;
(iii)   the right to inspect the union's accounting records;
(iv)   failure to conduct a political fund ballot properly or unlawful use of political funds;
(v)   the use of union funds for indemnifying unlawful conduct by union officials;
(vi)   failure to conduct ballots properly for the principal executive committee.

(g)   Employment and training

The Manpower Services Commission was renamed the Training Commission which would have 16 members as Commissioners with increased representation for employers.

21.   ACCESS TO MEDICAL REPORTS ACT 1988

This Act came into effect on 1st january 1989. It applies to medical reports by a medical practitioner for employment or insurance purposes. Individuals get four main rights under the legislation.

(i)   Before approaching a Doctor the employer must notify the individual in writing, seeking consent to approach the Doctor and informing the individual of the right to refuse permission and the other rights under the Act;

(ii)   the individual, if consenting, has the right to demand access to the report before it is supplied to the employer or potential employer. The individual must exercise this right within 21 days of notification to the medical practitioner;

(iii)   the individual may request amendment of anything considered incorrect or misleading. The Doctor may refuse the request but, should refusal take place, the individual is entitled to add their own comments to the report;

(iv)   the individual may refuse to allow the report to be supplied at all.

These new rights only apply to the individual's own Doctor and do not apply to reports drawn up by an independent practitioner or company medical advisor. Following the model of the Data Protection Act access under this Act need not be given if the medical advisor is of the opinion that the disclosure would be likely to cause serious physical or mental harm, or would disclose the identity of a third party who has given information. This objection may only apply to part of the total report, in which caes the individual is entitled to see the remainder.

22. EMPLOYMENT ACT 1989

The main provisions of the Act were to
— remove restrictions on the employment of women and young people;
— help employers to create more jobs and be more competitive by removing some of the employment protection requirements;
— promote the Government's training strategy for the next cycle of the 1990s.

(i)   Discrimination

The Act removed or amended most of the legislation passed before the Sex Discrimination Act of 1975 which continued to allow either direct or indirect discrimination between men and women in both employment or vocational training.   In previous legislation the only lawful discriminatory clauses allowed subsequent to the 1975 Act, in relation to employment and training, were those which protected women in relation to pregnancy e.g. restrictions for working on board ships and aircraft, maternity e.g. returning to work in factories within four weeks of childbirth, and other risks relating to women e.g. exposure to lead and radiation. Now women are permitted to work underground in mines and quarries and are not prohibited from working on moving parts of machinery.   Women are now entitled to statutory redundancy pay up to the same age as men.
    The Act, however in Section 5 does allow,

— the appointment of Head Teachers in schools and colleges from a religious order where a restriction was contained in an instrument when it was established;
— in addition it permits different treatment of men and women in some educational appointments in Univesities and Colleges.

The legislation additionally contains provisions affecting any training provider or anyone who arranges training regarding sex and race discrimination. Thus it extends the Race Relations Act and Sex Discrimination Act provisions to include discrimination during the course of training. It also makes it lawful for training bodies to run training courses restricted to particular groups to enable them to enter employment in which they are underrepresented, without seeking the permission of the Secretary of State.

The Act also enables the Secretary of State to make orders exempting special treatment of single parents in training employment and enterprise schemes to prevent such schemes from being considered discriminatory against married people if special provisions are made e.g. making childcare payments to enable individuals to find time to develop themselves.

The Act in addition exempts turban wearing Sikhs from any non statutory requirements to wear a safety helmet on a construction site and restricts the liability if injuries ensue only to those that would have been sustained if they had been wearing a hard hat.

(ii)   Young people

Young people are defined as those over menimum school leaving age and their 18th birthday and the Act removes all restrictions on young peoples' hours of work, including maximum hours per day, per week, overtime, shiftwork, weekend and nightwork. Other provisions and requirements regarding young people also removed include

— restrictions on young females being enployed on certain factory processes,
— requirements to notify the Career Service when ypung people are employed in a factory,
— restrictions on the employment of young people in street trading, live performances and other entertainments.

(iii)   Amendments to the Employment Protection (Consolidation) Act 1978.

(a)Small employers with 19 or less employees are no longer required to provide, within 13 weeks of employment, written particulars of the disciplinary rules applying to them, nor the name of the person to whom they may apply if they are dissatisfied with a disciplinary decision. Once the firm expands to twenty employees or more, the 20th and subsequent employees are covered by the EP(C)A requirements but the original 19 are not.

(b)The qualifying length of service required to receive a written statement of reasons for dismissal if requested within 14 days is increased from six months to 2 years.

(c)Paid time off for officials of recognised trade unions is limited to that required for negotiations or time required for training about matters which fall within section 29(1) of TULRA 1974.

(d)All rebates to employers for redundancy pay are removed.

(iv)   Training

The Act dissolved the Training Commission and transferred all property and assets to the Secretary of State. It provided the ability to wind up the Industrial Training Boards so that they could be replaced by employer led non statutory bodies and facilitated the transfer of ITB staff and assets to these successor bodies.

23.   EMPLOYMENT ACT 1990

The Act had the following objectives,
— the abolition of the pre entry closed shop;
— the removal of all immunity for secondary industrial action;
— the control of unofficial industrial action by making unions responsible for unrepudiated unofficial action and by allowing the selective dismissal of unofficial strikers;
— the enhancement of the powers of the Commissioner for the Rights of Trade Union Members.

(i)   Section 1 of the Act makes it unlawful to refuse a person employment or refuse to offer the services of an Employment Agency because—
— the individual is not a union member,
— the individual is unwilling to join a union,
— the individual is not prepared to leave a union when employed,
— or the individual refuses to make payments to a union.

If these rights are infringed the person can complain to an Industrial Tribunal.
    The Act does not however prevent an employer from offering employment to a particular individual because of a previous reputation as a 'militant' or 'troublemaker'.
    It is also unlawful to indicate in any form of job advertising including word of mouth that unionists or non unionists are preferred or only to recruit union nominees. Complaints can be made to an Industrial Tribunal within three months.

(ii)   Secondary industrial action

Section 4 repealed the secondary action provisions of the Employment Act 1980, thus secondary action is now actionable in tort and not protected by the immunity provided by Section 13 of TULRA 1974. Secondary action is defined in the Employment Act 1980 Section 17(2). Under the 1990 Act liability will arise from inducing the employees of a secondary employer to break their contracts of employment and the definition of contract of employment is extended to cover the contract of a self employed person.

KEY ASPECTS OF CURRENT LEGISLATION

The only remaining, permitted secondary activity is peaceful picketing by the employees of the secondary firm or their union officials. The protection for action in tort will still be available to those who induce an employee of a supplier to break his employment contract by refusing to cross a picket line to supply goods or services.

(iii)   Union liability for unofficial action

The provisions in Sections 6 and 7 are aimed at wildcat or unofficial action and extend the potential liability of unions for industrial action authorised or endorsed by a responsible officer of the union whether or not that officer is acting within the rules of the union, unless the union repudiates the action. The Act thus amends Section 15 of the Employment Act 1980. Consequently, an act is considered authorised or endorsed by the union if it is done, authorised or endorsed by,
— any individual empowered by the rules to do, authorise or endorse such an act; or,
— the principal executive committee, president or general secretary; or,
— any other relevant committee of the union; or
— any other official, whether employed by the union or not.

Thus unions are made responsible for the actions of lay officials or shop stewards. The Act goes beyond this and defines a 'committee of the union' as any group created within the union's rules. It thus provides in a

'an act shall be taken to have been done, authorised or endorsed by an official if it was done, authorised or endorsed by, any member of, any group of persons of which he was at the material time, a member, the purpose of which included organising or coordinating industrial action.'

Therefore, if a shop steward was part of any group which may subsequently organise industrial action even when the shop steward has withdrawn from the group then the shop steward shall potentially be held vicariously liable for the action even if it was called in breach of the union's rules.

The act can be repudiated by the union, if it is repudiated by the principal executive committee, president or general secretary as soon as is reasonably practicable after learning of the action. This repudiation requires the union to do three things,

— to give written notice of the repudiation to the committee or shop steward as soon as possible
— to do its best, without delay, to give individual written notice of the repudiation to every union member who it has reason to believe is or might be taking part in the relevant action. This notice should read:

"Your union has repudiated the call(or calls) for industrial action to which this notice relates and will give no support to unofficial industrial action in response to it (or them). If you are dismissed for taking unofficial industrial action, you will have no right to complain of unfair dismissal."
— to give written notice to the employer of every union member,
— not to behave in any manner inconsistent with the repudiation.

In addition, a new subsection to the provisions of the 1980 EA., Section 15(9) gives to courts considering injunctions against a union the power to require the union to take any steps necessary to ensure that there is no further inducement to take unlawful industrial action. The union can be required to discipline the offenders either by fining them or expelling them from their office or the union itself.

(iv)   Selective dismissal for industrial action

In circumstances of unofficial industrial action an amendment to the EP(C)A 1978 (Section 62(a)) permits the selective dismissal of those taking part in unofficial action where the action has been repudiated by the union concerned. Thus Industrial Tribunals will have no jurisdiction to hear unfair dismissal claims, even where selective dismissal of only the real 'troublemakers' has taken place.

(v)   Immunity from industrial action in support of dismissed unofficial strikers.

The Act removes all immunity from industrial action which is subsequently called in support of any unofficial strikers dismissed as a result of the unions repudiation, even where a ballot has been taken and is in favour of support. Section 13 TULRA immunity therefore does not apply.

(vi)   Industrial action and other trade union ballots

The requirement for trade unions to ballot members who might be induced to take part in industrial action is extended to include those who work under contracts for services i.e. the self employed. If a ballot should fail to include such workers, it can be challenged in the High Court to stop the industrial action continuing or taking place at all, and the industrial action itself is likely to be considered unlawful and not protected from actions in tort.
    Trade unions are also required to ensure that any members of the workforce that have been seconded to Northern Ireland when am industrial action ballot takes place are given the right to vote in the ballot.
    Whilst generally an industrial action ballot is only valid if industrial action

commences within four weeks of the ballot, the 1990 Act extends the validity for up to 12 weeks, in those cases where court action challenges the validity of the ballot and the court extends the time period of validity. The union requirement to appoint independent scrutineers to supervise the conduct of political fund and union executive ballots is extended to require the union concerned to state the scrutineer's name on the ballot papers. Also before the scrutineer is actually appointed the union must circulate each member with the name of the nominee, to enable the members to challenge the appointment should they wish to. (The qualifications for being an independent scrutineer are laid down in the Trade Union Ballots and Elections (Independent Scrutineer Qualifications) Order 1988 Statutory Instrument 1988/2117.

(vii) Commissioner for the Rights of Trade Union Members
Section 10 of the Act extends the powers of the Commissioner to cover any action arising out of an alleged or threatened breach of the union's rules, where other members might have been similarly affected. Assistance may therefore be offered in relation to
— appointment or election or removal from office in the union;
— disciplinary proceedings of the union;
— authorising or endorsing industrial action;
— balloting union members;
— the use of the union's funds or property;
— the imposition, collection or distribution of any levy for the purposes of industrial action;
— the constitution or proceedings of any union committee or conference.

(viii) Redundancy Fund
The Redundancy Fund was wound up and its assets transferred to the National Insurance Fund.

(ix) Work Experience
Children can now be employed for work experience from the beginning of the term preceding the start of the school year in which they become entitled to leave school.

STATUTORY SICK PAY ACT 1991

This Act reduces the State's responsibility to pay for those on short term sickness absence. Under the Statutory Sick Pay Act of 1983, employers were given responsibility for administering payments for the first 8 weeks of sickness. Whilst employers bore the administrative costs the State reimbursed employers for the cost of Statutory Sick Pay as an amount offset against national insurance contributions. Due to the 1991 Statutory Sick Pay Act the employer can now only reclaim 80% of the cost.

CHAPTER TEN

ROLE OF GOVERNMENT AND GOVERNMENT POLICIES IN THE UK

The attitude and behaviour of Government plays a very important part in stimulating and controlling the economic and social environment within which organisations operate. It is hard to get Government behaviour into perspective, because inevitably individual policies are influenced by political affiliations. Before we examine the current political affiliations of the UK population, we should examine the influence and objectives of Government. Governments operate in a number of ways which affect the economic stability and growth of an economy.

Governments can be said to have the following roles in our society:

1. PROVISION OF PUBLIC SERVICES

They have a responsibility for the provision and maintenance of public services, which either may be uneconomic when left to private organisations, or which are so essential to the community at large that Government must, of necessity, control them. In our society we expect the Government to be involved in the maintenance of law and order; the provision of roads, schools and a public health system; to provide and run the basic transport system; to influence through consumer organisations the provision of power through the Gas and Electricity network; and to encourage the provision of basic water and sewerage facilities through the Water Authorities. Thus, the output of some organisations and the work they do may be considered important enough to be centrally controlled, because they yield benefits for the community in terms of overall health and welfare which are in excess of their potential monetary returns. Governments over the last ten to fifteen years have become increasingly concerned with the profitability and efficiency of nationalised industry which has led to privatisation and has reformed increased efficiency in the public sector in general.

On the one hand, it has been suggested that the public sector is producing vital goods and services and that the community should not be asked to pay excessively for those services; they should be subsidised through taxation. On the other hand, it is argued that the public sector is consuming too much of our gross national product and that this is preventing the private sector from developing in the way that it should, because the tax burden on industry is too heavy. Thus, the public sector should become more efficient and those parts of it which actually provide a saleable good or service should be expected to conform to profit or monetary targets so that public sector investment is self-funded. The public sector is a major employer, employing almost 27% of the UK labour force as the following table illustrates:

Table 5: Employment in the UK Public Sector, 1989

	Numbers (000's)	% of total UK Labour Force
Central Government	2303	8.6
H.M. Forces	308	1.2
N.H.S.	1221	4.6
Other Central Government Depts.	774	2.9
Local Authorities	2934	10.9
Education	1440	5.4
Health & Social Services	411	1.5
Police	196	0.7
Other Local Authority Depts.	769	2.9
Public Corporations	727	2.7
Total UK Public Sector	6081	22.7
Total UK Private Sector	20222	75.5
Total UK Labour Force	26765	100.0

Source *Economic Trends* adapted

2. INFLUENCE THE ATTITUDES AND BEHAVIOUR OF BUSINESS AND THE POPULATION

Attitudes to work, to saving, to family size, to foreign trade, to equality of treatment, to social mobility, to new technological methods can all be influenced by Government action through the provision of services; the encouragement and provision of finance; and through legislative protection.

Every Government has to be concerned with questions as to whether it favours large scale or small scale enterprise; a competitive or monopolistic market; public or private enterprise etc. The legal system will inevitably reflect societal attitudes and consequently there are laws which relate to contract, to companies, to partnerships, to protection against monopolies and restrictive practices, to property and to the employer/employee relationship. The Government also administers a framework of agencies and departments which either regulate business activity, e.g. the Monopolies Commission, or assist with money, advice or guidance for enterprises (e.g. Department of Trade and Industry, ACAS), or individuals and organisations within the society (e.g. Commission for Racial Equality or the Commissioner for the Rights of Trade Union members). Common attitudes and approaches can be developed through organisations like the National Economic Development Council (NEDC).

Role of National Economical Development Council (NEDC)

The Council is composed of the Chancellor of the Exchequer, who is the Chairman, the Secretaries of State for Trade and Industry, Energy and Employment, management representatives, those nominated by the TUC, independents, and the National Economic Development Office's Director General.

The combination of the NEDC, the Economic Development Committees (EDCs) and the National Economic Development Office – forms the economic advisory group to the Government of the day with the nomenclator of NEDDY. The functions of NEDDY are to:

— consider the country's economic performance and industrial and commercial prospects.
— to discuss the problems hindering faster economic growth.
— to find ways to improve industrial efficiency through consultation between management, trade unions and Government.

The NEDC meets monthly and reviews the medium and long term industrial, commercial and economic situation. It does not concern itself with day-to-day matters formally. In order to arrive at the overall picture, it may request the Economic Development Committee for specific sectors, e.g. Agriculture, or Electronics to carry out particular studies for it. In addition, the NEDC may set up working parties to examine particular subjects.

The EDCs and their sub-committees meet on a regular basis to review the progress and potential threats and opportunities in the industries with which they are concerned.

Each one has a Chairman, who is from outside the industry which is its predominant concern, representatives of the industry, including management and employees, and Government appointed officials.

The National and Economic Development Office is an independent body which is financed by public funds – controlled by a Director General. It is divided into three operating divisions.

— The Economic Division examines issues concerned with economic growth, prepares papers for NEDC discussions and gives advice and statistical support data to the EDCs.
— The Industrial Division does support work where necessary for the NEDC and provides a secretariat for the EDCs.
— The Administrative division does the administrative work of NEDDY, including providing a secretariat for the NEDC and involves itself in public relations functions.

3.   CONTROL OF THE MONEY SUPPLY

When money consisted primarily of precious metals, there was little need for the Government to control the money supply. This was limited by the supply of those precious metals and its value was based on theirs. In Britain, up to 1914, the supply of extra currency depended on the amount of gold coined at the Mint. From that time, money has been made of materials whose intrinsic value is far less than their face value and, although up until about 1931 the amount of money in circulation was based on the holding of reserves of gold bullion into which notes could be converted, from that time the link has been broken and the Government now regulates the amount of money in circulation through the Bank of England. Other banks are required to operate within a certain liquidity ratio, which issues Government securities to increase the money supply. The Government also controls the money supply by its taxation and transfer payments. e.g., the form of social security and policies. If the quantity of money is not controlled, inflation tends to be fuelled. This is the fundamental belief expressed in monetarism.

A current political issue is the international movement of capital and whether there should be more controls on investment overseas. The recent position on capital movement is as follows:

Table 6: Import/Export of Capital 1979 to 1989

Year	Export (£m)	Import (£m)	Net balance (£m)
1979	3030	5889	-2859
1980	4355	4867	-512
1981	2932	6005	-3073
1982	3027	4091	-1064
1983	3386	5417	-2031
1984	-181	6033	-6214
1985	3865	8456	-4591
1986	4987	11780	-6793
1987	8681	19128	-9447
1988	9218	20685	-11467
1989	18344	19365	-1021

4.   TO INFLUENCE THE USE AND DEVELOPMENT OF RESOURCES

Governments have some influence on the use and development of resources to ensure that they are economically used and dispersed in a socially acceptable way. Society may demand that some resources are conserved for the benefit of future generations, e.g. land, water, oil and other minerals. To this end governments have established conservation areas and green belts, and have passed anti-pollution laws to protect the community against ruthless exploitation.

Some productive systems may not be economically viable in a free market economy and it may be necessary to protect these activities by means of subsidy or, perhaps, nationalisation, or through the placing of Government contracts to ensure their continuance. This may be done either for strategic or defence purposes, e.g. British Aerospace.

Other organisations may require Government investment or loans to encourage them to develop resources or products which would otherwise be too expensive for these to fund themselves.

Generally, governments will attempt to create an economic environment which encourages investment in technological changes and improvements in business and managerial efficiency. Small firms and large firms face different problems in coping with the prevailing economic situation.

Small firms

The small firm, if it is efficient in meeting the demand for its products or services, will require access to capital in order to expand. In most cases this will require it to go into debt. Governments can help firms by means of their control of the level of interest rates and the availability of grants of one sort or another. Throughout the 1970s and 1980s, governments provided generous tax-based investment incentives to British industry to stimulate growth and maintain full employment. On the other hand, growth can be hindered by increases in taxation or any other policies which require firms to hold high levels of liquid funds. Thus, for example, it has been argued that the Incomes Policy operated by the Edward Heath Government in 1972-1974, which was based on threshold payments, had just that effect because of uncertainty about rises in the cost of living index. This triggered the threshold payments and reduced the propensity of small firms to invest in new productive assets, mainly because of uncertainty over how much cash they would require for wages and salary bills on a month-to-month basis. Conservative policy in the 1980s was to try and limit the legislative impact on small businesses in ordr to try and enhance employment in this sector.

There was a growth in the number of businesses registered for VAT in 1989 to a total of 1,611,000 which was an increase of 89,000 over the 1988 figures. A certain failure rate amongst small businesses is inevitable and these failures tend to occur in the second and third years of registration due to
— the effects of high interest rates and other finance related issues;
— the perceived problems of coping with government regulations and paperwork, and
— an inability to attract skilled and trained employees.

All regions have experienced a growth in the numbers of small businesses over the period from 1980 to 1989 ranging from 16% in the North West to 40% in the South East, with around 30% in East Anglia and the South West and 28% in the East Midlands. In the same period however there was a decline in the number of agriculture related businesses but 'other services' and financial and professional services showed the highest growth rates.

Government policy in the 1980s was to try and limit the legislative impact of individual labour law on small businesses in order to try and enhance employment in the sector.

In the past GB has tended to have a much smaller number of small firms than other countries but it is evident that the growth in this sector in the 1980s has narrowed the gap. In 1990 the European Commission published a report entitled "Enterprises in the European Community" which contained the results of a study of the size distributions of businesses in the 12 Member States in 1986. It showed that in all sectors other than agriculture that whilst the proportions of businesses and employment in the smallest firms in lower in the UK in comparison with the aggregate of the other Member States the differences were narrowing and the UK developments since has probably tended to reduce the gap further.

Table 7: Share of Enterprises and Employment UK compared with Europe 1986 (%)

	Very Small (0-9)	Small-Medium (10-499)	Large (500+)
Enterprises			
UK	90.1	9.7	0.2
EUR 12	91.3	8.6	0.1
Employment			
UK	23.2	46.8	30.0
EUR 12	26.9	45.0	28.1

Source: *Enterprises in the European Community report 1990*

Large firms

Large firms, on the other hand, which are an increasingly familiar feature of the UK economy, are usually more able to cope financially with short term difficulties because they can adapt their policies to changed political and economic conditions. Yet, longer term economic uncertainty and lack of economic control can lead to a preoccupation with 'survival' planning to the detriment of innovation, technological progress and growth. Survival can be bought by reducing high risk investment in new products, new production technology and the development of new markets at home and abroad and by not increasing their core labour force but by using overtime and part-timers to meet their needs.

Governments thus have a responsibility to reduce economic uncertainty in the market place and to attempt to encourage demand by the operation of appropriate economic and fiscal policies.

5. MAINTENANCE OF THE STABILITY OF FOREIGN EXCHANGE

The UK lacks many of the natural resources which are essential for the nation's survival. There is coal and, in recent years with the development of technology and investment in the North Sea, we have been able to extract oil and gas. We produce some of our basic foodstuffs. Yet, for many years, we have been increasingly reliant on imports of raw materials and other items which we either do not possess at all or cannot produce in sufficient quantities. The effects of this were especially evident during the Second World War when overseas assets, like Argentinian Railways and Malaysian rubber plantations, had to be sold off to pay for the essential goods we required for our survival. We thus need to export to produce sufficient foreign currency to pay for those things we need to import. Britain is now far more dependent upon her own industrial and commercial ability that it was a century ago when the 'Empire' produced exclusive sources of raw materials and we, in return, had tied markets for the disposal of the goods and services made from those raw material imports. Two world wars and the emergence of powerful new competitors, the USA, Japan and Germany in particular, plus the demand for political and industrial autonomy from most countries in the old Empire, which has broken many of the old trade relationships, has required British governments over the last thirty years to involve themselves consciously in helping the direction of our trading efforts to prevent balance of payments difficulties. Key influences on all governments since the mid 1950s have been our regular balance of payments deficits, inflation and the consequential effects on the value of sterling ever since our joining the European Exchange Rate Mechanism.

To facilitate trade to earn foreign exchange and maintain the value of the pound, governments have adopted various policies to try to contain prices at home and to ensure our competitiveness abroad. Until 1972, when the £ was allowed to float, governments tried to maintain the value of the currency at a fixed rate. In the immediate post-war era this was $4 to £1; then later $2.80; and then, from the devaluation of 1967, $2.42 to £1. Although, since 1972 until our joining the European Exchange Rate Mechanism in 1990, the pound has floated, the Government has tended to maintain the value of sterling at certain levels by dealing in the international money markets through the Bank of England.

Table 8: Sterling exchange rates annual averages

	US Dollar	Deutschmark
1979	2.12	3.89
1980	2.33	4.23
1981	2.03	4.56
1982	1.75	4.24
1983	1.52	3.87
1984	1.34	3.79
1985	1.30	3.78
1986	1.47	3.18
1987	1.64	2.94
1988	1.78	3.12
1989	1.64	3.07
1990	1.78	2.87

Source: *Economic Progress Reports* various issues.

In 1990 the UK finally agreed to join the European Exchange Rate Mechanism. This mechanism requires all member states to maintain the value of their currency within certain bands. Each currency has a central rate of exchange against other currencies in the mechanism and currencies can move in a percentage band up or down on this central rate. Central Banks agree to maintain their currency within the parameters of these bands by buying or selling the currency or by changing interest rates. If market pressures become too great and the policies required or attempted to maintain exchange rates within their bands become unsustainable, then a realignment conference may be called to consider and negotiate changes in parities.

6.   INFLUENCE THE DISTRIBUTION OF INCOME

A balance must be found between protection for those groups whose bargaining power is low relative to other groups whilst, at the same time, attempting to ensure that incentives for effort are available. We can identify three sources of income for individuals and families in the UK:

(a)   earned income, which can include all income from the employment relationship and from self-employment, including fringe and non-monetary benefits (e.g. pensions, free housing, use of a company car);

(b)   unearned income, which comes from ownership of assets and includes rent from the ownership of land or property and interest from investments;

(c)   transfer income: this is not paid in return for work or the use of an individual's assets but consists of benefits paid by the State, e.g. State pensions, family allowances, supplementary benefits, unemployment benefits, etc.

All households pay both direct and indirect taxation. *Direct* taxes are paid through income tax and national insurance contributions, and *indirect* taxes are paid through value added tax (VAT) and duty and through local community charges. Companies also pay taxes both directly and indirectly. Those taxes are used in Government expenditure from which the community as a whole benefits through the national health service, housing and food subsidies and payments of benefits and allowances in cash.

The main intention of expenditure on items such as pensions, supplementary benefits and unemployment benefits is to support people during periods of reduced earning, and their net effect is to redistribute earnings to the less well-off with low income families benefiting most. Similarly, the net effect of direct taxation, which rises as income rises, is that the better-off households pay more tax and income is redistributed to the less well off. In addition, in theory, indirect taxes take more from the higher income groups who spend more, and less from the lower income groups.

Evidence from the Royal Commission on the Distribution of Income and Wealth, 1975 and various issues of 'Social Trends', shows that the combined effect of the tax system, with the receipt of cash benefits, subsidies on rents and other benefits, does create some redistribution of income.

Table 9: Wealth distribution

Marketable wealth owned by wealthiest	1971 %	1976 %	1982 %	1983 %	1985 %
1%	31	24	20	204	20
5%	52	45	40	40	40
10%	65	60	55	54	54
50%	97	95	96	96	76
Total wealth (£ billions)	140	263	602	745	863

Source: *Social Trends*, various issues.

7.   TO MAINTAIN FULL EMPLOYMENT

Government policy, from the White Paper *Employment Policy* (Cmnd 6527), 1944, was to stimulate economic growth to 'maintain a high and stable level of employment' and this remained a priority of all governments until the mid 1970s, when unemployment began to increase substantially. However, the ability of a government to pursue a policy of full employment is influenced by the general world trade situation.

One of the major problems which all governments have to face is that the prosperity of each nation is linked to the world economy and, throughout the western world, unemployment is increasing. The movement of prices for international commodities has a significant impact on the prosperity of all economies, however large. This was particularly evident in the steep rise of international oil prices in the mid 1970s.

In addition, increasing independence of the emerging nations and now the Eastern Bloc in producing their own consumer goods, often financed by large multinational organisations who are taking advantage of relatively low labour costs and the availability locally of raw materials, has posed a threat to the security of employment of large sectors of the population in the traditionally-industrialised nations. Workers especially affected are those in vehicle manufacture, iron and steel production, the textile and electrical manufacturing industries.

In March 1985 the Government published the White Paper *Employment: The Challenge for the Nation* which was the first White Paper for forty years on employment, but reflected that the following words in the 1944 White Paper were still true.

'Employment cannot be created by Act of Parliament or by Government action alone. Government policy will be directed to bringing about conditions favourable to the maintenance of a high level of employment... but the success of the policy... will ultimately depend on the understanding and support of the community as a whole and especially on the efforts of employers and workers in industry; for without a rising standard of industrial efficiency we cannot achieve a high level of employment combined with a rising standard of living.'

The following points were emphasised in the White Paper:

— Jobs come from customer demand, i.e. when businesses produce goods and services that people want at prices they can afford;
— Public Sector Employment, however valuable, has to be paid for through taxation of both businesses and individuals;
— Adaptation to change is inevitable and something to which every part of society has to contribute;
— The role of Government, however crucial, is unfortunately limited. Its role is:

ROLE OF GOVERNMENT/POLICIES IN THE UK

(i) To provide a sound and stable framework of economic and industrial policy; to encourage sustained economic growth through an industrial environment in which organisations can flourish and industry and commerce can compete successfully and raise output. Thus a primary aim has to be to control inflation.

(ii) Within the economic framework the Government has to encourage jobs by removing obstacles which hinder employers taking on workers or prevent individuals using and developing their potential, and to modernise training so that job seekers are able to acquire the necessary skills for the future.

(iii) To take direct action to tackle problems of unemployment especially amongst those groups affected by changes in industry.

The White Paper listed the steps which were being taken or needed to be taken to improve the movement in the labour market. The task it suggested was to improve the workings of the labour market in several ways.

(a) In quality and incentives, so that people are neither prevented from pricing themselves into jobs (possibly by accepting lower wages than currently paid) nor deterred from taking them up.

(b) In flexibility, so that employers and employees adapt quickly to new circumstances.

(c) In freedom, so that employers are not so burdened by regulations that they are reluctant to offer more jobs.

Thus:

— The educational system has to recognise the importance of the wealth creating business and improve the level of vocational training for young people and adults. To this end the White Paper Education and Training for Young People 'April 1985 — *Better Schools*' suggested further modernisation of the school curriculum and the examination system, e.g. through the Technical and Vocational Education Initiative (TVEI) and more recently the Technical Vocational and Education Extension (TVEE) and developments in in-service training. In higher education development of plans for producing more graduates in the technological industries were felt to be needed.

— all young people should be offered training;

— industry need to constantly monitor its training requirements;

— flexibility should continue to be developed in patterns of worth with employers and trade unions cooperating with each other to facilitate it.

— employers need to ensure that pay rises which may damage competitiveness should be resisted and rises only linked with productivity.

— the growth of new enterprises should be encouraged.

— government training initiatives should be constantly monitored to maintain their effectiveness.

8. GOVERNMENT AS A CONSUMER OF GROSS DOMESTIC PRODUCT

The problems of the British economy over the last twenty-five years or so have led to increasing concern about the levels and distribution of public expenditure. In 1900, of the £10,380 millions of Gross Domestic Product the public authorities spent £1,164 millions, or 10% of GDP. In 1981, of the £260,000 millions the Government spent £129,000 millions, or 47% of GDP, by 1988/89 the proportion of the GDP had fallen to 39%.

Table 10: Public Expenditure as a Percentage of Gross Domestic Product 1963–1994 (%)

Source: Autumn Statement 1990

1963/64	37.0%
1969/70	41.0%
1975/66	49.0%
1978/79	44.0%
1981/82	49.0%
1984/85	47.0%
1988/89	39.0%
1993/94	39.0% est

This represents a major influence upon the economic and financial policies within industry and commerce. The Government obtains its funds primarily by forms of direct and indirect taxation; by selling goods and services; and by borrowing for example, in 1989, taxes accounting for about 81% of the total receipts of the Government and were obtained as follows (£1 billion = £1000m) in cash terms from 1986–1989.

Central Government income 1986––1989 (£ billion)

	1986	1987	1988	1989
Income tax	52.3	55.8	61.9	69.8
Expenditure taxes	62.9	69.1	76.0	80.1
Social Security contributions	26.1	28.6	32.1	32.8
Gross trading surplus/deficit	0.2	-0.1	-	0.1
Rent, dividend, interest etc	9.9	10.4	10.3	10.6
Other	2.8	3.1	3.4	3.7

Government expenditure in 1989 was as follows:

Table 12: Government Expenditure in 1989

Expenditure on:	£ billion
Subsidies	4596
Benefits & grants to local authorities	24106
Grants & benefits abroad	4814
Debt interest	17991
General public services	3935
Defence	20463
Public order & safety	2589
Education	1217
Health	23889
Social security	2369
Transport & communication	689
Other	4083

With revenue and expenditure levels this high, and in many cases growing, it is inevitable that there will be differences of opinion as to how far the development of the public sector has affected the competitiveness of British industry generally and how we should use our overall resources to regenerate our ability to compete in world markets.

9.   SOLVE ECONOMIC PROBLEMS

The potential solutions to our economic problems are varied and inevitably influenced by political viewpoints. Some would suggest that the only way that British industry can become more efficient in the long run is to protect it for a considerable period by a combination of import controls and tariffs. Meanwhile some would argue, the Government should intervene in the economy financially and by encouraging the development of planning agreements, through the operation of a National Enterprise Board. This will require more public ownership to protect the weaker but essential industries, and more central control and intervention. The other extreme position sees the future in the development of an economy which encourages competitiveness to improve overall efficiency; reduces taxation to encourage innovation, investment and profitability; and thus reduces the restrictions on enterprises, especially high income taxes which are said to demotivate the creation of additional effort, and corporation taxes which reduce potential efficiency. The change in the impact of taxation and national insurance on a married man with two children earning the average weekly wage illustrated as follows:

Year	Tax & National Insurance Contribution as proportion of income
1955	3.0%
1975	25.0%
1983	22.5%
1990	23.5%

If one considers the effects of all taxation and includes Income Tax, National Insurance and VAT etc. as a drain on income, figures produced by the House of Commons library in July 1985 show that the proportion of earnings taken by tax in 1978/9 was 37.4% for the average family man and 41.2% in 1985/6. In order to reduce the tax burden most argue that this would require a reduction in public expenditure and a shift in the balance of resources from the public to the private sectors of the economy. Part of the reduction in public expenditure can be achieved by improving the management of resources within public sector organisations.

Which strategies will be adopted from time to time will depend on the political leanings of the Government in power. One difficulty which is faced by governments generally is that they have to work within a five-year timetable, although many of the problems they face are so complex that the answers require a longer time scale. Governments often, however, feel it necessary to take action of temporary effectiveness to achieve immediate results. Several post-war governments, representing both political parties, have introduced incomes policies which have a short term effect but tend, in the longer term, to create higher wage demands as people try to recoup what they think they have lost.

Whatever strategies are adopted in the future, it is inevitable that governments will take economic action to facilitate employment and influence business activity: as the manager of the economy as a whole and the watchdog of our overall competitive economic position, it has no choice. Ultimately it has the responsibility for creating an industrial economic

Table 13: Annual rate of change of wage rates, retail
prices and gross domestic product 1953–90

Year	Hourly wage rate Oct–Oct (Male married)	Retail prices all items (Oct–Oct)	GDP at cost (year on year increase)
1953	4.4	1.7	4.2
1954	4.8	2.8	4.1
1955	7.0	5.3	3.3
1956	7.9	3.9	1.1
1957	5.8	4.3	1.7
1958	3.7	2.1	-0.2
1959	1.1	-0.2	4.6
1960	5.4	2.0	5.4
1961	6.4	3.9	1.8
1962	4.0	2.9	1.4
1963	2.8	2.3	3.2
1964	5.7	4.1	6.1
1965	7.2	4.8	2.7
1966	5.4	3.8	1.8
1967	5.4	2.0	1.8
1968	5.5	5.6	4.3
1969	5.6	5.4	2.0
1970	11.6	7.4	1.6
1971	11.7	9.4	1.5
1972	15.5	7.9	3.2
1973	11.3	9.9	6.1
		(Jan–Jan)	
1974	22.1	15.0	-1.8
1975	25.4	19.9	-1.9
1976	15.8	23.4	2.1
1977	5.1	16.6	2.5
1978	18.0	9.9	3.0
1979	–	9.3	–
1980	20.7	18.4	-2.3
1981	13.0	13.0	-1.3
1982	9.4	12.0	2.1
1983	8.4	4.9	3.3
1984	7.3	5.1	2.8
1985	.	5.0	3.5
1986	.	5.5	3.0
1987	.	3.6	4.9
1988	.	3.3	4.6
1989	.	7.5	2.7
1990	.	7.7	.

environment to ensure adequate and sustained growth for the benefit of all. It must, therefore, be concerned with education, manpower planning, regional development and technological innovation and with helping organisations to cope with the problems of rapid change. Progress in our type of economy should not mean profits and benefits for the few and hardships for the many. Thus, it is also a duty of governments to ensure that there is an equitable distribution of the nation's wealth and that there are basic safeguards against hardship for those who are affected adversely, despite planning. The Government should also ensure that legislation provides the framework required to make the employment relationship equitable and should ensure that those areas where collective bargaining power is weak should not suffer too much in comparison with those whose collective bargaining strength enables them to improve their standard of living.

A Government should encourage economic activity and increase Gross Domestic Product whilst, at the same time, attempting to control the retail price index so as not to increase the pressure on wages caused by inflation. The annual rate of change in wage rates, retail prices and GDP from 1953–1990 can be seen in Table 13.

CHAPTER ELEVEN

THE UK POLITICAL SYSTEM

1. INTRODUCTION TO THE UK POLITICAL SYSTEM

It has long been recognised that if individuals are going to live together in a community some rules must be developed to lay down the acceptable parameters of behaviour. In order to derive those rules and control their application, some sort of leadership or government has to be established. Politics exist because individuals and groups have different interests and hold different beliefs and attitudes towards the aims, objectives and rules of their society. In order to turn the expression of their views into the reality of practice, individuals, as members of groups, have to acquire the power necessary to achieve their political objectives. It is through power that things can be done and power can be obtained by the force of the gun on the one hand or the cut and thrust of reasoned debate leading to success in a democratic election on the other.

The nature of political institutions and the manner in which they operate is influenced by the culture in which they have developed and reflect and embody the beliefs and mores of the society over time. Britain, it must be remembered, has a long history of independence and national unity and its institutions have not been affected by the wars and revolutions which have significantly influenced other societies; it has been protected from foreign invasion since 1066. Britain uniquely amongst the world nations does not have a written constitution or body of rules and practices which regulates its Government. There are, however, numerous statutes which influence the composition and powers of particular institutions. Thus for example:

— The Magna Carta of 1215 provided certain rights. Article 39 reads:

'No free man shall be taken or imprisoned or deprived of his lands or outlawed or in any way destroyed, nor will we go upon him nor put upon him, except by the lawful judgement of his peers or the law of the land'.

The free men of the Magna Carta did not include serfs but the principle was the same. The King had rights, free men had rights and even serfs had rights and no one might infringe those rights.

— In 1628 the Petition of Right prescribed that taxation could only be levied by Parliament;

— The powers of the Monarchy were limited by the Bill of Rights of 1689 and the Act of Settlement of 1701;

- The powers of the House of Lords were defined by the Parliament Acts of 1911 and 1949;

- The modern electoral system was regulated by the Representation of People Acts of 1948 and 1949.

Other individual rights have developed through a process of evolution, enforced by the judges in the Courts, based on the principles of Common Law.

Additional rights are laid down by other Acts of Parliament which establish fundamental rights and freedoms and limitations on behaviour.

The British system of Government has authority resting in a single legislative organisation — Parliament, which comprises the House of Commons, the House of Lords and the Monarch. Supreme power lies with Parliament which has direct control over legislation and indirect control over the actions of the Cabinet and the Civil Service (EEC membership has imposed some limitation on the sovereignty of Parliament, if UK legislation is found to be in conflict with EEC rights and freedoms). No Parliament can bind a future Parliament and in the UK the Government is ultimately accountable to the people and can be removed by the people.

In theory, the powers of the Sovereign to use the Royal prerogative and act without consulting Parliament are very wide. In practice, that power is restricted and the Monarch only acts on the advice of the Government members. The Monarch has power to summon, prorogue and dissolve Parliament but normally does so on the advice of the Prime Minister. Technically, the Monarch has power to select and appoint all Ministers, including the Prime Minister, but these decisions are invariably made within the Party winning an election and the appointments are confirmed by the Monarch. Thus, the influence of the Monarch these days is only indirect through the weekly meetings with the Prime Minister of the day and her reading of State Papers. All Acts of Parliament however have to receive the Royal Consent.

The House of Lords is the upper house or second chamber within Parliament and comprises hereditary peers, life peers and the Archbishops and Bishops; in essence the House of Lords is the successor of the Great Councils of the Monarch in the 11th Century. Until 1911 the House of Lords had virtually the same powers as the Commons and it could veto legislation, but by the Parliament Act of 1911 the upper house had its rights limited to delaying Bills for two years and this was reduced to one year in 1949. There are three functions of the House of Lords:

(i) It revises Bills sent to it by the Commons and sends them back to the Commons for reconsideration. This is useful because many Bills are not given a full enough debate in the Commons because of pressure of time on the discussion, and amendment and tidying up of legislation by the Upper House is generally welcomed by the Commons.

(ii)   It saves the time of the Commons by giving a first hearing to non-controversial Bills introduced by the Government.

(iii) It constitutes a chamber in which major issues of national policy can be debated without the pressure of time that influences the Commons.

The House of Commons consists of 650 elected members of Parliament whose major role is to scrutinise and criticise the activities of the Government. This role can be split down into three parts:

(i)   Parliament provides a system where Government can explain its policies to the electorate and where the policies can be questioned and discussed so that they can be amended, approved or rejected.

(ii)   Parliament can also influence and restrain the Government by its ability to control the raising of money, primarily through taxation and its spending of that money.

(iii) Parliament is a forum through which individual members of the electorate, via their MP, can air their grievances.

One of the major functions of Parliament is, of course, to pass legislation. Every law starts as a Bill and only becomes an Act when it has been read, debated and approved three times in both the Commons and the Lords and has received the Royal Assent.

Because the MPs in their formal debates cannot give detailed consideration to all aspects of Bills and public administration in general, there are within the House of Commons a variety of sub-committees:

(i)   *Standing Committees,* which are appointed for each Parliamentary session. They consist of 30/40 MPs from all political parties chosen to try to refllect the distributions of the Parties, with a Chaiman apointed by the Speaker. These committees discuss and investigate the Bills proceeding through Parliament.

(ii)   *Select Committees,* which inquire into specific aspects of Government can be of two types:
       — *ad hoc* committees set up to inquire into specific issues, which are disbanded once the investigation and report is complete;
       — *permanent committees* of whom are set up to monitor the work of Government departments and others which, for example, look after matters such as privileges, European legislation, House of Commons services, Public Accounts and Statutory Instruments.

Not all legislation is totally comprehensive and many Acts of Parliament confer powers on Ministers or local authorities to make further rules, regulations and orders within the limits and purposes of the statutes. These laws, when made by Ministers, are generally known as Statutory Instruments and can be drawn up through consultation to meet changing situations or to comply with EEC legislation without having to go to the lengthy process of amending Acts through new Bills. They are known as 'delayed legislation' because they are made through the authority given by Parliament and there are some 2,000 or more Statutory Instruments a year. The Select Committee on Statutory Instruments, chaired by a member of the opposition, and which includes members from both the House of Lords and the House of Commons, monitors these before they are laid before Parliament whence they become Law, if they are not challenged, after 40 days.

The relationship of Government can be represented as follows:

Figure 32: Relationships of Government bodies/roles

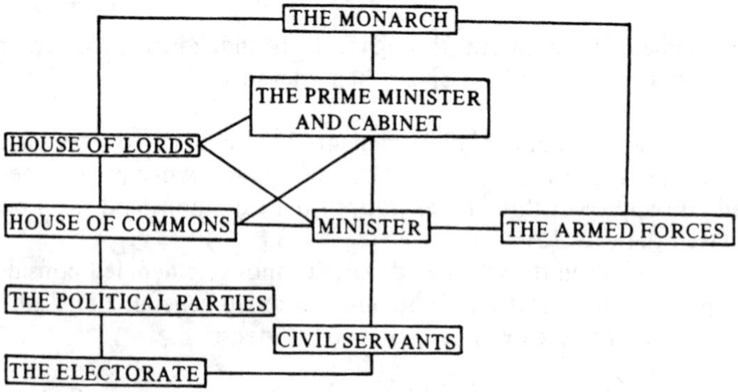

The British system of Government is referred to as a liberal democracy in that:

— Limitations are put on Government action and the power of the State by the constitutional obligations that have been established.
— Individuals and groups are tolerant of the political views and opinions of others and those views can be expressed openly as there is a recognition that society is pluralist (i.e. consists of divers views) and conflict of ideas is seen as creative.
— Periodic elections are held at least once every five years in accordance with the 1911 Parliament Act.
— There is universal franchise; since 1969 everyone over the age of 18 has the right to vote and any individual in society over the age of 21 can stand for election.

- Basic civil liberties — freedom of association, freedom of speech and freedom from arrest — are protected.
- Elected representatives, whatever their political allegiance, have to be accountable to, and represent, all members of their constituency.

The Government consists of some 100 or so ministers (a maximum number of 95 of whom can sit in the Commons); of these ministers 20 or so are the Cabinet which is headed by the Prime Minister and which meets regularly once or twice a week. It is the Cabinet which formulates and establishes Government policy. It is, therefore, the responsibility of the Cabinet which is chosen by the Prime Minister:

- To reconcile the demands of ministers and coordinate the work of departments;
- To establish the priorities of Government action;
- To further the objectives of the party in power's manifesto;
- To modify policy in the light of the current situation;
- To deal with unforeseen problems and crises,and
- To generally look after the well being of the nation.

A number of Cabinet Committees of either an ad hoc or a permanent nature are set up to help expedite the business of Government. These enable non-Cabinet ministers to influence policy decisions.

The ability of Parliament to control the Government is limited for the following reasons:

(i)   MPs of the Government party very rarely, in divisions of the House of Commons, vote against their party. This is particularly important where a Government has a slender majority.

(ii) Amendments to legislation are often fought by the Government, unless the objectives complement the proposed legislation, as they may be seen as ministerial defeats.

(iii) The procedure of the House requires that at Question Time each MP is restricted to one supplementary question which enables Government ministers to evade problem question's to give themselves time to respond in a more informed way.

(iv) The Government controls the Parliamentary timetable.

(v)   Government ministers are much more able to be better informed on matters than the average back bench MP, which gives them a greater edge in Parliament.

2.   VOTING PATTERNS IN POST-WAR BRITAIN

Until relatively recently, political commentators on British post-war politics have argued that we have a two party political system and that the dominance by one party in Parliament – the House of Commons – is crucial to the idea of responsible Government and the ability of the Cabinet to run the country. This belief can no longer be maintained as a general trend has been discernible away from the two-party domination of politics since June 1951 and the formation of the SDP and the SDP/Liberal Alliance in 1981/82 and later the realignment into the Liberal Democrats has produced a threat to Labour/ Conservative domination. This can be illustrated by Tables 14 and 15.

Table 14: Party votes as percentages of electorate 1951-1987

	1951	1955	1959	1964	1966	1970	Feb 1974	Oct 1974	1979	1983	1987
Conservative	39.6	38.2	38.9	33.5	31.7	33.4	29.9	26.1	33.3	30.8	31.8
Labour	40.3	35.6	34.5	34.0	36.4	31.0	29.3	28.6	28.0	20.0	23.2
Lib/SDP											17.0
Liberal	2.1	2.1	4.6	8.6	6.5	5.4	15.2	13.3	10.5	18.4	
Other	0.6	0.9	0.7	1.0	1.2	2.2	4.4	4.8	4.4	3.4	3.2
Abstentions	17.4	23.3	21.3	22.9	24.2	28.0	21.2	27.2	23.8	27.3	24.7

Table 15: Votes cast and members elected at general elections 1951 – 1987

Year	Conservative Votes	Seats	Labour Votes	Seats	Liberal Votes	Seats	Others Votes	Seats	Total Seats
1951	13718199	321	13948883	295	730345	6	198966	3	625
1955	13310891	345	12405254	277	722402	6	3211822	2	630
1959	1350875	365	12216172	258	1640760	6	254845	1	630
1964	12002642	304	12205808	317	3099283	9	349415	0	630
1966	11418455	253	13096629	364	2327457	12	422206	1	630
1970	13145123	330	12208758	288	2117035	6	873882	6	630
Feb 1974	11872180	297	11645616	301	6059519	14	1762847 *	23 *	635
Oct 1974	10462565	277	11457079	319	5346704	13	1922756	26	635
1979	13697753	339	11509524	268	4313931	11	1799582	17	635
					Lib/SDP Al				
1983	13012612	397	8456504	209	7793778	23	1320590	21	650
1987	13763066	376	10029778	229	7341290	22	1702005	23	650

Source: various

(* NB: due to realignment of the Northern Ireland Unionists.)

THE UK POLITICAL SYSTEM

The argument that electoral support for the two major parties — Labour and Conservative — has reduced, can be made for a number of reasons:

(a)   these two parties now win fewer votes and seats;

(b)   The turnout at elections has generally declined. Turnout at elections is however generally higher in rural areas than in urban areas and is particularly low in the inner cities.

(c)   bye-election results specifically show evidence of disenchantment with the two major parties;

(d)   opinion polls underline the loss of support for the major parties;

(e)   surveys have shown that voters are less inclined to identify themselves as Conservatives or Labour.

Despite these statements, the majority of people still tend to vote for one or other of the two major parties, but their share of the vote has steadily declined over the last 30 years. Thus, for example, in 1951, 97% of those who voted, voted either Labour or Conservative, yet in October 1974 only 75% voted for either of these two parties, and by the General Elections in 1979 and 1983 70% showed allegiance to the two major parties with omly a small reversal to 73% in 1987.

The proportion of the electorate who turn out to vote at a General Election has also declined from 82.6% in 1951 to 76.2% in 1979 and 72.7% in 1983 and 73.1% in 1987. This has paralleled the decline in the Labour/Conservative party vote share. For example, in October 1974 the largest party vote was for the Labour Party and the second largest group were those who abstained. The Conservatives effectively came third in popularity.

There has also been an increase in those voting for other parties. In 1951 only 2.7% of the electorate voted for other parties, in February 1974, 19.6% voted for other parties; in 1983 30.1% voted for the other parties and in 1987 27.1%. The increase in the number of Members of Parliament representing parties other than Labour or Conservative has acquired increasing importance because it has occurred at a time when the difference in the numbers of MPs returned by the two major parties has been declining. Hence, the smaller parties are increasingly liable to hold the Parliamentary balance.

In the aftermath of the indecisive election of 1974, in order to try and retain power, Ted Heath sought an agreement with the Liberal Party, but his offers were rejected and in 1977, when the Labour Party lost its overall majority in Parliament, the Labour and Liberal parties agreed to the LIB–LAB pact of March 1977. This lasted until the end of the 1977–78 Parliament and enabled the Labour Party during that time to retain Government.

Statements by the Liberal Democrats in 1991 suggest that in return for a move towards Proportional Representation (PR) they are prepared to form alliances with either of the other major Parties.

This increase in electorate voting for other parties has opened the debate about our current method of electing representatives. Our method at present is 'first past the post', but other methods debated have included preference voting' where the votes of the weakest candidates are transferred to other candidates according to the preference of the voters and the one which has been argued should be adopted by the Liberals — proportional representation — in which the seats won are proportional to the votes cast. These arguments have occurred because the votes captured by the parties other than the major two have increased much more dramatically than their number of Parliamentary seats. This is especially evident in the February 1974 election when the Liberals gained the support of 15.2% of the population, but only obtained 2% of the Parliamentary seats. 1987 saw the SDP–Liberal Alliance obtain 22.6% of the votes cast and only 22 seats. It is also evident on a regional basis for, in 1979, the Scottish Nationalist Party — the SNP — obtained 17.2% of the Scottish vote, but only returned two MPs to Parliament and, in 1970, the Welsh Nationalist Party — Plaid Cymru — obtained 11.5% of the Welsh vote, with no MPs returned.

No party since 1945 has won 50% of the votes cast and in March 1974 the Labour Party was able to form a single party Government with only 37% of the votes cast. It can be ascertained that had a system of PR operated at the time of the 1987 election the final result would have read as follows;

Conservatives with 42.3% of the actual votes cast	279 seats
Labour with 30.8% of the actual votes cast	202 seats
SDP/Liberal Alliance with 22.6% of the votes cast	149 seats
Other Parties with 4.4% of votes cast	20 seats

Bye-election results have also shown loss of support for the two main parties. Since 1964 bye-elections have shown that the party of Government is likely to lose even safe seats with large electoral swings, although the seats may return in the next General Election; for example, between 1964 and 1970 the Labour Government lost 16 of the 31 seats it defended, and between 1974 and 1979 it lost 7 of the 21 seats.

In an article 'Partisan Realignment in Britain 1964–74' in the *Scottish Journal of Political Science* Vol 7, 1977, Ivor Crewe, using survey data gathered over a 10 year period from 1964–74, found a weakening of the willingness of manual workers and workers in general to think of the Labour Party as their party, and an increase in the proportion of the electorate who consistently voted for the minor parties as an alternative to the main parties. There was also evidence of a substantial growth of those who switched from voting to abstention and the article hinted that this could be the result of an increased scepticism amongst the electorate about politicians. The 1987 election showed some evidence of tactical voting by the electorate which seemed to be maintained in the Bye-elections which followed and in the Council Elections of May 1991.

Despite the election results of 1983 and 1987 many commentators would argue that the alternation of the two major parties in office alone is becoming a more arguable presumption, especially with the formation of the Social Democratic Party in January 1981, and the SDP–Liberal Alliance which was so formidable in the total share of the votes in 1983 and 1987 despite the problems posed by the concept of a joint leadership under David Steele and David Owen which eventually proved untenable. The Labour Party has apparently lost the old working class traditons of loyalty and solidarity which once gave them so many safe seats and the Conservatives have lost the confidence of many of the influential institutions which once backed the party. Both parties are unable to rely on the loyalty of large numbers of supporters. Particularly influential have been the geographical influences on the Parties of the Scottish and Welsh Nationalists and also the influence of the realignment of Northern Irish Unionists who, until 1974, voted in Westminster with the Conservatives. The Conservative Party is stronger in the South East including East Anglia, the Midlands and Southern England, whereas the Labour Party is stronger in the North West, Scotland, Wales and Northern England. The 1983 & '87 elections produced the following results:

Seats	Conservative		Labour		Others	
	1983	1987	1983	1987	1983	1987
N.W. Britain	103	81	150	170	18	22
S.E. Britain	294	295	59	59	13	6

One of the problems which occurs with our political system is that elections must be held at least every 5 years. The dominance of the two parties has tended to produce adversary politics with the opposition party criticising and attempting to replace the existing governing party. This electoral system results in discontinuities in Government policy between both parties, and constant attention to the opinion polls from halfway through office. This can lead to decisions being made with the next election in mind, rather than necessarily what is required for the long-run benefit of the economy and the population in general.

Neither of the two main parties appears able to generate the conditions for overcoming Britain's economic decline or managing the recession in a way that wil restore faith in Parliamentary Government and the parties themselves. So long as the central economic problems of a low annual growth rate obtains, compared with our major competitors, there will be a readiness of electors to switch their votes and party allegiancies. Annual rates of growth are given in Table 16.

REAL GROSS DOMESTIC PRODUCT
Table 16: Annual percentage growth rates 1960–1982
TOTAL

	1960–68	1968–73	1973–79	1979–82
USA	4.5	3.3	2.6	0.1
Japan	10.5	8.8	3.6	4.1
West Germany	4.2	4.9	2.4	0.2
France	5.4	5.9	3.1	1.0
UK	3.1	3.1	1.4	-0.5
Italy	5.7	4.6	2.6	1.2

PER HEAD OF POPULATION

	1960–68	1968–73	1973–79	1979–82
USA	3.2	2.2	1.6	-0.9
Japan	9.4	7.3	2.5	3.3
West Germany	3.3	4.0	2.6	0.1
France	4.2	5.0	2.7	0.5
UK	2.5	2.8	1.4	-0.6
Italy	5.0	4.0	2.1	-0.9

Source: *OECD Historical tables* 1960–1982 OECD Paris

Election campaigns are becoming increasingly sophisticated as the media campaigns develop. Election expenditure of the main parties for 1983 and 1987 had the following costs;

Party	1983	1987
Conservative	£5.7m	£11.8m
Labour	£4.0m	£6.7m
Alliance	£3.5m	£4.2m

2.   THE CONSERVATIVE PARTY

The Conservative Party structure can be represented as in Figure 16. The Conservative Party has been more often and longer in Government in the 107 years since the extension of the voting franchise in the 1884 Third Reform Act than any of the other parties who have held Government in that time.

Either alone or in coalition, they have held office for 72 years and have won fifteen of the twenty-eight elections. In order to maintain this record Conservative leaders have had to operate an electoral strategy which appeals to all sectors of the community and which ensures a substantial number of working class votes, although office holders within the Party tend to be primarily middle class. Estimates by D Butler and P Kavanagh, in *The British General Election 1987*, Macmillan, 1988, have suggested that in 1987 54% of management and professional classes (A,B + C1), 40% of the skilled working class (C2) and 30% of the unskilled working class and others (D and E) voted Conservative. Thus, in 1987, nearly 40% of the voters did not vote for the party of their social class. It was also estimated that 30% of trade unionists voted Conservative (Data from MORI polls), a drop in 2% from 1983.

Figure 33: Structure of the Conservative Party

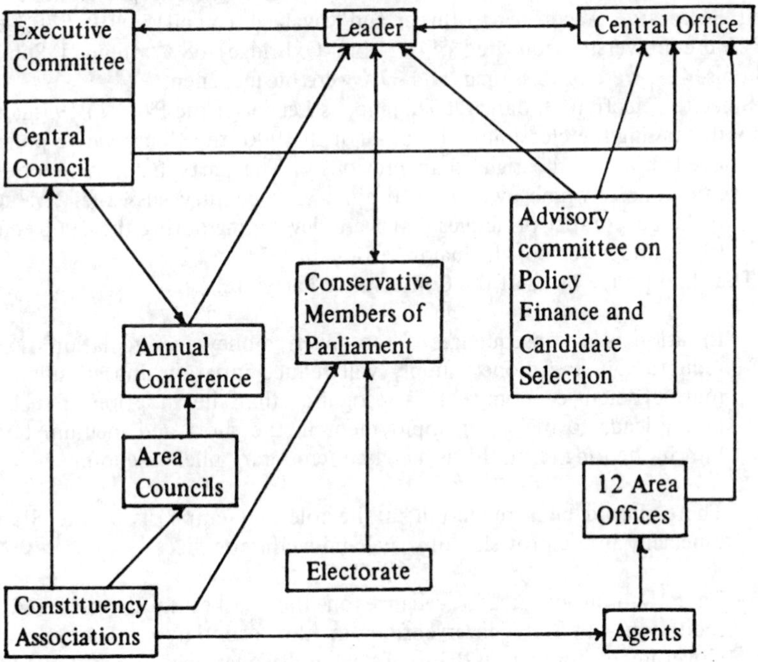

Source: A R Ball *The British Political Parties* Macmillan, 1981

Conservative leaders have tried to ensure that the party does not consider itself to be an instrument of any particular part of the electorate. There is a tendency to identify it as the party of big business finance but it has a following amongst all class groups thus, for example, in 1983 and 1987 members of the relatively affluent working class who were car owners, employed in the private sector, and buying their own houses, tended to vote Conservative.

Home-ownership was especially significant. MORI found that, whereas council house tenants voted 57% Labour and 25% Consevative, the figures amongst working class voters owning or buying their own homes were 32% Labour and 44% Conservative voting.

All important powers in the party are concentrated in the hands of the Leader to whom all the major Committees, Central Office departments and area offices report. The Cabinet is appointed by the Leader as is the Chairman and all the other leading officials of the party. Financially it is the wealthiest of the political parties.

Members of Parliament are in class and social terms unrepresentative of their electorate. According to Butler and Kavanagh (op.cit) in 1987 70% of MPs were university educated (44% from Oxbridge) 68% attended Public Schools, 42% were professionals and 37% were businessmen.

Since the election of Margaret Thatcher as Leader of the Party in 1975, and notwithstanding the election of John Major in 1990, the Conservative policy has moved more to the right than previously. The party has now adopted economic policies which owe more to nineteenth century laissez-faire values than to the corporatist principles that were developing during the 1960s and early 1970s under both of the major parties.

The chief policy bases of the Conservative Party are:-

(a) Inflation is a consequence of too much money in circulation, so a reduction in the money supply will reduce inflation and stimulate a more efficient economy. It is recognised that the adoption of such a policy leads to higher unemployment in the short and medium term but, in the long term, this is merely a temporary phenomenon.

(b) There should be a reduction in the role and emphasis of the State, especially in the provision of social and welfare services.

(c) There should be greater reliance on the market mechanism and a reduction of State intervention in the economy. The sale of Government holdings in British Telecom, BP, National Freight Co. Ltd., privatisations of British Airways, British Gas, British Transport Docks Board are examples. As a consequence, major State aid to ailing sectors of the economy should be reduced. This is set to continue with the proposed privatisations of British Coal and British Rail.

(d)   There should be a shift from direct to indirect taxation to encourage the individual enterprise necessary for industrial reorganisation.

(e)   Trade unions should be controlled so that they do not use their monopolistic position to hinder free market economic forces and impinge on the freedom of individual citizens. To quote from the Conservative election manifesto, Conservatives are 'committed to redressing the balance in industrial relations by curbing the abuse of Trade Union power wherever it occurs and by tackling some of the uniquely privileged positions of Trade Unions under the law'. The 1980 and 1982 Employment Acts go some way towards protecting individuals against the collective power of the Trade Unions and the Trade Union Act 1984 aimed at increasing democracy in Trade Unions and the 1988 and 1990 Employment Acts removing the influence of the Closed Shop. The proposals to require public sector workers to give 14 days notice of industrial action will continue the theme.

(f)   There should be continued reduction in public spending with more direct control of Local Goverment spending.

Summary of Tory Party Policy:
— free market economy;
— trade union reform;
— cuts in public expenditure and taxation;
— sale of nationalised industry (privatisation);
— economic liberalism to create a climate of profitability and enterprise to encourage small businesses;
— rigid monetary targets to control inflation;
— no interference in wage negotiation;
— no help to failing enterprises;
— the unity of the UK;
— continued membership of the EEC;
— continued support for NATO;
— emphasis on encouraging training and retraining.

There are inevitable conflicts between the different wings of the Party on these economic policies, but these differences tend to represent differences of emphasis rather than differences of fundamental ideology. The so called 'wets' were heirs of those who believed in Keynesian economic policies and who are less sure of the validity and desirability of allowing free market forces to operate. Broad agreement exists over the need for public spending cuts, reform of trade unions, and inflation control, but they disagree about the primary reliance on monetarism as the way to bring these objectives to fruition.

4.   THE LABOUR PARTY

The structure of the Labour Party can be depicted as in Figure 34.

Figure 34: Structure of the Labour Party

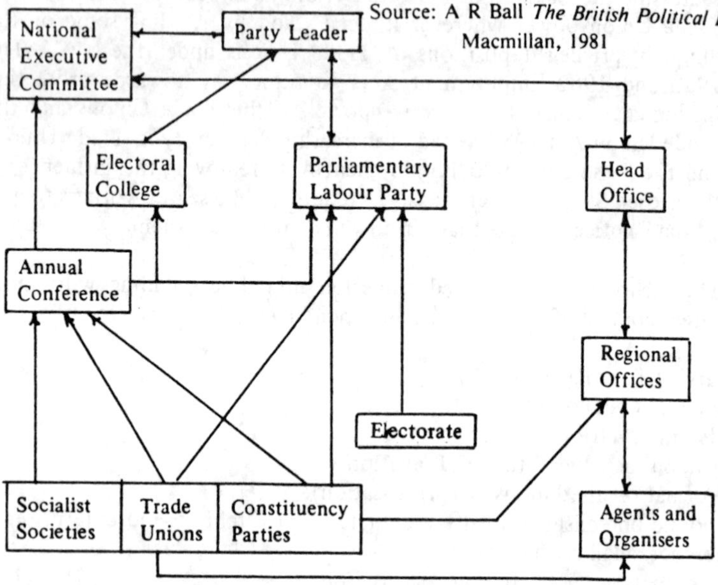

Source: A R Ball *The British Political Parties* Macmillan, 1981

The Labour Party Constitution is formal and elaborate and attempts to control the Leader. It is based on the assumption that the Leader is in office to carry out the wishes of the members of the party. In practice, policy is decided by the National Executive Committee which the Annual Conference elects.   The Leader must be re-elected every year when the party is in opposition. The party franchise in the selection of the party leader and the deputy leader has been extended and the choice is not left entirely to MPs. More power has been given to the NEC and the Constituency parties. More power has also been given to the NEC in the drafting of the election manifesto and re-selection of MPs takes place by constituency parties between General Elections, thus giving more power to the rank and file. Trade unions control 40% of the votes for Leader, the constituency parties 30% with the Parliamentary Labour Party the other 30%.

The Labour Party was founded in 1900 and grew originally out of the political desires of the trade union movement. After its foundation in 1900, it was more of a pressure group than a political party and its hopes of political success rested on its ability to persuade other parties to legislate on its behalf. Both in 1924 and 1929, the party took office without having a majority in the House of Commons and, as a result, it found it had the responsibility of governing without the power to govern.

The Labour Party is a coalition of socialists and was formed to express the views of the trade union movement and progress their social and political objectives. The unifying beliefs of the groupings within the party can be said to be the use of Parliamentary means for achieving power; the goal of economic equality of opportunity in income, wealth and living standards; the elimination of poverty; protection of working class interests; and a vision of society as one in which the means of production, distribution and exchange are publicly owned. Divisions exist over the range of policy options and the extent to which socialist ideals should be promulgated in Government.

Labour Party support is broad but its greatest support comes from amongst the working classes in general, especially amongst the unskilled. Thus, in 1987, according to Butler and Kavanagh (op. cit.) 18% of the social classes AB + C1 voted labour, 36% of the C2's, and 48% of the D's and E's voted for the party. Labour therefore reflected only a portion of the working class, only 38% of manual workers and 42% of trade union members – blue collar and white collar – voted Labour.

Crucial to the strength of the Labour Party are the trade unions. They provide the party with 79% of its finance. In 1983 6.0 million of the Labour Party's 6.4 million members were affiliated to the party as members of trade unions. The unions dominate the seats on the National Executive Committee. Unions also sponsor MPs and, in 1987 there were 129 union-sponsored MPs in the Parliamentary Labour Party, out of a total of 229 Labour MPs in all. The figures from 1983–1987 can be seen in Table 17 and the figures for 1900 to 1987 in Table 18.

Unions influence Labour voting by their participation in the Annual Conference and their influence on the election of the National Executive Committee. Communication takes place with those unions who are not directly affiliated to the Labour Party but which are affiliated to the TUC by the Existance of the Labour Party – TUC Liaison Committee. On this Committee sit 9 members of the Parliamentary Labour Party, 10 representatives of the NEC and 7 representatives of the TUC.

The social background of the Labour MPs elected in 1987 was more cosmopolitan than that of their Conservative colleagues, according to election studies; 53% went to University, 14% had been to Public School; 40% were professionals, 10% businesspeople; 29% were manual workers and 21% were white collar workers and others.

Table 17: 1983 & 1987 Elections: union sponsored candidates

Union	Total		Elected	
	1983	1987	1983	1987
TGWU	30	44	25	33
AEU	27	14	17	12
NUM	14	13	14	13
GMB	14	12	11	11
ASTMS (now MSF)	11	9	10	8
NUR	12	9	10	8
NUPE	10	16	4	9
APEX	3	3	3	3
COHSE	3	8	3	4
EETPU	7	3	3	2
NCU	3	2	3	2
SOGAT	82	2	2	2
USDAW	2	9	2	8
UCATT	2	1	1	1
OTHERS	11	19	6	16
TOTAL	154	164	115	129
COOPERATIVE PARTY	17	20	8	10

Table 18: Union sponsored MPs, 1900–87

Election year	No of Labour MPs	No of Union—Sponsored MPs	% of MPs who were Union Sponsored
1900	2	1	50.0
1906	30	21	70.0
1910–1	40	38	95.0
1910–2	42	39	92.8
1918	57	49	85.9
1922	142	86	60.6
1923	191	102	53.4
1924	151	88	58.2
1929	287	115	40.1
1931	46	32	69.5
1935	154	79	51.3
1945	393	121	30.8
1950	315	110	34.9
1951	295	105	35.6
1955	277	96	34.6
1959	258	93	36.0
1964	317	120	37.9
1966	364	132	36.3
1970	287	114	39.7
1974 Feb.	301	127	42.2
1974 Oct.	319	129	40.1
1979	269	133	49.6
1983	209	115	55.0
1987	229	129	56.8

Not all trade unions are affiliated to the Labour Party and, in 1990, only 53 trade unions had a political fund. This does not mean that, of those 54, all their members are affiliated to the Labour Party, as many members go through the process of contracting out of the political levy. Thus, for instance, in 1990 only 45% of MSF members were affiliated, whereas 99% of UDM members were.

Table 19: Political allegiances of Trade Union members

	Oct. 1974	May 1979	June 1983	June 1984	June 1987
Labour	55%	51%	39%	51%	42%
Conservative	23%	33%	31%	26%	30%
Liberal/SDP	16%	13%	29%	21%	26%

Source *MORI* 84 and 1987

The main features of Labour Party policies could be summarised as follows;

— increased public investment including transport, housing and energy conservation;
— increased investment in industry especially in new technology with some steering of jobs and industries to areas of high need. Creation of a National Investment Bank;
— new job subsidies and allowances to encourage employment and training;
— a Department of Industrial and Economic Planning with a 5 year National Plan in consultation with employers and trade unions;
— repeal some of the Conservative legislation on industrial relations and make provision for introducing industrial democracy;
— common pension age of 60 to be introduced;
— return to public ownership some public assets sold off by the present Government;
— improve social services;
— increase spending on education;
— introduce positive action programmes to promote women's rights and opportunities and the rights and opportunities of racial minorities;
— on defence — new initiatives to promote peace and development;
— strengthen Britain's position in the EEC.

Conflict can occur between the left of the party, organised around the Tribune Group, and on the right of the party, those organised around the Manifesto Group. The close relationship with the trade unions does not ensure an ability to obtain total cooperation from the unions, as the events in

1969 over *'In Place of Strife'* and 1979 over Incomes Policy show, although agreements like the Social Contract and the Concordat of 1979 are more likely with Labour than the Conservatives. Tensions within the Labour Party as to policy can influence its share of the vote, which dropped in 1983 to 20% of the electorate – the smallest poll percentage since 1931. The tensions within the Party in the run up to the 1987 election produced the second lowest number of MPs and the second worst performance in votes since 1945. However the 1987 election campaign was fought in a very professional way and arguably they won the media campaign. In addition the steady expansion of home ownership and the growth in the white collar labour force has undermined some of its traditional support. In the last four years much useful work has been done to try and develop more modern policies to attract the voters back.

5. THE LIBERAL PARTY latterly THE LIBERAL DEMOCRATS

The Liberal Party was strong in British politics from the mid-nineteenth century to the outbreak of the First World War, but it declined to a minor position in the 1930s, 1940s and 1950s. Liberal policy for a long time has talked of a partnership between capital and labour and some form of industrial democracy; it has long advocated membership of the Common Market.

Since the Second World War the number of Liberal MPs at Westminster has varied between 6 and 14, yet the actual share of the votes which the Liberals have gained has been increasing and Liberals have judged their performance on this ability to gain votes rather than the winning of Parliamentary seats. Their share of the vote has been as low as 2.5% in 1951, and as high as 19.3% in February 1974 (see Table 20). Yet only at one election in October 1974 has the party fought all the Parliamentary seats. During the 1960s it tended only to fight 50% of them. Seats were fought or left unfought depending on local decisions, which reflect organisational preparedness and the political confidence of the local constituency. For the first time in 1983 and then in 1987 all the Parliamentary seats on the mainland were fought by the Liberal/ SDP Alliance.

Evidence suggests that there is a hard core Liberal vote which spans all the social groupings but with an emphasis particularly in the lower middle classes, especially professionals, and then a much larger group of Liberal sympathisers. After the break with the SDP the Liberals after some soul searching changed their name to the Liberal Democrats.

Most evidence suggests that the floating Liberal Democrat vote is a result of dissatisfaction with the other major political parties and especially those with a central (as distinct from left or right) belief on many economic and social issues. Thus, the emphasis on moderation rather than extremism by the Liberal Democrat Party attracts votes. Interestingly enough evidence suggests that the Party does best when the Conservatives rather than Labour have been in power, especially at bye-elections. This has tended to reinforce the view amongst many Liberals that it is more in opposition to the Conservatives than to the Labour Party and explains the Lib-Lab pact of 1974.

Liberal Democrat candidates tend to pursue a policy of 'community politics' and concentrate on local issues which are of direct concern to the local voters.

LIBERAL DEMOCRAT PARTY POLICIES

The main features of Liberal Democrat Party Policies could be outlined as follows:

— worker participation and profit sharing (in firms of 50) are seen as important. Thus, every company of 20 employees should have a Works Council with a statutory right to information, consultation and joint decision making;
— supervisory Boards would be introduced in all companies of 200 employees, with no requirement that the only channel for elections would be through the union;
— introduction of electoral reform;
— decentralised public sector pay bargaining;
— civil liberties and fundamental freedom should become a constitutional right;
— local income tax
— decentralisation in decision making to the Regions with Regional and Community Enterprise Boards;
— stronger statutory protection of the environment including pollution taxes;
— expansion of public spending, especially in the development of new technologies, training and retraining, new building programmes and education
— potential increases in taxation to pay for increased public expenditure;
— retention of membership of the EEC; support for the single European currency
— support the NATO alliance, the establishment of a Nuclear free zone; increased educational opportunities.

Liberal Democrat MPs are overwhelmingly middle class. MPs come predominantly from the professions and business people. Generally, the Liberals fail to get consistent working class support. In the 1987 election 26% of their vote came from the AB and Cs and 20% from trade union members.

Table 20: Liberal election results 1950–1987

Election	Seats won	% vote	No of candidates	No of lost deposits
1950	9	9.1	475	319
1951	6	2.5	109	66
1955	6	2.7	110	60
1959	6	5.9	216	55
1964	9	11.2	365	52
1966	12	8.5	311	104
1970	6	7.5	332	184
1974 Feb.	14	19.3	517	23
1974 Oct.	13	18.5	619	125
1979	11	13.8	577	284
1983	17	13.8	322 *	7
1987	17	22.6	327	n/a

* Seats split with SDP

Source: D E Butler and A Sloan – *British political facts 1900–1979* Macmillan; D E Butler & D Kavanagh *The British general election of 1983* 1984, Macmillan, D. Butler and D. Kavanagh *The British General Election of 1987,* 1988, MacMillan.

6. THE NATIONALIST PARTIES: SCOTTISH NATIONALIST PARTY (SNP) AND PLAID CYMRU (PC)

The fortunes of the Liberal Party in the 1960s and 1970s were to some extent mirrored by the SNP and PC, who experienced increased electoral participation in local and national elections. There followed a slow ebbing of support with defeats in the 1975 EEC referendum, while the devolution referendums of March 1979 constituted a reversal for the SNP and disaster for PC. Table 21 gives vote shares for SNP and PC. The nationalist parties in 1987 obtained 1.7% of the UK vote.

Table 21: Vote shares for the Scottish Nationalist Party & Plaid Cymru 1959–1983

| | SNP | | PC | |
	Seats	% Scottish vote	Seats	% Welsh vote
1959	0	0.8	0	5.2
1964	0	2.4	0	4.8
1966	0	5.0	0	4.3
1970	1	11.4	0	11.5
1974 Feb.	7	21.9	2	10.7
1974 Oct.	11	30.4	3	10.0
1979	2	17.3	2	8.1
1983	2	11.8	2	7.8
1987	3	14.0	3	7.3

The Nationalist Parties have been the recipients of a negative protest vote and have reflected the reactions to regional economic difficulties – both Scotland and Wales have a feeling of neglect at Westminster. The SNP case was helped enormously by the development of North Sea oil, for it can be argued that an independent Scotland would not suffer enormously from a break up of the UK. PC has no such advantage but its support is rooted firmly in the principality's culture and language, and is greatest in the Welsh speaking areas.

7.   NORTHERN IRELAND PARTIES

Before 1972 Northern Ireland enjoyed a measure of self government and therefore the elections to the Stormont Parliament were more important than Westminster elections. Economic and class factors play an unimportant role in Northern Ireland. Political allegiance and voting behaviour occurs because of religion: Protestants vote for the various Unionist parties and for the maintenance of links with Britain, whereas the Catholics (33% of the population) tend to vote for Unification Parties.

Until the 1970s the Unionist parties in Northern Ireland were indistinguishable from the Conservative Party, but with the 1972 suspension of the Stormont Parliament, these old alliances broke up and the Ulster Unionist Party fragmented into different units. The old Nationalist Party disappeared and its place was taken by the Social Democratic and Labour Party (SDLP). After 1974, the Protestant MPs refused to follow the Conservative Party whip and there are now 17 independent MPs who do not specifically align themselves with any of the other majorparties.

In contrast to the position in the rest of Great Britain, turnout in the 1983 General Election rose compared with 1979 but in 1987 fell to 67.4% the lowest since 1966..

Northern Ireland voters had the choice of 6 political parties for the 17 seats which were contested in 1987 — the results were as follows:

— the Official Unionist Party (OUP) — 9 seats — 37.6% of the vote;
— Provisional Sinn Fein — 1 — 11.4% of the vote;
— Alliance Party — 9.9% of the vote;
— Democratic Unionists Party (DUP) — 4 — 11.7% of the vote;
— Social Democratic and Labour Party (SDLP) — 3 — 21.5% of the vote;

8.   SOCIAL DEMOCRATIC PARTY

A new party was formed in January 1981 by some disaffected Labour MPs and ex MPs who were concerned with the increasing involvement of the 'left' in the design of the Labour Party's policies, especially the arguments for unilateral disarmament and to discontinue membership of the EEC. The initial founders of the party — the 'gang of four' were ex MPs (at that time) Shirley Williams, Bill Rodgers, David Owen and the ex Labour MP and President of the EEC, who in the Dimbleby Lecture in November 1979 had argued for a party of the 'radical centre', Roy Jenkins. In March 1981 the party was formally established supported by 14 ex Labour MPs and one Conservative. By 1982 the SDP MPs numbered 29 and opinion polls showed the SDP in alliance with the Liberals as a powerful embryonic force in British Politics. In the 1983 General Election, 23 out of the SDP MPs were not re-elected. The 1987 election was fought in a joint alliance with the Liberal Party under the banner of the Alliance with David Owen and David Steele as joint leaders. The Party with the majority of MPs to determine the Prime Minister.

At the General Election in 1983, the SDP — Liberal Alliance polled 25.4% of those voting and in 1987 22.6%.

SDP ELECTION RESULTS 1983 AND 1987

	Seats	% rate	Number of Candidates	Lost Deposits
1983	6	11.6	311	6
1987	5	shared with Liberals	306	n/a

Of the MPs elected, 3 came from the professions and the other 2 came from middle class white collar jobs; 4 went to university (3 Oxbridge) and 2 had attended Public Schools.

As a result of the differences of opinion as to the reasons for the relative decline in the Alliance vote during the 1987 election the Alliance was broken up and several of the SDP MPs transferred their alliegance to the Liberal

Democrats. Only the results of the next election will show whether David Owen's party is finally dead, he is not standing.

THE GREENS

Environmental issues are increasingly being seen as important both in the UK and in Europe and the World in general. More and more organisations are being questioned on their policies regarding the environment. Public awareness has been raised by a number of ecological disasters in recent years. The burning of the oilfields in Kuwait, the Exxon Valdez affair, Chernobyl etc. Some advance has thus been made by the Green Party which was formerly known as the Ecology Party. Their share of the votes in the last three General Elections was as follows;

	1979	1983	1987
No. of candidates	53	108	133
Overall votes	39,918	54,299	89,753
% vote	1.5	1.0	1.4

9.   EFFECT ON PERSONNEL MANAGEMENT

With the reduction in the vote for the two major parties over the last 25 years or so, it is increasingly likely that the balance of power in future Parliaments will be held by the minority parties. This could have the effect of reversing the trend where one party, when it gains power, either repeals, in entirety employment legislation passed by the other party, or amends the legislation to limit what are seen as the excesses of the previous Government. It thus will be less easy to forecast the likely effects on labour legislation with changes in Government. This was illustrated in the period of the weak Labour Government, under Harold Wilson in 1964, which only had a majority of 3 over all the other parties after 2 months of office. Priority was given to winning the next election and policies were therefore much less radical than people would have expected.

The issues would be clearer if either of the two major parties were returned to power, although how far they could fulfil their manifesto promises would depend on the levels of economic activity and the pressures of inflation, the balance of trade and the value of sterling and levels of unemployment. Only if we can increase the growth in our gross domestic product, whilst at the same time, holding down increases in retail prices (which are inevitably affected by the price Government charges for its services), can we reduce pressures on wage rates and allow organisations and their personnel staffs to devote their time to the other crucial issues of productivity and the introduction of technological innovations.

The increasing involvement of Government in public sector terms and conditions settlements and the consequential financial and manpower cut backs have adversely affected relations between the employers and the trade unions in those industries. Disputes in recent years in the local authorities, the coal mines, the railways, the NHS, education, fire service, water industry, etc., have left scars which, in the present economic climate, will be slow to heal. Issues like control of wages and privatisation will continue to cause problems for some time.

CHAPTER TWELVE

THE INFLUENCE OF THE EUROPEAN COMMUNITY

1. THE EUROPEAN COMMUNITY

The European Community can trace its origins back to the Treaty of Paris which was signed in April 1951, when France, Germany, Italy, Luxembourg and the Netherlands created the European Coal and Steel Community (ECSC) which operated from 1952. This Treaty placed the coal and steel industries of these countries under the control of a common European body. Whilst it was recognised that such an arrangement would potentially bring considerable economic benefits, the underlying objective of the Treaty was to remove from the individual nations sole control of key industries which were necessary to sustain any future war. The central coordinating body of the ECSC, the High Authority, was allowed to impose production quotas, introduce minimum prices and set import ceilings when circumstances required it.

As the initiative seemed to prove successful the Foreign Ministers of the six member states of the ECSC at a conference in Messina in 1955 set up a committee to study ways in which a United States of Europe could be developed. The Committee reported in 1956 with a proposal to construct a customs union between the six countries. This was translated into action on the 25th March 1957 when the two Treaties of Rome were agreed and signed, the one setting up the European Economic Community (EEC) the other the European Atomic Energy Committee, Euratom. The broad objectives of the Treaty were,

— the creation of a customs union,
— the elimination of all tariff barriers between Member States, and
— the construction of a common external tariff.

There was also an inferred longer term objective which was to attempt to develop common economic policies and the convergence of the management of the national economies. These aims can be derived from the Treaty preamble which present the original goals of the Community as follows,

"To lay the foundations of an ever closer union between the peoples of Europe... to ensure economic and social progress by common action to eliminate the barriers which divide Europe."

This was expanded in Article 2, as follows

"The Community shall have as its task, by establishing a common market and progressively approximating the economic policies of Member States, to promote throughout the Community a harmonious development of economic activities, a continuous and balance expansion, an increase in stability, an accelerated raising of the standard of living and closer relations between the States belonging to it."

Further expansion can be found in Article 3 which defined the intended activities as,

"(a) the elimination......of customs duties and quantitative restrictions on the import and export of goods, and of all measures having equivalent effect;
(b) the establishment of a common customs tariff and of a common commercial policy towards third countries;
(c) the abolition....... of obstacles to freedom of movement for persons, services and capital;
(d) the adoption of a common policy in the sphere of agriculture;
(e) the adoption of a common policy in the sphere of transport;
(f) the institution of a system ensuring that competition in the common market is not distorted;
(g) the application of procedures by which economic policies of the member states can be coordinated and disequilibria in their balance of payments remedied;
(h) the approximation of the laws of the member states to the extent required for the proper functioning of the common market;
(i) the creation of a European Social Fund in order to improve employment opportunities for workers and to contribute to the raising of their standard of living;
(j) the establishment of a European Investment Bank to facilitate the economic expansion of the community by opening up fresh resources;
(k) the association of the overseas countries and territories in order to increase trade and promote jointly economic and social development."

The Merger Treaty or Treaty of Brussels in 1965 led to the merger in 1967 of the executive bodies of the ECSC, Euratom and the EEC into the European Community. In 1970 the Werner Report proposed closer monetary union of the six Member States but further development of the idea was stultified by the period of relative economic stagnation initiated by the oil crisis of 1973. The Community grew in 1973 with the accession of Denmark, Ireland and the UK, in 1981 when Greece joined and in 1986 with the accession of Portugal and Spain to comprise currently a community of 12 countries.

The Single European Act was signed in February 1986 and amends and develops the previous Treaties. This Act outlined certain Community objectives for greater cohesion of the member states. These were,

— the completion of the European internal market, an area without frontiers by December 1992,

— the development of further technological interchange,

— further progress towards economic and monetary union,

— the strengthening of economic and social cohesion,

— the improvement of the ecological and working environments,

— enhanced cooperation in foreign policy.

The Act defines the Single European Market as,

"an area without frontiers in which the free movement of goods, persons, services and capital is ensured in accordance with the provisions of the Treaty [of Rome]".

2. THE INSTITUTIONAL SYSTEM OF THE EUROPEAN COMMUNITY

Before examining the role and activities of the various institutions within the Community it is useful to examine the following guide on page 296 to the legislative process which operates.

1. The Commission.

The Commission is composed of 17 members representing at least one citizen from each Member State of the Community. The number of Commissioners which each country is entitled to varies based on size, thus Belgium, Greece, the Netherlands, Denmark, Ireland, Portugal and Luxembourg each have one whilst Germany, Spain, France, Germany, Italy and the UK each have two. The two current UK Commissioners are Sir Leon Brittan and Bruce Millan.

Each Commissioner is appointed for a potentially renewable term of four years with the mutual approval of the various Community governments. Once appointed they are required to act solely in the interest of the Community as a whole and they take an oath of independence from their own government and therefore cannot be expected to act upon instructions from their own country's legislators.

The Commission is subject to the overall supervision of the European Parliament which is the only organisation which has the power to force the Commissioners to resign en masse. Decisions are taken by the Commission as

Figure 35: Legislative Process of the European Community

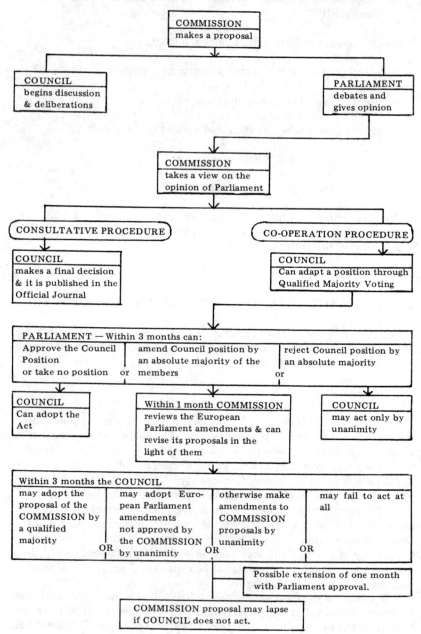

a whole although each Commissioner is designated with areas of responsibility in overseeing the work of the 23 Directorates General which comprise the administrative arm of the Commission. These are

DGI	External relations
DGII	Economic and financial affairs
DGIII	Internal market and industrial affairs
DGIV	Competition
DGV	Employment social affairs and education
DGVI	Agriculture
DGVII	Transport
DGVIII	Development
DGIX	Personnel and administration
DGX	Information, communication and structure
DGXI	Environment, consumer protection and nuclear safety
DGXII	Science, research and development
DGXIII	Telecommunications, information industries, and innovation
DGXIV	Fisheries
DGXV	Financial institutions and company law
DGXVI	Regional policy
DGXVII	Energy
DGXVIII	Credits and investments
DGXIX	Budgets
DGXX	Financial control
DGXXI	Customs union and indirect taxation
DGXXII	Coordination of structural instruments
DGXXIII	Enterprise policy, distributive trades, tourism and cooperatives.

The Commission's main roles are as follows.

1. It is the 'guardian' of the Treaties and is the primary organisation which has responsibility for ensuring that Community legislation is correctly and properly implemented. If it finds that a company or even an individual has broken Community rules or principles, it can impose fines, Appeals from these fines can be made to the European Court of Justice. Member States which break the rules and their obligations can be taken to the Court of Justice for censure.

2. It also has an 'initiating' role. It makes proposals to the Council of Ministers on Community policy and legislation in the areas of social policies, regional policies, agriculture, energy, industry, research, the environment, foreign affairs, external trade, economic and monetary union and any other matters of concern. These proposals are made after consultation with professional organisations, experts and the Commission's

legal service. It is then up to the Council to discuss them and consult with the European Parliament and, if considered appropriate, to amend or adopt the proposals.

3. The Commission also has an 'administrative' role in implementing Community policies whether these are based on Council decisions or are direct provisions of the Treaties. Thus for example it has wide powers in sectors such as steel and coal over decisions on investment and price control and it has the responsibility for ensuring that there is fair competition within the Community by scrutinising monopolies. In addition it manages and implements Community programmes through
   - the European Agricultural Guidance and Guarantee Fund to modernise agriculture;
   - the European Regional Development Fund to encourage regional and industrial development;
   - European Coal and Steel Community grants;
   - the European Social Fund to assist in the implementation of policies aimed at equipping the Community's workforce with the necessary skills required for the development of the economic wealth of the Community. Thus financial help is provided towards vocational training, guidance, recruitment, wage subsidies and resettlement;
   - the Framework Programmes for Research and Technology development for promoting scientific research;
   - the European Development Fund and food aid programmes for overseas relief.

4. It also has a 'representative' function and maintains contact with other international organisations. It operates under instructions from the Council to negotiate commercial treaties with organisations outside the Community.

3.   THE COUNCIL OF MINISTERS AND THE EUROPEAN COUNCIL

The Treaty of Rome designated the Council of Ministers as the prime decision making body of the Community consisting of Ministers from the individual states. Each government acts as the President of the Council in rotation each six months. The relevant participants in the meetings vary with the topic under consideration, thus farming matters are handled by Agriculture Ministers, employment matters by Employment Ministers and so on. The Foreign Affairs Ministers in their Council maintain a coordinating role over the special interest Councils.

Twice a year, the Heads of State or Government and their Foreign Affairs Ministers meet as the European Council with the President of the Commission and other Commissioners to discuss and make decisions on areas of policy. The Council has authority to

(i)   issue Regulations and Directives;
(ii)   make Decisions; and
(iii)   formulate Recommendations and Opinions.

(i)   Regulations.

These have general application, are binding in every respect and are directly applicable in all Member States. Through Regulations the Community can therefore legislate directly onto member countries without being required to operate through national parliaments. Regulations are published in the Official Journal and are binding either, on a specified date, or, 20 days after publication.

(ii)   Directives.

These are binding on any Member State to which they are directed but they leave the national Government to decide for themselves the precise form and means of implementation which has to be completed within a stated time period. Failure to implement Directives into national law could lead to enforcement proceedings.

(iii)   Decisions.

These are binding in their entirety on those to whom they are directed. Decisions can be directed at Member States, enterprises and individuals and those enforcing financial obligations are enforceable through the Court system of the Member State concerned.

(iv)   Recommendations and Opinions.

When these are made they have no binding force and express the view of the institution that issues them, they therefore have informal rather than formal influence.

The Single European Act amended the original voting form of the Treaty of Rome to encourage and espouse the more frequent use of the system of *qualified majority voting* from 1987 rather than requiring unanimity in making decisions. Unanimous voting is still required for those matters relating to taxation, the free movement of people within the Community, and workers' rights. Other decisions, particularly in relation to the completion of the internal market, research and technology, regional policy and improvement in the working environment, e.g. health and safety, can be made on the basis of majority voting. 54 votes are required out of a total of 76 votes in qualified majortiy voting in order to adopt a Commission proposal. The votes allocated to each country are as follows;

- 10 votes UK, Germany, Italy and France;
- 8 votes Spain;
- 5 votes Belgium, Greece, The Netherlands and Portugal;
- 3 votes Denmark and Ireland;
- 2 votes Luxembourg.

It is therefore now possible for two of the major countries to be outvoted by the remainder of the Community. The system of qualified majority voting only applies to the following Articles of the Treaty;

- Article 54(2) which are directives abolishing restrictions on freedom of establishment;
- Article 56(2) relating to coordination of national measures providing for special treatment of foreign nationals on grounds of public policy, security or for health reasons;
- Article 57 on mutual recognition of formal qualifications (excepted access to the professions) and on coordination of national measures concerning the pursuit of jobs as self employed people;
- Article 100A which addresses matters concerned with completing the internal market;
- Article 100B regarding proposals relating to national measures not harmonised by the start of the single market in 1993;
- Article 118A concerning the adoption of basic requirements for the implementation of improvements in health and safety at work;
- Article 130E on the implementation of decisions relating to the European Development Fund;
- Article 130Q(2) which relates to other programmes in the arena of regional development.

4. COMMITTEE OF PERMANENT REPRESENTATIVES

In carrying out its legislative functions the Council of Ministers is assisted by the Permanent Representative Committee known collectively as a COREPER. It consists of civil servants from each of the Member States most of whom have the rank of Ambassador. The overall duties of this group include,
- communication with various Community institutions the views and interests of their own government on the matters being discussed;
- having discussions with relevant interest groups to ensure that any proposal being deliberated upon by the Council has the potential approval of their government.

Generally, therefore, the overall aim is to attempt to ensure that any opposition or reservations are resolved as far as possible before they are debated in their final form by the Council of Ministers.

5. THE EUROPEAN PARLIAMENT

Until 1979 the European Parliament was made up of nominees from national parliaments. Since that time it has been elected directly by the citizens of the individual Member States however the European Parliament does not have the same legislative powers as our parliament. The 568 seats are allocated on the following scale;

- 81 seats, Germany, France, Italy and the UK.
- 60 seats, Spain;
- 25 seats, The Netherlands;
- 24 seats, Belgium, Greece and Portugal;
- 16 seats, Denmark;
- 15 seats, Ireland;
- and 6 seats from Luxembourg.

European MPs however take their seats on the basis of broadly similar political groupings as follows.

Table 22: Main Political Groupings in the European Parliament from 1979—1990

	1979	1981	1984	1987	1990
Socialists	112	124	130	166	180
European People's Party	109	117	110	113	121
Communists & others	44	48	41	48	42
Liberal Democrats & reformists	40	38	31	46	49
European democratic alliance	22	22	29	29	22
Rainbow	11	12	20	20	14
European right	—	—	16	16	17
Non attached	10	10	7	14	10
European Democrats	64	63	50	66	34
Greens	—	—	—	—	29
Total	412	434	434	518	518

Taking the figures for 1990 the next table shows the source country of MEPs.

Table 23: Main political groupings in the EC by Country (1990)

GROUP	UK	Portugal	Nether lands	Luxem bourg	Eire	France	Spain	Greece	Germany	Denmark	Belgium	Italy	Total
Socialists	46	8	8	2	1	22	27	9	31	4	8	14	180
Euro. people's party	1	3	10	3	4	6	16	10	32	2	7	27	121
European democrats	32	.	.	.	.	.	.	.	.	2	.	.	34
Communists & others	.	3	.	.	1	7	4	4	.	1	.	22	42
Liberal democrats & reformers	.	9	4	1	2	13	6	.	4	3	4	3	49
European democratic alliance	.	.	.	.	6	13	2	1	.	.	.	.	22
Rainbow	1	.	.	.	1	1	2	.	1	4	1	3	14
European Right	.	.	.	.	.	10	.	.	6	.	1	.	17
Non attached	1	.	1	.	.	1	2	.	.	.	.	5	10
Greens	.	1	2	.	.	8	1	.	7	.	3	7	29
Total	81	24	25	6	15	81	60	24	81	16	24	81	518

The Parliament meets in Brussels or Stasbourg and its role includes the following.

1. A legislative function: It participates in the formulation of Directives, Regulations and Community Decisions by considering the Commission's proposals and based on the debate amongst MEPs the Commission can be asked to amend its proposals. The Single European Market in addition provides for an enhancement of the cooperation procedure between the Council and the Parliament. Under the new procedure the Council adopts a common position on a Bill taking into account the opinions of Parliament. Parliament then has three months to adopt the proposal, which if it does so (or if it decides to take no action) passes into law. However, if the MEPs reject the Bill or propose amendments on its second reading by Parliament, the Council can only pass the original version by unanimous vote, otherwise it must adopt the Parliament's version or totally reject the Bill.

The Single European Act also added a new 'assent' procedure whereby the conclusion of international agreements between the EC and non EC countries or the admission of new members into the Community are subject to the ratification by European Parliament.

2. A political function: Together the Euro MPs represent the views of some 325 million people within the Community. Parliament thus has the ability to influence policies of the Commission and Council. Within their Member States the members of the Parliament are able to influence the policies of their own parties as they develop their expertise on European wide matters.

3. A budgetary function: Parliament is the organisation which can adopt or reject the Community Budget which is prepared initially by the Commission. Euro MPs exercise joint control with the Council on non obligatory expenditure, i.e. outside the farm expenditure which is obligatory in the original Treaty, and on which the Council has the final say. Parliament has the right to reject the Budget in total which it did in 1979 and 1985.

4. A supervisory function: Parliament has the power to ask questions about and comment on the Commission's programme. It has the power to force the Commissioners to resign en bloc if it adopts a censure motion by a two thirds majority.

Whilst its powers have certainly been enhanced by the Single European Act the Parliament is still not the pan European legislating body which some would like it to be, the Council still retains the primary power.

6. EUROPEAN COURT OF JUSTICE

The European Court of Justice consists of 13 judges representing at least one from each Member Country and 6 advocates general. These are nominated by the individual States and serve for terms of six years. The Court which operates in Luxembourg is the guardian of the Treaties and is the supreme legal body of the Community. It can operate at a number of different levels and can act as

— a constitutional court;
— a labour tribunal;
— a court of appeal from Community decisions; and
— as a court of interpretation for the assistance of national courts.

It is able to hear complaints from the Commission, a Member State against another Member State, an enterprise operating within the Community and any individual from a Member State.

The first stage of the procedure involves a written complaint and defence. This is followed by an oral hearing at which the evidence is presented to the judges. In the third stage, the Advocate General gives an opinion and finally the judges deliver a verdict which can be based on a majority vote. Judgements of the court are binding on each Member State and have primacy over national law and can therefore be used as precedents.

As Community law becomes more and more reflected in the laws of the individual Community countries the decisions of the Court of Justice are becoming more important to national courts.

7. COURT OF THE FIRST INSTANCE

In July 1988, the Council of Ministers agreed to the establishment of an EC Court of the First Instance which has jurisdiction over a number of Community areas especially in the area of competition. It is hoped it will take some of the delay out of progressing issues and some of the load off the Court of Justice.

8. ECONOMIC AND SOCIAL COMMITTEE

This Committee was set up as the primary forum for discussion of consumer, labour and employer interest groups so that their views could be passed on to the Community decision making and formulating institutions. Thus before a Commission proposal on matters relevant to the Committee can be made, an opinion must be sought from the ESC. The Council would also consult it before making final decisions. The Committee is thus a consultative body, it has 189 members who represent employers, trade unions, farmers and consumer interest groups.

9. COURT OF AUDITORS

The Court of Auditors is based in Brussels and is made up of 12 members who are appointed for six years by agreement of the Council of Ministers. It supervises the management of the Community budget. It has extensive powers to ascertain the legality of spending and to ensure that money is not mismanaged. The finance for the Community comes from a proportion of VAT collected in each of the Member States and from customs duties and levies on goods imported into the Community.

Table 24: Community Expenditure 1973 & 1989 (in ECU)

Item	1973		1989	
	ECUm	%	ECUm	%
Agriculture and fisheries	3627	80.6	30032	67.0
Regional policy	-	-	4294	9.6
Social policy	249	5.5	3232	7.2
Research, energy, and industry environment and transport	70	1.6	1536	3.4
Development cooperation	61	1.4	1032	2.3
Miscellaneous	250	5.5	2562	5.7
Administration	248	5.5	2153	4.8
Total	4505	100.0	44841	100.0

10. EUROPEAN INVESTMENT BANK

The European Investment Bank (EIB) is an independent organisation within the Community with its headquarters in Luxembourg. It's role is to encourage Community development through its policy on loans. It obtains funds from the capital markets and relends on a non profit making basis to finance development in the following areas;

— regional development,
— urban landscaping and regeneration,
— improvements in the transport and telecommunications infrastructure,
— protection of the natural environment, e.g. water projects,
— protection of architectural heritage,
— strengthening industry's international competitiveness,
— development of advanced technologies,
— and help for small and medium sized industries.

During the 1970s and 1980s amongst the major UK borrowers from the EIB were the Electricity and Water Boards, Local Authorities, British Gas, British Rail, British Steel, British Telecom and the Post Office.

11. EUROPEAN SOCIAL POLICY BODIES

A number of organisations are involved with the Commission and the Economic and Social Committee in consultations over the Community social policy.

THE INFLUENCE OF THE EUROPEAN COMMUNITY

(a) Standing Committee on Employment.
This was established in 1970 with the aim of providing a consultative forum where employers and trade union representatives could meet and share opinions on employment matters. Enthusiasm for the Committee has generally not been high amongst employers, who have expressed the view that it should be abolished. Trade unions on the other hand believe the Committee could be a useful forum and the trade unions have tried, so far unsuccessfully, to raise the status and reputation of the forum.

(b) Sector Committees.
Each committee, of which there are currently eight, is composed of equal numbers of employers and labour representatives recommended by national associations. The purpose of these committees is to hold meetings of those with specialist interest to discuss matters of common concern. The current Committees are;

— Joint Committee for the Harmonisation of Working Conditions in the Coal Industry;
— Joint Committee for the Harmonisation of Working Conditions in the Iron and Steel Industry;
— Joint Committee on Social Problems for Agricultural Workers;
— Joint Advisory Committee for Social Problems in Road Transport;
— Joint Advisory Committee for Social Problems in Inland Navigation;
— Joint Committee on Social Problems in Sea Fishing;
— Joint Advisory Committee on Social Problems in the Railways.

(c) Advisory Committees.
These committees were created to serve a variety of purposes which include,

— offering advice on the implementation of particular policies;
— fulfilling the overall structural policies of the Community;
— dealing with recommendations on the approximation of laws;
— contributing to the development of EC Social Policy.

There are currently a number of Advisory Committees on,

— vocational training;
— safety, hygiene and health protection at work;
— mines health and safety;
— general health and safety;
— the European Social Fund;
— social security and migrant workers;
— free movement of workers.

(d) European Foundation for the Improvement of Living and Working Conditions.
This organisation is primarily a research and policy centre with the aim of disseminating knowledge on working conditions and technological change in order to assist in the development of living and working conditions in the Community. This entails,

— encouraging the exchange of information and experience;
— encouraging contact between educational establishments;
— setting up working parties;
— providing financial assistance for pilot projects;
— and organising courses, conferences and seminars.

It's management committee is tripartite and includes representatives of the trade unions, employers and the Commission itself.

(e) European Centre for the Development of Vocational Training (CEDEFOP).
CEDEFOP is also a tripartite body, including representation from trade unions, employers and the Commission. Located in Berlin it has the following roles;

— to assist the Commission in encouraging at Community level the promotion and development of both vocational training and continuing education;
— to compile and disseminate relevant research in the field of education and training;
— and to encourage the exchange of information and experience relating to Member States' education and training policies and practices.

12. EUROPEAN INFLUENCE GROUPS

(a) Union of Industries in the European Community (UNICE).
UNICE was formed in 1957 and is the European equivalent of the CBI in Britain. It's role is to attempt to influence the decisions made by the main Community Institutions. The main policy areas of UNICE include;

— the successful completion of the Single European Market;
— the creation of a favourable climate within which enterprises can operate, including encouraging the improvement in adaptibility of the labour market, a reduction in State and Community intervention where considered unnecessary, and reduced interest rates;
— the promotion of technological research and development to increase Community competitiveness with the outside world;

— the convergence of national economic policies and increased financial and monetary integration;
— to encourage the Community to play an enhanced role within GATT to encourage greater world trade liberalisation;
— to challenge outside the arena of health and safety many of the principles of the Social Charter.

UNICE represents 33 employers' confederations from 22 countries.

(b) European Trade Union Confederation (ETUC).
The ETUC was formed in 1973 and it's Constitution states it's aims as being to

"represent and promote the social, economic and cultural interests of workers at the European level in general, and in particular in respect of all European Institutions, including the European Communities ......"

and further,

"to safeguard and strengthen democracy within Europe."

It broadly supports the move towards the Single European Market and argues that a social dimension is a critical part of the process because it believes that otherwise there will be industrial and geographical within the Community. It believes that the European social programme should include;

— an increased protection to help with genuine collective bargaining;
— social legislation that improves economic and social cohesion to ensure that all employees in the community are covered by a collective agreement;
— an increase in investment to ensure economic and social cohesion within the Community;
— an increase in economic planning at all levels;
— more approximation of vocational and educational initiatives to raise the overall skill levels available to the Community;
— legislation creating maximum daily and weekly working hours, rationalisations in overtime and general reorganisation of working time;
— implementation of comprehensive health and safety measures for all sectors of employment;
— measures to recognise the employee contribution to organisational success, in the form of industrial democracy.

THE INFLUENCE OF THE EUROPEAN COMMUNITY

Membership of the ETUC is not confined only to the trade union centres within the existing Community, it also includes representatives from other countries. These include Cyprus, Iceland, Austria, Norway, Sweden, Finland, Malta and Denmark. It therefore represents 37 unions and union Federations from 21 countries.

Organisation and initials	Country
Fédération Générale du Travail de Belgique (FGTB)	Belgium
Confédération des Syndicats Chrétiens (CSC)	Belgium
Cyprus Workers' Confederation (SEK)	Cyprus
Cyprus Turkish Trade Unions Federation (TURK-SEN)	Cyprus
Landsorganisationen i Danmark (LO)	Denmark
Fällesrädet for Danske Tjenstemänds- og Funktionärorganisationer (FTF)	Denmark
Deutscher Gewerkschaftsbund (DGB)	Germany
Union General de Trabajadores de España (UGT)	Spain
Solidaridad de Trabajadores Vascos (STV-ELA)	Spain
Confédération Générale du Travail- Force Ouvrière (CGT-FO)	France
Confédération Francaise Democratique du Travail (CFDT)	France
Trade Union Congress (TUC)	Britain
Greek General Confederation of Labour (CSEE)	Greece
Irish Congress of Trade Unions (ICTU)	Ireland
Althydusamband Islands (ASI)	Iceland
Bandalag Starfsmanna Rikis og Baeja (BSRB)	Iceland
Confederazione Italiana Sindacati Labaratori (CISL)	Italy
Confererazione Generale Italiane del Lavoro (CGIL)	Italy
Unione Italiana del Lavoro (UIL)	Italy
Confédération Generale du Travail de Luxembourg (CGT-L)	Luxembourg
Lunzbuerger Chrësteche Gewerkschafts-bond (LCGB)	Luxembourg
General Workers Union (GWU)	Malta
Confederation of Trade Unions (CMTU)	Malta
Federatie Nederlandse Vakbewegining (FNV)	Netherlands
Christelijk National Vakverbond (CNV)	Netherlands
Landsorganisasjonen i Norge (LO)	Norway
Österreichischer Gewerkschaftsbund (ÖGB)	Austria
Uniao Geral de Trabalhadores (UGT)	Portugal
Schweizerischer Gewerkschaftsbund (SGB)	Switzerland
Christlichnationaler Gewerkschaftsbund der Schweiz (CGS)	Switzerland
Toimihenkilö- ja Virkamiesjärinestojen Keskusliitto (TVK)	Finland
Suomen Ammattiliittojen Keskusjärjestö (SAK)	Finland
Landsorgaisationen i Sverige (LO)	Sweden
Tjänstemännens Centralorganisation (TCO)	Sweden

EEC Implications for HR Staff

Over the next decade the implications of the Single Market will increasingly influence political and economic decisions to be made at national and local level. Those with a human resource role will have to constantly monitor these decisions as they will have an effect on the ways we manage and utilise labour as a primary resource.

For employers membership of Employers Associations or Federations and other pressure groups is going to be important in developing cooperation on a pan-European basis in order to be capable of influencing, both directly and indirectly, the decision making institutions of the Community. European Community Regulations and Directives and draft Directives will need to be built into the undertaking's strategic decision making.

Social Charter

Particularly influential could be the endorsement of the Social Charter by all of the Member States, excluding the UK in December 1989 (The Community Charter of the Fundamental Rights of Workers) with its 12 initiatives which could lead to far reaching influences on human resource practices and costs throughout the Community. The 12 Rights posited are;

1. Right to freedom of movement; throughout the Community for family or occupational reasons, without loss of rights for social security or tax purposes. In addition, wages and conditions of service prevailing in the host country should apply to all workers from other Member States.

2. Right to fair remuneration; decent wages should be established by either law or collective agreement at whatever level regional, occupational, industrial or at company level. The current position with Minimum Wage fixing machinery is as follows;

Country	System/date of operation
Belgium	Since 1975
Denmark	n/a
Spain	yes
France	since 1970
Greece	since 1982
Ireland	for those not covered by collective agreement joint labour committees and Labour Court minimum wages set for each industry.
Italy	since 1944
Luxembourg	since 1986
Portugal	since 1974
Germany	n/a
UK	since Trade Boards Act 1909, Wages Council industries only.

3. Right to improvement in living and working conditions; including flexibility of working hours, redundancy or layoff rights, paid leave rights. Benefits or rights should be transferred to all forms of employment including fixed term, seasonal, temporary or part time workers.

4. Rights to social protection; every adult, whether in or out of work, should have adequate social protection providing a basic standard of living.

5. Right to freedom of association and collective bargaining; including recognition of the right to belong freely to a trade union or professional association, freedom to negotiate through the process of collective bargaining and the right to strike in the event of conflict of interests.

6. Right to vocational training; all workers should have access to training or retraining on a regular basis in order to minimise the social impact of industrial restructuring and technological change.

7. Right to equal treatment; for men and women in all aspects of remuneration, employment access, social security, education and vocational training.

8. Rights to information, consultation and participation of workers; this should apply especially in areas such as technological change, industrial restructuring, mergers and takeovers and any other changes which are likely to have direct employment implications.

9. Rights to health and safety protection in the workplace; everybody should be able to work in satisfactory working conditions.

10. Rights for children and adolescents; there should be a minimum employment age of 16 years, with equitable remuneration and complementary vocational training within working hours.

11. Right to a decent standard of living for the elderly; all citizens of Member States should have a reasonable income commensurate with a decent standard of living.

12. Right to integrate for the disabled; the disabled should be helped to integrate fully into the working environment, through vocational training and improved accessibility, which includes transport and housing.

The Social Action Programme which emerged as a result of the endorsement of the charter, listed 47 initiatives which the Commission intended launching in order to progress the implementation of it. 17 of these are proposals for new EC Directives — the majority in the area of health and safety; 3 in the form of Regulations and 3 in the form of Decisions. The remainder was intended to be progressed by means of non statutory methods.

The Directives proposed are as follows;

(a) Atypical contracts. Directives on employment relationships other than full time employment contracts — three draft Directives were published in 1990.

(i) The first aiming at the approximation of EC laws relating to employment conditions regarding consultation on hiring atypical workers, equal access to training and benefits for all and priority access to full time work.

(ii) The second aims to approximate laws to prevent distortions in competition. It would provide for those working eight or more hours per week, pro-rata terms and conditions to those working full time in statutory and occupational pension schemes and pay and benefits generally. It would also impose a three year limit on temporary contracts.

(iii) The third would give atypicals the same health and safety protection as full timers with regard to the work to be undertaken, the qualifications required and training needed.

(b) Working time; this is a proposal of minimum daily and weekly rest periods between working hours. It proposes an 8 hour night work limit with no overtime. It suggests that exceptions will be allowed if agreed through collective bargaining.

(c) Health and safety on board vessels; this proposes requirements for minimum standards for medical assistance on board vessels.

(d) Health and safety on mobile work sites; proposes minimum standards.

(e) Health and safety for exploration and drilling; proposals to provide minimum safety standards.

(f) Health and safety in quarrying and open mining; Proposes harmonisations of standards of health and safety.

(g) Health and safety on fishing vessels; proposes minimum standards.

(h) Safety signs at the workplace; a directive aimed at updating current requirements in the light of enhanced mobility of labour.

(i) Protection against dangerous substances; directives on information for workers who may be exposed to dangerous substances and on exposure to risks caused by biological agents.

(j) Asbestos; proposes amendments to the 1983 Directive on risk protection.

(k) Health and safety in the transport sector; a draft directive aimed at providing minimum harmonised standards.

(l) Protection of young people at work; aimed at the protection of young people from exploitation at work.

(m) Collective redundancies; aimed at updating the 1975 Directive which is currently reflected in the Employment Protection Act 1975 provisions in the UK.

(n) Protection of pregnant women at work; this draft is aimed at protecting pregnant women or women who have recently given birth. It defines minimum paid maternity leave at 14 weeks and suggests no qualifying period for a right to return to work.

(o) Proof of an employment relationship; proposes that all those working for more than eight hours per week should be entitled to written confirmation of employment terms and conditions.

(p) The establishment of a European Works Council to consult employees in Community scale organisations; this proposes that all organisations employing 1,000 or more employees, with at least two establishments in two member states, each employing 100 staff or more , should set up a European Works Council.

(q) The handicapped; a draft concerning the improvement of conditions for the mobility of handicapped workers.

The three Regulations proposed are;

1. Right to residence; a proposal to amend current Commission Regulation 125/70 on the right of workers to remain in a Member State upon ceasing employment in that country.

2. Social security; to amend the current 1971 Regulation on Social Security.

3. Child care; this is a Recommendation on ways to enable workers to combine family and work responsibilities.

Influence on Human Resource Management.

The output of legislative devices of one sort or another from the Community is therefore likely to have a considerable impact on us within the next decade and will require constant monitoring in order to prepare ourselves for the changes which will be required.

We will not only have to consider the changes in Community legislation which will have a manpower implication but also the changes in the competitive environment with which we shall be placed. Free movement of capital, goods, services and labour will have their implications on competitiveness and profitability.

Companies will make decisions on location of their manufacturing sites based on unit labour costs, levels of unemployment and skill availability. Whilst the Cecchini Report, on the perceived benefits of the Single Market predicted overall job growth in time to the tune of 1.8 million jobs, many others argue that the short term will see substantial job losses as rationalisation takes place. Mergers and takeovers across national boundaries have already taken place within the Community and from outside companies have been acquiring European companies and development sites to obtain a foothold within the tariff wall.

Whilst free movement of labour is enshrined within the Treaty of Rome and is already a fact, we cannot expect the skills shortages which we currently perceive in the UK to be made up from within the Community. The shortages in the supply of young people are endemic throughout the EC. This will mean competition for staff at all levels, senior managers, graduates, technical and specialist staff and especially those with a dual or multilanguage facility will be at a premium. We shall thus need to hone our recruitment skills to draw from other Community countries. Those involved in the milkround will undoubtedly prefer Paris to Bradford and Rome to Ealing.

The quality and quantity of training effort will have to be enhanced in order to compete more efficiently and effectively with our German and French colleagues, thus language training and cultural awareness sessions are bound to be more prevalent activities over the remainder of the millennium.

Trade unions and employees will become more and more aware of the differences between terms and conditions of employment in the Member States, particularly those with transferable skills and qualifications. These trade unions and professional associations too, will wish to enhance their members' wages and conditions by reference to the best conditions within Europe generally and those in the employee relations field will have to develop the skills and knowledge required to cope with these pressures.

CHAPTER THIRTEEN

THE LABOUR MARKET IN THE UK

In 1988 there were 34.2 million people in Great Britain who were of working age. This is 2.3 million more than in 1976, due to a rise in the birth rate in the 1960s and the drop in retirements due to the low birth rate during the 1914–18 era. There were 26.5 million people either in employment or seeking employment, which was 5 million more than in 1951 and 2 million more than in 1976. The number of men in the labour force was around 15.5 million and the number of females around 11.7 million.

It is estimated by the Department of Employment that the population of working age will rise by about 500,000 from 34.3 million in 1991 to 34.8 million in the year 2001.

Although the focus of personnel management is upon individuals and groups of people in organisations, it is important to remember that these individuals and groups are members of a much larger number of people – the UK labour force as a whole. Over time, changes occur in the total labour force, both in terms of its age and sex distribution and in the skills available within the community. This is partly due to the level of demand from companies for certain skills and partly to the willingness of individuals to develop certain skills and to enter particular jobs. Manpower is a key resource in society and there is thus a need for governments to consider manpower in the forefront of their industrial and commercial strategy and planning.

Although it may appear callous, labour can be considered to be the same as other factors of production, e.g. materials and machines, in that it is bought and sold for a price. Features like unemployment, non-discrimination by race or sex in pay, and the effects of incomes policies in attempting to control the price of labour, must be examined within the context of the general social and economic forces which inevitably affect the working of the market.

1.   WHAT IS A LABOUR MARKET?

A labour market is a complex system with people offering themselves for work and with employers seeking to recruit and retain the workers they need by offering rewards or pay for services rendered. We tend to talk generally about the labour market, but the labour market in fact operates as a series of distinct markets with boundaries determined by geographical, occupational, industrial, and organisational boundaries. Whilst the boundaries of these markets tend to overlap in places, they can be regarded as separate entities. Sometimes there is little or no movement between labour markets, for example, the labour market for steeplejacks is different to, and separate from, the labour market for dress designers. We can expect little or no movement at all between them, even if there were vacancies for steeplejacks and an oversupply of dress designers. Conversely, other markets overlap considerably; so you will get semi-skilled car workers moving from the car industry into, for example, the electrical components industry.

The major influences on demand for labour within the market include the demand for products and services produced by the organisations which employ the labour; the technology which is used for producing those goods and services and whether it is labour intensive or not; the type of labour, in terms of skills that are available; and the degree to which organisations operate, what has been termed the internal labour market by Doeringer and Piore in *Internal Labour Markets and Manpower Analysis,* (1971), i.e. the extent to which employers try to insulate themselves from the pressures in the external labour market by favouring the employees inside their own organisations for higher level jobs in terms of skill, pleasantness and responsibility.

2.   INTERNAL LABOUR MARKETS

The factors which influence the extent to which organisations will operate internal labour markets include the cost of labour turnover, i.e. recruitment, selection and training costs; the influence of trade unions and staff associations in protecting the job security of their members; the custom and practice arrangements on seniority rights which have developed; and the degree to which training is specific to the organisation. As labour turnover is most likely to occur in the early months of employment, organisations will tend to prefer to utilise existing employees who can be retrained for more senior or more responsible jobs. They can reduce the costs of hiring labour (which could be scarce) by training existing staff who are already felt to be committed to the organisation. This provides an incentive for those people who wish to develop their skills further to remain with an organisation. Thus organisations will attempt to leave themselves with a situation where they only incur the costs of hiring, i.e. advertising and screening, for those skills which are more readily available in the open market and where the costs are likely to be lower.

In some industries, e.g. steel manufacture, where trade unions perhaps operate a closed shop and attempt to protect the job security of existing employees, they will only allow management to promote employees who have a certain length of service. Over the years custom and practice reduces the tendency of such an organisation to go into the labour market.

We can recognise an internal labour market at work by the following features:

— All jobs, except the lowest in certain skills categories, are filled through internal advertising, which leads to promotion and retraining for existing workers. There are thus what are called specific entry ports;

— The wage system will be based on rigid differentials, according to an internal grading system, and the wage differentials will have little relationship with external forces. Thus wages are linked to the job, not the workers themselves;

— Seniority rights are widespread. For example, labour reductions are often based on the concept of last in first out (**LIFO**); there are overtime possibilities for long service workers.

Good examples of internal labour markets exist in the public sector, e.g. for teachers, civil servants, nursing staff and hospital doctors. Internal labour markets can be said to have developed partly because within organisations skills, whether they are transferable or not, become developed within specific jobs and require training which is specific to the particular job or organisation and often acquired on the job. Experience with particular technologies can tend to be 'firm specific' because of the particular idiosyncrasies within each plant. Equipment use can generate training which has value only within one organisation, especially where particular rules, regulations and standards operate.

3.   DUAL LABOUR MARKET

Some people argue that the total labour market, apart from being divided on geographical, occupational, industrial and organisational or internal labour market lines, can also be sub-divided into two generally separate sectors, primary and secondary.

(a)   Primary labour markets

These markets contain the skilled and professional workers. Jobs tend to be performed within large firms; unionisation tends to be generally strong; wages are high; working conditions are good; job security and employment stability are high; and there are good prospects of advancement and training for promotion and to retain workers.

(b)   Secondary labour markets

These markets contain the less attractive jobs which tend to have a low skill or knowledge requirement. There tend to be few training or promotional opportunities; working conditions are poor with long hours and relatively low levels of payment for work done. Organisations in these markets tend to suffer from high levels of labour turnover because there is little economic and psychological satisfaction from employment. Individuals employed in the secondary labour market find it difficult to move into the primary market because their education and skills are of a low level. Doeringer and Piore, in *Internal Labour Markets and Manpower Analysis* (1977) argue that, within the primary labour market, workers are judged in relation to their skills and potential productivity, considering their employment. Lower skilled workers are less likely to obtain employment because organisations will require a basic level of skill and experience. Those workers who are unsuccessful in obtaining work in the primary sector will, therefore, be forced to seek work in the secondary sector, but this sector does not allow them to increase their marketability by increasing their skills because of the nature of work in the secondary labour market. They are forced to remain in that sector. Examples of the secondary sector include unskilled work in the hotel and catering and the construction industries. One of the features of the post 1970 era of de-industrialisation has been the willingness of production industry to sub-contract to the service sector activities which were previously carried out in-house. This trend seems set to continue as concepts like the core and peripheral labour force becomes operational in corporate policy making.

4. PUBLIC SECTOR INVOLVEMENT IN TRAINING

Employers have always been concerned with the provision of training, both for existing employees to update or uplift their skills, and for new entrants to industry. This enables a direct link to be made between the training provided and the needs of the job itself, which ensures some form of guarantee that training will be both realistic and cost effective. The role of the public authorities, therefore, should be to intervene and provide training where it is felt necessary to support, supplement or encourage the efforts of employers. It is argued that the role of public finance in training should be to provide additional funds, where necessary, not to enable employers to rely on training at public expense, instead of providing their own. Public training should help individuals to cope with labour market demand changes, which cannot easily be handled by industry itself, for example, in areas where there is a growth in demand for skills which outrun current supply; where there is structural labour market movement; and where there are geographical shifts in demands for skills, which workers are unable to follow.

(a) Investment in Human Capital

Both education and training give work skills to the labour force and the potential labour force. They represent a form of investment for society itself and for employers; this has been termed — investment in human capital. G S Becker, in *Human Capital,* Columbia University Press, 1964, suggests that the acquisition of education and training gives the individual a higher earnings potential, and thus the individual will invest his time and money in education and training which gives him the highest future return. (If we consider that the opportunity cost of education and vocational training, where not paid for by an employer, is the wages which otherwise could be earned if the individual continued working – even the individual studying in the evening may be passing up the chance to work overtime.) In economic terms organisations also will invest in any training which provides potential returns of increased productivity from the individual worker, which are greater than the costs of training. Costs include the costs of equipment; facilities; materials used in training; the value of the employee's wages whilst undergoing training; and the cost of the trainers. There are also less measurable returns on training which, although not completely relevant to the individual's job, encourage him to remain with an employer, perhaps because the training meets the individual's need and provides intrinsic satisfaction.

(b) Specific versus General Training

Becker (see above) also argues that we can differentiate between specific and general training.

(i) General training is useful to many other organisations besides those providing it, as it increases the productivity and effectiveness of the individual. There is thus a danger that those providing the training may not reap the benefits of it if employees take advantage of job opportunities elsewhere. In economic terms, it can be argued that firms will only carry out general training if it is heavily subsidised, either by low wages while the training is taking place (this is not normally possible due to both union agreements and the non-attractiveness of taking jobs at low wages), or because the State provides grants towards the costs of such training. Examples of general training include many professional study programmes, clerical and typing training and skilled and semi-skilled machine operating in engineering and other sectors.

(ii) Specific training. If training is completely specific, individuals will not be able to improve their job prospects by moving elsewhere. Organisations often regard such training as valuable because they will reap all the benefits and employment stability is likely to be increased. On the other hand, turnover is more costly in jobs where specific training has been undertaken because no equally skilled and efficient employee can be obtained. Firms may pass some of the benefits of specific training onto the employee by offering higher wages: employees will have less incentive to leave and organisations less incentive to dismiss them. Training can be specific to one organisation or specific to an industry.

Often where internal labour markets operate, which give preferences on promotion to existing employees, there will be specific training. For example, much of the training in the Civil Service could be considered specific. Can you think of any examples of specific training within your own organisation?

5. MOBILITY OF LABOUR

It can be argued that as employers, regions and occupations prosper and increase their labour demand, the chance of stable earnings and employment prospects will lead to an increased supply of people in those successful sectors or areas and reduced supply in less prosperous sectors as individuals adapt their skills and change their place of residence to take advantage of job opportunities. There are, however, many imperfections and rigidities in the overall labour market which prevent the demand being supplied by those with appropriate skills, knowledge and experience. This is partly caused by inadequate mobility of labour from one region to another, even though jobs may not be available to individuals in their current region. The following factors are likely to influence labour mobility:

(a) Inefficiency in information flow – jobs may be available in a particular organisation, area or occupation but recruitment methods are such that suitable workers do not know about them and are thus unable to take them. Although the it is argued that the job centre system is efficient in matching jobs to suitable employees, the Manpower Services commission report *The Employment Service in the 1980s* showed that the Employment Service only handled 18% of total engagements in 1976–1977, increasing to 20% in 1979.

(b) People may hear about vacancies, but may not have the relevant qualifications and skills to be eligible for them. At current levels of economic activity, organisations may not be prepared to give them the chance of acquiring skills, unless the jobs are those for which there is an acute shortage.

(c)   Individuals may not be able to afford the cost of moving house to work in another area, especially those who own their own homes and who are moving from an area which is hit especially hard by the depression and find it difficult to sell their existing house.

(d)   Psychologically, people may not be willing to move from an area where most of their friends and relatives live and where their roots are.

(e)   Higher skilled, managerial and professional workers are more likely to move than semi-skilled and unskilled workers, who may not be prepared to take the risk of moving.

(f)   Younger workers with few family ties may be more prepared to move or more able to afford to purchase or rent property, especially if they currently live in a high cost property area.

(g)   Employers and trade unions may impose restrictions on entry to specific jobs, which means that those technically qualified to fill them may not be able to do so.

6.   SUPPLY OF LABOUR

The total supply of labour in the UK is of major significance in determining the success of the economy. The supply is limited by the total population and its age and sex distribution and what is known as the participation rate or activity rate of those of working age. In addition, the legal framework of society determines the minimum age at which people leave school (at present at 16) and it may also influence the retirement age. Most men are entitled to a State pension at the age of 65 and most women at the age of 60. Social attitudes, often underpinned by legislation, can also influence the ability of minority groups, especially women, to obtain employment.

The size of the total population, which was around 54.3 million for the UK in 1981, sets the upper limit on the supply of labour. Within this figure are 26.3 million males and 28 million females (1981 census data). The population size is influenced by three major factors – the death rate, the birth rate and the level of migration, i.e. immigration and emigration.

7.   PARTICIPATION RATES

The *participation rate* or activity rate measures the percentage of those who can work, are of working age and who actually offer themselves as available for work to their appropriate labour market. The labour force surveys show that the over 60s have been leaving the work force rapidly during the 1980s. Thus, figures in the *Employment Gazettes* showed that economically active men aged 60–64 declined from 69.3% in 1981 to 56.7% in 1983 to 55.4% in 1985 and down to 54.6% in 1989. Overall, too, the proportion of men over school age who were economically active declined between 1981–89 from 89.1% to 87.0%, whereas the proportion of women marginally increased, especially in the 25–34 age group. Surveys also reported that over 50% of Britain's employed in 1983 were in non-manual occupations, the swing from manufacturing to service industries also being maintained with the retail trade, banking, finance, insurance, other services and hotel and catering showing the biggest increase. Economic activity by age group was as follows:

Table 25: Economic activity by age 1984 & 1989 labour force survey

% economically active i.e. employed or looking for work

AGE	MALE		FEMALE		ALL	
	1984	1989	1984	1989	1984	1989
16-19	73.5	75.0	69.4	73.7	71.5	74.4
20-24	85.0	87.1	70.2	75.1	77.7	81.2
25-34	93.7	93.8	61.1	69.3	77.6	81.6
35-44	95.4	95.1	70.9	75.0	83.2	85.1
45-54	93.0	91.7	69.5	72.2	81.2	81.9
55-59	82.5	79.8	51.8	54.3	66.8	66.9
60-64	57.3	54.6	21.8	22.9	38.6	38.1
65-69 (65+)	14.0	14.6	3.1	3.4	5.2	5.6
70+	5.6	5.5				
All ages	74.5	74.3	9.0	52.6	61.2	63.0

Labour economists would argue that most individuals decide to offer themselves for work through a household decision. A household allocates its labour resources and makes a choice between what can be called market work or non-market work, which includes housework, leisure and time spent in education. The decision on what proportion to allocate to market versus non-market work is influenced by a number of factors which can be listed as follows:

— The total household's financial resources and its perceived needs — some households will be able to purchase the necessities of life, based on one income, whereas some will have a higher level of needs or may not be able to manage on one income and will require two or more.

— The non-work sources of income, e.g. State social security benefits investment income and property income.

— The economic and social values placed on non-market activites and leisure. Some may be able to work but may prefer to use their time in other ways.

— The availability of work in the labour market.

In the UK the participation rates of males have fallen over this century due to increased education, voluntary early retirement and the lowering of the retirement age. The highest rate of participation occurs amongst males in the age group 20–60; between these ages almost all those who are not in full time education, and are not seriously physically or mentally handicapped, are working or registered as unemployed. Over the last 20 years the size of the labour force has steadily increased, except in 1982 and 1983. These increases have been dominated by a growth in the female labour force of some 1.6 million.

Although legislation, in the form of the Equal Pay Act 1970 (as amended by the Equal Pay Amendment Regulations 1983) and the Sex Discrimination Acts 1975 and 1986, has reduced the degree of sexual discrimination in the UK, there are still a number of jobs which can be identified as typically male or typically female. In addition, attitudes are slow to change as we can see if we chart some successes in the history of equal opportunity. For example:

1893	first female factory inspectors
1898	first female architect
1920	first female magistrate
1929	first female Cabinet minister
1945	first female prison governor
1958	first female bank manager
1966	first female racehorse trainer
1979	first female Prime Minister

The participation rate of unmarried females has fallen over this century due to increased education and earlier retirement. This decline has been offset by the increased participation rate of married women. Table 26 gives the percentages of the participation of married women drawn from official census figures:

Table 26 : Participation rate of married women 1911–1982

Year	Percentage of those in work or actually seeking work
1911	9.6
1921	8.7
1931	10.0
1951	21.7
1961	29.7
1971	42.3
1981	40.0

The reasons for this are complex, because the decision on married women's participation is often taken in a family context. Evidence suggests that the higher the level of the husband's wage, the lower the labour force participation of a married woman. Notwithstanding this evidence, wives' participation increases the higher the potential wage they can earn themselves. Additional factors, which also influence the work/non-work decision, can be listed as follows:

1. The availability of work locally: in some parts of the country there is very little work available. Married women tend to work closer to home than men because of family commitments.

2. The level of educational attainment of the individual woman: the higher the level of educational attainment the more likely a women is to work.

3. The level of family income: Mincer, in *Labour force participation of married women : a study of labour supply* (1962), argued that when family income was low in relation to the normal or permanent level, thus when overtime is cut or husbands become or are likely to become unemployed, wives tend, where possible, to enter the labour force, at least in the short term, to supplement family income. This effect was noticeable over the 1970s when high levels of inflation were reducing the levels of 'real' wages.

4. The ages of any children and the availability, either in the public sector or in the private sector, of child-care facilities.

5. Appropriateness of hours of work: labour shortages mean some organisations attempt to encourage the employment of married women by introducing special shifts and other acceptable arrangements for part-time work, including the right to take time off during school holidays.

6. As women tend nowadays to have their families later, their level of work experience tends to be greater. This helps in the job search process.

7. Improvements in household technology and the availability of labour-saving devices such as washing machines, automatic ovens and pressure cookers, plus the availability of fast foods and late night supermarket shopping, have reduced the time necessary for housework. Women have found it easier to substitute market work for housework.

8. There has been greater social acceptance for women working over the last thirty years. This has been underpinned by anti-discrimination legislation. As Tom King emphasised when the EOC code on equality of opportunity

THE LABOUR MARKET IN THE UK

was launched in April, 1985 (quoted in *Employment News* May, 1985):

"For Britain to succeed we do have to make the most of all the resources that we have; and one of the most neglected resources we have in the country is the skill, and intelligence of many women. What is needed is a revolution in public attitudes – a recognition that what matters is not whether an employee is a man or a woman but their skill and aptitude and acceptance that there is virtually no job that a woman cannot do. That cannot be achieved by changes in the law. It requires a constant process of persuasion and example by employers, employees and trade unions."

In the UK, after a decade of steady growth, the female labour supply fell from 1981 to 1983 before it continued its growth for the remainder of the decade. The labour force is expected to grow continuously until the end of the century at a slower rate than in the immediate past. Hence the concern with what has been termed, the 'demographic time bomb'. However the composition of the potential growth is distinctive, nearly all of it will be due to an increase in the female labour force and there will be a further narrowing of the gap between male and female activity rates.

Women's employment still tends to be heavily concentrated in certain occupations. Of all women workers in 1981 according to census figures;
- 29.1% are clerical workers, e.g. secretarial and typing;
- 23.2% are in service, sports and recreation, including canteen
- 23.2% assistants, and office cleaners;
- 11.9% are professional, technical or artistic workers, including teachers, and nurses;
- 10.7% are in sales and distribution.

Within occupations women account for:
- 96.8% of all canteen assistants, counter hands etc.;
- 91.7% of all charpersons, office cleaners, etc.;
- 91.6% of all nurses.

A Department of Employment and Shell UK report published in March 1987 showed that from 1981–1987 the number of self-employed women had risen by 70% to around 586,000.

If we accept that the demand for labour is derived demand, which is based on the level of economic activity, we can recognise that significant changes have occurred in the type of employment undertaken in the sectors which employ women. We can discern in the UK a shift in employment patterns from manufacturing to service employment. Since 1951 this has been especially represented in a decline in those manufacturing sectors which employ women. For example, there are now less permanent part-time jobs in the manufacturing sector generally, because of the increase in technology and the fall in demand for goods produced due to the economic recession. In addition, the textile and clothing industry, which has long been female dominated, has reduced in size. Two-thirds of all working women are in the service sector where there is extensive part-time employment. For example, in the distributive trades with extensions in the opening hours of shops and garages due to the need for employers to reduce variable overhead costs at low levels of demand, the use of part-time labour has increased.

Services associated with the Welfare State increased during the 1950s, 1960s and into the 1970s, at a time when male unemployment was low, so female labour was drawn into many white collar and blue collar jobs within the public employment sector.

Although unemployment increased from 1966 onwards, due to the decline in the manufacturing sector, women tended not to be employed in that sector in large numbers and were cushioned from this decline. Men did not move into the 'female' jobs in the service sector because many were deterred by the low pay and relative lack of skills and training required and because many of the jobs were traditionally considered to be 'female', e.g. shop assistants, typists, secretaries, nurses.

From 1974 onwards the economic recession became more severe and began to hit even the service sector, especially as concern increased over the levels of public and local authority expenditure. The total numbers of full-time female employees fell, yet this continued until recently to be offset by the continued availability of part-time jobs for women, as the service sector could see the benefits of employing part-timers rather than full-timers to reduce costs. At the same time, as there was a slowing down of the demand for female employees, the supply of women wishing to work increased. This was partly due to the lower birth rate; the availability of child-care facilities; the significant changes in the social attitudes to working women, evinced in the Equal Pay and Sex Discrimination Acts; and the effects of inflation on real incomes, combined with the decline in husbands' employment opportunities. These influences have led to a rise in registered unemployment amongst women, due partly to an increased propensity of women to register in order to be able to enter Government skills education programmes.

With the likelihood of increasing technological incursions into clerical and allied jobs, especially with the advent of the microprocessor, the prospects for female employment, if organisations decide to take advantage of such technologies and can afford to install it, is less growth in jobs to match the increase in those offering themselves for work. A report by Tannenbaum *Technology : the issues for the distributive trades,* (1982), showed that microprocessors are rapidly permeating through the distributive trades and affecting existing and future job numbers significantly. A further influence will be the likelihood of the male unemployed, faced with few opportunities in traditionally male-dominated activities, competing for those jobs traditionally held by women.

PART TIME EMPLOYMENT

There has been a significant growth in the use of part time employment in the post war period. It is fair to say that to a large extent this phenomenon has significantly been recognised in the area of female employment. Census figures illustrate this trend as follows.

Table 27: Employment trends in Great Britain 1951–1984 (000s)

Year	Males			Females		
	Total Employment	Part-time Employment	% p/t	Total Employment	Part-time Employment	% p/t
1951	15,366	45.3	0.3	6,797	753.7	11.1
1961	15,748	174.3	1.1	7,590	1,892.1	24.9
1971	15,031	572.1	3.8	8,701	3,151.8	36.2
1981	12,229	718.0	5.9	9,085	3,781.0	41.6
1984*	11,698	771.0	6.6	9,147	3,858.0	42.2

* Department of Employment figures.

The definition of part time work may vary. The Department of Employment defines as a part time worker those who are normally employed for not more than thirty hours per week. One difficulty with this definition is that with the length of the working week in most sectors is falling due to collective bargaining agreements, so the number of workers falling below the cut off figure increases naturally. The legislative definition is those working less than 16 hours per week. It is interesting in the context of the Single European Market to compare the figures for the UK with those of our Common Market partners.

Table 28: Part time employment as a percentage of full time employment

Country	All		Males		Females	
	1973	1981	1973	1981	1973	1981
Belgium	2.8	6.4	0.4	1.3	8.2	16.4
Denmark	17.0	20.8	1.9	3.0	40.3	43.6
France	5.1	7.4	1.4	1.9	11.2	15.9
Germany	7.7	10.2	1.0	1.0	20.0	25.7
Greece	n/a	2.1	n/a	1.1	n/a	4.3
Eire	4.0	3.1	1.8	1.3	10.1	8.0
Luxembourg	4.5	5.8 *	1.0	1.0 *	13.0	17.1 *
Netherlands	4.4	7.9	n/a	n/a	n/a	n/a
UK	15.3	15.4	1.8	1.4	38.3	37.1

* 1979 figures
Source; adapted from Eurostat Labour Force Sample Survey

As the table shows there is considerable variation within Europe in the utilisation of part time workers, although there is similarity in the proportion of males in part time work. Women patently contribute the greatest proportion of part time workers in all countries as the following table illustrates.

Table 29 : Women's share of part time employment (%)

Country	1979	1983	1986
West Germany	91.6	91.9	89.8
UK	92.8	89.6	88.5
France	82.0	84.6	83.0
Luxembourg	87.5	90.0	76.6
Netherlands	82.5	76.2	76.1
Eire	71.1	72.0	74.3
Italy	61.4	64.8	61.6
Greece	n/a	61.2	n/a

A number of factors have contributed towards the development of part time employment patterns in recent years. The most influential could be said to be

(i)   the change in the structure of industrial composition has meant a shift from manufacturing to the services sector where there may be greater possibilities and a longer tradition of using part time employees; thus Census of Employment data for 1984, published in the *Employment Gazette* in 1987, shows that nearly 89% of all part time workers were in the service sector, with 34% working in distribution and hotel and catering alone where some 57% of all female jobs were part time.

(ii) the introduction of employment legislation which differentiates between the rights available to full time and part time workers has also had an impact which has been accelerated by the changes made in recent years.

(iii) the changes made in the structure of personal taxation, and of National Insurance contributions towards individual assessment has increased the financial incentives for individuals, especially married females, to enter employment on a part time basis.

(iv) the use of flexitime systems may make it possible for child care arrangements to be made by the other partner thus releasing an individual to be able to seek part time work.

(v)   the recognition by employers of the cost and flexibility advantages of using part timers.

(vi) the recognition by some employers that an employee who is taking time off perhaps for family responsibilities may be able to do some work, rather than leave permanently. Brenda Stevenson of the EOC stressed at a conference in London in 1988, that losing trained workers can be a significantly costly mistake, she illustrated this by quoting training costs of £5,000 for a clerical officer and £13,000 for a nurse.

The questions we have to ask ourselves regarding our utilisation of part time staff include;

— do we enable them to progress through the organisation and be promoted?
— how far do we offer equal opportunities for training and development?
— are our remuneration packages and benefits packages flexible enough to ensure full time and part time benefits are integrated and we are not treating part timers as second class citizens?

The advantages of using part time staff include flexibility in matching manpower levels with demand and a certain amount of cost savings including National Insurance. However they require the same amount of administration and paperwork, turnover tends to be higher, it can be more difficult to arrange training, and it can be more difficult to communicate and to arrange meetings to include them.

OCCUPATIONAL DISTRIBUTION OF EMPLOYMENT

The structure of employment has changed over the last two decades. Information from the Warwick University Institute of Employment Research in their Review of the Economy and Employment 1988/1989 shows that there has been an increase in employment of managers and professional groups and a fall in manual work and that these changes are likely to continue this decade.

Table 30: Occupational employment 1971 and 1995 (%)

	1971	1995
Managers and administrators	12.1	18.4
Professional occupations	8.0	10.4
Associated professional and technical	7.4	9.2
Personal and protective services	6.9	7.4
Sales occupations	7.0	8.0
Clerical and secretarial	18.2	17.7
Craft and related	16.7	14.7
Machine operatives	12.3	9.4
Others	11.4	9.7

8. COSTS OF EMPLOYMENT

Most of us will recognise that the cost to an organisation of employing individuals to work for them is considerably more than the total cost of the wages and salaries paid. The amount of these additional cost has been growing in recent years and have therefore to be taken into consideration in planning recruitment activity. Some costs are incurred at the outset of employment — the initial cost of employment — and others continue throughout the time of employment — ongoing costs of employment.

(a) Initial costs of employment; every employer is faced with some costs in starting a new employee. The total amount of such costs will depend on the complexity of the role, the amount of skill required in the person specification, the type of organisation and its location and the degree of labour market competition for that type of labour. Included in these costs are:-

— advertising costs, printing and posting of application forms, the cost of interview in wages of the interviewers and travelling costs of the candidate, and possibly agency or headhunting costs.

— training costs, whether for on the job or off the job training, the payroll costs of the employee producing below established or experienced worker standard, training administration costs, the cost of trainer or instructor time, material costs ie. of waste while training and any proportional costs of training facilities.

— additional administration cost for putting and keeping the person on the payroll.

(b) Ongoing costs of employment; whilst every employer has to pay a wage, salary or fee, there are additional costs of various kinds which have to be paid to full time and permanent employees and possibly for part time and temporary employees. These include,

— pension contributions, National Insurance and sick pay contributions, holiday pay, absence coverage and additional leave allowances for domestic and statutory duties, all of which may be dependent on the level of remuneration.

— canteen facilities, other employee facilities, medical service costs, staff discounts and other costs which are not related to salary or wage level. In addition we can also identify other costs of employment which may be status related, including:

- permanent health or medical treatment insurance,
- company car costs
- travel and expense allowances
- house purchase assistance
- staff development costs.

All these costs have to be taken into consideration when considering the advantages and disadvantages of employing additional staff and the type on contracts we will offer any new employees.

9.   FACTORS INFLUENCING THE WORKINGS OF THE LABOUR MARKET

The efficient working of the labour market can be said to be impaired by the following:

(a)   Employment legislation which, in protecting the individual, fails to enable employers to shed labour immediately where necessary and has put up the cost of termination with rights to paid notice, redundancy pay, index-linked pensions, transferable and frozen pensions, unfair dismissal penalties etc.

(b)   Pay relativities – the existence of local, regional and industrial pay structures, which are quoted and defended by trade unions in their negotiations, affect the ability of employers to adjust payment rapidly.

(c)   Increased fixed labour costs – the cost of employing extra labour is said to be high because of the various national insurance contributions, pension schemes, increased holidays (including bank holidays) etc.

(d)   Reliance on sub-contracting and overtime – because of the high costs of employing labour with the above expenses (plus the range of other fringe benefits which are frequently offered) rather than employ additional manpower, firms can sub-contract suitable work, employ part-timers or utilise existing employees on overtime.

(e)   The inflexible use of labour because of demarcation and other rigid manning policies – trade unions are blamed for operating closed shop and rigid demarcation policies to protect their own members' employment to the perceived detriment of others.

(f)   Bad working conditions – it is suggested that certain jobs, which involve unpleasant conditions and long and unsocial hours, do not attract employees because of those working conditions and low levels of pay, e.g. hotels, the retail trade and other personal service jobs.

(g)   Low productivity – this prevents the production of goods cheaply and efficiently so that they sell against foreign competition and generate more employment.

(h)   Lack of manpower planning — organisations are often criticised for not attempting to plan their manpower needs more efficiently and for long enough into the future to enable them to signal skill needs to the labour market.

(i)   Lack of labour mobility.

(j)   The reaction of industry to cyclical and frictional changes — in past recessions industry has been prepared to reduce intakes of skills requiring long training, which has particularly created shortages of skills at various times. This has affected the ability of some young people to take apprenticeships because, by the time demand has picked up, they are too old to enter those occupations.

(k)   The constraints of incomes policy — firms have occasionally been prevented from adjusting wage levels, in times of low supply of essential skills, to attract people into those occupations.

(l)   The rate of technological change will have a differential impact from one industry to another. The impact of these changes is already being perceived in the type of work which is being offered. ACAS produced a survey of some 600 employers "Labour flexibility in Britain" in 1987, which showed that a significant number of organisations were developing skill flexibility amongst their staff. In one third of companies surveyed demarcation lines had been relaxed during the previous three years to produce craft flexibility and 25% of companies had production line workers carrying out routine maintenance tasks. A third of employers had introduced shift working and 3% of organisations had intriduced annual hours schemes. 14% of employers especially in banking, public administration, transport and communications had introduced flexible working hours. 40% of employers admitted that their use of part time and temporary workers had increased. On average 70% of organisations used part time workers although the use was higher in the South East with 80% of organisations using them. This requirement for increased flexibility increases training costs not only for those being required to be more flexible but also for those managing and supervising them.

CHAPTER FOURTEEN

UNEMPLOYMENT

This has been one of the key influences on governments over the last ten years and is likely to be so for the remainder of this century. In order to be able to examine the implications of high levels of unemployment, we need to understand the different concepts of the term.

The labour market, as we have inferred, is in continuous motion as people move from one job to another. In 1979 it was suggested, based on the number of P45's issued, that there were between 8 and 9 million job changes every year. Because unemployment and vacancies coexist, we cannot view unemployment as a residual state in the labour market which results when all vacancies have been filled. For, as the MSC illustrated in most of their annual reports, there are always a number of hard-to-fill vacancies in some sectors and regions. There are also variations in supply and demand in different labour markets. Unemployment is therefore a state through which most individuals pass within their lifetime. But, what is evident, is that some categories of employees have more frequent and longer spells of unemployment. It has been suggested that overall rates of labour turnover do not vary much over the economic cycle; what varies are the reasons for that turnover. Thus, when the economy takes a downswing, the lay-off or redundancy rate increases, i.e. involuntary unemployment, whereas, when the economy is booming resignations increase, i.e. the voluntary leaving rate increases.

1. VOLUNTARY VS INVOLUNTARY UNEMPLOYMENT

It has therefore been suggested by economists that policy makers need to distinguish between voluntary and involuntary unemployment, in trying to solve unemployment problems.

Voluntary unemployment: people leave because they do not think the prevailing wage rates or job opportunities within the organisation are adequate for their perceived level of skill and experience.

Involuntary unemployment: people cannot find work at a suitable rate of pay.

Some people are unemployed even where full employment exists, and the definition of *full employment* varies and has been considered over the years to exist when between only 1% and 5% of workers are unemployed. More realistically, it is a situation where, although demand exists for goods and services, supply cannot be increased because of labour shortages: there can be said to be a natural rate of unemployment, which is influenced by the industrial mix of the economy; the custom and practice arrangements regarding employment in the labour market, e.g., trade union/management agreements on the basic skills required for employment; the speed of technological and industrial change; and the preferences of the labour force as to their degree of participation. Thus, while the labour force adjusts to changes in the labour market and obtains the raw skills necessary for changed work practices and the search for new jobs, there will be an inevitable level of unemployment which will be difficult to avoid and to control.

2.   TYPES OF UNEMPLOYMENT

In order to consider the likely success of Government measures it can be useful to define other types of unemployment, based on reasons which can be broadly classified into:

(a)   Unemployment that occurs because of a *low level of demand for labour* − seasonal unemployment, cyclical unemployment and growth gap unemployment.

(b)   Unemployment which occurs because of *changes in skill requirements* and the necessary adjustments which take place in the labour market − hard-core unemployment, frictional unemployment and structural unemployment.

A.   Demand affected unemployment

(i)   *Seasonal unemployment:* occurs in those sectors of society where the work is of necessity of a seasonal nature; regular bouts of unemployment are likely, the pattern varying from industry to industry. The construction industry used to suffer seasonal unemployment but new techniques and improved raw materials have reduced the bad weather lay-offs which used to occur. A current example is the tourist industry where hotels and travel firms often take on staff only for the the summer season. Governments tend to adjust the unemployment figures to reduce the impact of seasonal unemployment.

(ii)   *Cyclical unemployment:* few economies or industrial sectors achieve a smooth trade cycle and thus there are always peaks and troughs through growth and deflation. Vacancies may exist, but in the 'wrong' jobs.

(iii)   *Growth gap unemployment:* growth gap unemployment or stagnation unemployment occurs when a country's economy has suffered from depression for a considerable period of time and there is little prospect of increasing economic activity. Thus, long term high rates of unemployment persist.

Sustained demand – deficient unemployment tends in the end to produce structural unemployment as production capacity and skills become obsolete.

B. Labour Market maladjustment unemployment

(i) *Hard-core unemployment:* this exists because any society has a number of workers who, because of their physical and mental conditions, age or work attitudes, are unlikely to be employed. These groups are possibly about 1% of the working population, according to the Department of Employment.

(ii) *Frictional unemployment:* or 'search unemployment' occurs because it takes time to match people and jobs' skill requirements; people have to either adjust their skills for the work which is available or adjust the wages at which they will offer themselves for employment. Each unemployed worker can technically be said to have a reservation wage which he feels represents the value of his skills; over time, if he cannot find work at what he considers an adequate wage, he may adjust his expectations and, therefore, his reservation wage has to be reduced to take account of the prevailing wage and salary structure as he perceives it. Because of poor information about available job opportunities, the job search process is hampered while individuals assess the extent of the market demand for labour. Economies are dynamic, therefore job mobility will be required as new firms and industries develop. There will inevitably be some level of frictional unemployment while the supply of skills adjusts to demand in the short term. Usually frictional unemployment implies that the number of vacancies exceeds the number of job seekers and that the unemployment period is of short duration. According to Labour Force Survey data job search methods include,
   – seeking employment via Government employment offices,
   – using private sector employment agencies,
   – answering advertisements in newspapers and journals,
   – seeking employment via professional bodies,
   – following up information from personal contacts and recommendations,
   – and cold calling on employers.

(iii) *Structural unemployment:* this can be thought of as a long term form of frictional unemployment. The unemployed have not the necessary skills for the available job vacancies and, in order to obtain work, they will either have to change their skills or change their location of residence. Throughout the period of industrialisation, industries have grown up and declined in importance in the economy. The skill requirements of society have developed, grown and declined in parallel. Few industries or types of work are guaranteed indefinite survival and, as an industry declines, the demand for labour falls quicker than the supply can readjust. Unemployment is created because the economy's industrial structure is itself changing. Often declining industries are grouped geographically, e.g. shipyards and, therefore, whole regions have a disproportionate level of unemployment because of these structural changes.

With structural unemployment it usually means that the worker has not left his job voluntarily but has been forced to do so. The shift in Britain from manufacturing employment has been an important feature in the unemployment distribution.

Table 31: Employees in Employment (Millions)

	June 1974	June 1979	June 1984	June 1990
Manufacturing	7.7	7.1	5.3	5.1
Construction	1.2	1.2	1.0	1.0
Distribution	3.1	3.3	3.2	3.4
Financial Services	1.5	1.6	1.9	2.8
Public Administration	1.9	1.9	1.8	2.0
Education and Health	2.5	2.8	2.8	3.2
Other	4.4	4.7	4.7	5.1
Total	22.3	22.6	20.7	22.6

Source: Department of Employment figures

Between 1974 and 1979 there was already a fall in employment in the manufacturing industry, but this was compensated for by both public and private services. However, between 1979 and 1990, the decline in manufacturing employment was very significant, a fall of about 33%. The position reversed somewhat between June 1982 and June 1990 as follows:

UNEMPLOYMENT

Table 32: Jobs: Gains and losses (June 1982–June 1990)

Sector	Numerical Change (000s)	% Change
SERVICES	+2749	+21.0%
Post and Telecommunications	+13	+3.0
Banking finance and insurance	+1042	+58.8
Retail distribution	+261	+13.1
Hotels and catering	+182	+18.9
Other services (public & personal)	+482	+36.9
Wholesale distribution	+99	+8.8
Medical and other health services	+225	+17.8
Transport	-45	-4.8
Education	+253	+16.4
Public Administration	+218	+11.9
MANUFACTURING	-643	-11.1
PRODUCTION INDUSTRIES	-872	-13.6
PRODUCTION & CONSTRUCTION INDUSTRIES	-880	-11.8
Paper, paper products, printing & publishing	-2	-0.4
Mechanical engineering	-35	-4.1
Office machine, electrical engineering and instruments	-92	-11.3
Metal goods (misc.)	-60	-15.5
Motor vehicles and parts	-50	-15.9
Timber, wooden furniture	76	16.0
Textiles, leather, footwear & clothing	-60	-10.4
Other transport equipment	-116	-34.4
Construction	-18	-1.7
Coal, oil, etc.	-171	-52.1
Electricity, gas & water	-46	-13.4
Agriculture	-61	-18.0
Chemicals and man made fibres	-49	-13.3
Food,drink and tobacco	-83	-13.0

From: Department of Employment figures.

3 . MEASUREMENT OF UNEMPLOYMENT LEVELS

Unemployment can be measured in a number of ways. There are two basic methods which have been used in the UK:

(a)   by surveys of individuals asking whether they have a job or if they are seeking work and what steps they are taking to find work,

(b)   by counting those recorded as unemployed at government offices.

A number of measures of unemployment exist, which can make comparisons of UK and other data difficult.

1. UK Official figures. The monthly count is based on the computerised records of claiments of benefits at unemployment benefit offices – including unemployment and supplementary benefits – on the second Tuesday of the month.

2. ILO/OECD definitions. The ILO/OECD definitions of unemployment include those who are (a) without a paid job; (b) available to start work in the next two weeks; and (c) had either looked for work in the last four weeks or were waiting to start work for which they were already selected.

3. Labour Force Survey definition. These figures include those who in the week preceding the survey interview were without paid employment and were either seeking work, waiting to start a new job or for the results of a job application or were prevented from seeking work only because of temporary sickness or holidays. This would include students in full time education who fall within the criteria.

There has long been criticism of official unemployment statistics: they are collected for two primary reasons. Firstly, as an indication of the demand pressures for labour, so that governments can help to lubricate the demand and supply in the labour market. Secondly, as a means of assessing cases of social and economic hardship and the amounts which have to be allocated for unemployment and social security benefit from Government funds.

In the UK, the Department of Employment calculates the unemployment statistics by counting the number of people who are registered each month as claiming benefit at unemployment offices. One of the intrinsic problems with statistics of registered unemployment is that people register according to their previous occupation. Thus, rather than measuring the true labour supply position for that occupation the statistics may actually reflect the number of people who have left that occupation. The figures may also not fully represent the extent of involuntary unemployment because they do not include in the employment count those who are not entitled to benefit for one reason or another. For example, some of those who will soon be entitled to retirement benefit may only register to obtain unemployment benefit to tide them over. In January,1991 there were 34,000 unemployed people who were 60 years old (and no longer required to register) but who would have been registered as unemployed had the definition of unemployment been those actively seeking work. Another problem with the official statistics is that, in including those actively seeking work, they do not count those 'unemployed' who are undergoing Government training and subsidy programmes of one sort or another, who technically would enter work if it were available.

In December 1990 the numbers involved in some Government employment measures were as follows:

Table 33: Numbers involved in Government employment measured December 1990 (GB)

Enterprise Allowance Scheme	55,177
Job Release Scheme	1,892
Job Share	1,531
Job Start Allowance	1,506

Source: Department of Employment figures

Estimates, from the General Household Survey, suggest that one-fifth of the unemployed are not entitled to benefit; these have been termed the *hidden unemployed*. They are defined as those who would like to work, but who have become so discouraged about finding jobs in the prevailing economic situation, that they have ceased active searching. This figure from the General Household Survey, although shocking enough, may be a gross underestimate for, if we take the monthly average unemployment rate for 1981, it stood at 806,800 people (the highest figure that year was for November when there were 926,100 unemployed), whereas the 1981 Census of Population showed that 1,366,000 people said that they were 'out of employment', an increase of nearly 41%! Groups which fall into the hidden unemployed category include married women, who would take suitable part-time work; those on an organisational pension, who are not eligible for unemployment benefit for it has run out, but who would take work if it was available; and those active people who are over the State pension retirement age who would work to supplement their pensions.

The statistics also ignore what has been termed *labour hoarding*. Organisations tend to retain surplus labour at the beginning of a depression to avoid incurring termination costs, for example, redundancy pay and redundancy enhancement and the potential future costs of recruitment, selection and training. They will thus tend to cut overtime first and then under-utilise existing employees. When organisations have a hierarchy of tasks they will, when faced with a continued decline in demand for their products, tend to retain the most skilled employees, especially those that they have invested in training, and will start the termination process with the least skilled who are easier to replace. The reasons for labour hoarding can be listed as follows:

UNEMPLOYMENT

(a)   Different sorts of employee have different sorts of contractual agreements with employers as, for example, in the Employment Protection (Consolidation) Act minimum notice periods.

(b)   In some processes a certain man/machine ratio is required. Unless production is rationalised and different methods introduced, it may not be possible to vary the ratios and organisations will initially introduce short-time working or get work done more slowly.

(c)   Hiring and training costs make employers unwilling to lay off skilled employees who will tend to be retained as a precautionary measure.

(d)   Workers tend to prefer stable employment and so organisations may be slow in reducing employment levels, to avoid an adverse reaction from trade unions.

At the onset of a recession, labour is not simultaneously cut back with output but labour utilisation will fall. With an upturn in the economy, increased output can be achieved without the need to obtain more workers because the labour utilisation rate can increase; there will thus be a lag in reducing unemployment levels. In the UK, manufacturing output declined slowly over the 1970s and initially labour hoarding took place but, as the depression deepened without any real signs of a recovery, organisations began the process of shedding labour. This has been continued in textiles, mechanical engineering, car manufacture and metal manufacture. In examining the numbers unemployed at any one moment in time we can also ignore the fact that there can also be an increase in those entering the labour maket. Thus the labour force in employment can increase despite high levels of unemployment. The GB labour force in employment has been increasing steadily since March 1883.

Changes have taken place in the unemployment counting methods since 1979.

Changes in the methods of calculation of unemployment

Changes	Estimated impact on unemployment figures
1979	
Benefits paid every two weeks	+20,000
Downwards adjustment to seasonal total	-20,000
1981	
Removal of those in training and temporary work from estimates	-495,000
Unemployed men 60+ removed	-37,000
1982	
Only benefit claimants counted	-216,000

UNEMPLOYMENT

1983

Men 60+ and not entitled to benefit not required to register at benefit offices to have NI paid	-107,000
School leavers disbarred from benefit for 1-3 months	-200,000

1986

Two weeks delay in announcing statistics	-50,000
New method of calculating unemployment %	-1.4%
Abolition of part-time unemployment benefit	-30,000

1988

Voluntary unemployment disqualification lengthened to twenty six weeks	-12,000
16 and 17 year olds disbarred from benefits	-90,000 to 120,000
Unemployment benefit contribution tests toughened	-38,000

1989

Ex miners not required to register	-15,000
Claimants required to prove they are seeking work	-25,000
Low wage levels no longer an acceptable reason for refusing work	-25,000
Change in the way earnings affect benefit	-30,000

The figures quoted are from various sources and there are many arguments between the Government and the opposition parties as to the real affect of the changes.

4. DIFFERENTIAL IMPACT OF UNEMPLOYMENT

What is evident is that the impact of unemployment will be felt with increasing severity on particular sectors of the labour market. In terms of the types of unemployment defined above, the current UK unemployment situation is, on the one hand, *growth gap unemployment,* caused by the general economic recession, but is also more fundamentally *structural unemployment,* which has hit hardest those with the skills once required by the declining industries.

Both these factors working together have led to an increase in the duration of unemployment. According to the 1985 White Paper, *Employment: the challenge for the Nation* (March 1985), more than 1.3 million in the UK had been out of work for at least one year, 760,000 for more than two years and 450,000 for more than three years. These figures can be compared with those of April 1989, April 1990 and January 1991 as follows.

Table 34: Number of unemployed by age and duration April 1989, April 1990 and January 1991 (000's)
Source: Department of Employment data.

YEARS	1989			1990			1991		
AGE	Under				Under			Under	
	25	25-49	50+	25	25-49	50+	25	25-49	50+
Duration									
0-6 mths	294.9	396.4	101.3	288.7	413.6	99.3	399.7	567.3	131.8
6-12mths	116.3	171.4	57.2	92.0	147.9	43.7	101.3	183.5	48.5
1 year +	119.2	378.4	246.4	84.5	283.0	172.3	85.4	286.9	152.5

Table 35: Number of unemployed by age and duration GB Jan 10th 1991

Weeks	Under 18	18-19	20-29	30-39	40-49	50-59	60+
less than 1	414	13591	44011	18883	13158	8382	1478
1-2	122	8071	27680	13009	10298	8314	1729
2-6	671	23966	88122	42551	31712	21142	3838
6-26	1335	79134	289840	220831	145202	70743	13332
25-52	104	33281	131954	68080	47596	38806	8146
52-104	16	10154	80636	46488	34705	33237	2981
104-156	0	106	27398	16818	13006	18594	535
156-208	0	19	11286	8462	7625	14392	344
208-260	0	0	5620	5095	5182	12384	235
Over 260	0	0	12722	21849	25311	58408	1123

(i) Skill distribution

In spite of low investment in the UK compared with many other industrialised nations, there has been a consistent trend in the British manufacturing
industry over the last decade towards new technologies and more capital-
intensive methods of production. This has been brought about because of
advances in computer systems technology and micro technology. This trend
is likely to continue and the occupations which are in decline, and which will
continue to decline, are those involving the least skill, whereas those on the
increase involve more skill and more training. In a study published by the
MSC in February 1980 *A study of the long term unemployed,* evidence was
gathered which showed that almost 75% of the long term unemployed interviewed in the survey had previously been manual workers, the majority of
whom had done semi-skilled or unskilled jobs. The prospects for those
people are slim for, within the employed labour force, there have been major
changes in occupational structure. For example, between 1971 and 1978 the

number of non-manual jobs grew by 1 million, whereas there was a loss of 900,000 manual jobs with the largest job losses among the least skilled occupations and those craftsmen from the declining industries with non-transferable skills. Blue collar jobs are fewer and white collar jobs outnumbered them before the end of the 1980s. The new technologies require a more highly skilled, better educated and more flexible workforce, in which a larger number of professional and technical staff will be supported by workers performing a range of tasks in a process industry rather than repetitive assembly or manufacturing jobs. Those who, either through State intervention or through opportunities being created for existing workers within firms (or through firms being willing to take on new employees to train), cannot obtain the new skills are likely to remain unemployed and certainly, as regards business and commercial organisations offering training, the long term and inexperienced unemployed will be the ones least likely to be given opportunities.

(ii) Sex distribution

Unemployment is more prevalent amongst the male than amongst the female working population. Within the broad industrial sectors, male and female employment moved in different ways over the 1970s and 1980s. In manufacturing the decline in employment affected males and females equally so that the shares of male and female employment were much the same at the end of the decade as they have been at the beginning. In the service sector, however, male employment only increased by 5%, whereas female employment went up 25%. In 1991 there are more woment than men employed in the service sector — almost 1.75 million women are employed in Local Government. The downturn in growth in the service sector in the 1990s is lilkely to lead to an increase in female unemployment due to the more prevalent use of information technology.

Table 36: Unemployment rate by sex 1981–1991

Year	Male	Female
1981	12.9	6.8
1982	15.0	7.9
1983	15.8	8.9
1984	15.7	9.4
1985	16.1	10.0
1986	16.4	10.0
1987	13.8	9.2
1988	10.7	7.1
1989	8.0	4.6
1990	7.5	3.8
1991 (Jan)	8.9	4.2

Source: Department of Employment figures

(iii) Regional distribution

There are different patterns of unemployment between regions, those hardest hit being the ones which have a high dependence on manufacturing industry (e.g. the North West and West Midlands); those with a reliance on metal processing (e.g. South Wales and the East Midlands); and those which are affected by the falls in shipbuilding output and the decline in demand for heavy construction for the oil industry. Nevertheless, the traditionally protected South East has also suffered over in the mid 1980s and at the beginning of the 1990s. Regional differences in unemployment are illustrated in Table 37.

Table 37: Unemployment rates by region April 1984, 1985 1986 and 1990

REGION	April 1984	PER CENT April 1985	April 1986	April 1990
South East	9.1	9.9	10.1	3.7
East Anglia	9.7	10.8	11.2	3.8
South West	10.9	12.0	12.2	4.2
West Midlands	14.6	15.5	15.5	5.8
East Midlands	11.6	12.8	12.9	5.0
York & Humber	13.6	15.0	15.8	6.8
North West	15.3	16.2	16.3	7.5
North	17.3	18.8	19.1	8.7
Wales	15.4	16.9	17.3	6.5
Scotland	14.2	15.7	15.8	8.2
Great Britain	12.3	13.3	13.6	5.5

Source: Department of Employment figures but they are
not directly comparable due to counting changes.

(iv) Age distribution

Young people usually face shorter unemployment periods than most of the other groups in the labour market. In recent years, however, young people have been finding it increasingly difficult to enter the labour market and periods of youth unemployment have become longer.

Unemployment is also highest amongst those aged under 34 (especially those under 18) and those who are aged 60 plus. The greatest concern presently is for the young unemployed who, without any significant work experience, or because they have been forced to take short term jobs, find it very difficult to find employment, even if an upturn occurs within the economy. The psychological effects of unemployment are damaging enough but, for the young person who feels rejected by society and who has no source of income, the effects are likely to be even worse. The unlikelihood of not obtaining employment, if the individual has few academic qualifications, is also likely to be reflected back into the school system and lead to lack of motivation, disinterest and potential discipline problems.

The changes in the Labour Market, with sectors becoming more efficient and needing a smaller number of employees to produce a given number of goods or services, is particularly affecting the young unemployed. New technologies are rationalising and eliminating jobs which once provided the first chance for young people entering working life.

Table 38: Number of unemployed by age — April 1990 & January 1991 (000s)

AGE	1990	1991
Under 18	*	*
18 and 19	131.0	166.4
20-24	334.2	420.0
25-29	268.4	335.1
30-39	323.8	400.5
40-49	252.2	302.2
50-59	286.7	297.9
60+	28.5	34.9
TOTAL	1626.3	1959.7

* included in 18 and 19 group

Source: Department of Employment figures

Table 39: Unemployment rates by age — April 1988, 1989, 1990 and January 1991 (%)

Age	1988	1989	1990	1991
18 and 19	14.3	10.5	9.3	11.9
20-24	12.7	9.9	8.6	10.8
25-29	10.3	7.8	7.1	8.9
30-39	7.4	5.7	5.0	6.2
40-49	6.1	4.6	4.1	4.9
50-59	10.6	8.4	6.6	6.8
60+	3.8	2.5	1.9	2.4
All ages	9.0	6.6	5.7	6.9

Source: Department of Employment figures.

(v)   Other groups

Disabled employees – During recessions the number of disabled people who become unemployed always tends to rise less quickly than general unemployment, partially because some organisations wish to maintain their quota and partially because many organisations operate a policy whereby the disabled are retained until the last possible moment.

Ethnic minority workers as a group have also tended to suffer disproportionately as Table 40 shows.   The problem is made worse by their age distribution as there is a high proportion of young people among these groups, and also by the fact that ethnic minorities are concentrated in certain regions which have been worst hit by unemployment e.g. West Midlands, Yorkshire and Humberside.

Table 40: Unemployment rates by Ethnic Origin 1987 from Labour Force Survey estimates (%) GB

	All	Male	Female
All origins	10.4	10.9	9.8
White	10.2	10.7	9.5
Ethnic groups	16.4	16.5	16.3
Of whom			
West Indian/Guyanese	17.0	19.0	16.0
Indian	13.0	10.0	17.0
Pakistani/Bangladeshi	29.0	30.0	n/a
All other origins	14.0	14.0	13.0

5.   UK UNEMPLOYMENT RATES COMPARED WITH OTHER COUNTRIES

International figures of unemployment are difficult to compare due to different methods of calculation and collection Table 41 however gives some idea of the differences.

Table 41: Unemployment rates in selected countries –
April 1986 & January, 1991

Country	% Rate of Unemployment	
	1986	1991
Belgium	16.2	12.5
Spain	22.2	16.4
Britain	13.2	6.9
Ireland	17.8	17.3
Holland	15.0	4.8
France	10.3	9.5
Italy	11.1	17.7
Canada	9.6	9.3
USA	7.1	6.9
West Germany	9.0	7.2
Australia	8.0	7.2
Greece	6.4	4.4
Japan	2.7	2.0
Sweden	2.8	1.8

Most industrialised countries have high unemployment levels in the 1980s, compared with the last 10–20 years, and are increasingly uncertain about growth. Over the last 25 years most industrial economies have experienced a steady shift in the balance of economic ability from manufacturing and agriculture into service industries. In each of the nine major industrial countries listed below there has been a decline in the proportion of GDP which is contributed by manufacturing output with the decline accelerating especially after 1970 (see Table 42):

Table 42: Share of manufacturing in GDP*

%

	1960	1970	1971	1972	1973	1974	1975	1976	1977	1978	1979	1980	1981	1982	1983
Canada	23.3	20.4	19.9	20.2	20.2	20.2	19.2	18.6	18.0	18.4	19.1	18.8	18.3	15.6	15.9
US	28.6	25.7	24.9	24.9	24.9	24.1	23.4	24.2	24.5	24.4	23.8	22.5	22.2	20.9	21.1
Japan	33.9	35.9	35.2	34.5	35.1	33.6	29.9	30.6	30.0	30.0	30.1	30.4	30.4	30.5	30.5
France	29.1	28.7	28.5	28.2	28.3	27.9	27.4	27.4	27.5	27.2	27.0	26.3	25.2	25.2	25.3
W.Germany	40.3	38.4	37.0	36.0	36.3	36.1	34.5	34.8	34.6	34.2	34.1	33.0	32.1	31.7	31.8
Italy	28.5	28.9	28.5	27.1	30.0	31.3	29.7	31.7	31.0	30.4	30.6	30.5	28.9	28.5	27.1
Netherlands**	33.6	28.2	27.2	27.1	26.8	25.5	23.7	23.9	20.9	19.5	19.0	17.9	16.9	17.1	17.0
Norway	21.3	21.8	21.1	21.5	21.5	21.9	21.7	20.1	18.9	18.0	18.2	15.6	14.7	14.3	13.7
UK	32.1	28.1	27.4	28.3	28.5	27.2	26.3	25.4	26.6	26.6	24.9	23.1	21.4	21.3	21.0

* Value added in manufacturing as percentage of current price GDP
**Figures for the Netherlands are estimates taken from national sources to reflect the exclusion of oil and gas extraction from the definition of manufacturing

Source: *OECD*

The share of manufacturing in total employment has also fallen in the same period and remains highest in West Germany with the UK being comparable to France, Italy and Japan but with a higher share employed in manufacturing than the USA. See Table 43.

Table 43: Employment in manufacturing

% of total civilian employment

	1960	1970	1971	1972	1973	1974	1975	1976	1977	1978	1979	1980	1981	1982	1983
Canada	23.7	22.3	21.8	21.8	22.0	21.7	20.2	20.3	19.6	19.6	19.9	19.7	19.3	18.1	17.5
US	27.1	26.4	24.7	24.3	24.8	24.2	22.7	22.8	22.7	22.7	22.7	22.1	21.7	20.4	19.8
Japan	21.5	27.0	27.0	27.0	27.4	27.2	25.8	25.5	25.1	24.5	24.3	24.7	24.8	24.5	24.5
France	27.5	27.8	28.0	28.1	28.3	28.4	27.9	27.4	27.1	26.6	26.1	25.8	25.1	24.7	24.3
W.Germany	37.0	39.4	37.4	36.8	36.7	36.4	35.6	35.1	35.1	34.8	34.5	34.3	33.6	33.1	32.5
Italy	23.0	27.8	27.8	27.8	28.0	28.3	28.2	28.0	27.5	27.1	26.7	26.7	26.1	25.7	24.7
Netherlands	30.6	26.4	26.1	25.6	25.4	25.6	25.0	23.8	23.2	23.0	22.3	21.5	20.9	20.5	20.3
Norway	25.3	26.7	25.3	23.8	23.5	23.6	24.1	23.2	22.4	21.3	20.5	20.3	20.2	19.7	18.2
UK	36.0	34.5	33.9	32.8	32.2	32.3	30.9	30.2	30.3	30.0	29.3	28.1	26.2	25.3	24.5

Note: figures for Italy 1960-1976 and 1983 and for the Netherlands 1971-1974 and 1983 are estimates based on different classifications of employment.

Source: *OECD*

6. ECONOMIC COSTS OF UNEMPLOYMENT

Money has been invested in the acquisition of skills, knowledge and experience of workers and not utilising those workers is wasteful and, therefore, is a cost to society. The cost of unemployment for society as a whole could be said to be partly made up from the value of production lost due to unemployment. In calculating such a cost we would have to consider a number of questions:

— Should lost production be calculated for the whole unemployed labour force? Perhaps not, because at any level of economic activity there is always frictional unemployment and hard-core unemployment.

— Would the unemployed achieve higher or lower production results than those currently unemployed? It is sometimes believed that the unemployed would have a lower productivity rate than those actually working because the unemployed have below average qualifications and efficiency levels. Yet it could also be argued that this underestimates the contribution which the unemployed could make to Gross National Product.

— How can we calculate sectoral change effects and changes in work patterns? Production results will vary between individuals, dependent upon their sector of work, due to differences in the degree of capital intensity. The costs would also be different if we changed work patterns from full-time to part-time or from five to four days a week. Other difficulties in calculating the true cost of unemployment include:

— The unemployment rate quoted by Government is not a total record of the unemployed. Evidence suggests that when the unemployment rate falls, the increase in employment is more than proportional to the reduction in the unemployment rate. This is due to the fact that, in such circumstances, not only do the unemployed find jobs, but also do other workers who were not registered as unemployed.

— Also, when the unemployment rate drops, the average number of hours worked increases because, as part of the process, some part-time jobs are turned into full-time jobs and labour hoarding results.

— In addition, as output increases, productivity tends to improve because improvements in economic activity lead to investment in new technology and an encouragement to use manpower more efficiently.

— Where a community or region suffers from high unemployment, the loss of purchasing power has a consequential effect on producers of other products, who may run down production targets before they too lay employees off. The turnover of the providers of other services — hairdressers, football clubs, cinemas etc. — will also fall, which is a loss to those groups.

Unemployment will also lead to increased Government spending as financial resources are transferred to unemployment and supplementary benefits. Government budgets are also affected by losses in income tax revenue, VAT and Social Security Contributions. Local government revenue is also reduced due to a reduction in income from the community charge. Actual unemployment expenditure is also affected by the structure of the unemployment.

— If a large proportion of the unemployed are new entrants on the labour market, the unemployment benefit cost is low because of the qualification rules.

— If a large proportion are long term unemployed many may not be entitled to supplementary benefits after unemployment benefit runs out after 12 months.

Other costs, however, include income tax rebates and subsidies like free school uniforms and school meals or uniform grants, and rent rebates.

These are not the only costs to the community or the Government, for the State will be forced to spend money on measures to try and stimulate employment; these will include training grants for individuals, the cost of operating training programmes in both the Government sector and the private sector and, perhaps, subsidies to create jobs, e.g. regional aid, and wage subsidies.

7. THE OVERALL INFLUENCE OF UNEMPLOYMENT

The problems of structural changes will not be easy to handle; redundancies in some of the traditional industries are heavily concentrated in particular regions, e.g. the reduction in steel manufacture and its effects on towns like Consett and Corby. Although it can be suggested that some of the decline in industries like motor car manufacture, steel production and in other manufacturing sectors is due to a degree of growth gap unemployment caused by the recession, other factors in the world economy could mean that, even with an upturn, there will not necessarily be an increased demand for those products. One significant effect is that the developing countries, who traditionally used to import many finished products, are creating their own home-based industries, often with the help of large multinational companies, to produce steel, motor cars and electrical appliances for themselves. This may, in the long term also result in an over capacity in the world supply of those goods and only the most efficient will survive. Unless we match their technology, productivity and prices, an economic upswing will not help employment very much in the UK.

A number of problems have been identified which are likely to influence the UK's ability to increase levels of employment:

(a)   Increases in product or service demand in the short term, because of labour under-utilisation, will mean only a small initial flow of additional job opportunities in those industries influenced as for a time remaining spare capacity is absorbed.

(b)   With developments in technology in many industries, less labour is likely to be required in the future to produce the levels of goods demanded. Evidence of this is already clear in new motor car production technologies using robotics and the use of *just in time* methods.

(c)   Public sector employment is falling because of public concern about the levels of public expenditure and the consequent privatisation and compulsory competitive tendering programmes.

(d)   Firms having suffered a fairly long term recession are likely to favour a more intensive use of their existing labour force as an alternative to recruitment or may only hire labour on a fixed term or emporary contract basis.

Of course, whether technological developments are likely to cause more serious unemployment is debatable. Historically, investment in technology created more employment through the creation of additional wealth and increases in gross domestic product; unemployment problems have, to a large extent, proved transitional, although employment is not necessarily created in the same industries and sectors. Technology can have long term benefits for the economy and for individual welfare. Technological developments can lead to investment and increased employment in those industries providing the technology and, if the technology lowers costs, and thus prices, it can have a beneficial effect on real incomes and demand can be stimulated overall with consequent further employment effects.

It is likely that the impact of information processing technology will be greater than before, especially due to its potential impact on the service jobs which previously have been areas of growth in employment. According to an institute of manpower studies report in mid 1985 by David Parsons, *Clerical Labour Markets: changes and trends in the UK*, between 1971 and 1981 clerical, secretarial and related work grew at 2.4% and, between 1980 and 1982, 250,000 clerical jobs were lost in the production sector. Examples of the actual effect of word processors on particular organisations are quoted by an article 'Jobs in Jeopardy and the Trade Union Response' in *Personnel Management* by Tim Webb (July, 1979).

"In Bradford Metropolitan Council (a 50% reduction in the number of typists in the word processor area) the British Standards Institute (33% reduction) and the Provident Financial Group (37% reduction in full-time typists and 79% reduction in part timers)."

A choice will inevitably have to be made in the UK between accepting and investing in the new technologies and of refusing or opting out of them to retain levels of employment. If we do not adopt them, and our competitors do, then there could be a resultant loss of exports, an increased threat from imports and, eventually, a more serious threat to levels of employment.

8. MEASURES TO REDUCE UNEMPLOYMENT

A number of measures have been suggested to attempt to deal with the problems of unemployment. The extent to which they are likely to be successful and the impact they are likely to have on organisations will vary. The measures also need to be evaluated against the causes of unemployment.

To some extent it can be argued that unemployment is a matter of definition; it presumes that employment means that people will work from the age of 16–65 (or 60); that they will work continuously; and that they will work a 35 to 39 hour week. The first set of measures deals with removing these parameters.

UNEMPLOYMENT

(i) Reduction in working hours

Logically, reducing the length of the working week would increase the amount of employment, but a reduction in working hours would not create more work if there was a corresponding increase in overtime. Certainly a reduction in working hours is favoured by the TUC as a way of reducing unemployment and, at the TUC annual conference in 1979, they passed a resolution which read:

> "Congress expresses its deep concern at the continued persistence of high unemployment...Congress notes that there was a general resistance on the part of employees to the 35 hour week clause in many unions' claims during the last pay round...Congress recognising likely technological developments, calls upon the General Council and its affiliated unions to give top priority in bargaining to reductions in the working week without loss of pay, with a reduction in overtime."

This reduction has already taken place in sectors of the economy due to the reductions in the working week in the Engineering industry in 1990/91.

Figures show that, although the working week in most industries and firms is technically between 36 and 39 hours per week, the average hours worked in manufacturing and certain other industries were as follows:

Table 44: Average weekly hours worked 1977–1990 full time manual males

Year	Hours
1974	46.5
1975	45.5
1976	45.3
1977	45.7
1978	46.0
1979	46.2
1980	45.4
1981	44.2
1982	44.3
1983	42.9
1984	43.5
1985	43.7
1986	43.7
1987	43.8
1989	44.5
1990	44.3

Reductions in hours of work need to be combined with overtime reductions or levels of employment are little affected.

Evidence, from the 3 day week in 1972, also suggests that a reduction in working hours may in itself lead to higher productivity from the existing workforce, with no consequential demand for additional workers. This is confirmed in a report by M White and A G Habadean 'Shorter working hours in practice' Policy Studies Institute, 1984, which was a study of firms who reduced working hours in 1981–82 in the engineering and printing industries and who reported higher productivity and yet no increases in unit costs.

The problems for employers of such a measure would be the effects on costs and competitiveness if those working fewer hours receive the same levels of pay as before, and there is no increase in productivity. The effect of employing additional labour to obtain the same output would be to raise unit costs, which could damage competitiveness and lead to higher unemployment.

Table 45: Percentage increase in labour costs resulting from reducing normal working hours, without loss of pay (%)

	35 Hours	38 Hours
1. Large employment	7.0	2.5
2. Intermediate employment (low productivity)	8.5	3.0
3. Intermediate employment (high productivity)	6.1	2.2
4. Small employment	6.4	2.2

(Source: Department of Employment Gazette)

Although the TU believes that costs will rise, it also believes that a reduced working week will lead to increased productivity. Figures for France and Germany compared with Britain seem to bear the TUC out, as in Table 46.

Table 46: Working time and productivity in major industrial countries

	UK	France	W.Germany
Annual hours 1975	1932	1831	1671
Annual percentage reduction 1976 – 1979	-0.5	-1.7	-1.1
Annual increase in productivity 1976 – 1979	1.0	2.8	3.0

(Source: Department of Employment Gazette)

(ii) Reductions in overtime

This could increase employment for, even with high levels of unemployment, overtime is being worked in many industries; it is thought to be, in the long term, a cheaper method of finding additional production than employing extra people. It has the benefit that it can be cut quickly, whereas the organisation will incur higher costs in terminating employees.

Table 47: Average overtime hours worked per week 1980–1989 (Manufacturing industries)

Year	Operatives (000s)	% of all Operatives	Hours of Overtime Worked	
			Average per Operative working overtime	Actual hours of Overtime (millions)
1980	1422	29.5	8.3	11.76
1981	1137	26.6	8.2	9.37
1982	1198	29.8	8.3	9.98
1983	1209	31.5	8.5	10.30
1984	1311	34.3	8.9	11.59
1985	1329	34.0	9.0	11.98
1986	1304	34.2	9.0	11.72
1987	1350	36.0	9.4	12.63
1988	1413	37.9	9.5	13.43
1989	1392	37.6	9.6	13.38

Source: Department of Employment figures

If we take the total overtime hours worked in week ending December 14th 1990 and presume that the average working week in manufacturing is 38 hours and that all overtime could be converted into jobs, then we could create, at a stroke, 333,000 jobs.

In some industries compulsory reductions in overtime could create employment where equipment is available for additional employees to operate, but, in some cases, if overtime were reduced, individuals might suffer because overtime can be a vital element in earning levels. Reductions in overtime do not necessarily create work where man/machine systems already have the required number of employees and there is no way of adding staff without incurring higher investment costs.

(iii) Job sharing or job splitting.

The following definitions apply to these methods of structuring work, based on the work of R.Clutterbuck and R.Hill *Remaking of work: changing work patterns and how to capitalise on them* Grant McIntyre 1981.

(a) *Job sharing:* The two employees have equal responsibility for the whole job and they accept that part of the activity is to coordinate and collaborate to ensure that the task is completed. They therefore have to negotiate between them to determine who does what and how they are going to ensure that nothing falls between them.

(b) *Job splitting* is where the two incumbents simply divide the job between them so it is always covered. There is little need for coordination between them as the task consists of a regular flow of largely routine activities.

It has been suggested that a combination of a shorter working week, longer holidays, early retirement and less overtime could provide employment opportunities for the out of work. Worksharing has its aim of redistributing the total work available more evenly among the population. One of the difficulties in Britain is that working time is not influenced by statute, except in the Wages Council Industries, nor are holiday entitlements, except the public holidays. Whereas countries, such as Belgium and West Germany, have legal limits to the amount of overtime worked, the UK only has such limits for young people under the Factories Act and the regulations regarding driver's hours under the Transport Act. Otherwise all these matters are subject to agreement in the UK by the process of collective bargaining and in recent years there have been some significant negotiations which have reduced the working week and increased holidays.

Trade unions generally seem to be in favour of shorter hours of work and many employees, when questioned, have argued that they would prefer to work shorter hours for the same pay than attempt to significantly increase their pay for current hours.

Job sharing is a form of employment whereby two or more worksharing individuals voluntarily share the responsibility for one full-time position with the salary and fringe benefits being split between them according to the time they work. One of the pioneers in the field of job sharing in Britain was GEC Telecommunications in their Coventry and Atcliffe plant. Many organisations in the public and private sector now have schemes. (A form of job sharing has been encouraged by the Job Share Scheme in the UK. Advantages of job sharing schemes include:

— the opening up of opportunities for part-time workers in areas where only full-timers were previously employed. (But are these opportunities going to help the registered unemployed or the hidden unemployed?)

— reduced labour turnover, increased efficiency and greater flexibility of employees.

— greater continuity and flexibility of work coverage as it is unlikely that the job shares will both be absent or leave together.

— can be a good way of helping the future retiree to wind down.

— reduction in costs to the Exchequer.

— retention of key staff.

— improvement in equal opportunities

Disadvantages include

— some jobs, especially of a managerial nature, require continuity and may therefore be difficult to split.

— part-time jobs are created, not full-time ones.

— may limit promotion opportunities.

— where less than 16 hours per week is worked, there is no protection under the EP (C)A 1978.

— more time and expense of training for employers.

— extra cost of payroll administration, protective clothing, facilities e.g. lockers, which cannot be shared.

Main opposition to worksharing has come from employers' organisations because they argue it will increase costs, and therefore reduce competitiveness, and hence mean lower profits.

N. M. Meltz, F. Reid and G. S. Swartz in *Sharing the Work,* an analysis of the issues in worksharing and jobsharing University of Toronto Press, 1981, suggest that there is evidence that worksharing does not necessarily lead to increased labour costs:

— when there is a leisure/income agreement and restrictions in overtime.

— worksharing can remove some of the administrative costs of holiday coverage, replacement problems when somebody leaves etc.

— by retaining workers during a recession and training new ones during periods of low demand, it helps to reduce the recruitment, selection and training costs once trade recovers.

— it may prevent the rusting of skills and problems of motivation amongst those who would be otherwise unemployed.

— shorter hours may reduce absenteeism.

— reorganising working time could allow more capital utilisation and greater flexibility, leading to higher productivity.

(iv) Raise the School Leaving Age

It is becoming apparent that to exclude young people from the labour market by keeping them within the educational system is not equally appropriate for all young people, e.g. the poorly motivated, and furthermore that not all families have the economic capacity to maintain their children in a financial sense.

This would incur increased economic costs for the Exchequer, for it is likely to require investment in more school buildings in some areas and the employment of extra teaching staff. Thought would also have to be given to what is done in that additional school time to improve the likelihood of young people obtaining work.

Certainly some moves have been made thus in November 1982 the Prime Minister invited the MSC to launch a major new educational initiative — the Technical and Vocational Education Initiative (TVEI) which has subsequently been extended by the operation of the extension scheme TVEE. The target group of TVEI is the whole ability range of the 14—18 age group. The general aim of the scheme is to give young people the knowledge and skills necessary to prepare them for the world of work. Thus the scheme attempts to promote a balance between educational and vocational needs, to develop each individual's personal effectiveness and link the work of schools with the world of business, commerce and the public services.

Whilst there are a variety of schemes with variation in content from area to area the common characteristics of schemes include a strong emphasis upon project based learning; the development of real and simulated experience of work problems, the development of problems; the development of problem solving, study skills, computer awareness, communication ability, numeracy, business management and technological initiatives.

The TVEI scheme has a counterpart in the Certificate of Pre-Vocational Education (CPVE) which is a one year programme, launched in 1984 and aimed at the 17 group. Its general aim is to assist the transition from school to work by developing in the students basic skills, experience, knowledge and the relevant personal and social competence which will be required outside of the education world. The CPVE provides a framework of knowledge and has three components:

1. To develop, core competence in the areas of personal development, communication, numeracy, information technology and industrial studies.

2. Vocational studies are organised in five main categories; business and administration services, technical services, production, distribution and personal services.

3. Additional studies which are based on individual choice.

The emphasis is on activity based learning, the development of individually relevant work experience and personal counselling support.

There is a danger however that extra education could raise individuals job aspirations to levels which may not be capable of being met by industry and commerce. Certainly, to keep people at school merely to keep them off the streets has limited value. To transfer back into the education system some of the existing training and work experience schemes could be an attractive proposition, but then we are incurring the costs even for those who can get work and not specifically for those who need it. It would also have repercussions for current apprenticeship and higher education processes.

Table 48: School leaving age (1990)

Belgium	14
Denmark	15
France	16
Germany	15/16
Greece	14
Ireland	15
Italy	14
Luxembourg	15
Netherlands	16
Sweden	16

UNEMPLOYMENT

(v) Lower Wages

The argument has been used by employers and politicians that young people especially, but also others (for example, in the Wages Council Industries) cannot be employed because the costs are too high. It was estimated by the Department of Employment in 1983 that a 1% fall in the wages rates of young males would lead to a 1.2% rise in their employment. Whilst it must be agreed that the cost of the employee is an important factor when deciding who and how many to employ, wages are only one element of cost. It is the demand for the product and service which is of crucial importance.

A number of studies, both in the UK and abroad, have shown that even where the young have relatively lower wage rates there is little impact on the levels of employment. For example a study by the Labour Research Department Bargaining Report 30 in December 1983 analysed the relative rates of pay of young people under 18 and, although these have declined, there has been no increase in employment in the UK.

Table 49: Under 18 gross weekly pay as % of adult average

Year	All Male	All Female
1974	38%	58%
1979	40%	58%
1980	39%	59%
1981	39%	55%
1982	38%	54%
1983	36%	51%

Source: Labour Research Department — December 1983

Even where studies have shown lower wages leading to small increases in youth employment, it is extremely difficult to ascertain whether this apparent improvement in the situation is at the cost of someone else's job or to the benefit of total employment in society.

(vi) Lower the retirement age

This also would have the effect of raising Exchequer costs; to retire people early increases social security spending and creates the need to develop leisure facilities. In July 1980, a written reply was given to the House of Commons on the costs of reductions in male pension ages by Reg Prentice, the then Minister for the Disabled. The reply was as follows:

"On the assumption that the pattern of retirement amongst men in the five years following the new pension ages would be the same as the present pattern amongst men aged 65 or 70, and that two thirds (the figure of two-thirds is assumed because not all retirements would create vacancies, and because some vacancies would not be filled, since there would be insufficient unemployed with the necessary qualifications in the right localities) of the jobs created by men in employment retiring earlier were filled by persons on the unemployment register, the net cost to Central Government funds for a full year, at November 1980 rates, would be in the order of:

Reduction of age to:	64	63	62	61	60
Cost £ million	300	600	900	1,300	1,800

However, in a situation of full employment, when there would be significant job replacement by persons on the unemployment register, these costs could rise considerably. To give some indication of this, if the effect of job replacement on the above calculations were disregarded, the costs, on the same basis as those above, would be of the order of:

Reduction of age to:	64	63	62	61	60
Cost £ million	600	1,200	1,900	2,600	3,600

These figures take account of the net cost to the National Insurance Fund, the loss of National Insurance surcharge, National Health Service, Redundancy Fund and Maternity Pay Fund income, a broad estimate of the loss of income tax revenue and a saving in supplementary benefits. There would, in addition, be important implications for occupational pension schemes."

According to the DHSS's best estimate in 1982, a male pension age of 60 would cut registered unemployment by 420,000, of which 200,000 would be currently unemployed 60–64 year olds. There is some doubt whether the other 220,000 jobs released would actually be filled by others on the unemployment register because it can be argued that many of these close to retirement are retained by organisations because of a perceived moral obligation to 'long serving' employees.

(vii) Employment Subsidies

Employment subsidies to reduce unemployment are based on the idea that employment is extremely costly in economic, psychological and social terms and that Government expenditure to support jobs is preferable to paying social security benefits. The arguments for subsidies as a weapon against unemployment are:

(i) Cash subsidies are a simple method of reducing the costs of hiring labour, (i.e. wage rate minus the subsidy); therefore, employment is stimulated because hiring costs are reduced.

(ii) They are cheap in terms of public finance — there are savings in social security payments, and income tax and national insurance revenue will increase as the level of employment rises.

(iii) They have a dampening effect on inflation:

— employment subsidies have a direct cost-reducing effect on unit labour costs of subsidised firms and, as prices tend to be linked to costs, employment s ubsidies work directly to keep prices down;
— employment subsidies means a lower Public Sector Borrowing Requirements (PSBR) as compared with the costs of unemployment benefits.

Whether there is a long term dampening effect on prices is debatable, as is the idea of reducing the PSBR. There is a danger that employment subsidies will be 'wasted' on employers who will have to reduce their labour force in the long run, for example, British Steel received the Temporary Employment Subsidy in the late 1970s. Subsidies which reduce the relative costs of one firm over another may discourage consumer expenditure on the products of non-subsidised firms, whose output and employment may be reduced: they could have an effect in delaying structural change in the rundown of older industries and distorting long term labour changes and investment decisions.

Although recruitment and training subsidies appear to have the advantage of accelerating the progress of firms who are expanding, rather than a subsidy which can help declining firms, it tends to favour those who are leading the recovery and this can induce a labour supply problem for those who recover later. Another major problem for a government is to know when to terminate the subsidies.

Even subsidies and training grants cannot create work where work does not exist, so their benefits may be illusory. There may be a substitution/displacement effect with employers retaining labour at public expense or, if subsidies are used to create jobs, changes in the pattern of labour demand to take advantage of public funds and displace normal recruitment policies.

(viii) Lower Unemployment Benefit

The idea has been put forward that people today are less interested in having a job because of the possible disincentive benefit of unemployment pay, which is said to increase the amount of voluntary unemployment. Yet the majority of serious investigations have tended to support the view that unemployment benefit at its present levels does not in most cases increase 'voluntary' unemployment (e.g. A. B. Atkinson *et al.* Unemployment Benefit Duration and Incentives in Britain: How robust is the evidence. *Journal of Public Economics* 1984 Vol 23 No.1/22).

The problem in setting unemployment benefit levels is the difficulty of ensuring adequate income for those unlucky enough to be unemployed whilst, at the same time, avoiding a disincentive to work.

There are two main state schemes that provide income support for the unemployed:

(a) National Insurance unemployment benefit is a contributory scheme for which an individual becomes eligible if in the previous tax year he has paid sufficient N.I. payments. It can be paid for a maximum of 52 weeks in a spell of unemployment and is a flat rate payment.

(b) Supplementary benefit depends, not on past contributions, but is payable if a claimant who when means tested, needs it. The degree of need is assessed, taking into account family circumstances and whether the claimant is the head of the household.

Once the need has been established, and provided the claimant's circumstances do not change, eligibility for supplementary benefit runs indefinitely from July 1982. Both National Insurance unemployment benefit and supplementary benefit have been made subject to tax.

The argument against an incentive to remain unemployed, created by N.I. Benefit, is made stronger when we realise that not all the unemployed at any one moment are receiving N.I. unemployment benefit. The reasons for non receipt of N.I. unemployment benefit include:

— awaiting the DHSS to determine eligibility for benefit.

— insufficient contributions — for example many married women who wish to enter the labour market after a break are not entitled to benefit and, in addition, those married women who have continued to pay the reduced N.I. stamp are not entitled.

— disqualification from benefit — disqualification for up to twenty six weeks may occur where a person quits his job voluntarily without just cause (i.e. the N.I. Commissioners would expect that the employee had made every effort to secure alternative employment before handing in his notice), or where an individual is sacked for misconduct (in general however a dismissal is assumed to be involuntary unless misconduct is proved).

— denial of eligibility for benefit where the claimant has entered unemployment with wages paid in lieu of notice.

Certainly OECD evidence from eight countries on young people's attitudes to work rejects the argument that young people do not wish to work because unemployment benefit is high. Thus CER, *Education and Work, the Views of the Young* Paris, 1983 concluded:

'We should perhaps be permitted to repeat one of the more important findings of the present enquiry, namely that evidence drawn directly from young people in eight OECD countries does not confirm the widespread belief that their attitude to work is largely one of rejection.'

(ix) Regional policies

Regional imbalances in the level of economic activity and the availability of work, and thus the level of unemployment, has been a feature of post- war Britain. Even in times of so-called full employment, there has been a higher than average level of unemployment in the development areas of Scotland, Wales, North and North West England, Northern Ireland and the South West, whereas the South East has tended to have a continuous shortage of labour for the last decade.

One of the main causes of this differential level of unemployment, in areas outside of the South East, has been that these areas have housed the declining industries, for example, coal mining (i.e. those pits which are considered no longer economical to mine), shipbuilding, textiles, and, latterly, steelmaking; the unemployment is thus primarily structural. It has also proved difficult to encourage new firms to move into these areas, mainly because of their distance from major markets in Europe and elsewhere and the costs of transportation or the unreliability or unsuitability of the transport available.

Methods used to tackle regional problems have included grants for investment, tax allowances against building and capital costs, cheap factories to rent and employment subsidies to reduce the cost of employing labour. Some local authorities have also refused to grant permission to firms to set up in specific areas, unless they were likely to create a significant amount of work. This has been tried by local authorities around the London area to prevent maufacturing units being replaced by warehouses. Individuals have been given financial assistance to move from high unemployment areas to those where jobs are more readily available.

Regional policies do not seem to have been very successful, especially in recent years, but this must be judged against the prevailing level of economic activity, and business uncertainty generally has been a reason for organisations' unwillingness to establish themselves in new areas or to expand.

(x)   Increased use of temporary work

Whilst temporary work has been a traditional feature of a number of industries (especially those where work levels follow a seasonal pattern e.g. retailing, tourism and agriculture) a view has developed that employers across a wide spectrum are making an increased use of temporary and fixed term contracts as part of a move towards more flexible manning strategies in work organisation.

The highest proportion of temporaries are found in the Service Sector with high concentrations in the educational professions, literary, artistic and sports jobs, sales, waiters, waitresses and shop stewards. Outside the service sector the construction industry especially includes temporaries.

The principal reasons for use of temporary workers include:
— to cover for absence, including annual holidays;
— to cope with seasonal workload peaks;
— to cope with a fluctuating workload when employers are unsure of the potential longevity of increased demand;
— to cover shortages while recruiting full-time staff;
— to ease problems of reorganisation or for short-term projects;
— to avoid a commitment to permanent employment in the face of uncertainty in future labour needs;
— to avoid the legislative requirements and responsibilities towards full-time staff;
— to increase the degree to which flexibility of manning is possible;
— whilst providing training.

It is, however, questionable whether temporary workers are reducing the numbers on the unemployment register or whether those who offer themselves for temporary work are a different category of worker who do not want a permanent job.

Unemployment figures are likely to remain high for the next four years as the repercussions of the single European market filter through and as the world adjusts to the opening up of Eastern Europe and the Russian economy. The numbers of long term unemployed will continue to rise but the levels will be difficult to asses. There is likely to be less stability in the growth of the service sector's absorption of labour and the shift from manual to non manual work may decelerate.

CHAPTER FIFTEEN

BRITISH INDUSTRIAL RELATIONS SYSTEM

No understanding of the context of the human resources function can be complete without some examination of the workings of the British Industrial Relations System. Whether the problems are unemployment, the level of wages, training and development of staff, the mobility of labour or the behaviour of individuals and groups within an organisation, the effects of the trade union movement are likely to be felt. However, this chapter can only give a very superficial introduction.

1. NUMBERS OF UNIONS

According to the Certification Officer's Report for 1990 there are 323 unions in the UK as defined by the Trade Union & Labour Relations Act 1974, ranging from small organisations (the Halifax & District Power Loom Overlookers Association) to the giants (the Transport & General Workers Union and the Amalgamated Engineering Union). Twenty-three unions have over 100,000 members (see table), a combined membership of 8,163,414 out of a total of 10,043,606.

Table 50: Unions with over 100,000 members as at 31.12.90

(Source: Certification Officer's report, 1990)

Union	No. of Members
Transport & General Workers Union	1270776
Amalgamated Union of Engineering Workers (now AEU)	741647
GMB	823176
National and Local Government Officers Association	741647
National Union of Public Employees	604912
Manufacturing, Science and Finance Union	653000
Electrical Electronic Telecommunication and Plumbing Union	367411
Union of Shop Distributive & Allied Workers	375891
National Union of Mineworkers (includes retired members & widows)	*123479
Union of Construction Allied Trades and Technicians	258342
National Union of Teachers	213482
Royal College of Nursing of the UK	285548
Confederation of Health Service Employees	209344
Society of Graphical and Allied Trades 1982	178382
Union of Communications Workers	202500

Civil and Public Services Association	127976
Banking, Insurance & Finance Union	170481
National Association of Schoolmasters and the Union of Women Teachers	163646
National Union of Railwaymen	102676
National Graphical Association (1982)	131647
National Communications Union (Engineering & Clerical Groups)	*157060
Assistant Masters and Mistresses Association	135930
National Union of Civil and Public Servants	115606

*1989 figures

2. UNION STRUCTURE

Each union has its own problems of control and representation: some believe in centralised control, whereas others prefer to decentralise. Some unions have a left-wing bias in their administration, others are much more conservative in their approach to particular issues. The unions who are affiliated to the Trades Union Congress, represent over 90% of trade union members.

It is customary to divide British trade unions into three categories – craft, industrial and general – but these divisions must be treated with caution because, on the whole, the unions do not conform to any one of these structures; they do not develop in a vacuum and the social and economic environment is a continuously varying influence on their growth and development (see Henry Pelling – *A History of Trade Unionism*. Some categories can be identified as:

(a) *Craft Unions* – customarily recruit their membership from some distinct skilled trade or occupation, normally entered through apprenticeship. The object, historically, was to protect the jobs within that craft for members of the trade union exclusively. In a dynamic economy the main focus of the craft is likely to be changed due to technological innovation and, to survive, the craft unions have had to change their boundaries. Examples of craft-based unions include the AEU, EEPTU and ASLEF. (Appendix 1 at the end of this chapter, gives some commonly used trade union acronyms.)

(b) *Industrial Unions* – seek to recruit all the workers within a given industry, regardless of their occupations. Industrial unionism is not very pronounced in Britain because craft sectional and occupational unionism, which developed in the 19th century, established itself across industrial boundaries or as tightly organised segments within industries before industrial union organisation really developed. The National Union of Mineworkers did represent the nearest approach to an industrial union until the Union of Democratic Mineworkers broke away in the mid 1980s; however, another example quoted is ISTC, the steel industry union, although it does not organise all steelworkers.

(c)   *General unions* – by definition, general unions recruit across all occupational and industrial boundaries and recognise no restrictions on their potential membership.   The largest union in the country, the TGWU, is a good example also GMB has a very wide coverage both horizontally in terms of industries and hierarchically in terms of skills. Nowadays the categories of occupational and white collar unions are often added to the list.

(d)   *Occupational unions* – organise workers in a particular occupation or related groups of occupations, without the rigidities of the old craft union system.   Some, like the Association of Professional Executive Clerical and Computer Staffs, cover many industries; others recruit only in one industry, e.g. Fire Brigades Union.

(e)   *White collar unions* – concentrate on non manual occupations, e.g. MSF, NUT, BIFU.   These distinctions, as we can see, are not perfect and other classifications exist in modern writings, e.g. horizontal and vertical unions, open and closed unions; but all classifications tend to be imperfect.

3.   DENSITY OF UNION MEMBERSHIP

There are around 10.04 million trade union members (about 45% of the UK working population), although trade union membership has actually declined since 1979, whereas between 1969 and 1979 membership increased by 28.8% due primarily to white collar union growth, whilst the number of unions declined by 24.4%. This overall density of trade union membership figures is somewhat misleading for there are differences between blue-collar union density and for white collar union density. Density in the proportion of the workforce in a sector who are union members as a % of the workforce in that industry who could be union members.

Table 51: Manual & non manual union membership and density
Selected years 1911-1979

| | Manual | | Non manual | |
	Membership (000s)	Density (%)	Membership (000s)	Density (%)
1911	2730.9	20.8	398.3	12.1
1920	7124.1	53.7	1129.2	29.4
1931	2544.0	25.0	1025.4	22.1
1948	7055.7	50.3	2062.1	33.0
1968	6636.9	49.8	3056.0	32.6
1978	7549.7	62.0	5029.1	43.9
1989	4153.4	43.0	4324.9	35.0

1911—1978 Source: Price R & Bain G.S *Union growth in Britain: Retrospect & Prospect* BJIR March, 1983
1989 Drawn from New Earning Survey

There are also wide variations in density between occupations and between full time and part time employees.

Table 52: Union density by occupation and Sex
Source: Labour Force Survey 1989

| Occupation | Density (%) | |
	Males	Females
Non Manual		
Managerial	37	49
Clerical	45	28
Others	29	28
Manual		
Skilled	52	38
General	56	—
Others	48	30

Table 53: Union — density amongst full time and part time workers
Source: Labour Force Survey 1989

	Male (%) density	Female % density	All % density
Full time	45	40	43
Part time	12	23	22

Size of workplace is also significant with figures from the 1989 Department of Employment, Labour Force Survey showing workplaces with less than 6 workers having a density of 11% and workplaces with 6–24 employees having a density of 23%. The larger the workplace the greater the density.

Density also varies significantly from industry to industry, industries with less than 40% density include:

Agriculture and forestry
Fishing
Construction
Distribution
Hotels and catering
Professional Services
Timber and furniture
Leather, Leather goods and fur

Whereas, for example, the following industries have over 80% of employees in trade unions:

Coal Mining
Footwear
Tobacco
Cotton and Man Made Fibrs
Printing and Publishing
Gas, Electricity and Water
Railways
Road Transport
Sea Transport
Port and Inland Water Transport
Air Transport
Post and Telecommunications
Education and Local Government
National Government

4.   OBJECTIVES OF TRADE UNIONS

One of the major issues in society over the last 30 years has been Government concern and action to ensure that trade unions do not reduce the ability of the UK economy to grow and develop. To consider this debate realistically, it is important to realise that trade unions develop and are in existence, to serve their members and to improve or maintain their terms and conditions of employment. Whilst some trade unions can be justifiably criticised for their internal trade union democratic processes, it is to the members that trade unions are directly responsible and they should be judged on their success in reaching their members' objectives and not on the degree of cooperation which they maintain with Government or employers.

We can perceive the following objectives of trade unions:

(a)   To prevent legal interference in the collective bargaining process

Britain's industrial relations framework is based primarily on the concept of voluntary collective bargaining and there are no stronger champions of this philosophy than the trade unions. For a significant period in post-war Britain there has been some form of restraint on bargaining, but this has not weakened their resolve that bargaining should be conducted freely between employers and trade unions. Whilst the unions and the TUC are prepared to tolerate Government intervention to create a more favourable industrial climate through new labour laws to protect workers, they have an inherent dislike of policies to restrict incomes even in the short term and do not largely want interference in the bargaining process.

Trade unions do have a number of legal rights established by some of the Acts of Parliament summarised in Chapter 9 (i.e. Health and Safety at Work etc. Act, the Employment Protection Act; the Employment Acts; the Transfer of Undertakings (Protection of Employment) Regulations; and the Employment Protection (Consolidation) Act 1978). These rights are:

— the right to appoint safety representatives and to establish safety committees;

— the right to be consulted on pensions if employers wish to have a pension scheme which is contracted out of the State Pension Scheme;

— the right to consultation on proposed redundancies;

— the right to information and consultation on business transfers;

— the right to disclosure of relevant information for collective bargaining purposes;

— the rights of trade unions and employers to apply to the Secretary of State for Employment for exclusion in respect of dismissal schemes and redundancy proceeding agreements;

— the right to hold secret ballots on employers' premises when there are more than 20 employees;

— the right to reimbursement of certain costs of postal ballots from public funds through the Certification Officer;

— the right of officials to time off for trade union collective bargaining and organisation duties.

(b)   To improve wages of members

All unions exist to try to improve the material wealth of their members, both in real and in money terms. The pressure on them to do so is greatest under inflation, which reduces the purchasing power of real wages. Often success has attracted an added bonus of increased membership.

(c)   To improve other terms and conditions of employment

Britain's unions can be fairly criticised for not widening the scope of collective bargaining, especially over the 1950s and 1960s. A concentration of cash in the wage packet has led to neglect of better fringe benefits. During the 1970s, however, under the constraint of incomes policies, other fringe benefits became the target of trade unions. This has continued in the 1980s. and 1990s. Policies for a shorter working week, early retirement, longer holidays, better pensions and sick pay schemes are being increasingly adopted; the first three being a direct result of high levels of unemployment.

(d)   To be involved in the determination of national economic
and industrial objectives

It is natural that trade unions should wish to be involved in the determination of national and economic objectives and in decision making on industrial strategy because, in the long term, it is going to have an effect on their members. Trade unions are now involved in a whole range of official institutions and have become so since 1962 when they were invited to sit on the National Economic Development Council (NEDC), the 'little NEDDIES', and industrial sector working parties. They also participate, along with management representatives, in such organisations as the Health & Safety Commission. The trade union movement is also prominent in the work of ACAS the Industrial Tribunals, and the Employment Appeal Tribunal.

Unions have generally agreed to participate in organisations set up by both the major political parties so that the viewpoint of their members can be represented in Governmental policy decisions.

(e) Health and safety at work
In the opinion of the Robens Committee in 1972, which examined health and safety at work:

"the most important single reason for accidents at work is apathy".

The appointment of safety representatives (since 1978) from the workforce, who consult with employers on organisational health and safety questions, has underpinned the role and responsibility of unions in this area. These rights were clarified in the Safety Representatives & Safety Committees Regulations 1977. The functions of safety representatives include:
1. to investigate potential hazards and dangerous occurrences;
2. to investigate employee complaints;
3. to carry out inspections of the workplace;
4. to make representations to the employer through a safety committee as well as on a day to day basis;
5. to receive information from the Health & Safety Inspectorate
6. to represent individual employees.

(f) Protection of members' job opportunities
Britain's unions are often criticised for their refusal to abandon restrictive practices, which is said to hinder technological change and a rise in levels of productivity. Overmanning is seen as a feature of the 'British disease' and union custom and practice, far more than lack of investment in plant and machinery, it often gets blamed for our lack of competitiveness. Yet unions must be seen by their members to be protecting job interests as far as possible and certainly demarcation disputes are of reducing importance in annual figures of industrial conflict especially as more and more flexibility arrangements are being agreed especially by unions like ISTC, EETPU and the AEU.

(g) To improve public and social services
Trade unions have to represent their members' needs and interests in the broader sense. Though their prime function is industrial representation, they have to take into account that workers are also consumers and parents; tenants and actual, or potential, homeowners; sometimes sick or unemployed; and, eventually, old-age pensioners. So trade unions have not only to fight against deprivation and inequality at work, they also have to act as a pressure group to ensure social justice in the widest sense. Inequality is, in any case, indivisible, whether it be in the place of work or in the community. Many sociological studies have shown how inequality in the workplace is at least in part shared by other inequalities – in family conditions, housing, education etc. A trade union movement which confined its concern to the workplace would not be furthering its members' interests. The era of the Social Contract especially demonstrated union concern with this wider role.

(h) To have a voice in Government

In their early years, trade unions preferred to use their industrial power, and it was not until 1900 that they formed a political party to represent their views. As the unions contribute to Labour Party funds, they have some influence over Labour as a political party and in staffing its national, regional and local machinery.

Under the Trade Union Act of 1913 as amended by the Trade Union Act 1984, trade unions are allowed to make donations for political purposes, providing they are made out of a separate political fund and there are regular review ballots every ten years at least. At the end of 1989 there were 53 trade unions with political funds and, apart from the Civil Service unions, the only major union not affiliated to the Labour Party was NALGO. Trade union members do not have to contribute into their union's political fund and must be allowed to 'contract out' of that proportion of their trade union fees.

The Annual Report of the Certification Officer for 1990 shows that in 1989, within the 53 trade unions who had political funds, something like 80% of members paid the political levy. This figure hides wide variations between unions, for example, in the TGWU, 97% pay the political levy, whereas in the NUM (Northumberland area) only 33% pay it.

Table 54: Trade union members paying the political levy (%) and political Fund Expenditure 1989

Union	%	Expenditure (£)
AEU	72.1	658,004
ASTWKT	96.5	2,707
ASLEF	94.6	29,082
Association of Agricultural Educn. Staff	99.0	0
ACTAT	23.2	21,409
Assoc. of HM Inspectors of Taxes	97.0	0
Bakers Food and Allied Workers Union	93.0	39,357
BETA	94.1	41,003
CATU	96.1	55,543
CPSA	n/a	n/a
Communication Managers Assoc.	97.6	10,141
COHSE	91.7	319,872
EETPU	88.0	195,350
Educational Institute of Scotland	97.4	894
FBU	74.2	45,228
FTAT	87.7	27,213
General Union of Associations of Loom Overlookers	75.0	407

GMB	93.5	1,915,437
IRSF	95.9	39,923
Inst. of Professionals, Managers and		
Specialists	97.5	0
ISTC	89.5	83,913
MSF	45.4	495,000
MU	94.7	20,433
NALGO	91.9	115,434
NACODS	95.0	18,865
NATFHE	82.9	1,500
NCU – Engineering group	77.7	262,009
NCU – Clerical Group	93.3	38,284
NGA (82)	57.5	87,365
National League of the Blind and		
Disabled	95.9	2,458
NUCPS	97.3	0
Nat. Union of Domestic Appliance		
and General Operatives	99.7	1,000
NUHKW	99.6	75,412
Nat. Union of Insurance Workers	85.4	0
Nat. Union of Lock Metal Workers	98.2	50
NUM	95.3	1,176,027
NUPE	96.5	1,592,030
NUR	97.8	292,728
Nat. Union of Scalemakers	0.2	0
NUS	97.6	22,272
NUTGW	87.0	83,665
NUFLAT	97.0	26,241
Power Loom Carpet Weavers and Textile		
Workers Union	97.3	5,837
Scottish Carpet Workers Union	77.9	0
SOGAT 82	60.5	188,848
STE	57.9	8,000
Society of Union Employees (NUPE)	98.8	0
TGWU	97.5	2,898,326
TSSA	83.5	64,408
UCW	95.1	349,435
UCATT	85.4	193,068
UDM	99.9	508
USDAW	92.3	534,984
TOTAL		11,957,744

* 53 trade unions with a membership of 7.3 million have political funds.

* 84% of their members, or 6.2 million, pay the political levy.
* In 1990, the income from the political funds was just over £14.5 million. Six large unions accounted for nearly 70 per cent of this.
* 82.5 per cent of the political fund is given to the Labour Party; 14 per cent is spent on administering the fund; 3.5 per cent is spent on other items.
* 79 per cent of the Labour Party's national income comes from the unions; 16 per cent is given by constituency parties and 6 per cent from miscellaneous sources.

The TUC has issued a statement of guidance to trade union affiliates which sets out clearly the action which trade unions should take to ensure their members are fully informed about their rights as regards the political levy.

(i)   Industrial democracy

Many, but not all unions, wish to increase their members' involvement in the decision making process in their work organisations. All political parties and many firms have stated their commitment to the principle of worker participation. In 1976 the Labour Government published the results of the *Committee of Inquiry on Industrial Democracy,* chaired by Lord Bullock, and published a subsequent White Paper in early 1978. So far, nothing has transpired from these discussions, partly because of the differences of opinion as to what system of worker participation we should introduce, and partly because in recent years trade unions have been more concerned with other issues. Under Section 1 of the Employment Act 1982 there is a requirement that all publically quoted firms with over 250 employees must make a statement in their Annual Reports as to what they are doing in the area of employee involvement. The European Social Charter may influence the further development of employee involvement rights for the remainder of the millenium.

5.   ORGANISATION OF UNIONS

For most members the union only matters at the place of work when something is going wrong and the person to whom they look for support is the local shop steward.   Yet, like all other organisations, unions have a hierarchical structure.

(a)   Branches

Each member of the union is a member of a branch which has the task of organising meetings where problems can be raised and strategems discussed;

organising elections for various officers; and acting as a medium of communication between the member and the senior officers of the union. Members may be allocated to a branch, either because of their place of residence, or because of their place of work. Branches will usually have a Chairman, a Secretary and a Treasurer who are lay officers of the union elected by the branch members; these will administer the branch operations. The attendance of members at branch meetings varies considerably from union to union, but it has been calculated that average attendance is no more than about 5% of the membership.

(b) District Committees
District committees act as a focal point for major decisions which affect a particular locality and coordinate activity within that locality; they also help to spread information on local conditions amongst the members. Membership of District committees can be determined in several ways, but the most common system is that each branch sends representatives to sit on the District Committee.

(c) Area or Regional Committees/Trade Group Committees
In some unions, above the district committees there are a network of Area or Regional Committees to act as a further coordination or communication body. In addition, some large general unions recognise the need for coordination between members of the same trade on matters of mutual interest and also have a series of Trade Group committees as well as regional committees (e.g. TGWU).

(d) National Executive Committee or Council
The senior council within the union may consist of a mixture of full time and lay trade union officials or may be dominated by one group or the other. There is normally a full time General Secretary who is the senior executive; he is be elected by union members under the requirements of the Trade Union Act 1984 as amended. He controls the administrative machinery of the union; acts as the chief negotiator and chief spokesman; and ensures that the union follows the policy laid down by the NEC. Other members of the Executive will be elected, either from constituencies based on regions or trade groups, or by votes cast at delegate Conference. The Executive sets out the policy of the union, based on the wishes of the membership as expressed by the members attending the delegate conference speaking on behalf of their branch, trade group of industry constituency.

(e) Delegate Conferences

The membership elect representatives to go to regular annual or biennial conferences to discuss the activities of the union over the previous period and to agree or initiate new union policies on wages and working conditions; social economic and political matters; and other matters which are considered urgent. These conferences enable the NEC to keep in touch with the grass roots' feeling of the union members and are useful for the informal and formal dissemination of information. Some unions e.g. GMB have industrial conferences for the same purposes.

6.   TRADE UNION CONGRESS (TUC)

At the centre of the trade union system in the UK is the TUC. It was initially founded in Manchester in 1868 and acts as the chief representative for the affiliated unions — 78 of them (1990) — with Government, government bodies and internationally.

Circular calling the first TUC 1968

The document which led to the formation of the TUC in 1868 read as follows:

PROPOSED CONGRESS OF TRADES COUNCILS

AND OTHER

Federations of Trades Societies

Manchester, February 21st, 1868

Fellow Unionists,

The Manchester and Salford Trades Council having recently taken into their serious consideration the present aspect of Trades Unions, and the profound ignorance which prevails in the public mind with reference to their operations and principles, together with the probability of an attempt being made by the Legislature, during the present session of Parliament, to introduce a measure detrimental to the interests of such Societies, beg most respectfully to suggest the propriety of holding in Manchester, as the main centre of industry in the provinces, a Congress of the Representatives of Trades Councils and other similar Federations of Trades Societies. By confining the Congress to such bodies it is conceived that a deal of expense will be saved, as Trades will thus be represented collectively: whilst there will be a better opportunity afforded of selecting the most intelligent and efficient exponents of our principles.

It is proposed that the Congress shall assume the character of the annual meetings of the British Association for the Advancement of Science and the Social Science Association, in the transactions of which Societies the artizan class are almost entirely excluded: and that papers, previously carefully prepared, shall be laid before the Congress on the various subjects which at the present time affect Trades Societies, each paper to be followed by discussion upon the points advanced, with a view of the merits and demerits of each question being thoroughly ventilated through the medium of the public press. It is further suggested that the subjects treated upon shall include the following:-

1. Trades Unions an absolute necessity.
2. Trades Unions and Political Economy.
3. The Effect of Trades Unions on Foreign Competition.
4. Regulation of the Hours of Labour.
5. Limitation of Apprentices.
6. Technical Education.
7. Arbitration and Courts of Conciliation.
8. Co-operation.
9. The present Inequality of the Law in regard to Conspiracy, Intimidation, Picketing, Coercion, etc.
10. Factory Acts Extension Bill, 1867: the necessity of Compulsory Inspection, and its application to all places where Women and Children are employed.
11. The present Royal Commission on Trades Unions: how far worthy of the confidence of the Trades Union interest.
12. The necessity of an Annual Congress of Trade Representatives from the various centres of industry.

All Trades Councils and other Federations of Trades are respectfully solicited to intimate their adhesion to this project on or before the 6th of April next, together with a notification of the subject of the paper that each body will undertake to prepare; after which date all information as to place of meeting, etc., will be supplied.

It is also proposed that the Congress be held on the 4th of May next, and that all liabilities in connection therewith shall not extend beyond its sittings.

Communications to be addressed to Mr. W. H. Wood. Typographical Institute, 29, Water Street, Manchester.

By order of the Manchester and Salford Trades Council,
S. C. NICHOLSON, President.
W. H. WOOD, Secretary.

(a)   The Annual Congress

Congress is composed of delegates from trade unions who must be members of the unions they represent. Moreover, under Congress rules and standing orders, delegates must either be working at the trade at the time of their appointment or be full time paid officials of the union they represent.

Congress always meets on the first Monday in September and four following days. Unions are entitled to send delegates on the basis of one for every 5,000 members (or part thereof), but only the smaller unions tend to take up their full quota. They vote according to their affiliated membership and, if there is a doubt about the view of the Congress on an issue after a show of hands, the matter is decided by a card vote. At a card vote each union casts a vote equivalent to its total membership; if the large unions vote together, they can dominate the smaller ones. The order of business of Congress is arranged by the General Purposes Committee of five delegates elected at the previous Congress – they are not members of the General Council.

Congress forms policy in two main ways:

(i)   by considering, paragraph by paragraph, the detailed Report of the General Council about their work in the past year; and

(ii)   by endorsing or rejecting motions submitted by affiliated unions, each union being entitled to submit two motions.

The report of the General Council and a list of the motions and amendments submitted by unions is circulated two weeks before Congress.

(b)   The General Council

In 1990 there were 52 members of the TUC General Council. Since 1989 the General Council has been chosen by a mixed system of automatic represent-ation and secret ballot.

(i)   Now all affiliated unions with over 100,000 members are automatically entitled to a seat on the General Council and a sliding scale of seats operates depending on size of union. Thus unions with
100,000 – 199,999 members have 1 seat automatically
200,000 – 399,999 members have 2 seats automatically
240,000 – 649,999 members have 3 seats automatically
650,000 – 899,999 members have 4 seats automatically
900,000 – 1,199,999 members have 5 seats automatically
1.2 million plus members have 6 seats automatically.

(ii)   In this category, any union with 200,000 plus members who have at least 100,000 female members must nominate at least one woman to be their representative in one of the automatic seats.

(iii)   Secret Ballot — there are two elements to this:

(a)   8 seats are voted for by the unions with a membership of less than 100,000 members, with each union having the right to make a nomination.

(b)   Consists of 4 women members who are voted for by all the unions with less than 200,000 members.

The remaining seat is that of the TUC General Secretary.

The General Council acts as the executive body of Congress and its ultimate responsibility is to carry out the decisions of Congress. However, on most matters which come before the General Council, it would not be possible to delay a decision pending a reference to Congress and the Council acts on matters as they arise, reporting back to the next Congress via the Report.

The General Council meets once a month and is mainly concerned with examining the detailed work carried out by its committees. The Standing Committees are composed entirely of General Council members; these committees are Economic, Education, Employment Policy and Organisation, Equal Rights, Finance and General Purposes, International, Social Insurance and Industrial Welfare.

There are a number of committees for major industries on which General Council members sit with representatives from affiliated unions — Construction, Fuel, and Power, Health Service, Hotel and Catering, Local Government, Printing, Steel, Textiles, Clothing and Footwear, Transport.

Finally, there are a number of joint committees on which representatives from other bodies of national importance (e.g. CBI, Health and Safety Executive, Commission for Racial Equality) sit with General Council and/or union representatives; Arts, Entertainment and Sports Advisory Committee, BMA/TUC Committee, CBI/TUC Committee, Media Working Group, National Council of Labour, NEDC, Nationalised Industries Committee, Public Services Committee, Race Relations Advisory Committee, Trades Councils' Joint Consultative Committee, Standing Advisory Committee of the TUC Centenary Institute of Occupational Health, TUC Labour Party Liaison Committee, Womens' Advisory Committee.

The top 20 largest unions in the TUC are given in Table 55:

Table 55: Top 20 TUC unions by membership 1985/1986 & 1989/1990

Union	1985–86 membership	1989–1990 membership
Transport and General Workers Union	1,490,555	1,270,726
Amalgamated Engineering Union	1,000,883	741,647
GMB	846,565	823,176
National and Local Government Officers' Association	766,390	750,502
National Union of Public Employees	673,445	604,912
Union of Shop, Distributive and Allied Trades	392,307	375,891
MSF (including TASS)	610,000	653,000
Union of Construction, Allied Trades & Technicians	249,961	258,342
National Union of Teachers	214,361	213,482
Confederation of Health Service Employees	214,321	209,344
Society of Graphical and Allied Trades' 82	210,462	178,383
National Union of Mineworkers	200,000	123,479
Union of Communication Workers	195,374	202,500
National Communications Union	166,483	157,060
Banking Insurance and Finance Union	154,579	170,481
Civil and Public Services Association	149,782	127,976
National Union of Railwaymen	136,315	102,676
National Association of Schoolmasters/Union of Women Teachers	126,435	163,646
National Graphical Association – (1982)	126,267	131,647
Society of Civil and Public Servants	85,957	115,606

Source: various

Independent Review Committee

The independent Review Committee exists to consider appeals from individuals who have been dismissed, and given notice of dismissal from, or of having been refused admission to, a union in a situation where trade union membership is a condition of employment. Established under the auspices of the TUC, and its secretariat drawn from the TUC, its members were appointed in consultation with the Secretary of State for Employment and the Chairman of ACAS. The Committee is completely independent in reaching its decisions.

The following procedure is part of the Committee's Terms of Reference:

(a)   The Committee must be satisfied, before considering an appeal, that an individual who has been dismissed has exhausted all internal union procedures;

(b)   The Committee will discuss the case with the union and the individual concerned and will try to resolve the matter by agreement;

(c)   If agreement cannot be reached, the Committee will make a recommendation about whether or not the individual should be admitted to the union, or in the case of a member who has been expelled, whether or not he should be taken back into the union and, if so, upon what conditions. There is then a clear responsibility on the part of the union concerned to act upon such a recommendation.

(c)   Regional and Local Structure of the Trade Union Movement

The TUC Regional Councils (of which there are eight regions in England) and the Scotland and Wales TUC form the machinery through which TUC policy is administered. These Councils are also responsible for the formulation and development of trade union policy in their areas on all matters solely affecting a particular region. They are composed of representatives of those TUC affiliated unions with members in the region. The general duties of the TUC Regional Councils are:

(i)   To make representations to bodies throughout the region including Government departments, Local Authorities and other bodies on economic, political, industrial, social and environmental questions pertaining to the region.

(ii)   To appoint representatives to bodies within the region designated by the TUC General Council.

(iii) To support such representatives and to receive and consider reports from them about the activities of the bodies of which they are members.

(iv)   To perform a public relations function for the trade union movement within the region.

(v)   To keep the TUC informed of developments within the region.

(vi)   To give effect to policies adopted by the TUC and to keep trade unionists in the region informed of these policies.

(vii) To promote an exchange of information between unions in the region.

(viii) To assist unions in the recruitment of members in the region.

(ix) To encourage unions to take part in the work of Trades Councils in the region.

(x) To give effect to any directions by the General Council.

(d) Trades Councils

In most areas trade union branches join on a voluntary basis to form a local Trades Council, the main functions of which are to provide, to affiliated branches, services on a wide range of industrial, social and community issues. They, in addition, make representation to local authorities and nominate representatives to a number of statutory committees and tribunals. They communicate TUC policies and feed back local reaction and opinion. There are about 400 recognised Trades Councils in England and Wales. Trades councils have been in existance longer than the TUC as it was the Manchester and Salford Trades Council which initiated the TUC.

7. CONFEDERATION OF BRITISH INDUSTRIES

The CBI is the major organisation of British employers. Founded in 1965 and incorporated by Royal Charter it combines the roles previously played by three former organisations:

1. The Federation of British Industries (FBI) which represented the larger private manufacturing organisations and trade associations.

2. The British Employers Confederation (BEC) which was primarily concerned with labour questions and had only employers organisations in membership.

3. The National Association of British Manufacturers (NABM) representing manufacturing firms and trade associations in commercial matters, and although there was no restriction in size, in practice the individual members tended to be small businesses.

In addition the CBI includes the main nationalised industries.

The objectives of the CBI as stated in 1974 are:

(i) to voice the collective views of its members;

(ii) to promote and protect its members collective interests;

(iii) to help its members play their full part 'in the creation, in a free market setting, of the wealth on which national prosperity and social progress depend.'

In fulfilling these objectives the CBI seeks to represent the interests of its members at national and international levels and to assist them individually with any problems concerning the running of business organisations. It is an independent body financed by its members in industry and commerce.

Membership

Membership includes individual firms, almost all the nationalised industries trade associations and employers associations. Some 12m people are employed by companies associated with the CBI either directly or indirectly through their trade association.

Structure and organisation

The governing body is the COUNCIL which meets monthly — approves the proposals that become official policy. Council has over 400 members including representatives from employer, trade and commercial organisations, the public sector, the Regional Councils and member companies.

Council is chaired by the PRESIDENT who is usually drawn from a major industrial company and is appointed for a two year period. In 1975 the machinery of the CBI was strengthened by the setting up of a PRESIDENTS COMMITTEE consisting of about 25 leading representatives form the main sections of its membership — large companies, small firms, associations, nationalised industries and its main committees. The President's Committee meets monthly and advises the President on major policy issues and keeps the CBI's public position and overall strategy under review. (It could be compared loosely with the TUC General Council.)

The Council is served by some 20 STANDING COMMITTEES and a wide range of WORKING PARTIES and STUDY GROUPS. Collectively the Standing Committees serviced by the DIRECTORATE are responsible for the detailed work on policy making.

CBI Directorates

The CBI has a permanent staff of about 450 whose executive head is the Director-General who is appointed by the President with the approval of Council. The Directorates include Economic; Education, Training and Technology; Overseas; Social Affairs; Administration; Information; Company Affairs; and Regional and Smaller Firms.

Administration Directorate: One of two Standing Committees, Finance and General purposes which control major aspects of overall external and internal policy.

Company Affairs Directorate: has some 10– 5 Standing Committees dealing with such aspects as Companies, Company law, Contracts, Industrial property, Energy policy, Environmental and Technical legislation, Transport, etc. In addition there are some 20 working parties and other subordinate groups.

Economic Directorate: has around eight Standing Committees including Economic policy, Financial policy, Economic situation, State intervention in private industry etc., with 16 working parties and other sub groups.

Education, Training and Technology Directorate: has four Standing Committees: Education and Training, Overseas and Scholarships Board, Production, Research and Technology, and 10 subordinate groups.

Overseas Directorate: Two main Standing Committees, overseas and Europe, and 10 subordinate groups.

Regional and small firms Directorate: Two Standing Committees, Smaller Firms Council and Marketing and Consumer Committee, in addition one subordinate group.

Social Affairs Directorate: has six major Standing Committees; Industrial Relations and Manpower, Employment policy, International labour, Labour and Social Affairs, Safety, Health and Welfare, Social Security and finally Wages and Conditions with 7 subordinate groups.

CBI Standing Committees

A representative organisation must work through a committee structure and therefore committees must be composed of members drawn from the industries or sectors of society which the organisation was set up to represent. At least 10% of the membership of a CBI Standing Committee must represent small firms interests. The functions of the CBI internal staff are to act as a secretariat, to provide central back up of services – research, information, publicity, etc. – and to carry out those policy decisions delegated to them by the committees to whom they are responsible. Each Chairman of committee is appointed by the President and committee members are appointed by the Director General.

Regional Councils

The CBI is also divided into 13 regions with the three largest areas by company membership being London and the South East, the West Midlands and Yorkshire and Humberside. Each region has a regional council which assesses membership opinions on proposed CBI policy and facilitates personal contact among local members and contact is maintained with local authorities, Government departments and constituency MP's.

The CBI nominates employer representatives to a range of public organisations including the NEDC, ACAS and Industrial Tribunals. It has extensive European and international affiliations and maintains an office in Brussels.

National Conference

In 1977 the CBI staged its first National Conference open to all its members. It is designed to provide a public platform for delegates from all sectors of British business, to project thinking on major issues and recommend action to the council.

Discussion

There are differences between the CBI and other employer and trade associations. In the majority of associations members of the functional committees are properly accredited representatives of their company. Members of the CBI committees, however, do not theoretically represent their own organisation. They are invited by the CBI to serve on the committee in question because of their perceived expertise in the subject. Naturally their opinions will be coloured by their own organisation's policy which they probably help to formulate and certainly assist to implement.

Nevertheless because the CBI aims to be the spokesman for the whole of industry, a truly representative system would not be practical, for the committees would have to be so large that they would not be able to achieve anything within a reasonable period of time.

Committees therefore are acutely conscious that they represent much wider interests than those of the immediate parent organisation which send the individual members. This is inevitable because the output of the committees deliberations go to the council where there is a reaction from a wide sector of industry. If the output from the committee is too narrow and insular it is likely to be referred back for moderation and amendment.

CBI's Weaknesses

1. Although it has a wide membership it has been unsuccessful in attempts to extend membership beyond the manufacturing sector so its membership coverage is not across British industry.

2. Even within the manufacturing sector the CBI is stronger in some spheres than in others. It is strongest among larger firms and despite the establishment of the Smaller Firms Council, the continued existence of a

separate entity, the Smaller Business Association indicates that the CBI is an organisation whose policies are dominated by large firms.

3. Doubts have also been expressed about whether the CBI does really represent the views of its member firms. There is always potential tension in the CBI between those members who would prefer to see the organisation follow a strategy of cooperating with government in the implementation of its policies in the hope of securing concessions, and those who would like the CBI to engage in more frequent and more outspoken criticism of government policy even if this impairs the organisation's ability to negotiate concessions from government.

8. EMPLOYERS ASSOCIATIONS

(a)   Employers Associations are defined in the Trade Union and Labour Relations Act 1974 in Section 28(2) as:

"........an organisation, whether permanent or temporary which either,

(a)   consists wholly or mainly of employers or individual proprietors of one or more descriptions or is an organisation whose principal purposes include the regulation of relations between employers of that description or those descriptions and workers or trade unions, or

(b)   Consists wholly or mainly of:

(i)   constituent or affiliated organisations which fulfil the conditions specified in paragraph (a) above (or themselves consist wholly or mainly of constituent or affiliated organisations which fulfil these conditions), or

(ii)   representatives of such constituent or affiliated organisations and in either case is an organisation whose principal purposes include the regulation of relations between employers and workers or between employers and trade unions or include the regulations of relations between its constituent or affiliated organisations."

They are thus those bodies which deal partly, primarily or even exclusively with labour and industrial relations masters. The list of employers organisations which complied with the above definition registered with the Certification Officer in 1990 included 135 organisations.

(b) The largest employers associations on that list in terms of income included:
1. Engineering Employers Federation and its local associations
2. Building Employers Confederation
3. Test and County Cricket Board
4. British Printing Industries Federation
5. Electrical Contractors Association
6. Federation of Master Builders
7. Motor Agents Association
8. Newspaper Society
9. National Federation of Retail Newsagents
10. National Pharmaceutical Association
11. Heating and Ventilating Contractors Association
12. Federation of Civil Engineering Contractors

Other large employers associations which were not listed at 31.12.89 included:
1. National Farmers Union
2. Freight Transport Association Ltd.
3. Chemical Industries Association Ltd.
4. Road Haulage Association Ltd.
5. British Jewellery and Giftwear Federation Ltd.

(c) The following table shows the year to year changes in the total employers associations listed between 1st February 1976 when the Certification Office was set up and up to 31.12.90:

Table 56: Total employers' associations 1.2.76 to 31.12.90

1.2.76	206
31.12.76	205
31.12.77	196
31.12.78	194
31.12.79	190
31.12.80	181
31.12.81	172
31.12.82	166
31.12.83	157
31.12.84	158
1.12.85	147
31.12.86	148
31.12.87	144
31.12.88	140
31.12.89	139
31.12.90.	135

In addition the number of unlisted organisations known to the Certification Office at 31.12.90 was 158 compared with 290 in 1979.

There in fact no advantages from being listed for employers associations whereas for trade unions listing is essential as a preliminary to applying for a *certificate of independence* under Section 8 of the EPA 1975 and also entitles them to tax relief for expenditure on provident benefits.

(d)   Historically employers associations were proactive bodies in British industrial relations and one of the greatest obstacles to the development of trade unionism was the hostility and collective action of employers. For example, in the 1850s and 1860s the 'document' became an important weapon of the employers in the engineering and construction industries especially, although its success was limited in the long term. Employers organisations were however often weak and temporarily established bodies but the 1869 Royal Commission encouraged the development of employers associations when it stated:-

> "The employers cannot fail to see the advantage which the trade unions, in the conduct of strikes, have in attacking the employers.... the strike is with this view directed against a single employer, or against the employers in a single district, the workmen on strike being supported by those in the employment of other masters, the intention being, on the success of the first strike to take others in succession. To defeat this policy the employers resort to such expedients as they deem best for their own protection. The ordinary course is to form an association of their own in which they agree, in the event of a strike against any member of the association, to close the workshops of all, and in some cases by a subscription among themselves, to give pecuniary assistance to the employer against whom the strike is directed."

Three main aims were identified for the early employers association:

(1)   By collective action individual firms could be protected from being 'picked off'
(2)   To preserve the power to manage in conditions of change and growth
(3)   To establish national procedural agreements to deal with disputes between unions and employers (often in advance of strong trade unionism)

The Donovan Report Para. 77, emphasised the innovatory role of employers associations prior to 1914 but added:

"By contrast from 1914... nearly every important innovation in industrial relations which was not the work of the
unions came from Government and individual companies."

This prompted the Commission to ask why many firms still wished to
belong to employers associations and it found the explanation in the
continued existence of industry-wide bargaining despite its reduction in
influence on the pay packet in many industries, the advice they offered
on commercial matters (in those instances where they combined labour
relations and trade association functions) and the general services and
advisory functions they performed in such areas on representing
members' views to Government, advising on the impact of legislative
changes, the provision of training facilities and access to disputes
procedures.

(e)   Advantages perceived for association membership:

1.   Negotiation of wages and other terms and conditions of service for
     all members of the association — especially in those industries
     which include large numbers of small firms e.g. electrical
     contracting and construction.
2.   Advice on general industrial relations matters.
3.   Local meetings to discuss issues of mutual interest.
4.   Representation to Government, Government departments and
     other national bodies.
5.   Representation to the EEC and other international bodies.
6.   The availability of training services.
7.   Access to information on wage rates and working conditions.
8.   Advice on legal problems.
9.   Representation on legal matters.
10. Exchange of information.
11. Advice on specific industry health and safety matters.
12. Economic and trade advice.
13. Centralised procedures for the avoidance of disputes.
14. Access to trained personnel e.g. Membership of the General
     Council of British Shipping.

9.   WAGES COUNCILS

Wages Councils, which are now governed by the Wages Act of 1986, were
originally established as Trade Boards in 1909 by Winston Churchill to
protect those working in the "sweated trades". Churchill argued in the House
of Commons on the 28th April 1909:

"Where you have no organisation, no parity of bargaining, the good employer is undercut by the bad, the bad employer us undercut by the worst... where these conditions prevail you have not a condition of progress but a condition of progressive degeneration... the degeneration will continue...for a period which compared with our brief lives is indefinite."

The two objectives of the Wages Councils are to:

− protect unorganised workers
− promote collective bargaining

Wages Councils are tripartite bodies which have equal representations of the trade unions and of the employers represented in the industry and three independent members appointed by Government, who hold the balance of power. They are empowered to issue orders which fix the minimum wage rates for those over the age of 21 and a basic overtime rate . Wages Councils now have a statutory duty to consider the impact of their orders on employment levels in the sector concerned. These orders are mandatory on the employers and the policing force to ensure that organisations are complying with the orders are the Wages Inspectorate.

The 26 Wages Councils existing in 1990 fix the minimum conditions for some 2.75 million people (11% of the working population). 90% of the employees covered are in clothoing, retailing and catering. These are all industries which are dominated by small firms where trade union organisation is currently weak and where trade union membership is expensive and difficult to organise. The TUC tries to coordinate membership drives.

10. STATUTORY JOINT INDUSTRIAL COUNCILS

The Wages Councils Act 1979 subsumes the provisions of the Employment Protection Act 1975, which provided the facility for Wages Councils to be converted after investigation by ACAS into a Statutory Joint Industrial Council (SJIC). An SJIC is similar to a Wages Council except there are no independent members, but disputes are settled by compulsory arbitration on the request of either the trade union representatives or the employers on the SJIC. Orders can still be enforced by the Wages Inspectorate. The SJIC was an attempt to create a half-way house between statutory wage fixing and free collective bargaining. Whilst there was a recommendation to create an SJIC in the Toymaking Industry, so far none have been created.

APPENDIX
Commonly Used Trade Union Abbreviations

ACTSS	Association of Clerical, Technical and Supervisory Staffs (white collar TGWU)
ASLEF	Associated Society of Locomotive Engineers and Firemen
AMMA	Assistant Masters and Mistresses Association
AEU	Amalgamated Engineering Union
APT	Association of Polytechnic Teachers
AUT	Association of University Teachers
BALPA	British Airline Pilots Association
BECT	Broadcasting Entertainment & Cinematograph Techniciana Union
BFAWU	Bakers, Food and Allied Workers Union
BIFU	Banking, Insurance and Finance Union
BMA	British Medical Association
CBU	Clearing Bank Union
COHSE	Confederation of Health Service Employees
CPSA	Civil and Public Services Association
DATA	Draughtsmen's and Allied Technicians Union
EESA	Electrical and Engineering Staffs Association (white collar EETPU)
EETPU	Electrical, Electronic, Telecommunications and Plumbing Union
EMA	Engineers and Managers Association
FAA	Film Artistes' Association
FBU	Fire Brigades Union
FDA	Association of First Division Civil Servants
FTAT	Furniture, Timber and Allied Trades Union
GMB	General Municipal & Boilermakers
GPMU	Graphical, Paper and Media Union
HCSA	Hospital Consultants' and Specialists' Association
IPMS	Institute of Professional Managers & Specialists
IRSF	Inland Revenue Staff Federation
ISTC	Iron and Steel Trades Confederation
MSF	Manufacturing, Science & Finance Union
MU	Musicians Union

NACODS	National Association of Colliery Overmen Deputies & Shotfirers
NAHT	National Association of Head Teachers
NALGO	National and Local Government Officers Association
NAS/UWT	National Association of Schoolmasters and Union of Women Teachers
NATFHE	National Association of Teachers in Further and Higher Education
NCU	National Communications Union
NUCPS	National Union of Civil & Public Servants
NUKFAT	National Union of Knitwear, Footwear & Apparel Trades
NUIW	National Union of Insurance Workers
NUJ	National Union of Journalists
NUM	National Union of Mineworkers
NUPE	National Union of Public Employees
NUT	National Union of Teachers
PAT	Professional Association of Teachers
POA	Prison Officers Association
RCM	Royal College of Midwives
RCN	Royal College of Nursing
RMT	National Union of Rail, Maritime & Transport Workers
STE	Society of Telecom Executives
TGWU	Transport and General Workers Union
TSSA	Transport Salaried Staffs Association
TWU	Tobacco Workers Union
UCATT	Union of Construction, Allied Trades and Technicians
UCW	Union of Communication Workers
UDM	Union of Democratic Mineworkers
USDAW	Union of Shop, Distributive and Allied Workers
WGGB	Writers Guild of Great Britain

REFERENCES & FURTHER READING

CHAPTER 1

C. **Handy** *The future of work* Basil Blackwell, 1984.

S. **Wood (ed.)** *The degradation of work* Hutchinson, 1982.

Nick Cowan Change and the personnel profession *Personnel Management*, January 1988.

Paul Sparrow et al. Changing patterns of human resource management *Personnel Management*, November 1988.

Mike Taylor Changing the personnel function to meet changing business needs *Personnel Management*, September 1988.

Paul Sparrow and Andrew Pettigrew How Halfords put its HRM into top gear *Personnel Management*, June 1988.

David Guest Personnel and HRM: can you tell the difference? *Personnel Management*, January 1989.

Paul Miller Strategic HRM what it is and what it isn't *Personnel Management*, February 1989.

Celia and John Stanworth *Work 2000—the future for industry* Paul Chapman Publishing, 1991.

Roy Payne Taking stock of corporate culture *Personnel Management*, July 1991.

T. **Keenoy** HRM: a case of the wolf in sheep's clothing. *Personnel Review*, Vol.19, No.2, 1990.

CHAPTER 2

E. H. **Schein** *Organisational Psychology* Prentice Hall,1980.

Shaun Tyson The dilemmas of Civil Service personnel management *Personnel Management*, September 1988.

Pamela Peacock Is business ethics a contradiction in terms? *Personnel Management*, November 1989.

Paul Miller Managing corporate identity in the diversified business *Personnel Management*, March 1989.

Sandra Fredman and Gill Morris The State as employer: setting a new example *Personnel Management*, August 1989.

Laurence Jackson Turning airport managers into high flyers *Personnel Management*, October 1989.

Chris Brewster and Christopher Smith Corporate strategy: a no go area for personnel? *Personnel Management*, July 1990.

Ian Kessler Personnel management in local government *Personnel Management*, November 1990.

Dick Mackie Personnel's role on the campus *Personnel Management*, May 1990.

Roger Seifert Prognosis for local bargaining in health and education *Personnel Management*, June 1990.

G. **Bannock and M. Daly** Size distribution in UK firms *Employment Gazette*, May 1990.

J. **Reyes and B. H. Kleiner** How to establish an organisational purpose *Management Decision*, November 1990.

I.P.M. *Competitive tendering in the public sector: the personnel implications* IPM 1986.

J. **Rogers** The lifeblood of the NHS *Personnel Management*, June 1991.

H. **Fullerton and C. Price** Culture change in the NHS *Personnel Management*, March 1991.

Susan Corby Civil Service decentralisation: reality or rhetoric? *Personnel Management*, February 1991.

G. **Johnson and K. Scholes** *Exploring corporate strategy* Prentice Hall, 1988.

Gordon Greeley *Strategic Management* Prentice Hall, 1989.

H. **Igor Ansoff** *Implanting strategic management* Prentice Hall, 1990.

D. **Torrington** et al. *Effective management* Prentice Hall, 1989.

Cliff Bowman *The essence of strategic management* Prentice Hall, 1990.

Sandra Dawson *Analysing organisations* MacMillan, 1989.

Laurie J. Mullins *Management and organisational behaviour* Pitman 1989.

P. **Armstrong and C. Dawson** *People in organisations: fourth edition* Elm Publications, 1987.

M. **Botterill** Changing corporate culture *Management Services*, June 1990.

Kathryn Riley and Martin Sloman Milestones for the personnel department *Personnel Management*, August 1991.

CHAPTER 3

G. **Oliver** *Marketing today: second edition* Prentice Hall, 1986.

M. **J. Baker** *Marketing strategy and management* MacMillan, 1985.

Gordon E. Greenley *Strategic management* Prentice Hall 1989.

CHAPTER 4

J. **Woodward** *Management and technology* H.M.S.O., 1958.

K. **Lockyer** *Production management* Pitman, 1983.

CHAPTER 5

W. **Brown** *Exploration in management* Penguin, 1975.

R. **Stewart** *Managers and their jobs* Pan Books, 1967.

R. **Stewart** *Contrasts in management* McGraw Hill, 1976.

R. **Stewart** It's not what you do.. it's the way that you do it: implications of the choices in managerial jobs *Personnel Management*, April 1983.

R. **Stewart** *The reality of management* Heinemann,1986.

Paul Carter and Cedric Lumsden How management development can improve business performance *Personnel Management*, October 1988.

John Burgoyne Management development for the individual and the organisation *Personnel Management*, June 1988.

Mike Day Managerial competence and the Charter Initiative *Personnel Management*, August 1988.

Thomas Furtado Training for a different management style *Personnel Management*, March 1988.

Nicki Fonda Management development for the individual and the organisation *Personnel Management*, December 1989.

W. David Rees A system for assessing work priorities *Personnel Management*, December 1989.

Graham Prentice Adapting management style to the organisation of the future *Personnel Management*, June 1990.

Carole Tietjen Management development in the NHS *Personnel Management*, May 1991.

Jacqui Lewis and Chris McLaverty Facing up to the needs of the older manager *Personnel Management*, January 1991.

E. Willis Should management development just be for managers? *Personnel Management*, August 1990.

Philip Sadler and Kevin Barnham From Franks to the future; 25 years of management training prescriptions. *Personnel Management*, May 1988.

CHAPTER 6

P. B. Crosby *Quality without tears* McGraw Hill, 1984.

J. S. Oakland *Total quality management* Heinemann, 1989.

Dale and Plunkett *Managing quality* Philip Allen, 1989.

R. Collard *Success through people* IPM, 1989.

IPM/IDS *Customer care; the personnel implications* IPM/IDS, 1989.

E. Giles and R. Williams Can the personnel department survive quality management *Personnel Management*, April 1991.

IDS Study 457 *Total quality management* Incomes Data Services, 1990.

D. Bone and R. Griggs *Quality at work* Kogan Page, 1990.

David Hutchings *In pursuit of quality – participative techniques for quality improvement* Pitman Publishing, 1990.

CHAPTER 7

Ward Griffiths Fees for 'in house' work – the personnel department as consultancy *Personnel Management*, June 1989.

Terence Kenny et al. Personnel management 20 years on *Personnel Management*, May 1989.

David Yeundle and Jon Clark Personnel strategy for an automated plant *Personnel Management*, June 1989.

Sir Leonard Peach A practitioner's view of personnel excellence *Personnel Management*, September 1989.

Barry Curnow Recruit, retrain, retain : personnel management and the three Rs *Personnel Management*, November 1989.

David Bell Why manpower planning is back in vogue *Personnel Management*, July 1989.

Rhiannon Chapman Personnel management in the 1990s *Personnel Management*, January 1990.

Michael Armstrong and Robin Cooke The search for strategic HRM *Personnel Management*, December 1990.

Nick Georgiades A strategic future for personnel *Personnel Management*, February 1990.

Catherine Hodges Metamorphosis in the NHS: The implications of trust status *Personnel Management*, April 1991.

Stella K. Nkomo Strategic planning for human resources – lets get started *Long Range Planning*, Vol. 21, No. 1, 1988.

Anat Arkin Personnel policies in partnerships *Personnel Management*, May 1991.

K. R. Allen How middle managers view the function *Personnel Management*, June 1991.

Stephen Briscoe Meeting the training needs of NHS personnel specialists *Personnel Management*, July 1991.

The following IPM Codes are also essential reading;

The IPM Code of Professional Conduct,

The IPM Recruitment Code,

The IPM Redundancy Code,

The IPM Statement on Human Resource Planning,

The IPM Code on Employee Data,

The IPM Statement on Continuous Development People and Work,

The IPM Code for Occupational Testing,

The IPM Statement on Principles of Improving Work,

The IPA/IPM Employee Participation and Involvement in the UK Code,

The IPM Equal Opportunities Code,

THe IPM Secondment Code,

Smoking Policies at Work an IPM Guide,

Age and Employment:an IPM Statement.

CHAPTER 8

Linda Dickens and Trevor Collins Why equality won't appear on the bargaining agenda *Personnel Management*, April 1990.

David Lewis *Essentials of employment law* IPM 1990.

CHAPTER 9

Lorraine Paddison The equal value amendment, a flawed law for an irrational system *Personnel Management*, October 1988.

Gregory Povall Personnel's role in managing disability *Personnel Management*, December 1988.

Geraldine Hackett Who'd be an equal opportunities manager? *Personnel Management*, April 1988.

Rose Reddell Why COSHH will hit hard on health and safety *Personnel Management*, September 1989.

Philip James Holding managers to account on safety *Personnel Management*, April 1990.

David Lewis *Essentials of employment law* IPM, 1990.

Michael Rubenstein Devising a sexual harassment policy *Personnel Management*, February 1991.

Health and Safety Commission *First aid work – Health and Safety (First Aid) Regulations 1981 – Approved Code of Practice and Guidance* HMSO, 1990.

C. M. Solomon Careers under glass *Personnel Journal*, April 1990.

Useful journals include;

Industrial Cases Reports

Industrial Relations Law Reports

Industrial Law Journal.

CHAPTER 10

A. Ball *The British political process* MacMillan Press, 1981.

D. Butler and D. Kavanagh *The British General Election of 1987* MacMillan, 1988.

S. G. Richards *Introduction to British Government* MacMillan, 1984.

CHAPTER 11

T. Mallier and T. Shafto *Economics of Labour Markets and Management* Hutchinson, 1989.

CHAPTER 12

Richard Underwood 1992; new frontiers, new horizons *Personnel Management*, February 1989.

Ron Johnson Are the British qualified to join Europe? *Personnel Management*, May 1990.

Peter Goldrick Collective bargaining and the new Europe *Personnel Management*, October 1990.

Keith Thurley Towards a European approach to personnel management *Personnel Management*, September 1990.

Mark Hall UK employment practices after the Social Charter *Personnel Management*, March 1990.

IPM/IDS *1992, Personel management and the Single European Market* IPM/IDS 1988.

Chris Brewster and Paul Teague *European Community Social Policy, its impact on the UK* IPM, 1989.

John Atkinson *Corporate employment policies for the Single European Market* IMS Report 179, Institute of Manpower Studies, 1989.

Amin Rajan *1992 – A zero sum game* Industrial Society Press, 1990.

CHAPTER 13

IDS Study 454 *Flexibility at work* Incomes Data Services, 1990.

Joanna Foster Balancing work and family: divided loyalties and constructive partnerships *Personnel Management,* September 1988.

Philip Lynch Matching worked hours to business needs *Personnel Management,* June 1988.

Chris Hendry and Andrew Pettigrew Multiskilling in the round *Personnel Management,* April 1988.

Gerald Kennedy Single status as a key to flexibility *Personnel Management,* February 1988.

Sheila Forbes and John Miller What should employers ask of the education system *Personnel Mnagement,* March 1988.

Jane Pickard The challenge of full employment *Personnel Management,* May 1989.

John Atkinson Four stages od adjustment to the demographic downturn *Personnel Management,* August 1989.

John and Celia Stanworth Home truths about teleworking *Personnel Management,* November 1989.

P. Prowse Assessing the flexible firm *Personnel Review,* Vol.16, No.9, 1989.

N. Meager Job sharing and job splitting; employer attitudes *Employment Gazette,* July 1988.

NEDC/TA *Defusing the demographic time bomb* National Economic Development Office, 1989.

R. Waite and G. Pike *School leaver decline and effective local solutions* IMS Report 178, 1989.

IDS Study 461 *The shorter working week* Incomes Data Services, 1990.

D. Parsons Winning workers; rising to the demographic challenge *Employment Gazette,* February 1990.

P. Leighton and M. Syrett *New work patterns; putting policy into practice* Pitman, 1989.

IDS Study 440 *Job sharing* Incomes Data Services, 1989.

Training Agency *Training in Britain; a study of funding, activity and attitudes: Main report* HMSO, 1989.

P. Tolfree *Employment in the 1990s – making the best of employee resources* Croner Publications, 1990.

Jane Pickard Annual Hours: a year of living dangerously? *Personnel Management,* August 1991.

CHAPTER 14

IDS Study 456 *Industry links with schools* Incomes Data Services, 1990.
John Cassels *Britain's real skill shortages and what to do about it* Policy Studies Institute, 1990.

CHAPTER 15

Ewart Wooldridge The Donovan Analysis; does it still hold good *Personnel Management*, June 1989.
John Purcell Managing decentralised bargaining *Personnel Management*, May 1989.
D. Fillingham When bargaining is a life or death issue *Personnel Management*, March 1991.
D. Farnham and J. Pimlott *Understanding industrial relations* Holt, Reinhart and Winston 1990.
ACAS *Annual Reports*
Certification Officer *Annual Reports*
Reports of the Commissioner for the Rights of Trade Union Members

INDEX

EMPLOYEE RELATIONS

an introduction

Ken Whitehead

Employee Relations describes the system by which employers
and Trade Unions seek to resolve their differences,
and reveals that disputes are not entirely concerned
with a particular workplace or set of rules.
Rather problems at work are a focal point of wider
issues arising from the very nature of industrial society.

CONTENTS

Book - isbn 0 946139 76 8 £8.95

Tutor's Pack of tested exercises, notes, overhead projection
transparencies and other materials to support and extend
the textbook - isbn 0 946139 81 4 £39.00

WORK FOR WORK

A workbook for the mature job seeker

Michael Weatherley & Michael Ryan

Designed to help managers, professionals and other mature
people to find work. Starting with self-analysis, it
takes readers through the complex process of looking for a new
job, career or business opportunity, giving sound, practical
on organising and mounting a successful search.

It is a workbook, not a textbook. Tasks are set at each stage
so that individuals can develop and test their expectations,
perceptions and skills; analyse the market; evaluate their
own campaigns; and find appropriate, satisfying work.

Work for Work is based on successful courses for the mature
unemployed. It has been helpful to those wishing to
change career or to make an effective transition into
work which is new and rewarding.

Some of the topics covered:

the database
managing your career
decision making
alternatives to employment
the interview
offers/no offers
starting work

Wire bound (for ease of use)   £6.95   isbn 0 946139 51 2